Citizenship in Contemporary Times

This book engages with evolving definitions of borders and citizenship in the public discourse in the South Asia region.

The traditional understanding of citizenship and belonging in the Indian context has been fraying in recent decades. The book offers an analysis of discussions on India's contested zones, the anxieties around identity and the implications of and reactions to the National Register of Citizens (NRC) and the Citizenship Amendment Act (CAA) in different regions in the country. It interrogates the concepts of belonging, ownership and dissent through an analysis of the anti-CAA protests, the Namasudra movements, the life of Tibetan refugees in India and the precarious lives of many communities in India who are identified as stateless, refugees, migrants or outsiders.

Interdisciplinary and topical, this book will be of interest to students and researchers of sociology, political science, law, refugee studies, borderland studies, migration studies, public policy, social policy and development studies.

Gorky Chakraborty is a Faculty at at the Institute of Development Studies Kolkata (IDSK), India. His research is primarily focused on development-related issues in North-East India.

Citizenship in Contemporary Times

The Indian Context

Edited by Gorky Chakraborty

Routledge
Taylor & Francis Group
LONDON AND NEW YORK

First published 2023
by Routledge
4 Park Square, Milton Park, Abingdon, Oxon OX14 4RN

and by Routledge
605 Third Avenue, New York, NY 10158

Routledge is an imprint of the Taylor & Francis Group, an informa business

British Library Cataloguing-in-Publication Data
A catalogue record for this book is available from the British Library

Library of Congress Cataloging-in-Publication Data
A catalog record has been requested for this book

ISBN: 978-1-032-34712-7 (hbk)
ISBN: 978-1-032-39969-0 (pbk)
ISBN: 978-1-003-34515-2 (ebk)

DOI: 10.4324/9781003345152

Typeset in Sabon
by SPi Technologies India Pvt Ltd (Straive)

In memory of
Professor Partha Sarathi Datta
for foreseeing the outlines of turbulence
in the name of citizenship
in North-East India

Contents

Preface x
Acknowledgements xii
List of Contributors xiv

PART I
Introduction 1

Introduction 3
SAMIK ROY CHOWDHURY AND GORKY CHAKRABORTY

1 The 'Outsider' Within: Emerging Politics of Citizenship in India 16
SAMIK ROY CHOWDHURY AND GORKY CHAKRABORTY

PART II
Statelessness: Emotions and Anxieties 37

2 Citizenship Question in the Transnational Context: Literary Perspectives 39
HIMADRI LAHIRI

3 Cities of Refuge; Republics of *Char*: Stateless in South Asia 55
NANDINI BHATTACHARYA

4 *Miya* Poetry: Poetics, Politics and Polemics 71
ABDUL KALAM AZAD AND GORKY CHAKRABORTY

PART III
Persistent Fault Lines: The Unique Case of Assam 89

5 Postcolonial Modes of Nation Making: The Politics of Disowning Citizens 91
SAJAL NAG

6 Legislating Anxiety: The History of Citizenship Conundrum in Post-colonial Assam 112
BINAYAK DUTTA

7 Citizenship in the Fabric of Hindu Nationalism in Assam 128
BHUPEN SARMAH

8 From 'Filthy Migrants' to *Khilonjiya Musalmaan*: The Saga of Citizenship Question in Assam 145
SHOFIUL ALOM PATHAN

PART IV
Tracing Lived Experiences: The Curious Case of West Bengal 161

9 Disaggregating the "Anti-Immigrant Consensus": Party–Community Relations and the Politics of Citizenship in Contemporary West Bengal 163
HIMADRI CHATTERJEE

10 Muslims Between Citizenship and Media Bias: Insights from Anti-CAA Protest Sites 183
MOHAMMAD REYAZ, KAIFIA ANCER LASKAR AND FURQUAN AMEEN

11 'Rights', 'Lived Worlds' and Citizenship: The Case of Kolkata's Muslims 201
ANASUA CHATTERJEE

PART V
The Citizenship Question: Borders and Border Crossings 215

12 'To Be or Not to Be': Tibetans and the Question of Citizenship 217
JIGME YESHE LAMA

13 Citizenship Dilemmas of the Nepalis(ese) of Darjeeling Hills and Beyond 230
BISWANATH SAHA

14 Border and Belonging: Historicizing the Question of Indigeneity and Citizenship in Manipur 247
PUM KHAN PAU

15 Between Legality and Illegality: Citizenship and the Chakmas in North-East India 260
ANINDITA GHOSHAL

Index 278

Preface

In contemporary India, the *aporia* between an over-arching electoral democracy and a seemingly receding constitutional democracy appears palpable, affecting the lives of citizens perhaps like never before. One question. Is this India of 1947 that woke up to freedom after a protracted struggle through various means, which now looks at itself in a majoritarian mirror? Is this India of the freedom fighters that opted *jus soli* as it embraced its colonial subjects as citizens of a free nation but now looks askance at declaring judicial death on its own people? Is this the India that debated in the Constituent Assembly to bestow adult franchise to its citizens irrespective of class, caste, ethnicity, gender and religion that now proclaims to categorise its people into 'outsiders'? Is this the India, the 'jewel in the crown', that fought colonialism to take pride in 'we the people' that now intends to manufacture 'non-citizens' from within?

This *aporia* of the contemporary that we live in our everyday life lies fixated in respective utopias, where it is embedded, for some in partition, few others in centuries of servitude and a few more in Anglicised notions of nation building! Their causes, either perceived or real, vary, but under their cumulative weight of actions and inactions, the liberal-institutional democratic framework of India appears to be in tatters. This assault, however, is far from the *front* but constructed from within, curiously maintaining the semblance of the institutions at least for the time being. In these otherwise traumatic times, the generations that bequeathed us India will question our generation about whether we will bequeath the same republic with its pledge of '*we the people*' to our following generations.

Negotiating exasperations related to the crisis of his times, W. B. Yeats penned that when the "ceremony of innocence is drowned; the best lack all conviction, while the worst are full of passionate intensity", there is the *Second Coming*. In contemporary India, even this poetic expression of the *coming*, although discrete, falls short as a comforting thought when compared with the enforced changes, imposed on us, in the grammar of imagining the nation. For those of *us*, whom T. S, Eliot poetically ascribes as "hast nor youth nor age . . . dreaming of both", the words of the South Asian poet, Faiz Ahmad Faiz continues to seem nostalgic and long for *nahin nigah mein manzil to justuju hi sahi, nahin visal mayasaar to arzu hi sahi . . . gar intezaar kathin hai to jab talak ae-dil, kisi ke vaada-e-farda ki guftagu hi sahi* (if the destination eludes us, its longing is enough, if an embrace of thy beloved is difficult, the aspiration seems enough, if the wait turns arduous, then my heart, the (false!) promise of meeting tomorrow, is enough).

This volume is a testimony to the *aporia* of the contemporary times when India remains in the thraldom of a dystopic vision exemplified through the changing discourse and exercise on citizenship – a humble effort by diverse scholars in analysing the angst, pathos and chicanery associated with such a conundrum for the present and the unborn.

Gorky Chakraborty

Acknowledgements

With my existential roots in the Brahmaputra Valley, I was attuned to the acts of *acceptance* and *disowning* in the nationality formation in Assam. While the social history of my valley taught me about the inclusionary process, whereby the *Horu Koch* (Lesser Koch) were gradually elevated into *Bor Koch* (Higher Koch); the political history simultaneously opened my eyes to the fault lines of a bureaucratic model, eager to determine identity guided by political expediency and exclusion.

In geographical terms as well, acceptances and exclusions in identity formations were *reflective* of the flow patterns of our lifeline, the *Bor Luit* (the Brahmaputra). What it eroded also got bestowed on the fertile plains, through accretion. But the *bolia baan* (deluge) that started affecting the valley and the state during the last decade was far from a hydrological event. It has been a human-induced disaster, activated through political machination, where organs of the state arguably moved in tandem to institutionalize 'suspicion' and eventually disown its inhabitants, as if the *Bor Luit* disowns the very existence of the water, silts and values of the streams and tributaries, which feeds into it.

In one such agonizing moments of this continuous deluge, in an informal interaction with *Sajal da* (Prof Sajal Nag), my angst slowly got shaped into an academic discussion, which culminated in proposing for a National Seminar on Citizenship at Institute of Development Studies Kolkata (IDSK) in November 2019. I am thankful to Professor Nag for providing me with a meaningful academic *alibi* to fathom out as well as, to listen to the deliberations of scholars, who remained anxious about the state of affairs in Assam and India at large. I appreciate the efforts of my colleague Dr Anwesha Sengupta who helped me in organizing the seminar along with ICSSR-ERC for supporting the academic program.

Eventually, to our utter dismay, the pandemic appeared from the blue; it not only disconnected my efforts in planning a volume based on the seminar presentations but also catapulted us in a disjointed world where coherent thought and actions became almost *un*natural. My agony in the unfolding regime of 'sanitizing' citizenship now got overlapped by a continuous process of sanitizing oneself from the virus. Fellow travellers fell away, distance got negotiated only online and the architecture of thought for a volume on citizenship almost got dismantled. Until *Himadri da* (Prof Himadri Lahiri) patiently motivated me to think afresh on citizenship, not only through legalistic interpretations but also with affect theory and the *truthfulness* of emotion in a *state of exception*. I remain indebted to Professor Lahiri for negotiating patiently through the haze of my discipline-based ignorance.

I remain grateful to our student Samik Roy Chowdhury for illuminating me with the conceptual clarity on citizenship, many such issues that I lived through in the Brahmaputra valley but fell short in expressing myself academically. Since I continue to remain agonized by the state of the republic which my generation will hand over to Samik and his generation, I have opted to keep him ahead of myself in dreaming together for upholding the otherwise fading ideals. Hope, as Samik puts it, is destined to have a future too.

A special thanks for the contributors of this volume, many of whom I did not know before but connected with only through this academic exercise. It is only for their untiring effort and intellectual exercise that *our* volume is in your hands. I sincerely hope I can carry the academic alacrity of the young contributors like Abdul Kalam Azad, Biswanath Saha, Furquan Ameen, Samik Roy Chowdhury and Shofiul Alom Pathan, as well as the intellectual maturity of scholars like Anasua Chatterjee, Anindita Ghosal, Bhupen Sarmah, Binayak Dutta, Himadri Chatterjee, Himadri Lahiri, Jigme Yeshi Lama, Kaifia Ancer Laskar, Md Reyaz, Nandini Bhattacharya, Pum Khan Pau and Sajal Nag.

Heartfelt thanks to my colleagues at IDSK who have been a constant motivation with their intellectual insights in finalizing the volume.

The team at Routledge, especially Shoma Choudhury and Shloka Chauhan, along with the anonymous reviewers, deserves a special mention for their excellent advice, support and encouragement in adding value to the volume.

Gorky Chakraborty

Contributors

Furquan Ameen is a New Delhi–based journalist and associate editor at *Land Conflict Watch*, where he oversees reportage on issues of land, resources and governance. He has written at the intersections of politics, identity, conflict and social exclusion for mainstream Indian and global news outlets such as *The Telegraph India*, *IndiaSpend*, the *Hindustan Times*, *The Caravan* and *Al Jazeera English*. He has also worked as a researcher with the International Center for Journalists and been a fellow at the Reuters Institute for the Study of Journalism, University of Oxford.

Abdul Kalam Azad is a postdoctoral fellow and Lecturer at Vrije Universiteit, Amsterdam, The Netherlands. He identifies himself as a Miya poet and has been one of the founding members of the Miya Community Research Collective.

Nandini Bhattacharya is Professor in the Department of English and Culture Studies, The University of Burdwan, West Bengal, India. She is also the coordinator of the UGC SAP-DRS II Programme of Department of English and Culture Studies, whose focal thrust is partition and border studies. She is the curator of a permanent border crossing exhibition and the director of the Scottish Studies Centre in the department. She specializes in translation, genre, forced migration and ethics studies with particular reference to 19th-century colonial Bengal. She also specializes in law and literature studies, offering courses in the National University of Juridical Sciences, Kolkata, India, on the same. Her latest books are the *Annotated Kankabati: A Translation of Trailokyanath Mukhopadhaya's Modern Fairy Tale* (2016); *Rabindranath Tagore's Gora: A Critical Companion* (2015); *Borders and Border Crossings: Reading Partition, Reading Diaspora* (2017). Her forthcoming book *Strange Familiarities* is on the 19th-century postal revolution in South Asia.

Anasua Chatterjee is currently Assistant Professor of Sociology at RKSMVV, Kolkata. She has done her PhD in sociology from Jawaharlal Nehru University, New Delhi, India. Her research interests include the transformations underway in the South Asian city, with a focus on diversity, socio-spatial exclusion, citizenship, the aspects of identity and belonging. Her doctoral research on the socio-spatial segregation of Muslims in Indian cities has been published by Routledge as a monograph titled *Margins of Citizenship: Muslim Experiences in Urban India* (2017). Her work has also appeared in journals such as the *Economic and Political Weekly*, the *Journal of South Asian Development, Contemporary South Asia* and the *Seminar*, as well as in other edited volumes on urban space in India.

Himadri Chatterjee is a researcher and teacher of political at Department of Political Science, University of Calcutta, India. He is interested in the interplay between citizenship, migration, local economies, caste and electoral politics. His doctoral thesis explored the connections between urban development, refugee rehabilitation and citizenship struggles led by Dalit activists in peri-urban Kolkata. He seeks to work between the archive and the field in order to generate ethnographic understanding that is anchored in long-term historical trends. Very often he finds his archive on the field, in unnumbered files and undated photographs.

Binayak Dutta is a faculty member at the Department of History of North Eastern Hill University (NEHU) in Shillong, India and a senior fellow at Asian Confluence, Shillong. Before joining NEHU, Binayak was an advocate at the Gauhati High Court. He was also Visiting Fellow at the ICSSR's OKD Institute of Social Change and Development in Guwahati. His research includes studying the cultural and social dimensions of partitions in North-East India between 1947 and 1971 and how these could be seen through the lenses of law and citizenship.

Anindita Ghoshal is Associate Professor of History at Diamond Harbour Women's University, Kolkata, West Bengal. Her area of research includes partition and refugees' studies with special emphasis on eastern/north-eastern India and Bangladesh. She is the recipient of several awards and grants, and her recent publications include *Refugee, Borders and Identities: Rights and Habitat in East and Northeast India* (2021) and *Revisiting Partition: Contestation, Narratives and Memories* (editor; 2022).

Himadri Lahiri is a former professor in the Department of English, University of Burdwan, West Bengal, India. Currently, he is Professor of English at the School of Humanities, Netaji Subhas Open University, Kolkata, India. He has written extensively on diaspora studies and Indian English literature. His recent publications include *Asia Travels: Pan-Asian Cultural Discourses and Diasporic Asian Literature/s in English* (2021) and *Diaspora Theory and Transnationalism* (2019). He is also interested in postcolonial literature and 20th-century British poetry.

Jigme Yeshe Lama is currently Assistant Professor in the Department of Political Science, University of Calcutta, India. He completed his PhD at the Centre for East Asian Studies, School of International Studies, Jawaharlal Nehru University, New Delhi, India. His research interest lies in China-Tibet ties, the study of religion and politics in the Himalayas and Tibetan democracy in exile.

Kaifia Ancer Laskar is a PhD in Mass Communication with her dissertation titled 'Mediated Mythical Discourses in Television Soap operas'. She has been teaching Journalism and Mass Communication at Aliah University, Kolkata, West Bengal, India since 2016. She takes a keen interest in qualitative research methodologies for analysis of gender and myth in fictional television and film texts, fake news, and C4DSC. She has published research papers in several books as well as for many peer-reviewed Indian journals.

Sajal Nag is Professor and Head of the Department of History and Dean of the School of Social Sciences, Assam University, Silchar, India. He was the first Netaji Subhash Chandra Bose Chair Professor of Social Sciences, Presidency University, Kolkata, India and a former Commonwealth Fellow 2004–05, Charles Wallace Fellow at the University of Cambridge, UK 2008 and Senior Fellow at Nehru Memorial Museum and Library, 2013–2014. Some of his publications include *The Uprising: Colonial State, Christian Missionaries, and Anti Slavery movement in North East India, 1907–1950* (2016); *Bridging State and Nation: Politics of Peace in Nagaland and Mizoram*, with Rita Manchanda and Tapan Bose (2015); *Blending Region and Nation; Essays in Honour of Prof Amalendu Guha* (2019); *The Beleaguered Nation: Making and Unmaking of the Assamese Nationality* (2016); *Pied Pipers in North East India: Bamboo Flowers, Rat Famine and Politics of Philanthropy* (2008); *Playing with Nature: History and Politics of Environment in North East India* (2016); *Forces of Nature: Essays in History and Politics of Environment in India* (2016), *Contesting Marginality: Ethnicity, Insurgency and Sub Nationalism in North East India* (2002); and *Making of the Union: Integration of Princely States and Excluded Areas 1947–50* (2004).

Shofiul Alom Pathan is a PhD candidate at the Indian Institute of Technology Kanpur, India, and a sociologist with research interests in collective identity and violence, ethnicity, citizenship and the sociology and concerns of Muslims in North-East India.

Pum Khan Pau is Associate Professor at the Department of History, Manipur University, India. His research interests include frontier and borderlands studies, the two World Wars and local participation, colonialism and missionary endeavours in the Indo-Burma frontier, among others. Pau is the author of *Indo-Burma Frontier and the Making of the Chin Hills: Empire* *and Resistance* (2020) and co-author of *Forgotten fighters: Heroes of the Anglo-Kuki War, 1917–1919* (forthcoming). He has also published in many reputed journals.

Mohammad Reyaz is Assistant Professor in the Department of Journalism and Mass Communication, Aliah University, Kolkata, India. He was the 2021 Study of the United States Institutes (SUSI) Fellow at Seattle University and has completed an ICSSR-IMPRESS project recently. A former journalist, Reyaz continues to write articles in different media, besides research papers in journals and edited volumes. He works at the intersectionality of (new) media, society and (identity) politics in India and larger Eurasia.

Samik Roy Chowdhury has completed an MPhil in development studies from the Institute of Development Studies Kolkata, India, and is an independent researcher working on political theory, citizenship and border studies.

Biswanath Saha has completed his PhD at the Institute of Development Studies Kolkata, India, and currently associated with the Department of Geography, Sikkim University, India. He is interested in understanding ethnopolitics, culture and geopolitics of the Eastern Himalayan borderlands.

Bhupen Sarmah has been on the faculty of the OKD Institute of Social Change and Development, Guwahati, since 1998. He has extensively worked on India's North East, especially in the areas of ethnicity, democratic decentralization and agrarian questions. Professor Sarmah has contributed a large number of papers to many national and international journals and edited volumes and has authored/coauthored and edited several books.

1

Introduction

Introduction

Samik Roy Chowdhury and Gorky Chakraborty

I

This volume on citizenship has been conceptualised and compiled during prolonged moments of unfamiliarity and disassociation in the Indian citizenship discourse. This haze of unfamiliarity facilitated the volume to engage with multiple and often ignored spaces, not only on citizenship but statelessness as well. Key to understanding the source of this unfamiliarity is to engage with the multiple and at time's adversarial manner in which sentiments of uncertainty, precarity and anxieties are felt and articulated by multiple stakeholders vis-à-vis an imagined notion of the nation state. This feeling/sentiment of unfamiliarity can be mostly attributed to the uncertainties regarding the questions of belonging which now manifest themselves emphatically within the legal field of citizenship.

Recent times have seen figures and categories like the illegal migrant and refugees become central to the Indian citizenship discourse, casting a spell of unfamiliarity and disassociation over the entire society. On one hand, the most recent amendment to the Indian citizenship law has revived polarised debates on the basic principles of the Indian nation state, simultaneously; the growing paranoia regarding the presence of the illegal migrant within Indian territory has proved to be a fertile breeding ground for suspicion that in the last decade has been internalised not only by institutions but also by the public. The citizenship landscape in contemporary India is, therefore, marked by an unfamiliar sense of disassociation from the long-held perceptions of the nation and of its neighbour.

These conditions point to an ongoing moment of metamorphosis leading to the creation of an unfamiliar terrain of citizenship. It can be claimed that the present state of the citizenship discourse in India is on the cusp of a transformation, and it is in this moment between the death of the old citizen and the emergence of the new that we place this Introduction and the volume. Within this ongoing transformation towards the emergence of the new citizen, it is essential that we analyse how this new landscape of citizenship would interact with often ignored spaces of citizenship and statelessness. Citizenship, in essence, has always manifested itself as a spatially exclusive

DOI: 10.4324/9781003345152-2

and internally differentiated category and it is essential that we understand how the impulse of exclusivity is rearticulated by appropriating the differentiated narratives of citizenship. In this Introduction we intend to look at certain events and themes that have dominated the citizenship discourse in the last decade. The earlier decades in Indian politics had seen fierce public debates on sub-fields of citizenship, that is issues of affirmative action, land reforms, poverty alleviation and so on. The first decade of the 21st century, in contrast, has seen the very character and identity of the citizen change. While it would be myopic to claim that this shift in the citizenship discourse occurred singularly due to the events of the last decade, it still, remains an essential decade that saw fundamental changes in the manner in which citizenship rights were articulated and practised. Therefore, the intention of the Introduction is to carefully look back at the themes and events that have affected the Indian citizenship discourse during the last decade and understand how these themes and events, all of which originate in specific contexts, relate to one another and move towards the articulation of the new citizen.

When one looks back on the events and the developments during this time period, two major themes stand out. The more recent and maybe the more prominent theme relates to the basic identity and the definition of the Indian citizen. The central questions that these debates intend to answer relate to contestations regarding the legal membership. Central to this theme are the rules and regulations that define the limits and the exceptions to acquiring legal membership in India. The second and the older theme relates to the issues of institutional inefficacy. This theme became a prominent subject of public debate during the early parts of the last decade and was directly responsible for long-lasting political and social changes that allowed for the question of legality to become central in contemporary times. In the Introduction, we introduce the questions of legal membership and then trace our steps back to the events of the early 2010s to better highlight the linkages between these two discourses.

II

As mentioned earlier, the question of legal membership has emerged as a central theme in the national discussions on citizenship. This present curiosity can mainly be attributed to the most recent amendment to the Indian citizenship law that has proved to be one of the most polarising legislations of this century. The historical significance and the contemporary intricacies of this particular amendment are, unsurprisingly, dealt with comprehensively in this volume and this chapter will not delve into the specific politics of this particular amendment. Here, we are more concerned with the manner in which this amendment became one of the most polarising legislations in Indian history. One of the major points made against this particular amendment is the perceived exclusion and threat to the Indian

Muslim community. This perceived threat led to multiple protests all over India, especially Shaheen Bagh. Added to this, it was also the first time that the limited nature of citizenship and acquiring citizenship in India's borderlands became a national issue. By marking certain groups as refugees, with a legal path to acquiring citizenship, this amendment highlights certain unresolved dynamics of the partition (1947), which, till recently, were before this amendment limited to a regional issue.

Moreover, while the amendment in itself would have been controversial enough, one of its most controversial elements was related to the manner in which it was articulated vis-à-vis National Register of Citizens (NRC). This in itself occupies a grey area both in legal and social terms. The NRC was introduced in the 2003 amendment to the Indian citizenship law. The 2003 amendment to the Indian citizenship law allowed for the creation and maintenance of the NRC. Interestingly, the 2003 amendment did not lead to a polarising response like the most recent amendment, and it can be claimed that this particular amendment has not gained much national notoriety. The more recent salience of the NRC is instead related to the developments in the state of Assam. The histories of the NRC in Assam and the contestations regarding illegal migration constitute another important theme of this volume. The most recent incarnation of the NRC was born out of the Supreme Court judgement in the Assam *Sammillita Mahasabha* case. In this judgement, the Supreme Court ordered the central government to update[1] the NRC in Assam. The demand for an updated NRC had been one of the central demands of the Assam movement.[2] The NRC, according to certain sections of the Assamese society, was supposed to provide a remedy to the problem of illegal infiltration into Assam by differentiating the legitimate citizen and the illegal migrant. The Supreme Court in instituting the NRC agreed with these demands and acknowledged the threat of illegal infiltration from Bangladesh. This was not the first time that the Supreme Court had highlighted the threat of illegal infiltration from Bangladesh. The court had made similar insinuations in the *Sarbananda Sonowal* judgement (2005). In both these instances, the court cited the 'alarming' growth of the Muslim population in Assam as evidence of illegal infiltration marking the Bengali-speaking Muslim as a suspect citizen.

Sections of the Assamese society, a society that has had a long history of in-migration, have regularly complained of illegal migration into the state, which they claim, to be a threat to their citizenship rights. The figure of the illegal migrant has not only been a persistent presence within the policy-making circles but has also become embedded in the language of mobilisation. The emergence of the illegal migrant as a failure of the citizenship regime has been highlighted by the rise of multiple movements/organisations that have demanded that the central government take appropriate measures to not only stop illegal migration but to also identify and deport individuals who entered India illegally. According to these movements/organisations, the presence of the illegal migrant has had an adverse effect on the actualisation of citizenship rights of the legitimate residents of India. These movements/organisations have also disputed/questioned the mechanisms involved in the identification and deportation of illegal migrants. At the heart of these narratives is the claim that the Indian state has continually failed to protect the rights of the Assamese people. This grievance regarding the institutional failure had been central to the Assam movement and subsequent contestations of citizenship, but barring the peak of the Assam movement, this was mostly a regional sentiment.

The intrusion of the NRC in the national public consciousness can be attributed to the tendency of certain prominent public figures to link the NRC, as a tool to combat illegal infiltration and with the Citizenship Amendment Act (CAA), a law, intended to fix the historical injustices of partition. This sentiment was clearly visible when the home minister claimed in a tweet: "First we will pass the Citizenship Amendment bill and ensure that all the refugees from the neighbouring nations get the Indian citizenship. After that NRC will be made and we will detect and deport every infiltrator from our motherland". These narratives of citizenship intend to articulate citizenship in a narrower but more flexible manner. In other words, these laws when linked together seem to articulate citizenship in limited demographic terms while simultaneously expanding its cartographic scope. The CAA and the NRC when linked in this manner revives the debates emerging out of the partition and challenges the basic grounds on which citizenship had traditionally been articulated, while by reiterating the threat of the infiltrator, it crystallised suspicion within the public perception. Therefore, the present citizenship discourse seems to be in a transitional phase where it intends to disassociate itself from prior narratives of national membership.

III

To understand how the Indian citizen reaches the point of disassociation it is essential to understand the narratives of institutional inefficacy that emerged during the initial parts of the decade. The very beginning of the 2010s saw large-scale mobilisations against corruption and inaction in governance. The India Against Corruption (IAC) movement that demanded the adoption of a 'Jan Lokpal Bill' gained mainstream attention partly due to its prominent placement in Delhi and partly due to the multiple acquisitions of corruption against the then central government. The timing of the movement was even more pertinent as this took place during the peak phase of coalition politics. The then United Progressive Alliance (UPA) government was portrayed as an inactive/incapable government, which had failed in dealing with the challenges posed by issues like corruption due to the restraints put on it by the inner workings of coalition politics. This directly led to the decline of coalition politics and initiated the domination of the Bharatiya Janata Party since 2014.

The ramification of the IAC and the subsequent changes in Indian politics can in no way be understated as this allowed for the emergence of the *impatient* citizen. This impatient citizen would gather at Jantar Mantar. This citizen would get frustrated by the long-drawn-out negotiations between the government and the representatives of IAC. This citizen would take offence to rapes, and only rapes, which took place in 'his' country. This citizen was tired of government inaction on the economic slowdown and 'policy paralysis' and wanted to give a mandate to a leader who could take strong measures to kick-start the economy. This citizen wanted a 'strong leader' who would make sure that the 'corrupt' bureaucracy functions in an orderly manner. This citizen was vocal in 'his' demand for a strong, utilitarian government that could provide a quick resolution to whatever infected the body politic, even if, it meant circumscribing deliberation. This citizen was not bothered about the very precariousness of the multicultural democracy and the mechanisms that kept it afloat; rather, he was more concerned with grand actions and tangible 'development'. This citizen was so tired of the existing order of things that he ignored the communal injustices of the 'Gujarat model'. This citizen wanted his leader to give voice to his dearly held beliefs even at the cost of the others. This citizen wanted to be heard, represented and, most important, acknowledged at any cost.

By giving a platform to this impatience, the IAC movement would initiate a self-fulfilling prophecy as the impatient citizen, instead of practising restraint and deliberation to deal with critical issues, would get embroiled in witch hunts for scapegoats. And, while this scapegoat may momentarily satiate the thirst of impatience, it would keep going further and further away from the principles of deliberative democracy. The relevance of this citizen was not contingent on the values or traditions of a deliberative democracy; rather, this citizen wanted to cure inaction and hence emerged and evolved in conjecture with half-backed calls for action. This citizen is not necessarily a representation of the larger Indian society, but this citizen became the most visible figures of the early 2010s. This action-oriented, impatient citizen wanted a solution to their problems in the swiftest possible manner, and in essence this impatient citizen would effectively initiate the transformation towards the new citizen.

The new emerging citizen would want to 'right the wrongs' of the partition and beyond while also purifying it by weeding out the 'unclean' elements. The primary intention of this volume is to locate contested zones of citizenship within the newly emerging discourse of citizenship and governance and in the process extract the terms of membership that emerged through these interactions. In many ways, it is extremely fascinating to observe and understand how the *forgotten* citizens, mentioned in this volume, would interact with the impatient and anxious citizen that emerges during the last decade or two.

IV

In the global scale, too, during contemporary times, citizenship has once again become one of the most popular topics in social sciences cutting across disciplinary bounds. Concomitantly, it has yielded a vast and diverse literature in the field of citizenship studies as citizenship emerged as a contested topic, which noticeably, has become an inseparable part of social organisation too. This essentially pointed to two aspects of citizenship: malleability and indeterminacy, where the latter has been identified as a hallmark of modern democracy (Lefort, 1988). So citizenship, as a ritual of state making has been in practice as a tool for social engineering and in the process, a tool in redefining the nation too. Issues related to citizenship, therefore, will have to be understood in the specific contexts within which they manifest, necessitating a flexible and thick methodology that is beyond the bounds of a consistent theory. The first section of this volume, the **Introduction**, introduces similar themes. The Introduction, in other words, initiates the analyses of the metamorphosis in the public perception of citizenship and the citizen, along with the public intellectuals, academicians and researchers, who fell short of providing answers to questions that, remained latent, and have not been posed earlier. In this process of churning on the emerging discourse on citizenship, the sole purpose of this volume is to encourage discussion and interdisciplinary engagements on these issues. While the Introduction relates it to the Indian context, especially during the first two decades of the 21st century, the chapter "The 'Outsider' Within: Emerging Politics of Citizenship in India" contextualises the Indian experience into the global context, where Samik Roy Chowdhury and Gorky Chakraborty sheds light on certain unspecified and often ignored spaces of citizenship through a multidiscipline approach. The polyrhythmic impulses that citizenship policies and practices generate are paradoxically bound to the existence of the state, principles of public sovereignty and seemingly contradictory relationship between citizenship and territoriality. This chapter relates to a process of the changing relationship amongst citizenship, space and territoriality. While scholars (Turner, 1967; Benhabib, 2004; Hoffman, 2004) have argued for the withering away of the inherited geography of state territories with a focus on denationalisation of citizenship, Chowdhury and Chakraborty exemplify that the definition and the scope of the citizen continue to hinge on statist territorialist epistemologies. Accordingly, generating an identity that remains steeped in deep cartographic and demographic anxieties. The chapter thereby introduces the notion of 'outsider' as a representation of these anxieties and relates this category in analysing the citizenship discourse in the Indian and the South Asian context with special reference to Assam, which has undergone a transformation from *wastelands* to *borderlands*, and now 'aspires' to introduce the category of 'non-citizens' in the Indian citizenship discourse.

V

At a macro scale, it is now almost a truism in social sciences that contemporary globalisation has reconfigured the interplay of the social and the spatial relations at multiple scales and has resultantly complicated the issues related to migration, citizenship and statelessness. The corpus of writings under such a scenario that relates to the issues of citizenship and statelessness from a literary perspective however remains limited. Section II titled **Statelessness: Emotions and Anxieties** is an attempt in minimising that gulf. The chapters in this section dealing with the experiences of several communities located in diverse geographies highlight how the rituals of citizenship has been weaponised by the state and majoritarian political mobilisations, leading to an apparent situation of statelessness. These exercises are undertaken in the name of redefining the nation. In this process, the anxieties associated with the incarcerated communities are expressed in different forms as a response to the so-called nationalist sentiments that are generated through the emotional manipulation of the majoritarian sentiments. Himadri Lahiri's chapter "Citizenship Question in the Transnational Context: Literary Perspectives" relates to similar contexts by analysing two literary texts, the autobiographical narrative *Nisei Daughter* (1953) and the historical fiction *Chinatown Days* (2018, originally published as *Makam* in Assamese) through the critical lens of affect theory. He posits the issue of statelessness of two communities within a global perspective, located in different spatiotemporal frames. The chapter foregrounds on analysing how emotions are built up to fathom out majoritarian passion as well as experiences of emotional turmoil of the victims during such processes of 'nationalist' assertions. The next chapter *Cities of Refuge; Republics of Char: Stateless in South Asia*, by Nandini Bhattacharya, focuses on the emotive tradition of the subcontinent's history of multiple border makings and the process of creating layers of stateless and deterritorialised people. The chapter engages with an alternative vision rooted in the cultural genealogy of *chars* in Bengali narratives, poetry myths and movies to envision an ideational *char-ghar*, as an aterritorialist critique to the statist anachronism towards hard border making that ultimately generates illicit and unaffiliated people giving rise to statelessness and crisis of citizenship. Abdul Kalam Azad and Gorky Chakraborty's chapter "Miya Poetry: Poetics, Politics and Polemics" discuss the poetic response of a community towards statelessness. A threat that looms large over their head due to the emerging patterns of state-mediated processes of determining belongingness, allegiance and place making in Assam. The chapter showcases how a community, whose members have often been vilified with the slur *Miya*, decided to transform it into an identity through poetics, written in the language of the masses. Azad and Chakraborty, through their retrospective individual auto-ethnographies, in-depth life history interviews with six *Miya* poets and a pool of selected *Miya* poems, trace the birth of a new genre of protest poetry that celebrates a slur and the existential anxieties of the community members in an era of NRC regime in Assam.

VI

North-East India, in more than one way, reflects the confluence of historico-geographical traditions of South and South-East Asia. Cross-currents generated out of such traditions are reflected culturally in identity and nationality formation of communities and population groups. Fluidity and flux have accompanied the existential realities of the region. Assam, the largest state in terms of population in the North East, is an example in this direction. Waves of migrants have poured into the fertile Brahmaputra river valley at different historical times that have influenced the process of nationality formation through absorption and assimilation, giving rise to the great Assamese cultural community. Colonialism, with its territorial, strategic, trade, revenue extraction and military interests introduced ruptures to this process of cultural formation. Gradually, conditions thereafter became ripe that facilitated the 'construction' of the *other* vis-à-vis a cultural *core*, and the proximity to the core determined the acceptance of the other within the Assamese fold. While colonialism initiated this process, partition and post-colonial political machinations under the caste-Assamese hegemony, not only aggravated but consolidated it further. Now, it has achieved a newer dimension, where the effort is for a seamless confluence of the Assamese national question into the over-arching Hindutva agenda. Chapters in the third section, **The Persistent Fault Lines: The Unique Case of Assam**, analyses such a process. Sajal Nag's chapter "Postcolonial Modes in Nation Making: The Politics of Disowning Citizens" analyses how the assimilation process gets disrupted through a persistent effort of disowning in Assam. His chapter traces how the caste Hindu Assamese elite have been consistent through both violent and non-violent means to disown population groups from within. He elucidates that the contemporary exercise of NRC, has been far from an isolated phenomenon but the latest means towards fulfilling the aspiration to disown. Bhupen Sarmah in the chapter "Citizenship in the Fabric of Hindu Nationalism in Assam", on the other, illustrates how the political mobilisation centring around *Axomiya* national identity has transformed from anti-*bohiragoto* (outsider) supposedly for the protection of Assamese 'culture' to anti-*bidexi* (foreigner) movement with clandestine communal tone targeting the Muslim population hailing from erstwhile East Bengal (present day Bangladesh). Sarmah further explains how the apathy of the state failed to uphold the sanctity of the 'Public Law Contract' arrived at through the Assam Accord, which now led to a process where the convergence of the Assamese aspiration into the fold of the Hindutva agenda gets portrayed as 'natural'. Binayak Dutta's chapter "Legalising Anxiety: The History of Citizenship Conundrum in Post-colonial Assam" highlights that the politics in North-East India has long been dominated by contestations over belongingness and citizenship, since the alarm raised by the census superintendent, C S Mullan in 1931, when he suddenly identified the demographic threat of a relentless 'invasion' of Assam from East Bengal. Despite several attempts through legislative and judicial processes, the bogey of invading illegal immigrant has remained etched in the imaginaries of the dominant discourse in the state and the region. Dutta engages with the historical-legal framework of the citizenship question under such a 'threat' and relates how the anxieties and antagonisms of the bygone era colours the citizenship practices in the present. Interestingly, Shofiul Alom Pathan's chapter "From 'Filthy Migrants' to Khilonjiya Musalmaan: The Saga of Citizenship Question in Assam" shows how the issue of perceived Hindu victimisation, which is rampantly utilised by the proponents of Hindutva in India is used by the state in pitching one group of Muslims against the other in Assam, and the recent state-led census of Muslim communities is a glaring example in that direction. Pathan brings to the fore the dual process associated with identifying the Muslim identity in Assam. While on one hand, Muslims are identified as violent, the 'cultural polluter', the element of demographic threat and the everyday 'other', on the other, there is an alternative image of a 'good Muslim' who is culturally and linguistically similar to the caste Assamese core. The chapter interrogates the trajectory of politics associated with such a discourse concerning citizenship and the Muslims in Assam.

VII

Conventional theories of citizenship drawn from Western experiences interpret citizenship in terms of rights and duties that citizens enjoy vis-à-vis the state. As a result, the emphasis remains more on analysing the evolution of formal citizenship rights rather than understanding how these rights are actualised in lived contexts, especially in societies where trajectories differ significantly from those in the Western world. Anthropologically grounded works highlighting on 'informal' ways in which members of societies, particularly those from the dis-privileged sections (who otherwise remain entrenched in structures of social exclusion), negotiate citizenship rights and perceptions through lived experiences by forging networks, is fast emerging as an interesting area in citizenship studies in South Asia. Section IV, titled **Tracing the Lived Experience: The Curious Case of West Bengal**, is an addition in this direction. Himadri Chatterjee's chapter "Disaggregating the 'Anti-immigrant Consensus': Party-Community Relations and Politics of Citizenship in Contemporary West Bengal" unpack the negotiations between various political parties and the Namasudra community that are otherwise belaboured by a history of anti-immigrant politics in West Bengal, over the last 50 years. Studying grassroots Matua Namasudra activism the chapter traces back to the times of CAA 2003, which significantly introduced the phrase 'illegal immigrants' in Indian legal parlance beyond Assam and has also been the precursor to CAA 2019. Chatterjee explains how contradictions at multiple scales adversely influence the overall architecture of immigration policy and politics, often creating an impasse, as exhibited in the case of Namasudra mobilisation in West Bengal. Mohammad Reyaz, Kaifia Ancer Laskar and Furquan Ameen's chapter "Muslims Between Citizenship and Media Bias: Insights From Anti-CAA Protest Sites" analyses the everyday life surrounding mobilisation and protest against the CAA 2019. Drawing on field-based narratives from Shaheen Bagh, Delhi and Park Circus, Kolkata, the chapter elaborates how women's assertion of identity, rights and its loss, both perceived and real, galvanised the masses cutting across religious, ethnic and cultural backgrounds, all those who realised that the act vitiates the secular credentials of their republic. The role of the mainstream media is also critically looked at through its reportage and briefings, which according to the authors posited itself between ignorance and prejudice and, at times, reducing itself into an organ of the state. In this regard, the role of social media as an alternative source in forging alliance and networking amongst the protestors is also an insightful everyday lived experience elaborated in this chapter. Anasua Chatterjee in "'Rights', 'Lived Worlds' and Citizenship: The Case of Kolkata's Muslims" draws extensively from her ethnographic work in Park Circus, one of the many socially segregated '*musholmanparas*' (Muslim neighbourhoods) of Kolkata, and explores the different ways through which the idea of citizenship is perceived, accessed and vernacularised by its residents. It is observed that most of the residents have considerable difficulty in grappling the formal legalities of various terms associated with citizenship policies and practices. Chatterjee foregrounds these issues in the changing narratives on citizenship among the residents of this neighbourhood in the past and thereafter focuses on the contemporary debate on the Citizenship Amendment Act, 2019, which further escalated anxieties around belonging and everyday access to the developmental state.

VIII

Ideally, in territorialist epistemology, a citizen is differentiated from the 'other' by means of the territorial borders. But, what happens in a scenario where the borders remain open, unmarked or in the process of *making* over a long stretch of time? One of the best sites to examine such a situation appears to be South Asia where decolonisation has not only been long but also through multiple phases resulting from lack of clinical operations, what van Schendel refers as "ill-defined nations with frayed territories" (2007:37). Partition from India has not only been messy and a long-drawn-out process, as Joya Chatterjee (1999) reminds us, but also been accompanied by events that are little discussed in national histories, for example the separation of Burma in 1937. Chapters in Section V, titled **The Citizenship**

Question: Borders and Border Crossings, deal with such frayed geographies and nationalities. Jigme Yeshi Lama's chapter "To Be or Not to Be: Tibetans and the Question of Citizenship" discusses the intricacies of citizenship after the Chinese takeover of Tibet in 1950 and the 'escape' of the Fourteenth Dalai Lama and thousands of Tibetans to India in 1958 in the aftermath of a failed uprising. The establishment of the CTA (Central Tibetan Administration), as the government in exile has been in existence for over the last six decades spread in settlement camps in India, Nepal, Bhutan and several Western nations. Lama discusses various mechanisms that the CTA adopts to construct 'citizenship in exile' and further elaborates how by creating 'refugee citizens', it perpetuates its rule over the Tibetan subjects. But this generates precarious existential problems for these Tibetans in different spheres of their life. He observes that while the monks, reincarnated as the Lamas, obtain multiple citizenship due to their role as religious leaders in spreading Buddhism, the ordinary Tibetan encounters several problems in their everyday life as 'refugee citizens'. Biswanath Saha highlights another aspect of the citizenship conundrum of the Eastern Himalayas in "Citizenship Dilemmas of the Nepalis(ese) of Darjeeling Hills and Beyond". Saha explains the overall ramifications of a long process of state-making across the Indo-Nepal, Indo-Bhutan and Indo-Sikkim borders through treaties that encouraged mobility and migration of population groups. These histories, when compared with contemporary nationality and citizenship concerns, raise several question marks. It gets further complicated when one suffices that more than one lakh Gorkhas were declared 'foreigners' in Assam as their names failed to appear in the NRC exercise along with continuing uncertainties associated with the Nepali(ese) identity at various localities in the Eastern Himalayas considering India's open border with Nepal. Pum Khan Pau's chapter "Border and Belonging: Historicizing the Question of Indigeneity and Citizenship in Manipur" turns our attention to the boundary-making process between India and Burma on the Manipur–Chin border and the issues of belonging and citizenship related to such a phenomenon. Pau argues that the question of citizenship today, which continues to haunt the hill–valley relations in Manipur, especially the southern part of the state, cannot be fully defined without understanding the power, influence and territorial extent of the erstwhile kingdom of Manipur vis-à-vis the Sukte chiefdom in northern Chin Hills before modern cartography came into application. On the other, the Chakma citizenship question also throws light on similar lines, of course emanating from a different geography in South Asia. Anindita Ghosal's chapter "Between Legality and Illegality: Citizenship and the Chakmas in Northeast India" discusses about the plight of the Chakmas of Chittagong Hill Tracts, who became the worst sufferers, along with the Hajongs, who migrated from East Pakistan (present-day Bangladesh) to North-East India. In this regard, the Chakmas and Hajongs, who landed in Arunachal Pradesh, continued to be regarded as 'stateless persons' as they were kept outside the purview of the Citizenship

Act of 1955. Ghosal analyses their precarious status, of being neither a refugee nor a recognized migrant, and caught up amidst several tensions between state–centre binaries, perceived tribal resentments in North East India and the threats of statelessness.

IX

As the citizenship discourse changes, it is essential that any analytical analysis disassociates itself from the generalised presupposition, and shifts its focus from macro narratives to the often ignored micro narratives. This approach then allows us to understand the politics of appropriation that is embedded in the concoction and the articulation of singular and polarised narratives of citizenship. Citizenship, both in theory and in practice, has and will forever be intrinsically tied to questions of belonging, cohabitation and territorial authority and to understand contestations related to it as simple questions of legal or economic rights fails to engage with the historical elements of violence, mobilisation and mobility. Most commentaries on citizenship in the South Asian context correlate the emergence of the citizen with the emergence of the nation state, ignoring the histories of association, mobility and, most important, antagonisms that have persisted and shaped contemporary Indian. The juncture of unfamiliarity mentioned in the initial parts of this introduction is not only inhabited by the 'general citizen' but also by the academic who now will be compelled to confront discourses that till now were ignored. Hopefully, this volume will bring the contemporary events into the academic gaze – beyond the parliament onto the detention camps.

Notes

1 As Assam had already undergone the process of NRC in 1951.
2 For more information see Venkataramakrishnan, R. (2019, December 20). Who is Linking Citizenship Act to NRC? Five times Amit Shah did. CAA protests: Five times Amit Shah linked the Citizenship Act to the NRC (scroll.in).

References

Benhabib, S. (2004) *The Rights of Others: Aliens, Residents, and Citizens* (The Seeley Lectures, pp. 1–24). Cambridge: Cambridge University Press. doi: 10.1017/CBO9780511790799.002

Chatterjee, J. (1999). The Fashioning of a Frontier: The Radcliffe Line and Bengal's Border Landscape, 1947-52. *Modern Asian Studies*, 33(1), 185–242.

Hoffman, J. (2004). *Citizenship Beyond the State*. New Delhi: Sage Publication India

Lefort, C. (1988). *Democracy and Political Theory*. Oxford: Polity Press/Basil Blackwell.

Turner, W. V. (1967). Liminality and Communitas. In Victor W. Turner (eds.), *The Ritual Process: Structure and Anti Structure* (pp. 94–130). Chicago: Aldine Transactions.

Van Schendel, W. (2007). The Wagah Syndrome: Territorial Roots of Contemporary Violence in South Asia. In Amrita Basu and Srirupa Roy (eds.), *Violence and Democracy in India* (pp. 36–82). London: Berg Publishers/Kolkata: Seagull Books.

Chapter 1

The 'Outsider' Within

Emerging Politics of Citizenship in India

Samik Roy Chowdhury and Gorky Chakraborty

1 Introduction

Citizenship has been one of the most popular topics of academic discussion in contemporary times. Unsurprisingly, this has resulted in the accumulation of a vast yet diverse literature in the field of citizenship studies. Over the past few decades, it has emerged as a multidisciplinary arena of enquiry (Desforges et al., 2005). This enduring curiosity has also meant that citizenship has emerged as a contested topic, which has become central to essential practices of social organisation. Based on these factors it can be certainly stated that citizenship, especially in the last three decades, has become one of the most essential and discussed concepts. Contestations associated with it signify the malleable nature of citizenship, due to which it has almost become improbable to concoct a consistent theory of citizenship (Kymlicka & Norman, 1994). Issues related to citizenship, hence, have to be understood in the specific contexts within which they manifest, necessitating a flexible and thick methodology. Due to these complications, any text dealing with contestations and issues in relation to citizenship has to look into multiple academic and historical discourses. This chapter attempts to shed light on certain unspecified and often ignored spaces of citizenship, through a multidiscipline approach, which are essential in constructing rituals of citizenship that, in turn, have become essential in understanding the contemporary discourse on citizenship in India.

The malleability and the scope of citizenship prevent it from being characterised as a static concept (Hoffman, 2004) while, somewhat paradoxically, citizenship is also bound to the existence of the state and, therefore, to a principle of public sovereignty (Balibar, 1988, p. 723). It is due to these seemingly contradictory impulses that the relationship between citizenship and territoriality (Sack, 1983) has been heavily scrutinized in the last three decades. The relationship between citizenship, space and territoriality has undergone a reimagining over the last few decades. A significant section of the literature dealing with citizenship in recent decades has argued for a more globalised and fluid understanding of citizenship. Various scholars (Benhabib, 2004; Hoffman, 2004; Turner, 1986) have argued for the withering away of

DOI: 10.4324/9781003345152-3

the inherited geography of state territories as a result of the emergence of new post-territorial geographies. One of the predominant ideas during this period has been a focus on denationalisation of citizenship.

The argument for a de-territorialised understanding of citizenship has been based on two assumptions. The first assumption runs on the fact that a growing cosmopolitan consciousness would overtake sentiments of national pride; second, it is also assumed that the contemporary globalised systems will provide the material conditions within which cosmopolitan interactions will be possible (Roy, 2010). While the recent trend of globalisation undeniably warrants a new understanding of citizenship, it by no means signifies an end of territoriality. This understanding of deterritorialisation does not take sufficient account of the historical complexities of territoriality. Additionally, the global flow of capital and goods cannot occur without various forms of *spatial fixity*, localization and re-territorialisation (Harvey, 2001). Second, a break with state-centrism is thus secured through the state's conceptual negation, a move that sidesteps the analysis of newly emergent, reterritorialized forms of state power and their associated political geographies (van Schendel, 2004). Brenner argues that the current wave of globalisation is leading to (1) the transcendence of the state-centric configuration of capitalist territorial organisation that prevailed much throughout the twentieth century and (2) the production of new configurations of territoriality on both sub- and supra-national geographical scales (Brenner, 1999, p. 41). Therefore, the efforts to escape the previously mentioned *territorial trap* (Agnew, 1994) of state-centrism cannot be based on the negation of geographical locus of social and political power. Rather, this requires a reinterpretation of both state territoriality and political space in the present times. In contrast to the globalised narratives of citizenship, the imaginaries and management of space remains central in defining the category of the citizen is intrinsically associated with *cartographic* and *demographic anxieties*. Due to the presence of these anxieties, the figure of the *outsider* becomes central to the progress of the citizenship discourse and state formation. Moreover, given its broad scope of application, citizenship has emerged as a malleable concept that is articulated by actors at both macro and micro levels. In this context, it becomes essential to further highlight two related dimensions of citizenship.

The understanding of citizenship in academic circles and its articulation by state institutions and individual citizens points towards two dimensions of citizenship. The first can be characterised as the *functional* dimension of citizenship, which relates to the questions of citizenship rights and entitlements. The second can be characterised as the *relational* dimension of citizenship, which majorly relates to the spatial dimensions of citizenship. In a similar vien, the pre-existing literature on citizenship can be roughly categorised into another pair of broad themes that correspond to these two distinctions. The first theme deals with the questions of boundaries, inclusion and exclusion as shown by the increased scrutiny on the relationship between citizenship and territoriality. This essentially relates to the relational dimension of citizenship as it critically engages with the relationship among individual citizens and between the citizen and the state or any other territorialising institution, that is *forces of globalisation*.[1] The second theme deals with the question of rights, democratic participation, security, justice and the like. Central to this theme in recent times has been the question of difference or group differentiated rights, which has allowed for a multicultural articulation of citizenship, which can be essentially classified under the functional dimension of citizenship. It is the interplay of these two dimensions that leads to the emergence of the citizen as not only a spatially distinct category but also as an internally differentiated one too.

These two dimensions of citizenship are not paradoxical to each other; rather, it is essential that these two dimensions substantiate each other. The relational dimension of citizenship in recent times has emerged as the bedrock for the globalised narratives of citizenship as it emphasises the necessity of accepting diversity and difference (Hoffman, 2004). But, the relational dimension of citizenship, ideally, needs to be substantiated/complimented by the functional dimension. As the relational dimension of citizenship manifests itself among the citizens it becomes essential that it is substantiated by a functional authority that can enumerate the discourses of rights and entitlement promised by citizenship. Hence, the emergence of citizenship or membership, in general, is always tied to an institution that can reproduce the relational dimension of citizenship and perform the functional dimensions of citizenship. This is true even for the globalised narratives of citizenship, which have emerged in the last three decades as much of the arguments for a globalised narrative of citizenship are based on the acceptability and the ability of non-traditional institutions to reproduce and perform both these dimensions of citizenship. Traditionally, the nation state has emerged as the institution that has been the most efficient in performing and reproducing these relationships.

Due to the interplay of these two dimensions of citizenship, it has meant that traditionally the category of a citizen has emerged as an instrument of legibility, for the state, that unfolds itself as an '*instituted process*' (Somers, 1993, p. 589) through which multiple groups and individuals assert their claims. It is also in this process of unfolding, that rituals of inclusion and exclusion get embedded within the institutional and social structures of a nation state. Success or failure of any modern state among various other factors depends on its ability to make the society legible.[2]The legibility of society enhances the capacity for large-scale social engineering (Scott, 1998, p. 2), through which the state gets further entrenched. This quest for legibility thereby requires the formation of distinct, singular and governable categories. Citizenship, within such a framework, remains tied to the process of state formation and affirmation of state power (Roy, 2010, p. 11). As citizenship is associated with the state, the emergence of the citizen as a distinct and privileged category is most often associated with a distinct spatiality.

This is to say that the privileges accorded to the citizen are primarily based on its association with a particular spatial configuration and hence central to the manner in which the state constructs singular governable categories. The category of the citizen can, therefore, be defined as a distinctive category that enjoys certain privileges due to its association with the state. More important, it is within this structure that demands of group differentiated rights are articulated. In this context, we can make a couple of observations regarding citizenship in contemporary times. First, as citizenship develops, in tandem with the state, it has to distinguish itself from the *other*, where the other is situated outside the territorial bounds of the state in stark contrast to the citizen who remains unquestionably attached to the state. Second, in order to claim privileges associated with citizenship, within the state, the citizenry has to associate itself with a distinct identity that is acceptable to the state and doesn't challenge the relational dimension of citizenship that the state articulates.

Having identified these two dimensions of citizenship and the ideal relationship between them it is essential to further investigate the manner in which the synchronisation of these two dimensions have taken place in the Indian context. For the nation state to construct a sustainable discourse of citizenship, it has to continuously respond to the diverse functional demands in a manner that doesn't disrupt the relational and spatially distinct narrative/logic of citizenship. Hence, understanding the relationship between these two dimensions of citizenship becomes essential to understanding how the inherent progressive momentum of citizenship (Hoffman, 2004) that allows groups to make specific demands in relation to citizenship gets internalised within the larger narratives of the nation state. Obviously, this process is riddled with conflicts (Sharma, 2019), and the intention here is to look into the contested spaces of citizenship in which the articulation of citizenship has either challenged the relational dimension of citizenship of the Indian state or have been overlooked by it, thus creating contested spaces of citizenship, where the identity of the citizen itself becomes dependent on the interaction between different groups and the state. The purpose of this chapter is to further investigate the question of distinctiveness and exclusion in relation to the refracted nature of citizenship in India and South Asia. In essence, it intends to highlight how the articulation of a spatially distinct and internally differentiated citizen necessitates the presence of an *outsider* that allows the state to restructure the definition of the other in certain contested spaces. Before delving into the contestations surrounding the question of the outsider it is important that we understand the manner in which the nation state comes into being in South Asia.

II Reframing the Nation

To understand the present discourse of citizenship it is essential that we trace the historical presence of the nation in South Asia. This becomes essential due to several factors, first, looking into the conditions and the events that have allowed for the creation of the tangible entity that we now refer to as a nation allows us to understand the exact relational and functional dimension of citizenship in this context; second, this would allow us to escape the territorial trap (Agnew, 1994;Sack, 1983) that most commentaries on citizenship and nationalism fall into by taking the nation state as a taken-for-granted frame of reference. Rather, this chapter highlights that the nationalist project portrays the nation to be natural and this remains central to their nationalist imaginaries (Goswami, 2004) and it is only by identifying contested spaces of citizenship that we see the manner in which the nationalist project *teaches* the nation. Essentially, how one rationalises/historicises the emergence of the nation state in India has huge implications for the manner in which one articulates citizenship (Sammadar, 2016). In many ways, the difficulty regarding any theorisation on nationalism stems from the fact that the nation as an entity can be both *imagined* (Anderson, 2006) and *taught*, a fact that is best exemplified by India. To overcome this complexity it is therefore essential that we identify spaces, where the nation is imagined and differentiate them from the spaces where the nation is taught. This differentiation of spaces may depend on multiple factors, including the specific experiences of colonialism or the specific history of decolonisation.

The national territories marked out by the colonial retreat lacked homogeneity, these territories, although part of the same nation, were distinctly diverse in terms of sociocultural identities. Hence, the process of state formation in India can be characterised as a continuing process of accommodation of regional differentiations within a narrow logic of belonging. The portrayal of the nation as a natural entity, therefore, requires the production and the propagation of ideal types. In this context, it becomes essential for the nation state to frame the abstract idea of a nation on a bounded physical scale. These geographic scales are produced, contested and transformed through an immense range of sociopolitical and discursive process, strategies and struggles that cannot be derived from any single encompassing dynamic (Brenner, 1998, p. 461). The centrality of territorial authority in the creation of scales ensures that the persistence of colonial structures of territorial governance. Here, we can identify a temporal dissonance between the emergence of a national community and the territorial state, as the state continues to use colonial markers of governmentality. This then leads to the creation of a zone of suspension (Krishna, 1994) between the nation and the state as the postcolonial discourse of citizenship is unable to completely separate itself from the colonial parameters of subject hood. This temporal dissonance allows us to better understand the relationship between the nation and the state and how they correspond to the two dimensions of citizenship. The spatial discourse of the state, which in the South Asian context carries over colonial sensibilities, is articulated within a temporal or in this case relational one (nationalism); (Shapiro, 2005, p. 278). In postcolonial South Asia, the colonial structures and sensibilities become essential in furthering the nationalist discourse and vice versa. In this context, it becomes essential to understand how the Indian state remodels and rationalises the demands of group identities (Jayal, 2019) that precede its own existence.

According to Goswami (2004), the nationalist project of teaching the nation involves transforming the abstract categorical conception of the nation into a 'taken for granted frame of reference' as it involves fixing collective identities in place and refashioning local and regional solidarities in accord with a larger national whole (p. 2).The identity of the nation state, in this formulation, manifests itself as a constructed entity that is gradually taught/inscribed and hence the legitimacy of the Nation is contingent upon its ability to integrate multiple and sometimes conflicting functional claims to citizenship. Due to this, the impulse of differentiated inclusion that is the acceptance of varied claims to citizenship, articulated within the overarching relational discourse of nation building, becomes essential in the sustenance of Indian nationalism. The logic of nation building in South Asia, it can be claimed, emerges from negotiated terms of separation, the acceptance of which depends on the moments of encompassment for its affirmation. The logic of encompassment works to resolve the contradiction posed by the diverse nature of Indian society. For democracy to work, universalism must transcend differences by defining each subject in abstract terms as equal before the law while simultaneously it must unfold and install itself among groups and individuals located in different social locations through a relational and dialogical ethic of care, compassion and responsibility (Yuval-Davis and Werbner, 2005, p. 10).Citizenship, even as it manifests itself as a distinguished and privileged category, has to constantly engage with the question of difference that is solved by the logic of encompassment (Yuval-Davis and Werbner, 2005, p. 10), which is then directly followed by moments of closure (Roy, 2008).The manifestations of these moments throughout the history of citizenship in India are not singular; rather, they manifest themselves in specific contexts. Due to the multiple occurrences of encompassment and closure, the emergence of the Indian citizen as a governable category necessitates the creation of exceptions that allows the state to rationalise diverse claims to citizenship. This mechanism of rationalisation is based on a system of appropriation rather than assimilation. This distinction between assimilation and appropriation is necessitated by the specific manner in which these multiple demands are perceived by the state itself. These multiple demands are not necessarily absorbed within the general discourse of citizenship; rather, these are constructed as exceptions and placed in an appropriate relationship with the assumed 'national core' (Pandey, 1998).

Gyanendra Pandey (1998) in his article 'Can a Muslim be an Indian' highlights two major points in the context of Indian nationalism. First, he observes that nations are established by constructing a core, which is portrayed or assumed to be natural to the nation. Second, the category of the minority is constructed alongside this assumed core. Hence, this allows for the construction of the unhyphenated natural citizen in contrast to the hyphenated citizen (Pandey, 1998, p. 608). The theory of encompassment, in this context, is not only essential in maintaining the inclusive thrust of citizenship, but in the context of postcolonial India, it also helps in understanding the legitimisation of the nationalist core. These observations provide the context in which the theory of encompassment is actualised in the Indian context. For the theory of encompassment to function within the context of postcolonial nationalism, it has to act as a link between the unhyphenated and the hyphenated citizens by embedding the ethic of care, compassion and responsibility within the nationalist discourse (Yuval-Davis and Werbner, 2005, p. 10).In this context, the categories of the hyphenated and the unhyphenated are understood to be flexible and may also be understood in accordance with the specific context.

Due to the multiplicities of identities, the scope of these differentiations/categorisations are directly related to the scope of the question ('Can a Muslim be an Indian?'); that is once the question is changed, the constitution of these categories also changes; for example one can replace the term *Muslim* with any linguistic identity like Assamese, Bengali, Punjabi and so on or any tribal identity like Bodo, Chakma and the like and subsequently the constitution of these two categorisations changes dramatically. Moreover, the challenges to the constructed national core have mostly come from linguistic (ULFA), ethnic (NSCN-IM), tribal (the Bodo insurgency) and even class-based assertions of identity (the Maoist/Naxal movement). To understand the present discourses of citizenship in the Indian context it is essential that we understand the spatial dimension of these two categories as this allows us to free the categories of the unhyphenated and the hyphenated citizen from the juxtaposition of the majority–minority dynamic that has characterised politics in postcolonial India.

III Consolidating the State: The Outsider in India

As mentioned in the introductory section of this chapter, the figure of the *outsider* becomes an essential component of the citizenship discourse in South Asia. This chapter differentiates between the '*other*' and the '*outsider*'. The use of the term *outsider* in this context mirrors Chantal Mouffe's use of the term 'constitutive outsider', building on what was construed by Jacques Derrida. According to Mouffe (2000)

> the outsider, unlike the other, cannot be reduced to a dialectical negation. In order to be a true outside, the outside has to be incommensurable with the inside, and at the same time, the condition of emergence of the latter. This is only possible if what is 'outside' is not simply the outside of a concrete content but something which puts into question 'concreteness' as such.
>
> (p. 12)

The distinction between outsider and the other becomes essential in the context of postcolonial India, especially due to the context of state formation in South Asia. To understand the contemporary discourses of citizenship in India, it is essential to highlight how and why the figure of the outsider appears to be a disruptive yet an ever-present element in the Indian citizenship discourse. As mentioned, the relationship between the other and the citizen is one of dialectical negation. The citizen and the other therefore manifest themselves as singular and distinct spatial categories, inhabiting demarcated spaces, where the relationship between them is entrenched in distinction but not exclusion. The recognition of this distinction is essential to distinguishing between the category of the other and the impulses that lead to the process of othering. These impulses of othering are directed towards figures that do not fit into the statist categorisations made by the state and these impulses inform the rituals of legibility. It is in this context that the figure of the outsider emerges as a challenge to the statist categorisations based on distinctiveness. In the Indian context, one can identify two traits that make the outsider. First, unlike the other, the outsider emerges within the territorial bounds of the state and the outsider is inherently dual in nature as it shares features with both the citizen and the other, thereby preventing it from being placed in any singular categorisation. Second, as the presence of such a figure cannot be categorised within the territoriality of the state therefore challenges the very logic of categorisation that emerges with the state's effort to create a legible society. This, in turn, contributes to the narratives of cartographic anxiety (Krishna, 1994), where the outsider becomes a threat to the cartographic integrity of the state.

Due to this anxiety, the outsider becomes increasingly embedded in the language of mobilisation within the nationalist discourse. This makes it essential for the state to transform the outsider into a singular and distinctive category. This is where the citizenship regime becomes dependent and contingent on the ability of the state to locate and transform the outsider into a singular and distinctive category. It is done by delegitimising any claim that the outsider may have to citizenship and the privileges associated with it. At this point, the outsider is converted into a distinct and identifiable non-citizen who can make no claim to citizenship and by extension to the territory of the state that classifies it as a non-citizen. It is essential to highlight that even as the figure of the outsider shares traits with both the citizen and the other, the de-legitimisation of its claims to citizenship does not necessarily associate the non-citizen with a pre-existing entity rather the non-citizen in itself becomes a distinguished other, and is placed in a liminal[3] zone of exchange (Turner, 1967) that originates in the very specific context of state formation in South Asia. Contemporary citizenship experience in India, particularly Assam is also an indication of this direction.

As pointed out by Schendel, decolonisation in South Asia was not a series of clinical operations producing four well defined national bodies. On the contrary, the four post-colonial states (India, Pakistan, Myanmar, Bangladesh) found that their physical separation was incomplete and that they had inherited ill-defined nations and frayed territories (van Schendel, 2007, p. 37). The logic of state formation in South Asia, therefore, originates from multiple phases of separations that have occurred during decolonisation. To be more precise, the rationale of nation formation in South Asia finds its origin in the terms of separation that evolved out of the process of decolonisation. It is then, essential, that these terms of separation get superimposed on the pre-existing social, economic and cultural modes of interaction that preceded the moment of separation. Furthermore, given the incomplete and ill-defined nature of separation, it simultaneously becomes logistically impossible to disentangle these entities. This history of incomplete separation leads to the creation of an absurd situation, where it becomes paramount for each of these postcolonial entities to legitimise its own distinctiveness vis-à-vis another postcolonial entity. This lack of separation between these postcolonial entities creates an inherent crisis of distinction that remains embedded in the very origin of these entities. Due to this history of entanglement, the emergence of the outsider is not restricted to any one state. Hence, the impulse of converting the outsider into the other is an essential assertion of the state's authority and this impulse is shared among the postcolonial nations that have inscribed themselves in South Asia. Once the outsider is transformed into the non-citizen, through rituals of legibility, it becomes essential for the state to dispose of them. This becomes a dilemma in itself as no state can unilaterally place the non-citizen within the territory of another state as referred above. To resolve this dilemma the 'liminal zone of exchange' is created as a buffer between the nation states where the individuals and groups that have been denied citizenship, like non-citizen, are placed. Hence, as the non-citizen is marked as a distinct category, it is simultaneously placed in the liminal zone of exchange. In addition, the liminal zone of exchange is been essential in controlling the movement, transfer and the exchange of population across the national borders in accordance with the specific demands of each nation state. The inhabitants of this space are well defined as they have already been converted into a particular category by any one of the nation state. In this context, the trait of liminality is only associated with the space and not its inhabitants. In simple terms, the liminal zone of exchange manifests itself in between the nation states where the states can deposit unwanted groups and assimilate groups that fit its discourse of distinctiveness. The most recent amendment to the Indian citizenship law is indicative of the 'dictinctive' thrust impulse of nation formation. In contrast, the recently concluded process of the National Register of Citizens (NRC) and the presence of detention camps, in Assam, point to the 'exclusive' thrust of state formation in South Asia. A further example of this can be found in the experience of the Chakma, the Tibetan community Rohingyas who have experienced both these impulses at different points of state formation in South Asia.

IV Modes of Nation Building –The Outsider in the Borderlands

In the earlier section, we highlighted the importance of the 'outsider' within the citizenship discourse in India and how it relates to the inherent cartographic anxieties of the nation state. This particular section investigates how the figure of the outsider becomes an essential tool of teaching the nation in borderlands. Borders have always been an essential component of state and nation building as they have been traditional markers of territorial authority and are, therefore, essential in defining the spatial limits of citizenship (Baud and Van Schendel, 1997). The manner in which a nation state decides to govern its borders has a direct impact on the norms and rituals of citizenship. Second, borders are also significant from a representational point of view; in other words, borders are central to the manner in which any nation state is articulated, visualised and represented both globally and internally. It is due to these conditions that borders and the policing of the said borders have been central to the citizenship discourse in India. The importance of these borders and policing within the citizenship discourse can be attributed to the postcolonial paradox.[4] To address this inherent paradox, it is essential for the state to develop the institutional capacity that enables firm control over mobility and the manipulation of citizenship norms as ways of establishing a clear national identity. Second, postcolonial states adopt tiered migration practices that overwhelmingly favour some population groups over others, particularly wealthier, higher-skilled citizens and so on. (Sadiq and Tsourapas, 2021).

Furthermore, borders in the context of South Asia have been mainly understood, remembered and articulated as constructs that emerged in particular moments of upheaval akin to tectonic shifts. Understandably, these constructs both in their continued existence and their sudden formation are associated with violence, militarisation and conflicts (van Schendel, 2004). In essence, the salience of these constructs within the nationalist discourse is not only dependent on their continued existence, but also, on the retelling of the violence that created these constructs in the first place. The sudden manner in which the borders were created, the ensuing violence/displacement and the resulting (cartographic) anxieties have been popular themes of academic discussions/literature on citizenship, some of which have informed prior sections of this chapter.

Unfortunately, further discussion on these discourses has been undercut by an over-emphasis on borders and border structures and an under-emphasis on the regional specificities of the colonial experience and how these experiences impact the perceptions of borders, citizenship and mobility. This has resulted in a gap between literature on citizenship and borderlands and the literature dealing directly with regional histories of the relatively young borderlands. This gap has, in turn, resulted in the persistence of methodological nationalism[5] (Goswami, 2004). This persistence of methodological nationalism is clearly visible in the manner in which questions related to mobility and citizenship has been addressed in the context of borderlands in South Asia. Due to the inherent anxieties of the postcolonial nation state, borders and borderlands are always marked by cartographic anxieties. It is this anxiety that guides the nation state's approach towards these regions. Given these circumstances, borderlands are governed through legal and cultural zones of exceptions, of which citizenship, both in terms of rights and status becomes an essential part. The articulation of borderlands as a zone of exception marked by a severe crisis of governability, which, in turn, requires differentiated citizenship norms, becomes integral to the manner in which the nation is taught and accepted in these regions. This narrative of exception often circumscribes an acceptable cultural and territorial space of citizenship that ignores the specific histories of mobility and association in the borderlands. Overtime, this narrative becomes accepted facts which are then reproduced in public and academic discourses of the region itself. This allows for the creation of an appropriated understanding of borderlands where questions of belonging and, by extension, citizenship become contingent on the ideal narratives of the nation state and its anxieties. The attainment of citizenship in borderlands, therefore, becomes contingent on the ability of different groups to define or associate themselves with distinct identities that are acceptable to the functionality of the state and the relational discourse of the nation, a process in which, the outsider becomes essential. It is due to these historical patterns of engagement that the categories of the unhyphenated and the hyphenated become flexible and fluid. Essentially population groups that reside in borderlands may ambivalently oscillate (Roy, 2010) between unhyphenated and hyphenated status. The extent of this oscillation depends on how efficiently each particular group differentiates, mobilises and defines themselves in relation to the figure of the outsider. The consolidation of the nation as a community in the Indian context and the South Asian context, in general, depends on a sequential process of unlearning pre-existing patterns of social interactions and remodelling them in accordance to the new nation state's anxieties related to the figure of the outsider. Hence, it is essential to understand the manner in which certain regional groups redefine themselves in accordance with the discourse of the nation state.

As mentioned before this synchronisation of the functional demands of specific groups and the relational narratives of the nationalist identity is essential for the sustenance of a uniform discourse of citizenship in the

Indian context. Achieving this synchronisation has been a tenuous process in the postcolonial context and has been stretched to its utmost limits. These difficulties and nuances of state and nation formation in borderlands are exhibited by the specific developments in Assam, a region, which has generally been described and articulated as an exception within the citizenship discourse in India. One can point out certain specific reasons as to why this region has seen one of the most polarised debates on the issue of citizenship and why it emerges as an exception. First, the location of Assam as a borderland makes it a natural exception within the discourse of Indian nationalism. Second, the region has seen a persistent mobilisation and articulation against the manner in which the citizenship infrastructure has functioned in the Assamese context (Dutta, 2012). These movements and articulations have persistently claimed that the citizenship regime has failed to protect the state and its people from the illegal demographic invasion (SarbanandaSonwal vs. Union of India [2005]) from the neighbouring country of Bangladesh. These sentiments were central to the demands made by the Assam movement which eventually led to the Assam accord and the eventual amendment of 1986 that inserted section 6A in the citizenship law. This particular section only applied to Assam, and therefore, Assam, in terms of rules and a regime of citizenship does present itself as an outlier within the Indian citizenship law.[6]

V Assam and the Bangladeshi

In recent decades, the presence and the 'threat' of the Bangladeshi have not only become an accepted and integral part of the general/popular articulation of citizenship but also, through various reports, policies, laws and judgements, the Bangladeshi has become an legally accepted and ubiquitous part of the legal norms of citizenship specific to Assam (Chakraborty, 2012a; Gogoi, 2022). One of the most intriguing examples of the manner in which the Assamese exception is articulated by both regional actors and the legal system (Dutta, 2020) can be found in the Supreme Court judgement in the SarbanandaSonwal judgement of 2005. The dispute was regarding the exact mechanisms used to identify 'foreigners' in Assam. Sections of the Assamese leadership believed that by putting the burden of proof on the complainant, rather than the accused, the act gave an advantage to the illegal migrants and made the task of identifying/deporting them extremely difficult. To highlight this, they pointed out that the Foreigners Act (1946) that was used for the detection of illegal migrants in other states had proved to be more 'efficient'. This dispute reached a decisive point when SarbanandaSonwal filed a writ petition in the Supreme Court. In this petition, he claimed that the inefficiency of the Illegal Migrants (Detention by Tribunals) Act, 1983 (IMDT) has allowed a number of non-Indians to reside in the state of Assam, which had changed the cultural and the ethnic composition of the area. The Supreme Court in its 2005 judgement highlighted the 77 per cent increase in the population of Muslims in Assam from 1971 to 1991 to 'emphasise' the extent of illegal immigration into Assam from Bangladesh and mentioned that no misconceived notion of secularism should come by way of emphasising the dangerous consequence of illegal immigration from Bangladesh. The judgement claimed that the silent demographic invasion into Assam may lead to the loss of geo-strategically important districts of lower Assam. Therefore, the Supreme Court declared the IMDT act as inefficient and unconstitutional and instead highlighted the importance of the Foreigners Act of 1946. As section 9 of this act places the burden of proof of one's citizenship on the accused instead of the complainant as was the case with the IMDT Act (SarbanandaSonwal vs. Union of India [2005]). This presence/threat of the Bangladeshi in legal judgements, that directly affect the legal norms of citizenship, is not a singular occurrence as the arguments used in the Sonowal judgement were referred to in the Assam SamhillitaMahasabha judgement of 2014 that directed the government to initiate the process of updating the NRC in Assam.

In both these landmark judgements and many other judgements like the Sarabari Begum judgement[7] the presence of the Bangladeshi becomes central to the manner in which Assam is articulated as an exception by both regional and national actors. Moreover these judgments are reflective of the manner in which judicial sovereignty (Mehta, 2007) has shaped popular perceptions of citizenship in Assam. Assam, as articulated by these stakeholders, becomes a borderland that faces an existential threat as a direct result of illegal infiltration which threatens the very social fabric of Assam. In essence, the crisis of 'Demography in Assam' becomes a direct consequence of it sharing international borders with an 'underdeveloped' county that leads to illegal migration due in search of better economic activities. To make the situation more complicated, the 'illegal' migrant and the 'actual' Indian belong to the same ethnic stock (SarbanandaSonwal vs. Union of India [2005]). Therefore, the 'illegal' migrant from Bangladesh in the present context emerges as the outsider who is assumed to be present within the territorial bounds of the nation and shares traits with the citizens which directly challenge the nation state's logic of categorisation leading to cartographic anxieties. Here, the contestations in Assam and the steps taken by the government to resolve the contestations prioritise the anxieties that develop in relation to cartography and territoriality. If anything, the steps taken by the Indian state have at best assimilated the discourse of demographic anxiety, which developed during the colonial rule and still informs narratives of Assamese nationalism, within its discourse of cartographic anxiety. The history of postcolonial Assam is one of assimilation in which its depiction and articulation as an exception by both regional and national actors ignore the colonial specificities of Assam.

This is not to say that the every effort of the Indian state to convert Assam into a national exception has been uncontested as shown by the reaction to the most recent amendment to the citizenship law. The case of

Assam is also representative of how specific functional demands made by a certain section of the nation state may disrupt the nationalised narratives of belonging. This is exemplified by the ongoing resentment against the Citizenship Amendment Act of 2019 (CAA) in the state of Assam. The ongoing resentment in Assam in regards to the CAA represents the most recent point of contention between the Assamese community and the Indian state. This resentment has directly followed the publication of the NRC in the state of Assam, which was a long-standing demand made by certain sections of the Assamese population as it was meant to identify the illegitimate citizens residing in Assam (Roy, 2019). Both, the publication of the NRC and the adoption of the CAA, represent a culmination of two tendencies, which have historically advocated two distinct and bounded forms of citizenship, that have largely coexisted in India as the state was more or less able to assimilate the demands of a certain section of the Assamese community. The NRC, which has till now only been conducted in Assam, introduces a hyphenated citizenship that traces the legitimacy of one's citizenship based on conditions of descent to one particular state (Assam) (Roy, 2016). The publication of NRC was perceived to provide a definitive end to the long struggle initiated by the people of Assam against the influx of immigrants within their territory by differentiating between the legitimate and the illegitimate claims to citizenship. The CAA, on the other, makes religion a central principle in the matter of granting citizenship by exempting six 'minority communities' namely the Hindus, Sikhs, Jains, Parsis, Buddhists and Christians from three neighbouring countries – Afghanistan, Bangladesh and Pakistan – from the category of illegal immigrants. By excluding these communities from the category of illegal immigrants, the CAA brought the citizenship laws in line with the various changes made by the government of India to the Passport (Entry into India) Act (1920) and Foreigners Act (1946) which ensured that the communities mentioned in the CAA were excluded from the category of illegal immigrants (Roy, 2019). While the process of NRC, in principle, was generally accepted by the people of Assam, the adoption of the CAA was perceived to be a dilution of the entire process of NRC. These sentiments led to an anti-CAA protest in Assam and its neighbouring states. Various groups in these states have raised concerns that by exempting the previously mentioned communities from the category of illegal immigrants and legitimising their claims to Indian citizenship the CAA endanger the cultural and economic foundations of these states.

The contrasting reactions to the NRC and the CAA not only highlight a rupture in the negotiations involved in creating citizenship norms, but it also highlights distinct, and in this case conflicting norms of, interpretations of territorial identities and rights. The general acceptance of the NRC and the rejection of the CAA in Assam represent a contradiction embedded in, within the nationalist territoriality of postcolonial India that has manifested itself within the field of citizenship due to the increasing pre-occupation of the Indian state to create and maintain a verifiable and legible identity of an

Indian citizen. The opposition to CAA in certain parts of Assam is deeply rooted in narratives of demographic anxiety that have developed in response to the specific nature of colonialism in Assam. Assam was largely viewed as a *wasteland* (Chakraborty 2012b) where the colonial government encouraged the migration of multiple communities. This led to a restructuring of the demographic fabric of the Assamese society, which, in turn, contributed to a growing fear of being overrun amongst a section of the Assamese people. The manifestation of these sentiments can be found as early as the late 19th century and thus by the time the 'creation of India' was negotiated, demographic anxiety had become a central sentiment within the Assamese society (Nag, 2018).

The retreat of the empire was also an important moment in the creation of contemporary Assam. The creation of India marked a transformative moment in Assamese history as the partition of 1947 not only reconfigured the territory of Assam but it also transformed Assam from a *wasteland* to a *borderland*. It is this transformation from a wasteland to a borderland that necessitates the coexistence of both cartographic and demographic anxieties. The multiple moments of conflicts between the agenda of the Indian state and certain sections of the Assamese society, including the most recent conflict, represent a situation in which these two anxieties have led to differing and conflicting impulses. As mentioned earlier, the legitimacy of the state and by extension the citizenship norms, depends on the ability of the state to transform the outsider into a singular and distinct category and therefore the presence of the illegal migrant from Bangladesh becomes an essential tool in ensuring that that nation is taught in a region marked with deep demographic anxieties and antagonisms.

VI Case Zero–Non-Citizen

This chapter has primarily focused on the statist rationalisations of citizenship. This by no means assumes that citizenship as a category is solely dependent on the actions of the state or regional elites. As highlighted by Joya Chatterji, 'citizenship was produced as a complex interaction between a bewildering plethora of actors' (Chatterji, 2012, p. 1050). Rather, by characterising citizenship as an 'instituted process' (Somers, 1993, p. 589), this chapter intends to highlight how these interactions, mentioned by Chatterji (2012), are rationalised/unified within a singular articulation of citizenship. The most recent amendment to the citizenship law along with the process of NRC, in Assam, were merely new additions to the long list of measures used by the Indian state to articulate a unified discourse of citizenship. The CAA and the NRC are not a sudden addition to the citizenship discourse in India; on the contrary, these two exercises are a culmination of the two basic impulses of citizenship that we want to highlight in this chapter. The CAA, essentially, articulates the distinctive nature of Indian citizenship by favouring specific communities in matters of granting citizenship. Interestingly, a section of these people already inhabit the liminal zone of exchange while the others emerge as the outsiders in the historical context of other nation states. The NRC, in responding to the demands of the Axomiya people, acknowledges the need to assimilate the Assamese exception within the discourse of Indian citizenship. While prior efforts to integrate the Assamese exception within the overarching narrative have been conflict-ridden, the Indian state has also shown ample flexibility in smoothing over these disagreements. What is interesting is the emergence/use of the term *non-citizen*.

The term *non-citizen* is by no means new; rather, it has existed as a well-defined and accepted category. According to the 'Office of the United Nations High Commissioner for Human Rights' (2006) the non-citizen is identified as 'a person who has not been recognized as having any effective links to the country where he or she is located'. Moreover, the term *non-citizen* as used by the United Nation Human Rights Commission (UNHRC) represents an umbrella term that includes different groups like permanent residents, migrants, refugees, asylum seekers, victims of trafficking, foreign students, temporary visitors, other kinds of non-immigrants and stateless people. In contrast, this term, in the Indian context, has come to represent a singular category rather than an umbrella term. In fact, the emergence of the singular non-citizen has been contingent on the Indian state's willingness to accept certain sections of refugees. As we saw in the context of the Illegal Immigrants (Expulsion from Assam) Act, 1950, the Indian state differentiates between justified and unjustified claims to citizenship by juxtaposing the refugee against the illegal immigrant. As this chapter points that the illegal immigrant is not necessarily a singular category, especially in the Indian context, it assumes the role of the outsider that needs to be converted into a singular and identifiable category, that category being, the non-citizen. Here, the term *non-citizen* is used to refer to any group or individuals, who through various constitutionally accepted means have been identified as foreigners who were found to be illegally residing in India.

Arguably, one can claim, that the entire process of NRC (including the Foreigners Tribunals) creates a distinguished and legible category of the non-citizen, which in no way should be confused with the category of the Indian citizen or the desirable refugee. This sentiment was echoed by the present chief minister of Assam who stated, in an interview to Express News Service (2021),

> till we send them back, we have to create a class of non-citizens. We have to allow them to enjoy fundamental rights, rights to health and education, rights to life and liberty; however they may be disenfranchised till the question of extradition to Bangladesh is finally resolved. And there must be some specific time frame.

The non-citizen, therefore, emerges as a singular category that is identified and created by the rituals of legibility instituted by the Indian state. The non-citizen in this context is distinct from the category of the refugee due to two basic reasons. First, due to the entangled nature of state formation in South Asia, the nation states will always look for desirable refugees to further their narrative of distinctiveness. Second, while both the non-citizen and the refugee enjoy certain rights, they are distinct in their origins. While the refugee may emerge due to state-sponsored persecution, which may be backed by the majority community, the non-citizen is created inside courtrooms. Hence, the emergence of the non-citizen in contemporary India provides a fertile field for further analysis of the various currents of citizenship.

Notes

1 As the forces of globalisation or the global flow of capital and goods cannot occur without various forms of spatial fixity, localisation and re-territorialisation (Harvey 2001).
2 The term legibility, in this context, is used in relation to statecraft.
3 The term liminality was first used by Arnold Van Gennep in his book Rites De Passage (1909) and was later expanded on by Victor W Turner. The term liminality generally refers to an ambiguous phase that exists between two points of separation and assimilation.
4 The postcolonial paradox is defined by two sets of tensions in states' post-independence migration management practices. First, the need to establish a modern sovereign nation-state defined by a clear national identity is constrained by weak institutional capacity to achieve it. Second, the establishment of citizenship norms that aim to address colonial and/or imperial injustices, oftentimes by being accommodative to co-ethnics outside the nation-state, contrasts with establishing sovereign territorial borders themselves (Sadiq and Tsourapas, 2021).
5 Goswami defines methodological nationalism as entailing the common practice of presupposing, rather than examining, the socio historical production of such categories as a national space and national economy and the closely related failure to analyze the specific global field within and against which specific nationalist movements emerged (Goswami, 2004).
6 See section 6A of the citizenship act. Also see section 4A of 2003 citizenship rule.
7 The judge from Guwahati HC stated "that it is no longer a secret or in the domain of 'doubt' that illegal Bangladeshis have intruded every nook and corner of Assam very often, they are protected by extending the protective lands of 'secularism' branding them to be Indian "minorities' in Assam. A strong political will to free Assam from illegal Bangladeshi is the need of the hour coupled with public activism in that direction" [Sarabari Begum (Mustt.) @ Syera Begum Vs. State of Assam (2008)].

References

Agnew, J. (1994). The Territorial Trap: The Geographical Assumptions of International Relations Theory. *Review of International Political Economy*, 1(1), 53–80.

Anderson, B. (2006). *Imagined Communities: Reflection on the Origins and the Spread of Nationalism*. London, New York: Verso.

Balibar, E. (1988). Propositions on Citizenship. *Ethics*, 104, 257–289.

Baud, M. and van Schendel, W. (1997). Toward a Comparative History of Borderlands. *Journal of World History*, 8(2), 211–242.

Benhabib, S. (2004). *The Rights of Others: Aliens, Residents, and Citizens* (The Seeley Lectures, pp. 1–24). Cambridge: Cambridge University Press. doi:10.1017/CBO9780511790799.002

Brenner, N. (1998). Between Fixity and Motion: Accumulation, Territorial Organization and the Historical Geography of Spatial Scales. *Environment and Planning; Society and Space*, 16, 459–481.

Brenner, N. (1999). Beyond State-centrism? Space, Territoriality, and Geographical Scale in Globalization Studies. *Theory and Methods*, 28(1), 39–78.

Chakraborty, G. (2012a). The "Ubiquitous" Bangladeshis. *Economic and Political Weekly*, 47(35), 21–23.

Chakraborty, G. (2012b). The Roots and Ramifications of a Colonial Construct: The Wasteland in Assam. *IDSK Occasional Papers*, 39, 1–32.

Chatterji, J. (2012). South Asian Histories of Citizenship. 1946-1970. *The Historical Journal*, 55(4), 1049–1071.

Desforges, L., Jones, R., and Woods, M. (2005). New Geographies of Citizenship. *Citizenship Studies*, 9(5), 439–451

Dutta, B. (2020). Recovering the 'Other Side of Silence': Citizenship Amendment Act, 2019 and the Refugee versus Immigrant Discourse of Post-colonial Assam. *Asian Confluence: Engaging the Third Space, AsCon Monograph005.*

Dutta, N. (2012). *Questions of Identity in Assam: Location, Migration and Hybridity*. New Delhi: Sage Publications India.

Express News Service. (2021, June 3). P.M told me to have 'Zero Hour' in Cabinet to hear negative feedback: HimantaBiswaSarma. PM told me to have 'Zero Hour' in Cabinet to hear negative feedback: HimantaBiswaSarma |India News, The Indian Express.

Gogoi, S. (2022). From Outsiders to Termites and Infiltrators: How 'Bangladeshi' Came to Signify Hate and Difference. *Scroll.in*. Retrieved May 21, 2022, from https://scroll.in/article/1023979

Goswami, M. (2004). *Producing India: Form colonial Economy to National Space*. Chicago: The University of Chicago Press.

Harvey, David. (2001). *Spaces of Capital: Towards a Critical Geography*. New York: Routledge.

Hoffman, J. (2004). *Citizenship Beyond the State*. New Delhi: Sage Publication India.

Jayal, N. G. (2019). Reconfiguring Citizenship in Contemporary India. *South Asia: Journal of South Asian Studies*, 41(1), 33–50.

Krishna, S. (1994). Cartographic Anxiety: Mapping the Body Politic in India. *Alternatives*, 19(4), 507–521.

Kymlicka, W and Norman, W. (1994). Return of the Citizen: A Survey of Recent Work on Citizenship. *Ethics*, 104, 257–289.

Mehta, P. B. (2007). The Rise of Judicial Sovereignty. *Journal of Democracy*, 18(2), 70–84

Mouffe, C. (2000). *The Democratic Paradox*. London, New York: Verso.

Nag, S. (2018). Ethnic Cleansing through Constitutional Means. *Analytical Monthly Review*, 16(6), 53–63.

Pandey, G. (1998, p. 608). Can a Muslim be Indian? *Comparative Studies in Society and History*, 41(4), 608–629.

Roy, A. (2008). Between Encompassment & Closure: The Migrant and the Citizen in India. *Contributions to Indian Sociology*, 42(2), 219–248.
Roy, A. (2010). *Mapping Citizenship in India*. New Delhi: Oxford University Press.
Roy, A. (2016). Ambivalence of Citizenship in Assam. *Economic and Political Weekly*, 51(26&27), 45–51.
Roy, A. (2019). The Citizenship (Amendment) bill 2016 and the Aporia of Citizenship. *Economic and Political Weekly*, 54(49), 28–34.
Sack, R. D. (1983). Human Territoriality: A Theory. *Association of American Geographers*, 73(1), 55–74
Sadiq, K. and Tsourapas, G. (2021). The Postcolonial Migration State. *European Journal of International Relations*, 27(3), 884–912.
Samaddar, R. (2016). Rule, Governmental Rationality and Reorganisation of state. In A. Sarangi and S. Pai (eds.), *Interrogating Reorganisation of states: Culture, Identity and Politics in India* (pp. 48–65). New Delhi: Routledge.
van Schendel, W. (2004). *The Bengal Borderland: Beyond State and Nation in South Asia*. London: Anthem.
van Schendel, W. (2007). The Wagah Syndrome: Territorial Roots of Contemporary Violence in South Asia. In A. Basu and S. Roy (eds.), *Violence and Democracy in India* (pp. 36–82). London: Berg Publishers; Kolkata: Seagull Books.
Scott, J. C. (1998). *Seeing like the State: How Certain Schemes to Improve the Human Condition Have Failed*. New Haven: Yale University Press.
Shapiro, M. J. (2005). Nation States. In J. Agnew, K. Mitchell and G. Tola (eds.), *A Companion to Political Geography* (pp. 271–288). Oxford: Blackwell Publishing Ltd.
Sharma, S. (2019). Territories of Belonging: Citizenship and Everyday Practices of the State in Bodoland. [Unpublished Doctoral Dissertation]. University of Cambridge.
Somers, R. M. (1993, p. 589). Citizenship and the Place of the Public Sphere: Law, Community, and Political Culture in the Transition to Democracy. *American Sociological Review*, 58(5), 587–620.
Turner, B. S. (1986). *Citizenship and Capitalism: The Debate Over Reformism*. London: Allen& Unwin.
Turner, W. V. (1967). Liminality and Communitas. In Victor W. Turner (ed.), *The Ritual Process: Structure and Anti Structure* (pp. 94–130). Chicago: Aldine Transactions.
Yuval-Davis, N. and Werbner, P. (2005). *Women, Citizenship and Difference*. New Delhi: Zubaan.

Legal Cases and Acts

1) Assam Sanmilita Mahasangha & Ors. Vs. Union of India & Ors, (2014) 2014 Latest Case law 792 SC
2) Assam Accord, (15th August, 1985)
3) Constituent Assembly Debate, 12th August, 1949, p. 414
4) LOK SABHA. (2016). Report of the Joint Committee on the Citizenship (Amendment) Bill, 2016. Committee: LokSabha (loksabhaph.nic.in)

5) SarbanandaSonowal vs. Union of India & ANR. (2005) 2005 Latest Case law 347 SC
6) Sarabari Begum (Mustt.) @ Syera Begum and Ors. Vs. State of Assam and Ors. (2008)2008 G.L.T 272
7) The Indian Evidence Act, 1872, No 1 of 1872
8) The Passport (Entry into India) Act, 1920, No. 34 of 1920
9) The Foreigners Act, 1946, No. 31 OF 1946
10) The Immigrants (Expulsion from Assam) Act, 1950, No. 10 of 1950
11) The Illegal Migrants (Determination by Tribunals) Act, 1983, No. 39 of 1983
12) The Citizenship (Amendment) Act, 2019, No-47of 2019

II

Statelessness

Emotions and Anxieties

Chapter 2

Citizenship Question in the Transnational Context

Literary Perspectives

Himadri Lahiri

1 Introduction

> Statelessness is in part the description of a status, fixed in its contemporary moment. But statelessness is also a condition that changes over time, dynamically created and re-created by sovereignties in their own interests, defining the vulnerable in ways that affirm the invulnerable, and in the process revealing changing domestic values and changing power relations across inter-national boundaries.
>
> (Kerber, 2005, p. 731)

> What are the state mandated markers of belonging in the beginning of the twenty first century and how do these markers play out along the axes of race, gender and religion in specific historical contexts?
>
> (Banerjee, 2020, p. 289)

In India National Register of Citizenship (NRC), Citizenship Amendment Bill (CAB) or Citizenship Amendment Act (CAA) have pried open the question of citizenship and statelessness as never before. In a country that constitutionally proclaims itself to be secular, the NRC, CAB and CAA seek to operate on the criterion of religion, the fallout of which is the creation of a huge number of stateless people. Linda K. Kerber, in a different national context, rightly points out that '[s]tatelessness is not a simple conceptual matter [only]; it now breaks along the fault lines of perceptions of state security, race and ethnicity, ideal workers, and gender' (Kerber, 2005, p. 744). One can add similar other factors, such as religion, to the list provided by Kerber. There are allegations of a partisan ideology-based politics of discrimination and bureaucratic mismanagement and manipulations in the context of the NRC, the CAB, and the CAA in India.[1] There is also a widespread concern that such attempts to manipulate citizenship in India are prejudicial to the secular credentials of the nation state. Questions that crop up about the citizenship issue in the current Indian context have multiple dimensions including legal, constitutional, political and ethical ones. As a student of literature, the author of this chapter is, however, more concerned

DOI: 10.4324/9781003345152-5

with the human, emotional and ethical dimensions of the huge political manoeuvres. In examining the political impact of the citizenship laws, humanitarian aspects usually get sidestepped. The emotional concern of the victimised which is intricately connected with the human rights is being manifested daily through expressions of disappointment, disgust, anxiety, anger and fear, emotions which may cause madness, can drive people to violence and may even lead the victims to suicide.[2]

Literary representations of such a humanitarian crisis can effectively bring out emotive issues arising out of majoritarian politics and state policies and ensure the readers' vicarious participation in the actions represented there. In a perceptive study of Kamila Shamsie's novel *Home Fire* (2017), which raises the question of citizenship and statelessness in the transnational space, Debjani Banerjee observes, 'Entitlements and rights of citizenship remain significant in the context of increasing statelessness and the national identities via citizenship are valuable manuscripts of agency and mobility' (2020, pp. 289–290). At the same time, she asserts that one cannot 'gloss over state articulations of ideology which are important because they affect economies, war, immigration policies and crucially people's daily lives' (Banerjee, 2020, p. 290). She stresses the need for identifying 'the state mandated markers of belonging in the beginning of the twenty first century' and how 'these markers play out along the axes of race, gender and religion in specific historical contexts' (Banerjee, 2020, p. 289). The state usually enters into a collusion with the mainstream community as to how to decide the 'foreigner' question and act accordingly. Thinking in terms of fictional representation of such issues, Banerjee argues, 'The disembodied character of policies and doctrines when refracted through fictional characters shine a light on human tragedy and incomprehensible loss' (2020, p. 290). She refers to R. Radhakrishnan's comment on the intersection of fiction and politics as '[a] space of reflexive specularity' (qtd. in Banerjee, 2020, p. 290). Radhakrishnan indeed observes that without this 'reflexive specularity,' 'reality can never make any truth claims about itself' (2012, p. 660). Configuration of a transformed future is possible in a fiction through the agential role of the author's skill to 'think with precision,' a phrase he borrows from Amitav Ghosh's *The Shadow Lines*. Banerjee points out that '[t]he real exists through representation, and, at least, one of the ways in which the real represents itself is through fiction. Therefore, to understand fiction, one needs to understand the underpinnings of the real – the matrices that scaffold our material existence' (2020, p. 290). She speaks of the need to understand 'the underpinnings of the real' in the transnational space as well as to develop a transnational framework to 'read literature in the context of nationalism as a site of contestation' (ibid, p. 290). While doing so, one has to necessarily examine the issue of citizenship and statelessness in the host nation.

In the present chapter, an attempt is made to explore this issue of citizenship and statelessness in the transnational space as manifested in two literary works – Monica Sone's autobiographical narrative *Nisei Daughter* (1953) and Rita Chowdhury's (2018) historical fiction *Chinatown Days*. Sone's *Nisei Daughter* presents the narrative of a second-generation Japanese American girl growing up in the United States during the 1930s and 1940s. Seen through the lens of this young Japanese American girl, Sone's work presents the story of how, based on mere suspicion, a majoritarian regime victimises the members of a minority community immediately after the Japanese bombing of Pearl Harbor in 1941. Chowdhury's (2018) fiction similarly speaks of the plight of the members of the Chinese community in India who were also victims of suspicion and were interned in the wake of Indo-Chinese war in 1961. These works raise the related issues of belonging, citizenship, and statelessness of two immigrant communities – Japanese and Chinese – in two diasporic spaces – the United States and India. Both the texts have the common theme of detention and speak of the emotional turmoil of the members of the two communities. They foreground how 'nationalist' sentiments build up through the manipulation of emotions of the mainstream communities. The citizenship status of the members of the affected communities is either ignored or violated in such contexts. The study of emotion and affect is going to be the mainstay for the analysis of the two texts.

II Emotion and Affect: The Process of Being and Becoming

Speaking of the role of communication network and how it affects 'political field opened up by political biopower' (156) and 'cultural politics of communication' (156), Tiziana Terranova observes, 'As with the masses, this political mode cannot but start with affects – that is with intensities, variations of bodily powers that are expressed as fear and empathy, revulsion and attraction, sadness and joy' (2004, pp. 156–157). The political mode, she continues, 'arises out of affective investments and works through an inventive and emotive political intelligence on the terrain of the *common* – the constituent terrain of the contemporary politics of communication' (ibid, p. 157; emphasis original). Two important points emerge from the extract quoted earlier: first, political modes of all kinds involve an 'affect' in the sense that it is the result of emotional investments of the important stakeholders in specific issues. Tim C. Well, Lauren Mark, and Jorge Sandoval argue that 'affect is thought of alongside encounters within a constantly *becoming* world' (2020, p. 31; emphasis added). Following Brian Massumi, they observe that affect is 'the capacity to affect and be affected' (Massumi, 2002, p. 31) and assert that affect 'has less interest in its symbolic meaning than in the *generative outcome* that an encounter affords' (ibid, p. 31; emphasis added). Through the circulation of affective emotions, a community may solidify its attitude towards a particular issue and may form, or destabilise, an alliance with another community. New contexts may generate new forms of 'becoming.' It may be said that contemporary statelessness is also the outcome of new forms of affective politics in emerging contexts. Second, the 'common' constituency of politics involves newer and faster forms of communications (such as the mass media) in the everyday life. This implies faster circulation of affective, emotional contents in the public space. The circulation of emotion and the issue of relationality lead to the temporary formation of emotion which is fluid and unstable but oriented towards given directions. Emotion such as hate is thus an all-pervasive element now in the field of politics.

In politics and statist ventures, creating an affect remains a focal factor, and for this, the role of persuasive gestures is a pre-requisite. Rhetorical exercises, either on grand, spectacular public platforms or in micro-level meetings and processions or on mass media such as television, and even in person-to-person contact, try to generate the desired emotional effects. Carefully prepared scripts with focus on sensitive issues which are expected to rouse desired emotional outbursts go a long way in creating a politically charged atmosphere and this is achieved through carefully manipulated language and appropriate performative display on the part of the speakers. Politicians and other stakeholders are often found 'preying on the people's hopes and fears, the two emotions that they are most likely to appeal to' (Thrift, 2008, p. 247). Peta Tait argues that 'rhetorical display repeatedly demonstrates that emotion is socially performable and therefore can be manipulated' and argues that it is important 'in the 21st century to investigate how emotions are crafted for effect in communication processes and in order to evoke feeling' (2016, p. 2). In nations where common people largely remain uneducated and vulnerable to uncritical reception of views, politicians and policy makers, through different strategies, including rhetorical exercises, can rouse the emotion of the public to achieve their own political goals. It is easier to ignite the public passion by drawing their attention to issues like displacement and dispossession such as the ones that happened during the partition of India. This is also true of the measures taken by the states in times of political crises, real or imagined, which may include actual or imminent foreign military attacks. During such crises, security issues are foregrounded and a perception of threat from within the state becomes evident. A link between the local agent/s and a foreign power is often perceived to be true or is deliberately circulated to target individuals and groups. The target group with some ancestral connection to the invading country or ethnic-religious associations with the people of that country is singled out for persecution. Most often, the politics of suspicion and hate activates, or is activated, more on state and popular perception rather than on any actual evidence of sabotage or animosity. State edicts, based on the perception factor, promise punitive actions. The citizens too are swept by a wave of distrust, suspicion and animosity which are fuelled and reinforced by the state action. The effect is achieved by some 'affective techniques, premised on making appeals to the heart, passion, emotional imagination, to and through a realm of affect that is co-present with the psychic and the emotional rather than the intellect and reasoning'(Thrift, 2008, p. 243). The 'use of symbols, images, flags, music, affirmations, phrases, speeches, and slogans' play an important role in this respect (Thrift, 2008, p. 243). The 'inflamed imaginaries' can really 'produce conspiracy theories' (Thrift, 2008, p. 241). In the production of the conspiracy theory, circulation plays the most crucial role. Sara Ahmed argues,

> [M]y model of hate as an affective economy suggests that emotions do not positively inhabit *anybody* or *anything*, meaning that 'the subject' is simply one nodal point in the economy, rather than its origin and destination. This is extremely important: it suggests that the sideways [spreading horizontally to other 'subjects' during the same period of time] and backwards [historical] movement of emotions such as hate is not contained within the contours of a subject.
>
> (2004, p. 46; emphases original)

Emotion, thus roused, gathering its strength from a supposed history of injury/injustice inflicted on the subject, circulates through networks and generates passions that get channelised towards the targeted community. The circulation of emotion thus creates a body of 'we' that is pitted against a perceived body of 'they' who supposedly do not belong. The latter is then variously designated as 'the other," the dirt," the excess," the termites' which, according to the roused/manipulated rationale, must be banished from the territorial boundary of the state or otherwise incarcerated or crushed. 'In other words, waves of affect are transmitted and received, transmitted and received ... as they cook up an affective storm' (Thrift, 2008, p. 243). With each circulation, affect receives 'surplus values'. A 'continuous biocultural contagion' (Thrift, 2008, p. 243) affects the everyday life of the citizens. The circulation of the emotion and the rhetorical hype generate the impression of an emergency condition, a situation of 'exception,' that makes state intervention in the form of legislation and/or incarceration seem urgent. This is how, in the words of Thrift, 'affect can be engineered to produce a politics which is able to act as a dark force which is part and parcel of the new liberal settlement' (ibid, p. 240). Thrift also speaks of 'performance management' (ibid, p. 241) which can be deployed to achieve maximum effect.

Sara Ahmed argues that 'emotions operate to "make" and "shape" bodies as forms of action, which also involve orientations towards others' (Ahmed, 2004, p. 4). 'Bodies,' shaped by radical emotions, look on 'docile' bodies which are affected by other kinds of emotions. Emotions, she further observes, 'shape the very surfaces of bodies, which take shape through the repetition of actions over time, as well as through orientations towards and away from others' (Ahmed, 2004, p. 4). I interpret the phrase 'surfaces of bodies' to include not only an expressed bodily action (such as beating, hugging, or grimacing) but also an emotional articulation that bodies forth in the form of oral abuse or expressions of hopelessness or sympathy. Ahmed's discussion takes us beyond the expressions of individuals to include the spread of particular emotions through public discourses so that these can settle down and sediment as dominant elements in the popular mind. This implies that in the case of contested issues involving race, ethnicity, or religion which play an important role in the matter of citizenship of a country, larger bodies of population, besides the government machinery with all its policymaking bodies, are involved, and politicians, as well as activists of different hues, are engaged in the formulation of discourses and articulation of discourse-fed emotions. Repetition of ideological articulations through public speech and print and electronic media consolidate emotions of rage, frustration, disgust and the like. The larger the body of receivers, the greater the impact. Emotions collected in individual bodies merge into the emotion of the communities. Community bodies, in the process, often turn into communal bodies. In periods of political stress and strain in particular, this ultimately serves the objectives of larger political bodies and/or the state machinery. At such junctures of national history, humanitarianism and ethical values are surrendered to political convenience or at the altar of false gods.

In the next two sections, I try to explore the operation of this process through a brief analysis of the two texts I have mentioned earlier.

III Monica Sone's *Nisei Daughter*

White American racist hate for the Japanese American community was simmering for a long time; the Japanese bombing of Pearl Harbor on December 7, 1941, brought it directly to the foreground. It played a crucial role in the internment of people of Japanese descent, many of whom were in fact American citizens. Japanese Americans were considered to be 'unmeltable' elements in the American melting pot. Legally speaking, children born in the US to Japanese parents were citizens of the country although most of their parents were not so – they were indeed stateless people. Monica Sone's *The Nisei Daughter* also foregrounds this generational split in the community. The narrator, for instance, states, 'I knew Father and Mother were not Americans, as we were, because they were not born here, and that there was a law which said they could not become naturalised American citizens because they were Orientals' (Sone, 1953, p. 113). But at the time of internment, it did not really matter whether a Japanese American was a citizen or a stateless person. The narrator states, 'I knew instinctively that the fact that I was an American by birthright was not going to help me escape the consequences of this unhappy war' (Sone, 1953, p. 146).

This knowledge created a sense of emotional turmoil in the younger generation. The children, along with their parents, were also sent to internment camps. This was a great injustice to the Japanese American citizens. In 'Toward a History of Statelessness in America' Linda K. Kerber observes,

> When adults are deported, their citizen children go with them. The most notorious example of this is the U.S. internment camps of World War II, where the birthright citizen children of Japanese-American parents (some of whom were themselves birthright citizens) were confined without recourse.
>
> (Kerber, 2005, p. 738)

This suggests that citizenship for the immigrants is not an unconditional privilege; in the diasporic space, statelessness and citizenship are contingent on the criteria of race, ethnicity, or religion as well as on the nature of the relationship between the home country and the host country. Sone's narrative thus raises the question of belongingness: to which nation do they really belong? Irrespective of their legal status of citizenship or statelessness, they are all clubbed together as a community of people who do not belong. The *issei* (first-generation Japanese American) and the *nisei* (second-generation Japanese American) generation in the book struggle against this nativist position. As an *issei* declares in the book, 'After the young ones were born, our roots sank deeper here. This is our children's home, and it has become ours' (Sone, 1953, p. 121). Despite this claim, the country turns into an unhomely home.

Ethnicity, and not the citizenship, was of paramount importance during the period. Affectively, it created self-hate, a debilitating human emotion that introduces an erosion in self-esteem and often leads to suicide. The narrator resents having 'Japanese blood' which she considers as 'the blood of an enemy' (Sone, 1953, p. 145). This was the feeling that ran through the nisei generation. The more the feeling was communicated, the more it gained in intensity. It led to the consolidation of a group of Japanese Americans that considered itself as 'others' against the hegemonic group of white citizens. As a result of their guilt consciousness, they became both 'defiant and apologetic' about their descent.

The white American society was mostly unsparing in its dealing with the Japanese Americans. Before the Japanese bombing in 1941, house owners refused to rent rooms to them. The police harassed them on one pretext or another. Such incidents are represented in Sone's work. The narrator's father, an upright hotel owner who resists corruption, is arrested on a false charge of bootlegging. Young Japanese boys and girls are discriminated in the job market. As American citizens, they swing between hopes and dejection. The narrator's mother, more experienced in the affairs of the world, however, tells them, 'You're young, Kai-chan, you know very little about the ways of *nations*' (Sone, 1953, p. 147; emphasis added). She knows that the state and its agents would pounce upon them. Personally, the narrator is riven within, she thinks of herself as a 'freak', a cultural schizophrenia taking hold over her, and she asks herself, 'Doesn't my citizenship mean a single blessed thing to anyone?' (ibid, p. 158). The issei generation, who are mostly stateless people, descends into silence. They also have a *shikata ga nai* (can't be helped) attitude. Much later when the *sansei* (third-generation Japanese Americans) grow up, they dig out the internment of their parents and grandparents out of the silence that covered their history for years. Kristine C. Kuramitsu writes that the members of the *sansei* generation 'were startled to find that these camps had [really] existed' and that their parents had carefully wrapped up this fact in silence. 'Anger against their country for its racism and their parents for their acquiescence welled up in the *Sansei*' (Kuramitsu, 1995, p. 621). Similarly, Hisaye Yamamoto, a nisei writer, speaks of how she experienced a belated emotional upsurge years after the incarceration:

> The camp experience ... is an experience in our collective life which wounded us more painfully than we realize. I didn't know myself what a lump it was in my subconscious until a few years ago when I watched one of the earlier television commentaries on the subject, narrated by the mellow voice of Walter Cronkite. To my surprise I found the tears trickling down my cheeks and my voice squeaking out of control, as I tried to explain to my amazed husband and children why I was weeping.
> (qtd. in McDonald & Newman, 1980, p. 22)

The affective aspects of the experience flowed across individuals and generations. It was a 'collective' experience, as Yamamoto confesses in the quotation cited earlier.

Sone's *Nisei Daughter*, as we have seen, describes the Japanese American experience immediately before the Japanese bombing of Pearl Harbor. The white prejudice and anger against the Japanese Americans had free circulation during the time; there was an excess in the political economy of this hate. The press helped in the circulation of this hate and prejudice which whetted the racist desire for the blood of the 'other.' Sone mentions how it spread stereotyped images of the Japanese:

> The editorial sections of the newspapers and magazines were plastered with hideous-looking Japanese. The Japanese was always caricatured with enormous, moon-shaped spectacles and beady, myopic eyes. A small moustache was perched arrogantly over massive, square buck teeth, and his bow-legged posture suggested a simian character.
> (1953, p. 119)

The affective strategy adopted here by the majoritarian media project larger than life image of the 'vicious' Japanese. The body of the wicked 'foreigner' is produced metonymically through such semiotics as 'beady, myopic eyes' the offensive character of which is magnified by 'enormous, moon-shaped spectacles,' a 'small moustache,' and 'massive, square buck teeth.' While all these are suggestive of the 'wickedness' in the Japanese figure, its less than human character is communicated by 'his bow-legged posture.' Such images also help legitimise the hate crimes. This is indeed an excellent example of 'bestialization of man' spoken of by Michel Foucault, and this, as Foucault asserts, is 'achieved through the most sophisticated political techniques' which ultimately 'authorize[s]a holocaust' (quoted in Agamben, 1998, p. 3). Crimes against the Japanese are projected as appropriate measures taken against dangerous 'animals,' and not normal human beings. This project of dehumanising the 'foreigner' also gets manifested through such cryptic messages showcased against store windows, such as 'We kill rats and Japs' (Sone, 1953, p. 160). The inflamed 'superpatriotic' discourses make impact on the mainstream Americans: 'A Jap's a Jap, no matter how you slice them. You can't make an American out of little Jap Junior just by handing him an American birth certificate' (Sone, 1953, p. 158). Cries braying for Japanese blood is heard on the West Coast:

> For years the professional guardians of the Golden West had wanted to rid their land of the Yellow Peril. ... As the chain of Pacific islands fell to the Japanese, patriots shrieked for protection from us. A Californian sounded the alarm: "The Japs are dangerous and they must leave ..."
>
> (Sone, 1953, p. 157)

This pretext of seeking security, as we have seen earlier, is the most usual note sung during such critical periods. It is true that no extermination programme like the Holocaust is undertaken but the racist outcries nevertheless lead to the next step: deportation and/or internment. The demand for the ouster of the community members, its widescale circulation, and the rumour of the Japanese Americans spying on behalf of the Japanese government are so strong that the state is not ready to think otherwise. Sone mentions that it conveniently ignores 'Edgar Hoover's special report to the War Department stating that there had not been a single case of sabotage committed by a Japanese living in Hawaii or on the Mainland during the Pearl Harbor attack or after' (Sone, 1953, pp. 157–158). President Roosevelt signs Executive Order 9066 which authorises the evacuation of anyone from designated military areas. In the Preface to the 1979 edition of *Nisei Daughter*, Monica Sone observes that in 1942 'they became prisoners of their own government, without charges, without trial' (Sone, 1953, p. xvi). The Pacific Coast was marked as one such designated area. About 1200,000 Japanese Americans were shifted to ten relocation camps in this region. There were both *issei* and *nisei* members among them. The camps located in semi-desert areas had barbed wire fences and watch towers. In the book the narrator and her family are first relocated to Yokohama, Puyallup and then to Minnidoka. They are given a number: 'Family # 10710.' This is an attempt at stripping the members of a family of their individual and family identities. The community is homogenised and viewed as an undifferentiated one, an act which helps the state machinery to ignore the *nisei* members who have justifiable claims to American citizenship. The focus is thus on ethnicity with 'foreignness' tagged to it.

These 'foreigners within' indeed represent a 'bare life' spoken of by Giorgio Agamben. 'Bare life,' as Agamben observes, 'remains included in politics in the form of the exception, that is, as something that is included solely through an exclusion' (Agamben, 1998, p. 11). The 'exclusion' in most cases takes the form of confinement to the camps or extermination or both. All these happened during the Holocaust. The Jews were exterminated because Hitler considered them 'as lice,' 'which is to say, as bare life' (Agamben, 1998, p. 114). He thinks that the camp is 'the realm of bare life' (Agamben, 1998, p. 120). The 'bare life' exists in the modern politics to validate the power of the sovereign. Living in the detention camp approaches the condition of the Jews during the Holocaust. In the incarceration of both Japanese Americans and Chinese Indians (the latter are discussed in the next section), the symptoms of the biopower are evident.

The overall situation during the critical period confirms how the statist policies and majority community work together to create the picture of the immigrant community as the dangerous 'other' who must be deported or sent to a detention camp for the sake of the security of the nation. It does not matter to the state whether they are the legitimate citizens of the country. Even if they are, they are reduced to stateless persons for all effective reasons.

IV Rita Chowdhury's *Chinatown Days*

In Rita Chowdhury's *Chinatown Days* (2018) the scene shifts to India of the 1960s. The incarceration of the Chinese in India took place in 1962, almost two decades later. It happened in the context of Sino-Indian War. Chowdhury's fictional work which represents the plight of the Chinese people in India is the English translation of *Makum* (2010), originally written in Assamese.[3] It is a retrieval narrative, an act of digging up the lost 'Chinatown days' which is archived secretly in the dark recesses of Indian history. Arunabh Bora, an Assamese fiction writer, finds himself face to face with an unknown chapter of Indian history when he meets Lailin Tham in Toronto, Canada. Bora is at a loss to explain the reason of Tham's exceptionally rude behaviour towards him. He begins to understand the reason when he meets Tham's mother. He comes to know that she is originally from Makum in Upper Assam and knows Assamese well – they, in fact, converse in the language – and that she, along with thousands of other Chinese Indians, were sent to an internment camp at Deoli, Rajasthan, in 1962. This silenced episode of history strikes Bora dumb, and he gets down to excavate the past. Through his meticulous efforts, this little-known history is revealed layer by layer during the course of the novel, which has a story-within-a-story pattern.

Bora's excavation into the debris of the past is launched as a result of the challenge thrown by Lailin: "Will you dare to speak up? Will you dare to speak about us who are standing on the Indian soil [*sic*]? Do you have the guts?" (Chowdhury, 2018, p. 2). This is stated in a moment of intense emotional turmoil. She says that she has only hate for all Indians who are responsible for the displacement of innocent Chinese Indians. One understands that along with this hate, she has residual bitterness and anger in her heart which emanate from the depth of her ancestral history. This affects Bora to no small extent. He gets into an investigation and meets a number of people of different age groups who are located both in India and abroad. He discovers that even the Chinese who settled in India since the first half of the nineteenth century and married Indians were violently uprooted from their homes. They lost everything including their properties. The displaced included even the few Chinese who had Indian citizenship.[4] A newspaper report cited in the fiction states that many retained 'Chinese passports because of the constant pressure from the pro-China people' (Chowdhury, 2018, p. 199).The same report confirms that 'the stateless Chinese of Calcutta', most of whom were 'simple working-class people', were found to be harmless '[a]fter thorough examination' (Chowdhury, 2018, p. 201). For the Chinese Indians who had been living in India for a long time, India is their home. As a Chinese Indian character in the novel asserts, 'We have no one in China. Even if there is, India is our land. We were born here. We have worked here, married here. Our birth place is our motherland' (Chowdhury, 2018, p. 199). Due to the complicated process of obtaining passports, most of them remain stateless. On the basis of prejudice and unfounded suspicion, state machinery is mobilised to harass and ultimately intern them. Security of the country becomes the prime object and the residents of Chinese descent begin to be perceived as spies. Based on this perception nationalistic feelings are whipped up and state machinery is geared up. One-dimensional affective emotion consolidates a state–people alliance and direct them against the perceived 'enemies within.' Sara Ahmed argues that underneath the hate of others (she examines immigrants and 'boatmen' in the white-dominated country such as the US) lies the subject's (in her case, white subjects) 'love' of everything that they possess. 'The presence of this other is imagined as a threat to the object of love' (Ahmed, 2004, p. 43). The subject feels that whatever they love such as, a secure future, security of the nation is being threatened by the presence of the 'other.' Thus, she observes, 'the ordinary or normative subject is reproduced as the injured party; the one that is 'hurt' or even damaged by the 'invasion' of others. The bodies of others are hence transformed into 'the hated' through a discourse of pain' (Ahmed, 2004, p. 43). This explanation, as we have seen, is applicable to the context of the hate politics that the Japanese Americans were subjected to. The demand for their deportation and internment was voiced and carried out in the US. In the case of Chinese Indians also, security of the nation and the well-being of the 'Indian' people (excluding, of course, the Chinese Indians) were the objects of love. These were the interests that got 'hurt' – and the people of Chinese origin were allegedly responsible for this 'injury.' Ahmed observes that in such a case 'emotions work as a form of capital' in circulation (2004, p. 45). With each exchange, with each circulation, a 'surplus' (an intensification of hate or anger or whatever emotion is involved) is created. One can easily understand how, with the intensification of hate and animosity, the Chinese Indians' position became more and more precarious. Their precarity, as we see it in the text, is evident in the attacks on their bodies and properties and results in their being sent to the internment camp in Deoli, Rajasthan where they undergo harassment and mental torture.

In any affective situation, relationality is an important factor, and in this instance, the relationality operates on two axes. The circulation of wild emotion and alliance between the state policymakers, government agencies and the common people continue a symmetrical line, forming a 'sameness' on the basis of their understanding of the issue at hand. In the novel radio news and newspaper reports contribute a lot to the formation of a 'nationalist' platform of the masses and anti-Chinese lobby. These at the same time accelerate the growth of a hate campaign against the Chinese Indians. Unfounded suspicion of these 'foreigners' helps the circulation of the emotion of hate. As a character notes, 'See how emotional the people have become. The love for the country is true, but it is impractical' (Chowdhury, 2018, p. 194). Interestingly, the same character points out the role of Nehru, 'Nehru had used our people in the freedom movement; now he is going to use them again in the same way' (Chowdhury, 2018, p. 194). It necessarily means that these actors, coming from heterogenous backgrounds and platforms, close ranks for the time being to form a homogeneous body that prioritises its 'patriotic' duty to ensure national security. '*It is the emotional reading of hate that works to stick or to bind the imagined subjects and the white* [in our case, Indian] *nation together*' (Ahmed, 2004, p. 43; emphasis original). Secondly, relationality acts on the basis of oppositionality. Chinese-origin people in India were constructed as 'outsiders' despite the fact that they have been living in India for generations and they do not have any effective connections with their ancestral country. On the contrary, many of them are inimical to the contemporary communist regime in China. But logic takes a backseat and emotion runs wild. The Chinese Indians form the only visible body that carries the signs of 'foreignness' and hence must be targeted and uprooted.

The ghost of this history of the incarceration and statelessness seem to reappear in the NRC which has already identified, through a questionable process, about roughly 19 lakh people. The names of these people are missing from the list of citizens and new detention centres are reportedly being constructed now in addition to the existing ones. The echoes of the harassment and detention of Chinese Indians are being heard in the India of the NRC/CAB/NAA. The developments in contemporary India go to suggest that the interlinked issues of citizenship/statelessness and the 'foreigner' question are deliberately and irrationally invoked at particular junctures of history in order to respond to the racial/ethnic/religious hysteria of a section of powerful people. Chowdhury's literary representation of history serves the purpose of reminding us how irrational human beings can be and how fanaticism and hysteria can be fuelled by *agent provocateurs*.

V Conclusion

The two works discussed above are thematically connected and have some common features: (a) they are all set against transnational (although different) backgrounds; (b) they speak of abject bodies/bare life, narrate the experience of the members of the victimised communities in detention camps and figure out the emotions prior to, and subsequent upon, the internment; (c) they foreground issues of citizenship and statelessness; and (d) despite having differences in time and space, these works reveal the role of the state which, in collusion with the dominant communities, marginalise diasporic groups on the basis of racial, ethnic, or religious considerations.

These two literary works also suggest that at particular junctures in the history of nations, the issue of citizenship is employed as a political weapon to decide the question of inclusion/exclusion of certain categories of people in the nation state. Rooted only in the present and amnesic of the past, hegemonic groups forget that the current demographic picture of a nation is the result of the aggregated inflows of migrants who arrived in the interest of the nations at different points of time and gradually became an inalienable part of the demography. To dismiss this history amounts to the denial of the nation's past. However, the act of denial/amnesia occurs on regular basis as part of the politics of majoritarianism. The exclusivist position usually revolves round the question of security of the 'injured' nation, the perception of 'foreignness' as a threat and the production of the figure of the 'foreigner.' During exceptional times, the state, which usually requires the 'foreigner' for economic reasons, and the dominant community, which views the 'foreigner' with suspicion, work in tandem, generating an affective condition both in the community of 'natives' and that of the 'foreigners.' This recurrent pattern is observed in the history of nations all over the world. The 'foreigner' question almost inevitably arises whenever the nation is embroiled in political or social crises, such as at the time of a foreign attack or during the time of medical emergency (e.g., a pandemic when members of a particular community are specifically marked for the blame game and hate campaign).[5] In the present Indian context of NRC/CAB/CAA which is the outcome of a specific religio-political ideology, the circulation of the politically engineered hate is so vicious and widespread that the 'foreigners within' become the target of regular attacks. This is indeed 'an affect which is visceral and bodily' (Ahmed, 2004, p. 58). The attacks are organised around the theme of violation of the sanctity of certain sacred symbols (such as cow slaughter, beef eating, or dealing in cowskin). Interestingly, these issues cease to be mere social and religious issues, they enter into the domain of the political and the sovereign. The political leaders and the sovereign State rake up these issues to foment emotional disturbances in the common people, polarise communities around religious trajectories and reap political and ideological dividends. Intricately connected with this is of course the discourse of legitimate citizenship. This seems to be a predictable course in the history of a nation. Sara Ahmed points out that in Britain, some political parties may address the 'legitimate' citizens of the nation in emotional terms, asking these people to identify themselves as 'us' and posit this 'us' against a constructed 'them' (the 'outsiders'). Such a narrative invites the 'legitimate' citizens to develop 'a certain rage against these illegitimate others, who are represented as "swarms" in the nation' (1). She argues that through such metaphors 'a group of subjects' may be made to 'identify themselves with the injured nation' (2). While in the UK, or for that matter in the US, the injured subjects may be bonded together, through the play of imagination around whiteness, into a familial or racial tie 'that recognises all non-white others as strangers, as "bodies out of place,"' (2), in a country like India a politico-religious identity (e.g. 'Hindutva') may be projected as a familial tie to shut out those who do not have the same religious affiliations. They are pushed out of the national imaginary. In India, it is of course more complicated as religious communities, such as Sikhs, may be perceived by the majoritarian politicians as having a religious affinity with the dominant religious group, and others such as Buddhists, Jains, and Christians may be considered as being too insignificant in numbers to matter in the overall game of emotions.

NRC/CAB/CAA has already dealt a severe blow to the concept of a secular India. In actual life, it has affected thousands of lives. The long legal battles are pending for the people who are suddenly rendered stateless. Details of lives in the detention camps in Assam are slowly but surely pouring out. It is not simply possible to measure the huge emotional disturbances. The corpus of literary works is not much visible yet, but the emergence of a new genre of poetry known as Miya poetry is perhaps an indication of what lies in the womb of future. This particular poetic genre born out of the matrices of real life as it is lived in an exceptional time is engaged in contestations of the majoritarian worldview. Miya poetry leaves a 'space of reflexive specularity.' The poetic representation is engaged in 'coordinat[ing] into existence a future' that will surely reflect the spectral presence of the contemporary time.

Notes

1 See, for example, Shoaib Daniyal's article 'Explainer: How exactly Does India's Citizenship Amendment Bill Discriminate against Muslims?' (*Scroll.in* published on Dec 05, 2019). There are innumerable published articles on this aspect.

2 In 'Suicides over the NRC: Trend Analysis' Talha Mujibi observes that 'many ethnic Bengali Hindus and Muslims [are] choosing death over life due to the tremendous mental pressure of being excluded from the NRC or from the strenuous process of proving their citizen status. It is a failure of the government's Mental Healthcare Act, 2017 and a flagrant abuse of human, civil and political rights' (*The Citizen*, 7 March, 2020).

3 For a detailed discussion of Chowdhury's Assamese novel *Makum*, see Ananda Mohan Kar and Himadri Lahiri, "Documenting Trauma: Depicting the Chinese Indian in the Assamese Novel *Makum*." *The Visva-Bharati Quarterly* 23.1 (April–June 2014): 86–101. This essay approaches the novel mainly from the perspective of trauma and does not explore the issue of statelessness and citizenship from the perspective of affect theory.

4 Citizenship in the form of legal documents was not an important issue in the colonial India. However, the issue became complicated in the independent India. In the late 1950s, the Union government issued orders for the registration of foreigners which required residential permits. The Chinese would also have to obtain 'passports from the People's Republic of China, after the Chinese communist revolution, which most were loath to do. Passports issued by the Kuomintang government in Formosa (Taiwan) would not be recognized' (Mahanirban 22). At this point the spectre of statelessness loomed large on the Chinese community (Mahanirban 21–22). The Indian government granted passports to some Chinese living in India for a long time. But about 3,601 Chinese in India reportedly 'had Formosan passports and in effect were stateless, while 66 had applied for Indian citizenship. ... But clearly, throughout this period, the overwhelming majority of Chinese people in India were either formally or in effect stateless. Paul Chung, a leader of the Chinese in Calcutta, says that trying to obtain an Indian passport remained extremely difficult even about a quarter of a century after the Chinese hostilities' (Mahanirban 24).

5 The Muslim community in India became the target of hate campaign during the Covid-19 pandemic. The Tablighi Jamaat Conference in March 2020, for example, was identified as 'COVID-19 hotspot' and it 'became the basis of the large-scale communalisation of the pandemic' ('Communalisation of COVID-19'). Bebaak Collective published a report documenting instances of such communal prejudice and discrimination. Shakuntala Banaji and Ram Bhat explain, in a London School of Economics blog, the pattern, 'The basic architecture of othering Muslims to constitute Hinduness and Hindu nationalism remains a historical fact. The affordances of platforms and devices, as well as new possibilities of differentiated mass distribution, present enormous potential to produce the idea of India as a Hindu nation with an internal enemy community in new ways. The fabricated association of Muslims with the spread of Covid-19 is a prime example' (Banaji).

See 'Communalisation of COVID-19 Led to the Discrimination of Muslims' published in *The Hindu* and 'Disinformation about Indian Muslims during the COVID-19 Pandemic' written by Shakuntala Banaji and Ram Bhat.

References

Agamben, G. (1998). *Homo Sacer: Sovereign Power and Bare Life*. (Trans. Daniel Heller-Roazen). Stanford University Press.

Ahmed, S. (2004). *The Cultural Politics of Emotion*. Edinburgh University Press.

Banaji, Shakuntala and Ram Bhat. Disinformation about Indian Muslims during the COVID-19 Pandemic. Media@LSE 24 Sept. 2020. https://blogs.lse.ac.uk/medialse/2020/09/24/disinformation-against-indian-muslims-during-the-covid-19-pandemic. Accessed on 13 April 2021.

Banerjee, D. (2020). From Cheap Labor to Overlooked Citizens: Looking for British Muslim Identities in Kamila Shamsie's Home Fire. *South Asian Review*, 41(3–4), 288–302. doi:10.1080/02759527.2020.1835141

Chowdhury, R. (2018). *Chinatown Days*. Macmillan.

'Communalisation of COVID-19 Led to the Discrimination of Muslims.' (n.d.). *The Hindu* (Mumbai) January 23. https://www.thehindu.com/news/cities/mumbai/communalisation-of-covid-19-led-to-discrimination-against-muslims/article33639018.ece. Accessed on 13 March, 2021.

Daniyal, Shoaib. 'Explainer: How exactly Does India's Citizenship Amendment Bill Discriminate against Muslims?' *Scroll.in* (Dec 05,2019). Accessed on 9 March 2021. https://scroll.in/article/944852/explainer-how-exactly-does-india-s-citizenship-amendment-bill-discriminate-against-muslims

Kar, A. M. and Lahiri, H. (2014). Documenting Trauma: Depicting the Chinese Indian in the Assamese Novel *Makum*. *The Visva-Bharati Quarterly*, 23(1), 86–101.

Kerber, L. K. (2005). Toward a History of Statelessness in America. *American Quarterly*, 59(3), 727–749.

Kuramitsu, K. C. (1995). Internment and Identity in Japanese American Art. *American Quarterly*, 47(4), 619–658.

Mahanirban Calcutta Research Group (CRG). (n.d.). A Brief Report on 'Mapping the Stateless in India' 2 Phase. http://www.mcrg.ac.in/Statelessness/Statelessness_Report_2011.pdf. Accessed on 28 Feb. 2021.

Massumi, B. M. (2002). *Parables for the Virtual: Movement, Affect, Sensation*. Duke University Press.

McDonald, D. R., and Newman, K. (1980). Relocation and Dislocation: The Writings of Hisaye Yamamoto and Wakako Yamauchi. *MELUS*, 7(3), 21–38.

Radhakrishnan, R. (2012). Modern Fiction and Politics. *Modern Fiction Studies*, 58(4 (Winter)), 659–667.

Mujibi, Talha. Suicides Over the NRC: Trend Analysis. *The Citizen*, 7 March, 2020. https://www.thecitizen.in/index.php/en/NewsDetail/index/15/18425/Suicides-over-the-NRC--Trend-Analysis'. Accessed on 9 April 2021.

Sone, M. (1953). *Nisei Daughter* (Reprint 1979). University of Washington Press.

Tait, P. (2016). Introduction: Analysing Emotion and Theorising Affect. *Humanities*, 5(3), 1–7. https://www.mdpi.com/2076-0787/5/3/70.

Terranova, T. (2004). *Network Culture: Politics for the Information Age*. Pluto Press.

Thrift, N. (2008). *Non-Representational Theory: Space, Politics, Affect*. Routledge.

Well, T. C., L. Mark, & J. Sandoval (2020). Affect, Space, and Everydayness: A Reconsideration of Waste in Academic Inquiry. *Taboo: The Journal of Culture and Education*, 19(3), 27–42. https://digitalscholarship.unlv.edu/taboo/vol19/iss3/3.

Chapter 3

Cities of Refuge; Republics of *Char*

Stateless in South Asia[1]

Nandini Bhattacharya

1 *Char-ghar*

This chapter proposes a specific resituating of ideas of refuge – statelessness within the geopolitical realities of *char* formations in the Gangetic Bengal area, and a recasting of such debates within the specificities of the subcontinental partition-historiography. With the birth of the nations of (East) Pakistan (afterwards, Bangladesh), Myanmar, and India in a post-British imperial scenario, these deltaic formations on the eastern borders of the subcontinent were, and have remained, the refuge choices of stateless, unfitted people.

In Bengali, *char* remains a fit-all term for outer islands in deltaic regions in the Bay of Bengal as well as riverine islands created through silt deposits as rivers meander through state-province 'bordered' national territories. These clusters of islands that rise and subside along with storms, high tides, and movements of great rivers such as the Ganga, Brahmaputra, the Matla, the Naf, and the Bay of Bengal are examined as vitally informing the partition continuum[2] (Lahiri-Dutt & Samanta, 2013).

Partition history is replete with all kinds of *char* occupation and brutal state action against these 'waste' people as they furtively occupy these 'waste lands as their refuge' (Chakraborty, 2012).[3] Perhaps, the most well researched of such *char* occupations by the wretched of the earth, in partition history of Eastern India happened in the 1970s. Waves of migrants (from East Pakistan/Bangladesh) rejecting the inhuman conditions of Dandakaranya camps (in Chhattisgarh, and Odisha of India)[4] (Elahi, 1981) claimed the outer islands of Kumirmari and Marichjhapi of the Sundarbans in West Bengal as their home. A night of brutal state action in 1979 was enough to wipe out these waste people and their hopes of a *char* of their own (Chatterjee, 1992; Ghosh, 2004; Halder, 2019; Mallick, 1999; Shaktipada, 2009).[5]

Given that *char* lands are constantly created and uncreated, therefore scrambling lines, borders, demarcations, these geospatial formations need to be re-examined in the light of state formation and refuge-related studies. Can *chars* be that place where one achieves clarity about geographical

DOI: 10.4324/9781003345152-6

territory as just that, and not claimed-named/legitimised-utilised by statist powers? The *char*'s fragile territorial ontology makes such land rise and submerge, often several times within a human lifetime; its uncertain juridico-political status may remind us of the reality, the very uniqueness of bare, unaccommodated, un-legitimisable land. Can these riverine islands within an active deltaic region of the Eastern part of the subcontinent be ideated as alterities of cosmopolitan refuge? The essay then also turns on its head, the commonly held politico-economic-juridical position that *chars* are 'waste-lands' for "waste people" and that their being turned into detention centres–cum–prison islands for the biopolitically non-pertinent (in this case the stateless) is only apropos.

This chapter traces a cultural genealogy of chars in narratives, poetry, myths, and movies of people of Bengali-language ethnicity, in an effort to give chars an ideational *ghar*, a *heim* within subcontinental emotive traditions. Finally, the chapter proposes that such an exploration, the task of ideating sustainable refuge domains for stateless people, is one of the primary ethical responses for our times.

II Repatriation to *Bhasaner Char* and the Possibilities of South Asian Refugium Discourses

This chapter was sparked off by the prime minister of Bangladesh, Sheikh Hasina Wazed's (1947–) express resolve to repatriate, by the December of 2018, more than a hundred thousand Rohingya refugees (Ibrahim & Muhammad, 2018).[6] Identified by the United Nations High Commissioner for Refugees as South Asia's most vulnerable stateless community, the Rohingyas are caught between a long drawn-out ethnic strife between the Myanmarese majority of primarily South-East Asian origin (espousing Hinayana Buddhism), and Myanmarese minority of South Asian origin, from North Arakan/Rakhine (espousing Sunni Islam) populace (Chowdhury & Mohanty, 2020; Lewa, 2009)[7]. Presently, about 1.2 million Rohingya refugees are clustered near Cox Bazar (near Dhaka city) in Kutupalong area camps, and the Bangladeshi government plans to 'rehabilitate' these Rohingyas, to a minuscule and newly risen island in deltaic Bengal, about 30 kilometres by sea from Cox Bazar. The riverine island, going by names as various as Bhasan, Jaliya and Thengar *char*, was being readied for a war footing, with rows of barracks as detention centres and dykes and shelters for refugee rehabilitation, given that this *char* is in midst of a cyclone zone and likely to submerge during inclement conditions. As all this activity continues at the governmental level, groups such as Amnesty International and several refugee groups protest that the Bhasan *chars* are nothing less than death camps, prone to devastating floods and cyclones, and that is not even speak of its sheer desolation and a lack of amenities. In a post-COVID-19 world, general squalor, unhealthy density of populace, and a lack of sanitary conditions have spiked death rates in these camps. Devastating fires that raged in these camps in 2021, have also led to a considerable loss of lives (Neuman, 2021).[8] There is also the growing perception-based discontent among the average Bangladeshi populace regarding the continuance of Rohingya presence, as such migrants 'eat into' Bangladesh's meagre national resources. While the readying of the Bhasaner *char* and repatriation of batches of refugees there, recent reports also speak of the resistance of the Rohingyas and Sheikh Hasina Wazed buckling under world opinion and **United Nations** pressures only to delay and defer Rohingya repatriation into the *chars* of Bhasan or Jaliya. Recent reports from Human Rights Watch indicate the repatriation of over a lakh of Rohingyas to Bhasaner *char* from December 2020 and Hasina Wazed's pressurising the UN to support the cost of maintaining the refugees through international non-governmental funding agencies. The real problem is again questions about the safety of the *char* itself. Formed only **twenty** years ago through silt deposit in the deltaic region, its shape and shorelines have shifted repeatedly and can also submerge or be cut off from the mainland in the case of severe cyclones. Hopes of refugees returning home to Myanmar remains an even more distant dream, now that the very Myanmar military generals that had spearheaded ethnic cleansing and conducted genocides in the Rakhine province are back in power, and the voices of democracy of the **National League for Democracy** (NLD) suppressed.

III Partition History of 'Bengali migrants.'

Contemporary South Asian crises of statelessness have the Rohingya (Rakhine state ethnic Muslims) forced migration, at its centre. Peaking in the phases, especially between 2010 and 2017, it was consequent to the ferocious ethnic cleansing pogroms (of Rohingyas) by the Buddhist majority government in Myanmar. Waves of Rohingya migrants spilled over into the Indian state, and especially the culturally congruent Bangladesh.[9] Both the Indian and the Bangladeshi governments have been pushing back of those immigrants across their borders even as Bangladesh has accommodated considerable numbers in camps in various parts of the country in the most humanitarian of responses (among South Asian and South- East Asian nations) to these waves of migrant influx. While this crisis of statelessness appears sudden and distinctive, it is embedded within a complex matrix of post-partition resolves to formalise 'national' borders and identities in the subcontinent by its majoritarian state actors. Loosely speaking, the devolution of power of the British Empire, led to the subcontinent breaking up into four sovereign nation states, India, Pakistan, Bangladesh (after 1971) and Myanmar (after 1948). The messily drawn Radcliffe line that partitioned off the Eastern part of the subcontinent has made it well-nigh impossible to adequately formalise national borders and fix national identities, given the porosity of South Asian borders, and their long history of cultural congruity and exchange. Built into these state-building, identity-fixing initiatives were unfulfilled promises such as the promise of a separate Muslim majority Arakan state (now Rakhine), as distinct from Buddhist-majority Myanmar. The free flow of Chittagongese Bangladeshis (then part of undivided British Bengal) into the Arakan region and *vice versa* has also made it difficult to distinguish ethnicities. In fact, the present Myanmarese government prefers to define these people as never-native to Myanmar but as 'Bangladeshi/Bengali/Rohingya Muslim infiltrator/terrorists!' The official stance regarding Rohingyas is one of absolute denial. The then Burma's prime minister, General Khin Nynt, informed the UNHCR in 1998 that "these people are not originally from Myanmar but have illegally migrated to Myanmar because of population pressures in their own country." The government-owned newspaper stated in an article that "there is no national race by the name of Rohinjya" in Myanmar (*New Light of Myanmar*, February 2009). The ethnic conflict between the Myanmarese Buddhists majority and the Rakhine state Muslims has given birth to refugee crises situation that has Myanmar at its epicentre but implicates the geopolitics of South and South-East Asia regions. That Bengalis may be ethnically similar in Bangladesh, Rakhine in Myanmar, in West Bengal and Assam or other parts of India, has mired the whole issue of who belongs to which nation state, in a never-to-be-resolved tangle.

The 'infiltration' of Bengalis/Bangladeshis/Rohingyas into the Indian state of Assam post-1971 (the birth of Bangladesh) has been addressed (partially) by the Indian state through the National Register of Citizens exercise, a process that required complex documentary proofs of being native to Assam (and India). This is something many of these hapless *sans papiers* have not been able to provide or their documentation proved faulty. The fate of such people, excluded in the process, hangs in a precarious balance. Islamic faith predominance among the Rohingyas has propelled them to migrate to Malaysia and Indonesia, both of which are Islam-predominant but not particularly welcoming of penniless hordes of refugees. Thailand, another Buddhism predominant state is also not quite welcoming to such refugees. India and China, the two superpowers in the region have invested heavily in Myanmar and support Aung San Suu Kyi's government and her hardline approach towards Rohingyas. Culturally speaking, Myanmar is the gate between South Asia and South-East Asia and population-distinction games are ping-pong balls being played between two contesting superpowers, China and India. The present military take-over of Myanmar and the delegitimising of Aung San Suu Kyi have done nothing to soften the Myanmarese statist stance towards the Rohingya populace.[10]

In 1982, Myanmar's government (and I am indebted to Chris Lewa's Arakan Project for most of my information) stripped the Rohingyas of their citizenship. This was followed by severe restrictions on Rohingyas marrying, and even more severe restrictions on their movements and other human rights. The Na Sa Ka, Burma's border security force grants marriage authorisations on payment of steep fees and bribes and which "can take up to several years to obtain... This local order also prohibits any cohabitation or sexual contact outside wedlock" (Lewa, 2009, p. 3). The refusal to call its own people Myanmarese, and a systemic denial of rights as a national before their extermination is a chilling reminder of Judeophobia and Jew exclusion that begun after the First World War in Europe.

IV *Eurocentricism* of Refugium Debates

In proposing the ideational centrality to *char* lands in deltaic borderlands as alterities of refuge space, this chapter is yet another iteration, another critical intervention in statelessness–refugium debates. It also debates the Eurocentricity of such debates in recent times.

The violence that accompanied processes of decolonisation, the drawing of new border lines, the birth of new states and the concomitant mass migrations in the Indian subcontinent were chronologically contiguous and commensurate in terms of human suffering (i.e. if any such equivalence of human misery can be enumerated) to the World War II–related European events. The realities/impact of subcontinental partition has been largely occluded within the primarily Eurocentric (and naturalised as 'universal') critical formulations regarding statelessness refuge-seeking conditions. What is more unfortunate is the uncritical use of these configurations while engaging with partition history or its afterlives by scholars of subcontinental partition history.

This chapter unpacks statelessness-refuge-related concepts that evolved as critical responses within European Judeophobic conditions; border restructurings, and majoritarian violence-induced forced migrations. It factors in Hannah Arendt's conceptualisation of statelessness-refuge (Arendt, 1943, 1951),[11] and its critical afterlives in **the postulations of Jacques Derrida and Giorgio Agamben**[12].

The similarity between the Rohingya situation and that of European Jewish refugees between the third and fourth decades of the 20th century propels me to critically engage with the Arendtian position in "We refugees" (1943). She reverses the hierarchy of the citizen national at the top, and the "stateless" at the bottom in response to European Jews being hounded out of Europe by the German Third Reich and not being welcome anywhere. In a hauntingly beautiful passage, she notes that the stateless, in accepting their condition accrue the advantage of knowing how history works. They expose themselves to "the fate of human beings who, unprotected by any specific law or political convention, are nothing but human beings." Arendt notes that the crisis of statelessness is not event-centric but systemic, and it is no longer a question of 'good states' 'providing hospitality' and 'rogue states' violently evicting minorities.' The very Enlightenment nation-state idea, in its conceptual embracing of territorial congruity, cultural homogeneity, and ethnic cultural unity as its essences, is, according to Arendt, the source of such marginalising practices and thus ethically wanting.

Jacques Derrida (who, like Hannah Arendt, had experienced first-hand the anxiety of statelessness and denial of humanity thereby) takes his cue from *Origins of Totalitarianism* (1951) and critiques the nation-state idea by conceptualising spatial alterities that stateless people may lay claim to, and inhabit. Derrida perforates the nation-state idea in proposing "cities" of alterity. This is a response to the overwhelming realities of statelessness in the contemporary Europe, and their unwillingness to engage with such a crisis (*On Cosmopolitanism*). Derrida draws upon the Biblical references to 'cities of refuge', evoking St. Augustine's *City of God* and European modernism's cultural foregrounding of the cosmopolitan city. This was a cosmopolis that people (unrelated by blood or ethnicity) could lay claim to. Central to European modernism's city idea is that of the *flaneur*, a *sui generis* figure, disconnected, disinterested, free from ties of territory, blood and ethnicity and a freedom that lends the *flaneur* her necessary creative perspective.

This ideating of chars an alterity of refuge space is a critical response to Derrida's "city of refuge" ideal. Politico-ideational tropes of cities-of-refuge are undoubtedly embedded in and productive of Judeo-Christian traditions of refugium and cosmopolitan space.

It would be a clever thing to redeploy Derrida's 'city' ideal, to respond to the inadequacies of the subcontinental nation state, its production of layers of 'illicit' people through cleansing pogroms. This would have been critically adequate, given that most subcontinental nation states (India, Pakistan, Bangladesh, Myanmar, Afghanistan, Sri Lanka) have, at some point of time, been part of an overarching British Empire. It is undeniable that they continue to be informed by European statist models, and their present statist structures are mediated by memories of 'colonial modernity.'

Derrida's city–refugium ideal might seem like a worthwhile to import, given that cities of India and Bangladesh have greater degrees of cosmopolitan veneer *vis-à-vis* their 'villages of darkness.' I note however, that Derrida's very next essay *On Forgiveness* (as anthologised in the volume titled *On Cosmopolitanism and Forgiveness*, (1997, Tr. Mark Dooley and Michael Hughes, London and New York: Routledge, Thinking in Action Series 2001) warns us of the dangers of **globalising** concepts of flattening out, universalising and normativising Eurocentric ideas, of deploying them unselfconsciously.

My minor point, *pace* Derrida's warning regarding dangers of flattening out concepts is that the *nagar*, *shahar* (city) was never a major conceptual dominant in terms of 'refuge' in subcontinental history, and particularly in the Indian scheme of things. Thus, its revivification, an echo of the European 'city of refuge,' might not be an adequate ethical response to the crises of statelessness in South Asia but merely an exercise in academic dilettantism.

Anti-colonial resistance was predicated on the idea of unethical wealth–power concentration in Indian cities (and in European metropolises thereby) at the expense and detriment of British India's marginalised and denuded villages' populace. Mohandas Gandhi's critique of the city as derivative, alienating and inadequate for Indian requirements in his *Hind Swaraj* (1909) demands a re-examination in this context. The idea of the colonial city, as economically ruinous and parasitical, owes its conceptual debt to Dadabhai Naoroji's *Poverty and Un-British Rule in India* and the works of other drain-of-wealth economists such as Romesh Chandra Majumdar. The colonial intervention as coeval to drain of cultural and economic wealth finds imaginative and cultural reassurance in Indian modernists such as Rabindranath Tagore (*Streer Patra*, 2014), R.K. Narayan (*The Guide*, 1958), Dhanpat Rai or Premchand (*Sevasadan*, 1919); Saratchandra Chattopadhay (*Srikanta*, *Devdas*, 1917). As the 'infantilized' village is ever present in the Indic city imaginary and the aspirational-though-corrupt city, ever present in India's denuded village imaginary, the European idea of a cosmopolitan city of refuge will not work in India or in most South Asian nation states. I say this in awareness of the thematic trajectory of cultural texts as Saratchandra Chatterjee's *Mahesh* (1916, in Bengali) or Mulk Raj Anand's *Untouchable* (1935 in English), both in which the city and its cosmopolitan milieu of mills, factories or urban houses with no manual scavenging but flush toilets (*Untouchable*) **appear** as liberating refuge spaces to the broken-by-tradition populace of the Indian villages.

Ashis Nandy's insights about the re-creation of village spaces within Mumbai *chawls* and the strong village nostalgia marking Indian cinema (Nandy, 2001), especially its landmark, Satyajit Ray's *Pather Panchali* (1955) and Raj Kapoor's *Awara* (1951), *Shree 420* (1955), *Jagte Raho* (1956) and in popular tele-serials such as *Nukkad* (aired between 1986–87), is equally relevant here. 'City' poets such as Bishnu Dey and Arun Kolatkar have remained lonely, isolated figures in terms of major cultural influence Incidentally, none of the subcontinental cities, Delhi Jammu, Dhaka, Silchar, Hyderabad, has been particularly kind to these new stateless people, the Rohingyas.[13] The recent incident of bulldozing settlements of primarily Bengali-speaking labourers in New Delhi's Jahangirpuri area on the suspicion of their having Rohingya/infiltrator/terrorist links is a case in point.

Ashis Nandy reminds us, that we have had a problematic engagement with the city as a cultural imaginary as older subcontinental 'cities' of Varanasi as *teerth* (pilgrimage) destinations, or Cochin as traditional trade destinations were replaced by the colonial cities of Calcutta, Bombay and Madras through a violent process of cultural denigration (*Ambiguous Journeys*, 2001).

I contend that the newborn colonial cities (that mimicked European urban spaces architecturally showcased the empire's arrogance and its bureaucratic and commercial moorings) were not simply alienating to the older power stakeholders (upper caste landholders and pundits, as Nandy claims) but to the already socially marginalised landless lower castes. Arvind Adiga's *The White Tiger* (2008) and Roy's *The Ministry of Utmost Happiness* (2016) are nuanced evocations of city–village continuum, and continuity-with difference, so far as systemic marginalising practices go.

Precarious groups in both the narratives vainly seek freedom from caste- and community-based oppressions in these anomic urban spaces. They discover that the patterns of exclusion are even more terrifyingly reinforced in those urban spaces and that the vulnerable are left even without the compensatory comforts of community contexts – a cover that they had enjoyed in their rural margins despite their extreme precarity. A wonderful Marathi movie *Sairath*, 2016 (later adapted as a Hindi film, *Dhadhak*), in which caste-based violence of villages follows the couple into the city, testifies to my claim that India is, still, all village. A popular new web series *Mirzapur* (2018, Series 1) that prioritises the small town in Purvanchal (East) of Uttar Pradesh in India, ultimately underscores the predominance of the mafia don, Akhadanand Tripathi, that is a Brahmin, over **Maurya, the law-enforcing** police officer of the **Indian Police Service. The latter as a 'lower caste' will have 'lower' social status in the context of the fictious Mirzapur of Uttar Pradesh, despite his exalted status as an officer of the elite police force of the Indian state** (Angshuman, 2018).

A not-so-new movie called *NH 10* (2015) has a police officer informing the asylum-seeking and stricken female protagonist from Delhi that, the 'law of caste' as dictated by the Hindu lawgiver Manu rules Gurgaon, even as it poses as a glitzy Westernised, mall- embellished city, and swears by 'secular' constitutional law. Some of the most successful and 'happy' mainstream movies in these times have been like *Dum Lagake Hainsa* (2016), *Bareilly ki Barfi* (2017), *Badhai Ho* (2019), *Subh Mangal Sabhdhan* (2017), *Subh Mangal Jyada Sabhdaan* (2019), *Bala, Ramprasadki Tervi* (2019) and *Pagglait* (2020), celebrate the small town, the undivided Hindu family and its being awash with village-like cultural ties.

A great new city novel, Arundhati Roy's *The Ministry of Utmost Happiness* (2016), celebrates the city of Delhi architectonically, as its narrative form (as admitted by Roy) mimics Delhi's unwieldy, unplanned spatiality. It celebrates that part of the city (or its graveyards, to be precise) being claimed as a state of refuge by people whom the nation state has violently excluded – Anjum a *hijra*, 'Saddam Hussein,' a construction-site security guard whose father has been lynched in Gurgaon, which is on the outskirts of Delhi, an *azadi*-seeking Kashmiri intellectual; Tilo, an anarchic architect; and an unnamed young girl child who is accidentally killed while watching the procession mourning the martyrdom of a Kashmiri militant. Anjum creates a *heim* for those internally displaced, even in terms of bodily longings, within that marginality of a necropolis. The violence that displaces every person is spatially urban in its origins but casteist, communal and rural in essence –violence-ridden Ahmedabad, Gurgaon on the outskirts of Delhi and Srinagar. Significantly, in India, the book has also not done as well as Roy's village book, *The God of Small Things* (1997)!

The present Indian state has provided a new twist to the village/city debate in its constant evocation of *gaumata* (cow as mother) and mandatory *gauseva* that is also recognising the centrality of the cow in village economy. I will not even make mention of the vigilantism, the lynching of 'cow smugglers' in broad daylight that the self-styled *gaurakshaks* have taken to. This goes alongside the introduction of bullet trains and prioritising of cashless digital economy further scrambling the city–village binary and culturally prioritising a Hinduised village within cities.

I engage with questions of refuge, of the choice of wastelands by waste people of the earth. I propose a revivification of the *char* idea, given their non-aligned, disconnected, politico-juridically liminal natures, as aterritories that are coeval of the stateless, disconnected bare lives. The *chars* are lands like those people that are 'human' and nothing more. The foregrounding, ideating a *char* of refuge, perforates the naïve notion of a sacral nation state, as well as a "naïve notion of the citizen and a people" (Agamben, 1993. Tr. Vincenzo Binetti and Cesare Casarino. *Means Without Ends: Notes on Politics*, in Theory Out of Bounds series, edited by Buckley, Hardt, Massumi, London and Minneapolis: University of Minnesota Press, 2000).

V The Republic of *char*: Alterities of Refuge Space for the Stateless in South Asia

I propose an imaginative alterity so far as refuge spaces in Eastern parts of the subcontinent are concerned in those occluded riverine islands that rise and submerge with the flow of the river or with the tides of the ocean. When I propose such alterities of envisioning aterritorial and post-national communities, I do so in awareness of the *chars* of this active delta have a long and complicated history as places of refuge and alternative living, much to the chagrin of various statist powers. A considerable body of economico-geographical work has now documented the life of inhabitants on these riverine islands and the inherently precarious nature of their existence, given the unstable ontology of the *char* lands themselves.

Recent events in Assam prior and posterior to the **National Register of Citizens** exercise show that such lands and legislation regarding its ownership and taxation patterns remain mired in contradictions. The lack of empirical data also generates hysterical myths about such people in the population of mainland. The post-colonial state refuses to empathise their cause, as the mainland/mainstream population groups are impervious to the fraught nature, the indeterminate nature of their existence. The very *chars* that they cultivate and make habitable, deny them legislative safeguards. As Willem van Schendel's notes "legally speaking too, the chars cannot be regulated as once submerged, it collapses as a legal entity, and the inhabitants of *chars* who have cultivated it originally can no longer lay claims upon that lands posterior to its re-emergence" (van Schendel, 2004).

I revisit Giorgio Agamben's reiteration of Arendtian ideas in his *Means Without End: Notes on Politics* (1996) where he notes that "refugee crisis is mistakenly seen as the crises of fleeing human beings rather than the crises of anachronistic political institutions." The European nation state that emphasises territorial contiguity, ethnic-cultural homogeneity and demarcated borders is that anachronism. It is the conjunction of nation-state territory and national subject that makes human beings illicit, and Agamben proposes an aterritorial *refugium* that, is conceptually topological rather than topographical. He ideates a structureless structure that is like an impossible -to-spatially- pin down Klein bottle or Mobius strip (Agamben, 1996. *Means without End: Notes on Politics* tr. Vincezo Binetti and Cesare Casarino "Beyond Human Rights," *Theory out of Bounds Series*, 20, Eds Buckley, Hardt and Massumi, 200, 24–25).

Are then *char* lands (**such as Bhasan-Jaliya of Bangladesh, the outer islands of Sundarbans of India**) to be imagined as prison islands that have existed and operated from colonial times in South Asia and territories where the 'waste people' of a biopolitically managed subject populace could be incarcerated, and hidden from public view? Are they to be seen as not-so-well-hidden pockets of the nation jacket, where biopolitically non-pertinent populace could be 'managed'?

Or could the *chars* be vivified as a liminal space where new life in its plurality, its variegated and creative splendour could be imagined? The *char*, its dwellers, as alterities of human habitation find their finest vivification in Bengali literature. Such vivification is strangely in awareness of their topographical liminality. I refer to Rabindranath Tagore's depiction of *chars* in Selaidaha in *Chinnapatra*, those luminous bits and pieces of letters (primarily addressed to his niece Indira Devi) where he vivifies such 'wastelands' as immensely productive spaces in creative terms given their utter isolation and beauty (Tagore, 1902).[14] It is such a *char* that constitutes the narrative fulcrum of his *unheimlich* short story "*Nishithe*" (At Night) and which again beckons to an alterity of perceptions.

The *char* as a central entity and not a wasteland but a place of refuge though often blighted, and fraught constitutes an entire tradition of Bengali narratives beginning with Sunil Gangopadhyaya's *Jaljangaler Kabya* (1950, A poem for the water and jungles), Sushil Jana's *Belabhumirgaan* (1964 A Song of the Sandlands), Shyamal Gangopadhyay's *Kuberer Bishoye Ashoye* (1967, The Assets of Kuber), Sadhan Chattopadhyay's *Gahin Gang* (1979–80, Deep Seas), Anil Ghorai's *Nun-badi* (1989, A House of Salt), Jhareshwar Chattopadhaya's *Char-purnima* (1995, Full Moon on the Char), and *Samudra Duar* (2001, The Gate to the Sea), Abdul Jabbar's *Ilishmarir Char* (2017, Char Where Hilsa Fish Are Caught), Sachin Das's *Nundariya* (Salt Seas), Hosen Sohrab's *Gang –Baghini* (2011, The Tigress of the Delta). Utpalendu Mandal's *Jaljangaler Baromasya* (The Diurnal Tale of Forests and Wetlands) and *Mandas* (1917, A raft of banana plants) and Amar Mitra's *Dhanapatir Char* (2016, The Char of Dhanapati). Mitra's latest, *Kumari Megher Desh Chai*, (2018, A Home for Virgin Clouds) is a heart-rending story of the *chitmahals*, those bits and pieces lands that have been caught between randomly drawn national borders. The *chitmahals* remain undefined and its people rendered stateless and rightless, even to the extent of rape victims being unable to lodge complaints, not having a police station of their own. Although not strictly about *chars*, *Kumari Megher desh chai* is an important ideational follow up to Mitra's *char* narratives, and portrayals of those caught in between by undefined border lines. Shaktipada Rajguru's *Dandak theke Marichjhnapi* (From *Dandakaranya to Marichjhnapi* 1980–1981) is an earlier narrative of the long march of refugees in their unrequited quest for char refugium. I mention Amitav Ghosh's *The Hungry Tide* (2014), at the end as it is already a globally recognised story of *char* Marichjhapi lives because it is written in English.

The most recent evocation life on char lands is Sourav Sarangi's docu-drama "Moddikhane char" (2012) and subtitled in English as *Char: No Man's Island* (Sarangi, 2012a). The movie takes its Bengali title from Tagore's poem *Notunkal* (New times, in anthology *Senjuti*, 1937) and where the poet speaks of "*epar Ganga opar Ganga, moddikhane char*" (the Ganga River from side and from that side and in between lies the river island). Tagore's poem intertextually evokes an old anonymous *chada* line "*epar ganga opar ganga moddhikhane char/tar moddhyebose ache Shibsadagar*" (the Ganga on two sides and Shib the merchant sits on that river island that is in between) and thus pointing at the density of the char image in Bengali literature.

Sarangi's movie traces the lives of desperately poor uprooted families trying to accommodate themselves within the borderlands of India and Bangladesh but unable to belong to none. Ruled by the local mafiosi of India and Bangladesh, they egg boys to drop out of schools and smuggle cows and rice across borders. The women ferry Phencydyl (also called 'Dyl' in these parts) – a cough syrup that is used as drug across the borders into the 'dry' Islamic Bangladesh. The banter and coy exchanges between the Indian Border Security Forces, Bangladesh Rifles soldiers and the women on this char in Sarangi's movie, are indicative of human trafficking/prostitution across the borders, enforcing thus the 'refugee body' as that point of transit, that volatile border.

The protagonists Sofikul and Rubel (that is if any such word can be used in a predominantly silent, imagistic movie) have either lost their fathers or find them debilitated as the documentary begins. Their families have relocated on this newly risen *char* islands on the Ganga River between the two nations due to uneven river water distribution, and the river taking strange twists and turns as a result of the Farakka barrage construction of 1967. Both India and Bangladesh have laid claims to this *char* as the international borders pass through the river and set up symbolic border posts, voluminous barbed wires and posted scary border security forces. The lives of people on these char lands are precarious because the very existence of the risen land, and the ferocious land erosion record of the Ganga 'due' to the Farakka barrage-induced vagaries. What the Farakka barrage does or debilitates remains a major area of contention between the nation states of Bangladesh and India, between the province-states of Bihar, Jharkhand and West Bengal, and between the territory states of North Bengal and South Bengal of the province of West Bengal. Prof. Kalyan Rudra, erstwhile chairperson of the West Bengal Pollution Control Board notes that "Deltaic rivers have a tendency to oscillate widely. ... The case of the Ganga in West Bengal is quite different. ... The mighty river even threatens to outflank the Farakka Barrage and open a new route through the presently moribund channels of Kalindi and Mahananda" (Rudra, 2003). This leads to potential floods and river bank erosion, along with silting and creation–destruction of riverine islands (Elahi & Rogge, 1990; Mukherjee, 2011; Rudra, 2003).[15] Malda is likely to have lost over **two-hundred and fifty sq** km of land, in this process but loss of land through river bank erosion is not considered a natural disaster and no governmental aid is forthcoming. What I have been able to get across is the extreme in-betweenness of char lands and the people that occupy them.

One of the central episodes of the documentary is the naming of *char*. Even though the actual place of Palashgachi is submerged by the erratic river-induced erosion, people on this char insist that this is Palashgachi. The possibility of the *char* disintegrating through natural ways of land erosion is evoked at the end of the documentary. Rubel admits that this char that they now inhabit, this 'now Palashgachi' will go underwater, even though the people on it might find other places and other means of living. The conceptual density of a Mobius strip, a Klein bottle (Agamben, 1993, "Beyond Human Rights," 24–25), an aform, an aterritory may help understand the *char* as a territory that is present and absent simultaneously.

The four thousand kilometere long "Bengal borderlands" as Willem van Schendel calls it (popularly known as the Radcliffe line) where Assam, West Bengal in India, Bangladesh and Myanmar have shared histories, ethnic congruities, and yet distinctive identity assertion desires, has led to an incredibly complicated and never-to-be-achieved-clarity regarding post-partition national identities. It is these *char* lands that rise and submerge, in between the Bengal borderlands and in its deltaic borders with the sea (Bay of Bengal) whose legal position is always liminal, where such complications of national identity may be resolved. I point to the impossibility of nation identity assertion in a post-partition South Asia. I also point towards the inevitability of such desires, given the global realities of ultra-national assertion trends. The *char* as an imaginary is vivified by these impossibilities that are inevitabilities that point towards our intertwined variegated lives and our necessities for refuge.

In "Beyond Human Rights" Agamben reiterates Arendt's position, noting that "refugee crisis is mistakenly seen as the crises of fleeing human beings rather than the crises of anachronistic political institutions" (24–25). The European nation state with its emphasis on territorial contiguity, ethnic-cultural homogeneity and demarcated borders is that anachronism. In the light of the present citizenship law debates and reinforcement of exclusion of people without territorial rights (the *ghuspetiya*), the aterritorial realties, of *charlands* as states of refuge for the disenfranchised, the waste people of the subcontinent, will assume even greater importance; as will the realisation of the untenable and anachronistic nature of nation-state formation.

Notes

1 This chapter was written in 2019, but its final form delayed and deferred due to the spread of Covid contagion. Most of the issues, especially those of Rohingya repatriation have therefore lost their immediacy and taken different critical dimensions given that the world and its actions came to a screeching halt with the spread of Covid 19.

2 See Kuntala Lahiri-Dutt and Gopa Samanta's *Dancing With the River People and life of Chars in South Asia*. (Yale Agrarian Studies Series, Yale University Press:2013) for a dense geographical idea of char formation in deltaic Bengal.

3 Territorially speaking, these *chars* have unstable, enigmatic qualities that problematise the permanence of lands and its laws; their juridico-political nature is equally ambiguous. *Chars* embody those foundational binaries in European epistemes, those posited between the state of nature, and state of culture; between what is 'wasteland' and what is 'garden;' between the 'savage' and 'civilised'; between that which is owned as property, mapped and, taxed, and that which is beyond. Intimately associated with these *char* formations are the legal questions of 'wasteland' and 'garden,' cultivable, stable land and that which is 'waste' or unstable. The questions of productivity, ownership of land can be traced back to Lockean ideas. Wasteland was a British juridical terminology indicating non-instrumentalised, unclaimed land. More recently Michel Foucault has revivified questions of biopolitical pertinence or the lack thereof. Stateless people are like non- pertinent, waste lands as they remain in that liminal zone, un claimed by nation states in terms of protections, but exploited, surveyed and instrumentalised as 'bare lives' without legal rights. See Gorky Chakraborty's essay "Roots and Ramifications of a Colonial 'Construct': The Wastelands of Assam" (*Occasional Paper 39*, Institute of Development Studies Kolkata, September 2012) for more on this.

4 See K. Maudood Elahi's "Refugees in Dandakaranya"(*The International Migration Review*, Spring-Summer, 1981, vol. 15, no. 1/2. *Refugees Today* (Spring–Summer, 1981) pp. 219–225, for more on the reasons for failure of the DDA rehabilitation project and its future in independent India.

5 See Shaktipada Rajguru's novel *Dandak theke Marichjhapi* (2008), Madhumoy Pal edited, *Marichjhapi: Chinna Desh, Chinna Itihaas*, Kolkata: Gangchil, 2009), Nilanjana Chatterjee's "Midnight's Unwanted Children: East Bengali Refugees and the Politics of Rehabilitation" PhD thesis, Brown University, 1992 Ross Mallick's "Refugee Resettlement in Forest Reserves: West Bengal Policy Reversal and Marichjhapi massacre" (The Journal of Asian Studies, Vol 58, No 1 (Feb 1999, pp. 104–125, Association of Asian Studies, https://doi.org/10.2307/2658391, Deep Haldar's *Blood Island*, Amitav Ghosh's *The Hungry Tide*.

6 Refer to Sk. Hasina's interview to *Voice of America* radio in September 2016; her statements to Natalia Kanem (Executive Director United Nations Fund for Population Activities) and William Lacy Swing, Director General of International Organization for Migration, that Rohingya refugees would be relocated by October 2018 to Bhasaner char. Also refer to the report "Rohingya Rehabilitation plan in Bhasaner Char at a glance" *Dhaka Tribune*, 3rdDecember, 2017. **This is not even to speak about the** tremendous resistance to housing Rohingyas in different parts of India (especially in Jammu in J and K, where its traders guild had given a call to "identify and kill" such settlers) and PM Modi's symbolic repatriation of seven Rohingya men on the 3rd of October 2018, identifying them as illegal infiltrators and not refugees.

7 See Chris Lewa's "*Statelessness: North Arakan: An Open Prison for the Rohingyas inn Burma*. She notes "The Rohingyas are an ethnic, linguistic and religious minority group mainly concentrated in North Arakan or Rakhaine)

State of Burma adjacent to Bangladesh, where their number is estimated at 725000. Of South Asian descent, they are related to the Chittagongian Bengalis just across the border in Bangladesh, whose language is also related. They profess Sunni Islam and are distinct from the majority Burmese population who are of East Asian stock and mostly Buddhists. Since Burma's independence in 1948, the Rohingyas have gradually been excluded from the nation building process" (Lewa, 1). Also see Azeem Ibrahim and Younus Muhammad's *The Rohingyas: Inside Myanmar's Hidden Genocide* (C. Hurst and Co, revised edition, 2018); Nasreen Chowdhury and Biswajit Mohanty's *Citizenship, Nationalism and Refugeehood of Rohingyas in Southern Asia* Singapore, Springer: 2020.

8 The Reuters, Associated Press and others reported that a deadly fire broke out in the Rohingya camps in the Balukhali section of the Cox Bazar area, on March 20th , 2021, destroying more than 45, 000 huts as well as 163 learning spaces within those camps, and leaving at least 15 people dead and of which a few are children. Louise Donovan, a spokesperson for the UNHCR estimated that more than 45,000 people had been displaced by the fire, What is heart rending is the newly installed barbed wire fencing around the Rohingya camps restricting the escape of the most vulnerable, from the engulfing flames (Scott Neuman's report "Hundreds Missing in Aftermath of Fire at Rohingya Refugee Camp" on March 23, https://www.npr.org, 2021/03/23).

9 Rohingya refugees have also sought refuge in Thailand, Malaysia, and South Korea.

10 The military imposed a state of emergency for one year on first of February 2021 at a time when the newly elected Myanmar lawmakers were about to conduct the first session of parliament. They have detained the erstwhile PM, and leader of National League for Democracy, Aung San Suu Kyi in an unknown location and cited massive voting fraud in the parliamentary elections to explain their actions (Alice Cuddy of BBC News reports on 2nd April https://www.bbc.com).

11 The 'statelessness' concept is usually traced back to Hannah Arendt's *Origins of Totalitarianism* (1951) but she had introduced this idea in far more nuanced and feeling manner in an earlier essay "We Refugees" (1943).

12 See Jacques Derrida's "Cities of Refuge" in an anthology entitled *Cosmopolitanism* and Giorgio Agamben's *Theory Out of Bounds*.

13 The tremendous resistance to housing Rohingyas in different parts of India (especially in Jammu in J and K, where its traders guild had given a call to "identify and kill" such settlers also in many ways fuelled the debates about identifying 'infiltrators' carrying out country wide National Registration of Citizens based on documentation and clear cut off dates regarding nationality. The Indian government's symbolic repatriation of seven Rohingya men on the 3rd of October 2018, identifying them as illegal infiltrators and not refugees at the height of the Assam NRC operations is a case in point.

14 Tagore's *Chinnapatra*, Letter no.10, Selidaha,1888, 32–38, Letter no.14, 1891, Patishar, 43–52, Kolkata, Viswabharati Press,1902.

15 See Kalyan Rudra's pioneering work, *The Encroaching Ganga and Social Conflicts: The Case of West Bengal, India* (West Bengal: Department of Geography Habra H.C. Mahavidyalaya, 2003 and K.M. Elahi and John Rogge's *Riverbank erosion Impact study* (Jahangirnagar University, Dhaka Bangladesh, 1990.Also see Jenia Mukherjee' "No Voice, No Choice: Riverine Changes and Human Vulnerability in the 'chars' of Malda and Murshidabad" (Occasional Paper-28, July 2011, IDSK 1–29).

References

Agamben, G. (2000). Beyond Human Rights. In *Means without End: Notes on Politics*, Translated by Vincenzo Binetti and Cesare Casarino. University of Minnesota Press, Theory Out of Bound Series (Vol. 20).

Angshuman, K. et al. (2018). *Mirzapur, Web Series (Season 1), performance by Pankaj Tripathi and Rasika Dugal.* Ritesh Sidhwani et al. (Producers), Amazon Prime.

Arendt, H. (1943). We Refugees. *The Menorah Journal*, *31*(1), 69–77.

Arendt, H. (1951). *The Origins of Totalitarianism* (Second Enlarged (1958) (Ed.)). The World Publishing Company. https://archive.org/details/TheOriginsOfTotalitarianism/page/n9/mode/2up

Chakraborty, G. (2012). *Roots and Ramifications of a Colonial 'Construct': The Wastelands in Assam* (IDSK Occasional Paper 39; September).

Chatterjee, N. (1992). *Midnight's Unwanted Children: East Bengali Refugees and the Politics of Rehabilitation.* PhD dissertation, Brown University.

Chowdhury, N., & Mohanty, B. (Eds.). (2020). *Citizenship, Nationalism and Refugeehood of Rohingyas in Southern Asia.* Springer.

Derrida, J. (1997). *On Cosmopolitanism and Forgiveness, Translated by Mark Dooley and Michael Hughes.* Thinking in Action Series, Routledge.

Elahi, K. M. (1981). Refugees in Dandakaranya. *The International Migration Review*, *15*(1/2 (Spring-Summer)), 219–225.

Elahi, K. M., & Rogge, J. (1990). *Riverbank Erosion Impact Study.* Jahangirnagar University.

Ghosh, A. (2004). *The Hungry Tide.* HerperCollins.

Halder, D. (2019). *Blood Island: An Oral History of the Marichjhapi Massacre.* HerperCollins.

Ibrahim, A., & Muhammad, Y. (2018). *The Rohingyas: Inside Myanmar's Hidden Genocide* (Revised). C. Hurst and Co. Ltd.

Lahiri-Dutt, K., & Samanta, G. (2013). *Dancing With the River People and Life of Chars in South Asia.* Yale University Press.

Lewa, C. (2009). North Arakan: An Open Prison for the Rohingyas in Burma. *Forced Migration Review*, 32, Statelessness. https://www.fmreview.org/sites/fmr/files/FMRdownloads/en/statelessness/lewa.pdf

Mallick, R. (1999). Refugee Resettlement in Forest Reserves: West Bengal Policy Reversal and Marichjhapi Massacre. *The Journal of Asian Studies*, 58(1), 104–125. doi:10.2307/2658391

Mukherjee, J. (2011). *No Voice, No Choice: Riverine Changes and Human Vulnerability in the 'chars' of Malda and Murshidabad* (IDSK Occasional Paper 28; Occasional Paper).

Nandy, A. (2001). *An Ambiguous Journey to the City: The Village and Other Ruins of the Self in the Indian Imagination.* Oxford University Press.

Neuman, S. (2021, March). Hundreds Missing in Aftermath of Fire at Rohingya Refugee Camp. *NPR 23.*

Rudra, K. (2003). *The Encroaching Ganga and Social Conflicts: The Case of West Bengal.* Department of Geography, Habra H.C. Mahavidyalaya.

Sarangi, S. (2012a). *Moddikhane Char: Char… The No-Man's Island, performance by Rubel Mondal and Sofikul Sheikh.* Saurav Sarangi, et al. (Producers).

Shaktipada,R.(2009).*DandaktbekeMarichjhapi*.https://documentcloud.adobe.com/link/review?uri=urn:aaid:scds:US:332b5dd7-ba46-44c3-a734-0bc9fb43db47
van Schendel, W. (2004). *The Bengal Borderland: Beyond State and Nation in South Asia*. Anthem Press.

Bengali

Chattopadhaya, Jhareshwar. (1995). *Char-purnima*. Kolkata: Dey's Publishing.
Chattopadhaya, Jhareshwar. (2001). *SamudraDuar*. Kolkata: Dey's Publishing.
Chattopadhyay, Sadhan. (1979–80). *Gahin Gang*.
Das, Sachin. (2011). *Nundariya*. Kolkata: Karuna Prokasani.
Gangopadhyay, Shyamal. (1967). *KubererBishoyeAshoye*. Calcutta: Karuna rakashan.
Gangopadhyaya, Sunil. (1950). *JaljangalerKabya* (1950) Calcutta: Nabapotro Prakashan.
Ghorai, Anil. (1989). *Nun-Badi*. Kolkata: Ananda Publishers.
Jabbar, Abdul. (2017). *Ilishmarir Char*. Kolkata: Universal Book Depot.
Jana, Sushil. (1964). *Belabhumir Gaan*. Calcutta: Bidyadoy Library Private Limited.
Mandal, Utpalendu. (2002). *JaljangalerBaromasya*., Kokata: Boiwala.
Mitra, Amar. (2016). *Dhanapatir Char*. Kolkata: Dey's Publishing.
Mitra, Amar. (2018). *MegherDesh Chai*. Kolkata: Dey's Publishing.
Pal, Madhumoy. (ed.). (2009). *Marichjhapi: ChinnaDesh, ChinnaItihaas*. Kolkata: Gangchil.
Rajguru, Shaktipada. *DandakthekeMarichjhapi*. https://documentcloud.adobe.com/link/review?uri=urn:aaid:scds:US:332b5dd7-ba46-44c3-a734-0bc9fb43db47.
Sarangi, Saurav. (2012b). *Moddikhane Char: Char… The No-Man's Island*. Documentary.
Sohrab, Hosen. (2011). *Gaang –Baghini*. Kolkata: Dey's Publishing.
Tagore, Rabindranath. (1902). *Chinnapatra*. Santiniketan: Viswabharati Press, 1902.

Chapter 4

Miya Poetry

Poetics, Politics and Polemics

Abdul Kalam Azad and Gorky Chakraborty

1 Introduction

Globalisation has facilitated the extension of social relations on a global scale, and it has also problematised the spatial parameters in which it occurs. This interplay is reconfiguring spatiality and social relations on an unprecedented scale (Brenner, 1999). Under such circumstances few emerging areas of enquiry may include: how is the relationship amongst state–people–territory negotiated? Has it widen the scope for transforming the issues related to entitlement and citizenship? Is it renegotiating the social relationship between the majority and the minorities within a nation? What are its implications on belongingness, allegiance and place-making? How do art and literature navigate under such circumstances?

Globally, concepts, practices and markers of citizenship are in flux, and so is perhaps the relationship amongst state–people–territory. The world, as it appears, is witness to a crisis of citizenship both at sub- and supra-national levels, and the emerging patterns of statelessness at varying scales point in such a direction. Recent studies around the world indicate that the state has been fast weaponising citizenship and nationality against their own citizens, where the victims have been largely from marginalised communities (Bhat 2020; Burnay and Pils 2020; Eyakuze and Said 2020; Dardani 2017; Liu 2017; Reyes 2020). While migration to escape war, famine, political turmoil and poverty still continues to be endemic at an unprecedented level beneath the glitz of neo-liberal globalisation, adding to citizenship worries and statelessness; another tendency has been simultaneously visible at national and/or the sub-national scales emanating from state-mandated markers of belongingness, allegiance and place-making that pushes "citizens beyond the boundaries of citizenship rights" (Banerjee, 2020, p. 299).

Literary works, for example Shamsie's *Home Fire* (Shamsie, 2017), and poetry, for example the emerging genre of *Miya* poetry, are a few examples that highlight the angst associated with the state-mandated markers of citizenship that potentially lead to statelessness. While *Home Fire* portrays the dilemmas associated with citizenship, both in terms of ideation and praxis of a Muslim identity in 'multicultural' Britain, those associated with *Miya*

DOI: 10.4324/9781003345152-7

Poetry are embedded in a search for claiming epistemic justice for those who are made to suffer from citizenship *blues* and are identified with a slur *Miya*, in Assam. Both these instances manifest how the state with its varying interpretation on citizenship vis-à-vis the national core (Pandey, 1999) ultimately creates conditions of statelessness within the ranks of its citizens. This chapter deals with *Miya* poetry, which emerges as a poetic exasperation resultantly to the anxieties and emotions accompanying the statist process of pronouncing civil deaths to a section of its citizenry in Assan in its zeal to redefine the nation.

II Context and Methodology

During the preparation of the National Register of Citizens (NRC), the *Miya* Muslim community faced discrimination and the risk of mass statelessness. The community leaders, social activists, researchers, authors, writers and poets started sharing their concerns about the discriminatory process of NRC through which hundreds and thousands of *Miya* Muslims were potentially at the risk of becoming stateless. One of the most important and powerful means of telling stories of suffering and injustice was through this new genre of poetry, which thereafter organically got associated with the name *Miya* poetry. Surprisingly, it rattled a large section of people, including public intellectuals, politicians, office bearers of Assamese literary bodies and socio-cultural groups, amongst a few others. Gradually, in 2019, it transformed into a huge debate, leading to a controversy that led to the filing of several police complaints in different parts of Assam. The poets were accused of portraying the Assamese society as xenophobic and in the process weakening the Assamese language and spreading hatred between communities, among others.

Ironically, this duality has been an observed pattern in Assam and the controversy surrounding *Miya* Poetry seems to be its latest manifestation. This in a way reflects what Anupama Roy (Roy, 2008) ascribes to the process of 'encompassment' and 'closure' in citizenship discourses. While the encompassing attributes of Assamese nationality sought to accommodate and assimilate the *Miya* population groups as *Na-Axomiya*, there has been a palpably strong tendency to create wide fissures seeking to exclude, as if the process of Assamese nationality formation has been a closed chapter in history both, continuing in a way, where one is a dialectical negation of the other, yet entwined together.

In such a context, this chapter intends to chart the course of the emergence of *Miya* poetry and the milieu that it is set in. We draw our argument from two data sets – our own retrospective auto-ethnography and in-depth interviews with six *Miya* poets. While Azad, one of the authors of this chapter, is himself a *Miya* poet and community worker with lived experience concerning what ails the community. His co-author, Chakraborty, on the other hand, has been working with the *Miya* community as a close observer and chronicler for the past two decades. They have conducted interviews with six *Miya* poets to understand how their poetry helps reclaim *Miya* identity. The interviews were guided by various socio-political events that have affected the community over decades. Apart from these two sets of data, the corpus also includes a set of selected *Miya* poems, in translated forms, to understand the politics and polemics associated with poetics that define this historical moment. The poems in Assamese and local *Miya* dialect were translated by Shalim M Hussain. We followed a step-by-step guide of thematic analysis for the analysis and writing of this chapter (Braun and Clarke, 2006).

III The Socio-Political Milieu

Contemporary citizenship practices often innately reproduce the angst associated with colonial expansion in Northeast India and Assam without fathoming out the ramifications of such disjuncture. If we consider the colonial construct of 'wasteland', a land that did not accrue revenue for the British Crown, that in a way changed the course of history in the region, the implications of such colonial intervention become clear. It is important to point out that vast expanses of land under the custodianship of the communities for whom territoriality was synonymous with bio-spatiality, appeared *terra nullius* (no man's land) to the colonial state, ultimately to be appropriated for revenue generation through the jurisprudential principles of *res nullius* (what is not assigned by the sovereign belongs to the sovereign); (Chakraborty, 2012a). This wasteland, so 'located', was then sought to be utilised through tea plantation by bringing in labour from various parts of Bengal and Madras Presidencies and United Provinces while subsequently acreage under food and commercial crops has been expanded through facilitating in-migration of communities from several adjacent districts of Eastern Bengal. Out of these two broad but separate streams of migrants into colonial Assam, the tea plantation labourers and the *Miya* communities now comprise the two largest sections of the working-class population in the state in contemporary times.

Sharing contiguous regions, economic and socio-cultural interactions between Assam hills and plains, Eastern Bengal has been known since historical times, but large-scale migration started fructifying when Assam and Eastern Bengal became one province due to the partition of Bengal (1905). As the colonial administration encouraged migration from the densely populated *zamindari*-administered districts of Eastern Bengal to wasteland-abundant Assam, the number picked up exponentially and so was the area under cultivation, crop profiles and commercial interest on land. To cut a long story short, it is estimated that up to 1951, the total number of migrants from East Bengal must have been about 1 to 1.5 million, which was between one-tenth to one-sixth of the total population of the state (Goswami, 1994), who were settled with nearly half a million acres out of the total 1.1 million acres of wasteland settlement with all the (im)migrants into Assam (Guha, 1976).

Along with these economic changes, the socio-political landscape of the state changed significantly. With the large-scale arrival of the Bengali-speaking *Miya* community in Assam, the demographic characteristics of the state altered noticeably. The Muslim population doubled from 12.04 to 24.68 per cent in between 1901–51. It also had the potential to generate fault lines in terms of dwindling the number of Assamese speakers in the state. Interestingly, the *Miya* community leaders exhibited tremendous foresight and accepted the Assamese language as their mother tongue in their census declaration to evade 'death and deportation' (Sharma, 1980). This saved the community from becoming a minority on both counts – religion and language in Assam. While this process in terms of acceptance of the language should certainly be regarded as a moment of 'encompassment' in Assamese nationality formation, duly acknowledged by cultural stalwarts of Assam, for example Jyoti Prasad Agarwala, who referred to them as *Na-Axomiya* (neo-Assamese), the crosscurrents of treating the members of the community as 'suspicious' mortals have been an inseparable part of the socio-political milieu of the state. The saga of community relations between the *Miya* community and the larger Assamese society at least in the post-colonial period has been a reflection of such 'pulls' and 'punches' in the emerging history of Assam.

What Pandey (1999) ascribes as the 'national core' for India surely has its own replication for Assamese nationality, where its core consisting of dominant if not hegemonic caste relations control the process of 'encompassment' and thereby determine indigeneity by calculating the 'distance' from the core. Ironically, while the reprisals from the core towards the *Miya* community have been unabated largely through evictions, for example the aftermath of The Immigrants (Expulsion from Assam) Act 1950, during the Prevention of Infiltration from Pakistan Scheme 1962, to name a few, the community, on the other hand, stood firm with the core in terms of its effort towards upholding the Assamese language, for example during the movement concerning Assam Official Language Act 1960, Medium of Instruction Movement 1972 and others. In this regard, the Assam Movement (1979–85) has been a turning point albeit slowly particularly after the Nellie massacre in 1983, followed by the experience of the community members due to the 'invention' of a unique category by the Election Commission, termed as the 'D' voter that created more than 3 lakh doubtful citizens and thereby the ghost of ubiquitous *Bangladeshi* (Chakraborty, 2012b). This alienated the *Miya* community further as they went through inhuman experiences at the hands of several agencies and civil society organisations in Assam. Suspicion of being a *Bangladeshi*, coercion to refute their organic link to the land and violence to establish them as alien became institutionalised and endemic to the lived experiences of the *Miya* community in the state.

With the bitter experience from the 'D' voter episode along with dealing with cases in Foreigners Tribunals, when on 5 May 2005, in a tripartite meeting comprising of the Union, State governments and All Assam Students

Union (AASU) in the presence of the Prime Minister Manmohan Singh decided to update the NRC of 1951, the community was taken aback. An undercurrent of 'hurt' realisation of being unnecessarily pushed into an administrative exercise that carried the potential to further intensify the episodes of epistemic violence on the community became evident. This angst drove the members to protest against the proposed pilot project at Barpeta under the banner of All Assam Minorities Students Union (AAMSU) resulting in the death of four protestors, as the agencies used excessive force to mute the mobilisation. This brutal excess led to a realisation that instead of challenging the administrative order on updating the NRC, pragmatism lay in enabling the process by making the community members conscious and aware through grass-roots engagements, particularly about the formalities and documentary process related to such an exercise. A large number of groups consisting of young, educated community members voluntarily assisted people in terms of filling up the forms, retrieving documents, arranging them in proper order and simultaneously acted as the liaison between many of these poorly lettered people and the government offices, for example NRC Seva Kendra, along with attending to hearing, filing claims and others.

It was during this voluntary engagement that many of these youth volunteers became aware of the life experiences of the *Miya* community members, which the latter shared spontaneously with the former. These volunteers appeared as harbingers of hope to the hapless millions. While the lettered wrote for local, regional, national and international media, the poorly lettered started penning their stories in their local dialect. For the first time, they started speaking, writing and sharing their angst in a language other than Assamese, in their own *Miya* dialect. The tone and texture of their writing now have been sharp and focused, where they were not bothered about the grammar and syntax of the Assamese language. The stories of suffering were soon followed by poems of despondency, hope too. Poet Khabir Ahmed wrote:

> After forty years of independence
> I have no space in the words of beloved writers
> The brush of your scriptwriters doesn't dip in my picture
> My name left unpronounced in assemblies and parliaments
> On no martyr's memorial, on no news report is my name printed
> Even in tiny letters.
> Besides, you haven't yet decided what to call me-
> Am I Miyah, AsoMiya or Neo-AsoMiya?
> ....

Followed by another poem, where Hafiz Ahmed portrayed betrayal:

> Milord
> Contrary to his claims

I am not his step-brother
Mother and son
Were not separated
When I was born
He has eavesdropped too often
On the whispers
Of friends and foes
And muddled his head
This might be why
He repeatedly declares me illegitimate.

IV The Trajectory

It is widely believed that the *Miya* poetry movement sparked off when poet Hafiz Ahmed penned the poem "Write down I am Miya" and posted it on social media during the NRC updating process. Nevertheless, newer insights from our fieldwork suggest that even before Hafiz Ahmed, there were few poets who composed poetry using the *Miya* dialect. They wrote highlighting the pain and sufferings of the community members. In 2011, a year after the killing of four protestors who raised their voice against updating of NRC in Barpeta, poet Siraj Khan wrote a poem "My Son Has Learnt to Cuss like the City":

They ask, 'Oie, what is your language?'
Just as the tongues of beasts and birds
Have no books, my language has no school
I draw a tune from my mother's mouth
And sing Bhatiyali. I match rhythm with rhythm
Pain with pain
Clasp the sounds of the land close to my heart
And speak the whispers of the sand
The language of the earth is the same everywhere.

Siraj Khan's poem nurtures the idea of the universality of pain and suffering. He moves beyond the acrimony surrounding language by focusing on his community members who have suffered historically as they were identified as aliens, others, foreigners and so on. He narrates how his organic association with Assam has always been contested and denied using various slurs. His poetry challenges these slurs that are ascribed to him and the community members and refuses to accept this contestation any further. He asserts that the new generation of *Miya* Muslims are educated, smart and hard-working. They will rightfully question such dehumanisation. Poet Khan writes:

O mister snake charmer
How long will you slither and slide

My son goes to college now
He has learnt to cuss like the city
He knows little but he knows well
The sweet twists and the sweet turns of poetry.

After the violence in Barpeta, the pilot project of NRC was put on hold. In the meantime, the public interest litigation filed in the Supreme Court came to the bench of Justice Ranjan Gogoi. Soon, the Supreme Court of India directed the government agencies to implement the updating process of NRC within a specific time frame. The community members initially thought that the direct supervision of the apex court may minimise arbitrariness of various agencies and organisations and thus reduce their suffering. However, soon their hopes were belied, as the apex court seemed to be apathetic towards their pain and agony. The members of the *Miya* community continued to narrate their stories through various mediums. One of the most powerful mediums was the *Miya* poetry.

In the last week of April 2016, Dr Hafiz Ahmed, the president of *Char Chapori Sahitya Parishad* (a literary organisation in the *char* areas of the Brahmaputra Valley) wrote a poem and posted on social media:

Write / Write Down
I am a Miya
My serial number in the NRC is 200543
I have two children / Another is coming
Next summer / Will you hate him
As you hate me? …

This poem went viral and had a mesmerising spell on the other young poets within the community, who responded in large numbers by writing newer poetry. Interestingly, poet Ahmed, has been one of the ardent supporters of promoting the Assamese language within the community. All through his life, he has popularised the Assamese language and Assamese literature among the *Miya* community in various remote corners of the state. However, when he wrote this poem, he had come under vitriolic attack from various quarters in Assam. In response, Shalim M Hussain, a young *Miya* poet and translator wrote back:

Nana, I have written attested countersigned
And been verified by a public notary
That I am a Miyah

Many among those who responded after Ahmed's poem were not even poets but wrote poems as a mark of solidarity. Aman Wadud, a young lawyer, followed suit and wrote a poetic response to attacks on Hafiz Ahmed. Wadud's poem chronicled the violence perpetrated against the *Miya* community in various places as well as how their identity has been weaponised against them.

> You murdered me in Nellie
> Because I am Miya
> You murdered me in Khagrabari
> Because I am Miya
> You abused me by calling me Bangladeshi
> Because I am Miya
> You denied me my rights
> Because I am Miya
> Here I am prouder than ever

A large group of young and educated people within the community posted their poems. These poems now moved beyond laments of their suffering but asserted the reclaiming of an identity, which thus far has been weaponised against the community and used as a slur over the past many decades. Noticeably, it was through these poems, the community members gained pride and dignity precisely with the term *Miya* that has long been weaponised against them. A chain of social media posts of poems symbolising violence, suffering and humiliation that the community has historically experienced suddenly became alive. As time passed, more poets wrote in various languages and dialects, including many in the *Miya* dialect. Poet and now political activist Ashraful Hussain posted:

> My father wears on his chin a handful of beard
> A topi on his head, a string of beads on his hand, a jute bag on his shoulders
> But because he wears on his jaw broken Assamese,
> He walks from work to the police station
> Sometimes as a Bangladeshi, sometimes as a fundamentalist

It was not just young people from the *Miya* community, some young people within the mainstream Assamese community also expressed their solidarity. College teacher El Biswajit and lawyer Nandita Talukdar wrote poems and became part of the movement. Dilip Chakravarthy, a doctoral candidate wrote "let us hope to see many more Miya poets asserting their identity and tearing down the prejudice and ethnocentrism." Gradually, it transformed into a full-fledged poetry movement and got recognised by other poets, critics and commentators.

The *Miya* Poetry movement was progressing along with the NRC updating process. As the NRC process was coming to a close, the stories of suffering intensified further and so was their narration through these poets and volunteers. Their poetics talked of violence and harassment meted out to the community throughout the post-colonial period in Assam and the emerging urge to stand up in solidarity with their brethren. In one such poem, "Everyday On The Calendar Is Nellie", Abdul Kalam Azad wrote:

> You have seen blood all your life, I tell my heart
> Why are you scared of blood?
> I close my eyes
> Another handful of fear rumbles in my belly …
> My world shivers in fear
> I cannot sleep
> lend me some strength, friends
> Lend me some false hope

V The Philosophical Roots

Interviewing the *Miya* poets and those associated with the movement provided us with a discrete sketch of the history, contexts and personalities that they referred to as positive vibes. Cultural and literary movements around the world, for example the negritude movement, the black arts movement and the Chicano movement, were referred to more than often. Similarly, recent parallels were drawn regarding various other groups who have used poetry as a means of expression particularly Dalits, LGBTQ+ community, Afro-American community and others. *Miya* poets felt that their thoughts converged at a point with these groups, as all of them, talk about discrimination and prejudice while seeking justice and acceptance (P. Das, 2021). In the initial days of the movement, when the poets and activists were debating the name of this new genre of poetry, some of them who were students in institutions of higher learning, felt inspired by their formal coursework in literary criticism and cultural studies, along with the movements and their icons. Abdul Kalam Azad, a *Miya* poet, mentions the same in an interview with a news website, quoting Langston Hughes "I am a Negro" poem, he argues that reclamation of the term *Miya*, which has been otherwise used pejoratively over the years, has hit the hearts of those who harass (N. Das, 2016). *Miya* poets and their associates were influenced by Harlem Renaissance poets like Langston Hughes, whose writings inspired and shaped the founders of the negritude movement. *Miya* poets in various occasions have spoken about their inspiration from these art and literary movements (Hassan, 2021). Azad narrates how the words of Aimé Césaire, inspired the *Miya* poets to reclaim their identity, which has been so far used to dehumanise them (Azad, 2019). Aimé Césaire wrote:

> We asserted that our Negro heritage was worthy of respect, and that this heritage was not relegated to the past, that its values were values that could still make an important contribution to the world.
>
> (Kelley, Césair, and Pinkham, 2000)

In their conversations, the *Miya* poets excitedly drew parallels with the negritude movement. They reiterated that between 1920 and 1930, black writers and poets from the French colonies met in Paris to take a stock of racism in the French colonies. Accordingly, they were introduced to the writings of Langston Hughes and Claude McKay of the Harlem Renaissance. Three black students from different French colonies: Aimé Césaire (1913–2008) from Martinique, Léon Gontran Damas (1912–1978) from Guiana and Léopold Sédar Senghor (1906–2001) from Senegal came together to initiate a literary movement to highlight the conditions of the black people. Aimé Césaire coined the term 'negritude' in his writing *Cahier d'un retour au pays natal* (Notebook of a Return to My Native Land; Jones, 1997). Writer and activist Paulette Nardal, her sister Jeanne Nardaland and their tea stall 'salon' played a vital role in facilitating discussions that built the philosophical foundations of the movement. People associated with the movement came from different backgrounds and professions including poets, journalists, activists and politicians, among others.

The *Miya* poets drew our attention to a situation where a group of young educated community members, many of whom were students of Assamese language and literature came together and tried to find new vocabulary to reclaim the slur '*Miya*' and reinterpret it with pride. Dr Hafiz Ahmed, who has been a brilliant student of Assamese literature at Gauhati University and has been awarded a doctorate degree in Assamese language, thereafter was one of the senior-most poets associated with this movement. Similarly, Dr Rehna Sultana, Dr Abdul Mazid Sheikh and Dr Shalim M Hussain were pursuing research on various aspects of the Assamese language and literature for their respective doctoral thesis. Kazi Sharowar Hussain, Gazi Rahman, Abdur Rahim, Siraj Khan and Aman Ali, among others, were also bestowed with excellent literary skills in the Assamese language and had been writing in Assamese for a long time before they started actively participating in the *Miya* poetry movement. All of them asserted that the *Miya* identity has been a stigma and now they want to adorn themselves with the term and thus poetically transform *thorns into roses*.

During our discussion with some *Miya* poets, it was pointed out that the person who coined the term *negritude*, Aimé Césaire, was a leftist political activist. He was elected as mayor of Fort-de-France and deputy to the French National Assembly for Martinique with the support of the French Communist Party (Viveros-Vigoya, 2020). His fundamental formulation of Négritude was drawn from Césaire's understanding of Marxism. He incorporated Marx's theories on consciousness, culture and alienation to formulate his arguments for the recognition of a unique black identity (Rexer, 2013). *Miya* poet Aman Ali draws similarity by pointing out that he himself is a left activist and has dedicated his life to the development of grass-roots organisation of the Communist Party of India (Marxist). For him, being a member of the political party and his *Miya* identity are not at loggerheads.

In fact, both are complementary to each other. Aman Ali dreams that his downtrodden *Miya* identity will help create a coalition of solidarity with other oppressed classes and groups in Assam. Ali emphasizes:

> Just assertion of Miya identity is not enough. We need to make a coalition with other communities based on the common issues like employment, education, health among other things. When you speak twice about the issues of Miyas, at least you must speak once for the rights of the Adivasi community. They are also not less oppressed. We must speak about them as well.

We tried to problematise the Miya identity in order to understand its criticalities. What makes someone a *Miya* or what is *Miya*ness? How is a *Miya* differentiated from the other? What is the common thread that binds all *Miya* together? Is the same *Miya* dialect spoken by all the people within the community? It was interesting to observe that there were several variations in the language spoken by the *Miya* people inhabiting different areas of the state. Similarly, a lack of uniformity was understood to exist in terms of culture and cultural practices as well. In other words, *Miya* people do not share a common culture. We also tried to situate the ideas of essentialism in order to understand the *Miya* identity, for example as essentialism seeks to locate a definitional uniformity to identify certain beings as one despite being in flux so that they are put under one category (Thinius, 2021). It was noted that the definitional thread that binds the categorisation of the community as one is the *slur* used by their oppressors, that is *Miya*! However, an equally strong contradictory tendency did accompany the start of the movement where people within the *Miya* community questioned: How can one form an emancipatory collective or community using a name which is not ours but bestowed by their oppressors? A term which is associated with the trauma and suffering of hundreds and thousands of people belonging to the community? Why would they own up an identity which is given by their oppressors and exploiters?

The *Miya* poets ascribed that it was during these discussions and debates that a minute observation of the negritude movement opened their eyes. Using the theoretical framework provided by subaltern theories helped them understand why they may choose to adopt the term *Miya* and reclaim this identity with pride. These poets elaborated and once again drew our attention to the historical context of the negritude movement. One of the advocates of the negritude movement, Aimé Césaire, refused to put their movement within the framework of essentialism. He argued that is not in essence but rather an in-suppressible reality. He said:

> Negritude, in my eyes, is not a philosophy. Negritude is not a metaphysics. Negritude is not a pretentious conception of the universe. It is a way of living history within history: the history of a community whose

> experience appears to be … unique, with its deportation of populations, its transfer of people from one continent to another, its distant memories of old beliefs, its fragments of murdered cultures. How can we not believe that all this, which has its own coherence, constitutes a heritage? (Césaire, 2020)

Similarly, the *Miya* identity propagated by the *Miya* poetry movement is not essentialist. There is nothing called "*Miya*ness" or "*Miya* essence" to define who is a *Miya*. The pride in the *Miya* identity is not because it is given by their oppressors but by not being oppressors themselves, the ability to remain humane. Poet Aman Ali says:

> When many people of Assam have taken arms, used political platforms and many other means to establish their rights and in such a time these people have chosen poetry as a medium for their movement. What a beautiful thing.

The common thread which is used by the *Miya* poets to unite their community is their untold suffering and marginalisation at the hands of their oppressors. Subaltern theorist Gayatri Chakravorty Spivak provides us with a new vocabulary to understand such a situation. She calls it 'strategic essentialism' when the oppressed group, recognising its need for group unity and a positive self-conception, intentionally promotes an essentialist identity (Nielsen, 2013). Nielsen (2013) further explains the advantage of moving from essentialism to strategic essentialism:

> Such a move is both therapeutic and strategic in nature. With respect to the former, a period of healing and regaining strength is necessary, given the suffering the group has endured. With respect to the latter, in order to accomplish their socio-political goals, the group must have time to solidify and develop its own distinctive voice, signature, discursive practices, and other unique features.

Miya poets understand the intensity of pain and suffering and the urgency to create a support system in solidarity yet simultaneously continue to learn the language to question the mighty state as well. *Miya* poet Gazi Rahman outpours this pain and suffering in his poem and urges for solidarity. Rahman's poetry uses it as a therapy for his 'ghost nation':

> I don't mourn my death
> I don't remember
> When last I was alive
> Look after my old mother
> And stay well, my country

On the other, young poet Kazi Sharowar Hussain fiercely narrates how his community is dehumanised and forced to live a life of rightlessness, as he talks about his people and their right to have rights, and his poem touches the imagination of the stories beyond the darkness of the detention centres:

> The land where a skull cap is radicalism
> A Miya is sub-human
> Every charuwa a Bangladeshi
> Where the earth is weighed and sold to
> Tatas, Birlas and Ambanis
> That land is mine; I am not of that land

Ashraful Hussain, *Miya* poet and political activist uses similar agony and pain but argues that such a strategic use of identity is neither against anyone nor does it fix the community into a singular level. This *Miya* poet argues that the assertion of his *Miya* identity doesn't clash with his Assamese identity as a resident of Assam, and Indian identity, as a citizen of the country or his affiliation to various other group identities. Similarly, poet Aman Ali narrates that his poems are not against any individual, community or group of people. He doesn't differentiate anyone and shouldn't be read as a threat to anyone else. Rather, these poems are a tool to ask questions to the state and those who are at the helm of power. Ali writes:

> We have lit this flame
> With the fires of our pain
> Why does this flame scare you?
> This flame will never burn your home-
> Your target and mine, is the king's palace.

VI Poetics, Politics and Polemics

Was the *Miya* community bereft of poetics prior to the emergence of *Miya* poetry? Were there no poets within the community, who penned the angst of these people? Our analysis revealed that the community lacked neither poetic expressions nor poets worth its name. Then, why has the contemporary moment of *Miya* poetry *been so different*? The difference perhaps lies in the process of self-conscious poetic expressions of a few poets, whose desire to channel their 'felt' sense of deprivation, indignity and fear of statelessness during the NRC moment in a 'language' that reflected the lived experience of the community. Their poetry could transform the "consciousness of the few into the consciousness of the community" (Datta, 1990, p. 18), a 'form' that caught the imagination of the community in a way that was unprecedented in the history of Assam. Poetics helped to transform an age-old slur *Miya*, which has been colloquially used to denigrate, into an expression of self-identity for the community. The latent cry that lay hidden in the depths of their heart was vented out through poetry. *Miya* poetry became the platform for self-identification without guilt, assuaging the community to be aware of their existential realities. Poetry, in these circumstances, provided them with the solace of rootedness in a milieu, which has been otherwise marked violently by the praxis of erasure. Poetics, during this contemporary moment of *Miya* poetry, ushered hope when the community suffered from the threats of rightlessness. This poetry thus being "the nascent self-consciousness" of the *Miya*, "not as an individual but as sharer with others of a whole world of common emotions ... emotions because it is common ... for each individual, an objective, and therefore pseudo-external existence" (Caudwell, 1937/1991, p. 21). The birth of *Miya* Poetry has precisely therefore been a birth of nebulous identity for the *Miya* community as well.

The apprehension of a threat to their citizenship rights that may ultimately be thrust on many, a state of statelessness after the updating of NRC, affected the psyche of the community and *Miya* poetry became one of the most popular forms of such expressions. Of course, it has been a moment of imagination and freedom too. But, as Radhakrishnan (2012) while commenting on *Modern Fiction and Politics* hints, a literary creation "has to carry its own burden of representation" (p. 60), and *Miya* poetry due to its unique name and language became contrapuntal in its representation. This genre of poetry visibly aggrieved the status quo in Assam, resulting in diatribes, intimidation and legal actions against *Miya* poets by cultural elites, activists and political functionaries. In a way, *Miya* poetry marked a moment when "politics [was] suspended and the political [was] inaugurated at the same time" (p. 62). Like fiction, the birth of *Miya* poetry also heralded the birth of the political as it took on the authorities. These poets and their poetry created polyphonic impulses. The discord lay not with their style, metre, rhyme, assonance or alterations of poetry but with the poets who embraced the slur *Miya* and became the *producers of knowledge* on behalf of the hapless community. The audacity of a community, which has thus far been historically oppressed and vilified, now dared to create their own imaginaries, an act that became difficult to fathom for its critiques. The poetics of counter storytelling irked the status quoist, as they wove a venomous campaign portraying the *Miya* poets as conspirators posing a threat to Assamese language, ethnicity and nationality.

Incidentally, if one peeks into history, the roots of these vociferous campaigns against *Miya* poetry get further *deconstructed*. It is understood that negotiating partition (1947) has been rather linear, which has been perceived on religion in large parts of India. For Assam, however, this negotiation lay frayed around the intersectionality of religion and language. The Sylhet referendum and its loss have been interpreted as a boon in disguise as it facilitated Assam to ward off the Islamic threat along with the linguistic one, since Sylhet was a Bengali-speaking area in colonial Assam. The urge to become a majority within a particular space, otherwise an inseparable urge underlying partition, seemed to be accomplished for Assam through this referendum. The euphoria was short-lived as large-scale Hindu Bengali migration became a post-partition reality. In such a circumstance, the *Miya* population who pragmatically adopted Assamese language as their mother tongue in various Census declarations became a natural ally to the 'core' Assamese nationality formation, which remained pivoted around language. Identifying the *Miya* in certain quarters as *Na-Axomiya* has been such an example. Concomitantly, the acts of "social discriminations, superiority complex of the caste-Hindu Assamese society [pushed] them away from the larger Assamese society" (Datta, 1990, p. 16). So, forceful eviction and harassment in the name of foreigners continued to be a perpetual affair in post-colonial Assam. These contradictory 'pulls' and 'pressures' went on unabated yet as indicated in this chapter, the *Miya* community could hardly dare to raise its voice of protest as they lay marooned within the precincts of the slur, *Miya*. Despite several political mobilisations, particularly the mobilisations under United Minorities Front during post-Assam Accord and All India United Democratic Front in the post-Illegal Migrants (Determination by Tribunals) (IMDT) Act period, the community members never vented their angst in a language beyond Assamese. It was only during the contemporary moment of *Miya* poetry, when rightlessness and statelessness hung like Damocles's sword over the *Miya* community, few poets used their spoken language, colloquially also referred as the *Miya* language, in order to be auto-reflective of the existential crisis that afflicted the community. So the apprehension of those casting aspersions on *Miya* Poetry lay somewhere at the intersections of language and religion, on one hand, and class and coercion, on the other.

Thus to conclude, it seems that the critics of *Miya* poetry in their polemics have missed both the history and historiography of the poetic movement. For they, in their "genre called history has failed to capture the historical" resulting in a "woeful disjunction of the existential from the epistemological" (Radhakrishnan, 2012, p. 2). The *Miya* poets, on the other, look for history not in history, for it has always denigrated them, but in romantic-existential poetry. *Miya* poetry has therefore been, to put in Arendt's (1958) expression, a momentary reprieve from a condition of complete rightlessness, whereafter they seem to be destined to be herded into ghettos and detention camps, where ultimately their right to life, too, gets challenged.

Acknowledgement

The authors would like to thank Shalim M Hussain for providing the English translation of the *Miya* poems and Kazi Sharowar Hussain, Wahida Parveez and Ayesha Siddika for their untiring support in organising the interviews and transcriptions.

References

Arendt, Hannah. (1958). *The Origins of Totalitarianism.* Cleveland and New York: Meridian.

Azad, Abdul Kalam. (2019). "Write… I Am a Miya." The Indian Express, August 11. https://indianexpress.com/article/opinion/columns/assam-miya-poetry-culture-nrc-5895176/

Banerjee, Debjani. (2020). "From Cheap Labor to Overlooked Citizens: Looking for British Muslim Identities in Kamila Shamsie's Home Fire." *South Asian Review*, 41 (3–4): 288–302.

Bhat, M. Mohsin Alam. (2020). "Twilight Citizenship." Twilight Citizenship. https://papers.ssrn.com/abstract=3603707

Braun, Virginia, and Victoria Clarke. (2006). "Using Thematic Analysis in Psychology." *Qualitative Research in Psychology*, 3 (2): 77–101.

Brenner, Neil. (1999). "Beyond State-Centrism? Space, Territoriality, and Geographical Scale in Globalization Studies." *Theory and Society*, 28 (1): 39–78.

Burnay, Matthieu, and Eva Pils. (2020). "Weaponizing Citizenship in China: Domestic Exclusion and Transnational Expansion." *State Crime Journal*, 9 (1): 4–28.

Caudwell, Christopher. (1937/1991) *Illusion and Reality: A Study of the Sources of Poetry*, New Delhi: People's Publishing House.

Césaire, Aimé. (2020). "The Négritude Movement." Black Then. May, 19, 2020. https://blackthen.com/aime-cesaire-the-negritude-movement/

Chakraborty, Gorky. (2012a). "Roots and Ramifications of a Colonial Construct: The Wastelands of Assam". IDSK Occasional Paper 39. Kolkata: IDSK.

Chakraborty, Gorky. (2012b). "The 'Ubiquitous' Bangladeshis." *Economic and Political Weekly*, 47 (38): 21–23.

Dardani, Ross. (2017). "Weaponized Citizenship: A Critical Race Theory Analysis of U.S. Citizenship Legislation in the Pacific Unincorporated Territories." University of Connecticut. https://opencommons.uconn.edu/dissertations/1671/

Das, Nabina. (2016). "For Better or Verse: Miyah Poetry Is Now a Symbol of Empowerment for Muslims in Assam." First Post. September 18, 2016. https://www.firstpost.com/living/for-better-or-verse-miyah-poetry-is-now-a-symbol-of-empowerment-for-muslims-in-assam-3007746.html

Das, Pranjit. (2021). "Miyah Poetry: A New Form of Protest Poetry." *International Journal of Humanities and Social Science Invention (IJHSSI)*, 10 (5): 4–8.

Datta, P. S. (ed.) (1990). *"Introduction", Ethnic Movements in Poly-cultural Assam.* New Delhi: Har-Anand and Vikas Publishing House.

Eyakuze, Aidan, and Khalifa Said. 2020. "The Weaponization of Identity and Citizenship: The Case of Tanzania." *Development*, 63 (1): 95–99.

Goswami, P. C. (1994). *The Economic Development of Assam.* Ludhiana: Kalyani Publishers.

Guha, Amalendu. (1976). "East Bengal Immigrants and Maulana Abdul Hamid Khan Bhasani in Assam Politics, 1928-47." *The Indian Economic and Social History Review* 13 (4): 419–452.

Hassan, Masha. (2021). "'We the Sons of Bitches Are Doing Fine': The Dissent of Miya Poetry." Jamhoor. August 7, 2021. https://www.jamhoor.org/read/we-the-sons-of-bitches-are-doing-fine-the-dissent-of-miya-poetry

Hughes, Langston. (2010). "Negro." The Atlantic, January 12, 2010. https://www.theatlantic.com/daily-dish/archive/2010/01/poem-for-the-day/191851/

Jones, Bridget. (1997). "Aime Cesaire: 'Notebook of a Return to My Native Land.'" *The Modern Language Review*, 92 (January): 212+.

Kelley, R. D. G., A. Césaire, and J. Pinkham. (2000). "Discourse on Colonialism." https://www.sahistory.org.za/sites/default/files/file%20uploads%20/aime_cesaire_robin_d.g._kelley_discourse_on_colbook4me.org_.pdf.

Liu, Franklin. (2017). "Weaponizing Citizen Suits: Second Circuit Revises the Burden of Proof for Proving Sham Citizen Suits in Apotex v. Acorda Therapeutics." *Boston College Law Review*, 58: 147.

Nielsen, Cynthia R. (2013). "Frantz Fanon and the Négritude Movement: How Strategic Essentialism Subverts Manichean Binaries." *Callaloo* 36 (2): 342–352.

Pandey, Gyanendra, (1999), "Can a Muslim Be an Indian?", *Comparative Studies in Society and History*, 41 (4), October.

Radhakrishnan, R. (2012), "Introduction". *Modern Fiction and Politics*, 58 (4): 659–667.

Rexer, Raisa. (2013). "Black and White and Re(a)d All Over: L'Étudiant Noir, Communism, and the Birth of Négritude." *Research in African Literatures*, 44 (4): 1–14.

Reyes, Paul. (2020). "Citizenship in the Twenty-first Century." *The Virginia Quarterly Review*, 96 (3): 8–9.

Roy, Anupama. (2008). "Between Encompassment and Closure: The 'migrant' and the Citizen in India." *Contributions to Indian Sociology / EcolePratique Des Hautes Etudes -Paris [and] Institute of Social Anthropology-Oxford*, 42 (2): 219–48.

Shamsie, Kamila. (2017). *Home Fire*. London: Bloomsbury Publishing.

Sharma, K. M. (1980). "The Assam Question: A Historical Perspective." *Economic and Political Weekly*, 15 (31): 1321–1324.

Thinius, A. C. (2021). "Genders as Genres: Understanding Dynamic Categories." https://dare.uva.nl/personal/pure/en/publications/genders-as-genres(3423aaa4-b224-4d51-bfe1-20f66fb049ca).html

Viveros-Vigoya, Mara. (2020). "The Political Vitality and Vital Politics of Césaire's Discourse on Colonialism: A Reading in Light of Contemporary Racism." *The Sociological Review*, 68 (3): 476–491.

III

Persistent Fault Lines

The Unique Case of Assam

Chapter 5

Postcolonial Modes of Nation Making

The Politics of Disowning Citizens

Sajal Nag

I Introduction

Hostility to outsiders and anti-outsiders movements are endemic in North-East India. It started in the colonial period itself and continues to this day.

> Among the stories of north east India, a compelling and untold bunch revolves around the experiences of the outsiders in the region. This is a fascinating story of role reversals; people from communities that are majorities in India or the countries around its north east live in the region as oft-persecuted minorities.
>
> (Gill and Samrat, 2018, p. x)

Indeed the history of north east is replete with anti-outsider riots.

> Ours is a story rarely told … this is a story about being a *dkhar* in Shillong … it is mine but it could also be the story of a *bangal* in Garo hills, a *Mayang* in Manipur, a *Vai* in Mizoram … commonly called non tribals by all tribes of the region we are people whose origin lie in the plains of India. …In my memory rings a popular phrase I heard as a child in Manipur: if you see a *mayang* and a snake, kill the *mayang* first. One has also seen as an adult in Shillong not many years ago, the graffiti – 'non tribal dogs get out in peace or in pieces' splashed in the walls in Laitumkhrah, the cosmopolitan part of Shillong.
>
> (Bakshi, 2018, pp. 135–136)

Indeed, the anti-outsiders movement is what distinguishes the politics of North-East India from the rest of India.[1] From colonial times to today, various restrictive devices like the Inner Line exists in the region to restrict the entry of outsiders into the region. Yet there is demand for more. Now, not just outsiders but also the communities are hostile to other communities of the region. Assam has disintegrated into seven new states. There is demand for more from the Bodos, Karbis, Dimasas, Koches and Ahoms. So far, 31 autonomous councils were granted succumbing to the autonomy demands

DOI: 10.4324/9781003345152-9

of the communities. The recent proposal by the Government of Assam wants to increase it to 45. Nine under the sixth schedule. Bodos, Karbi Anglong, Dimasa, Deori, Missing, Rabha-Hassong, Tiwa, Sonowal Kachari, Thengal Kachari.Rest of the Tribal areas were put under the Fifth Schedule of the Constitution. The communities who have been able to secure an autonomous council for themselves were the Moran, Mattock, Moria, Gorkha, Chutiya, Adivasi, Nath-Jogi, Koch-Rajbongshi, Bishnupriya Manipuri, Tai-Ahom, Mech Kachari, Manipuri, general castes, Singphoh (Man-Tai), AmriKarbi, Sarania Kachari, Barak Valley hills tribes, Tea tribes and ex-Tea tribes, Scheduled Castes, Chowdang, Modahi, Kumhar, Hajong, Sut, Garia, Barman-Kachari, and Karbis living outside Karbi Anglong, Hindi-speaking communities, Bangla-speaking communities and Julahas. Many more are in the line. In the Barak Valley, there are some too. Most of these wanted to graduate to full statehood. The six tribes, like the tea tribes and the Ahom and Kamatapuris, have been granted Scheduled Tribe status while other tribals oppose it. In Meghalaya, the minor tribes, like the Hajong, the Koch, the Rabha, the Boro and the Mann, have been excluded from the purview of the Sixth Schedule due to opposition from the major tribes. In the North East, exclusion has therefore been the dominant theme of vernacular politics, and Assam has been in the leader and inspirer of such politics. It is obvious from the preceding discussion that the North East has identified its external enemy. It is not the colonising white-skinned masters, not the postcolonial Indian state, which it often fights demanding sovereignty, not the rich of their own who captured power for decades and continually deprived the people and land of 'development' or the shuttling bureaucracy who get paid a special-duty allowance for working in this 'difficult region' but the displaced and struggling non-tribals who migrate to these hills for livelihood and settlement knowing fully well that they cannot buy an inch of land here for building a home, jobs cannot be procured as 80% jobs are for the local and the remaining 20 also would be given to the tribal locals and business has to be always *benami*. During the 1960s and 1970swhen the country was going through an immense crisis, there was turmoil in the region too. American political scientists and anthropologists who thronged to study the imminent disintegration of a new nation state saw it as a dangerous decade (Harrison, 1960) and saw the developments in Assam as a struggle of 'the son of the soil' (Weiner, 1978). Subsequently, Weiner saw the anti-plainsmen movements in North-East India as a response to the inability of the nascent nation state to control interstate migration and migrants as 'rejected and unwanted people' by indigenous natives (Weiner, 1978, pp. 1737–1746). Another discourse located the anti-outsider violence of the indigenous community in terms of the structure of polity, whereby numbers emerge as important determinants of power. Even though the indigenous community are a majority, who are otherwise a national minority, there is constant fear of the outsider minority, who are a majority in the national context, of becoming dominant. The majority then perceives itself as a 'threatened majority' and mobilization takes place on such understanding (Appadurai, 2006, pp. 51–53). When a majority experiences a challenge – real or imagined – to its majoritarianism, wholeness, and purity, Appadurai (Appadurai, 2006, pp. 51–53) explained in an earlier essay, the visible presence of the 'Other' can become a discursive flashpoint for its own anxieties and uncertainties. In this context 'violence can create a macabre form of certainty' by distinguishing, in the clearest of ways, the 'them' from the 'us.'

> By mobilizing an understanding of itself as a threatened majority. This kind of mobilization is the key step in turning a benign social identity into a predatory identity. ...They are claims about cultural majorities that seek to be exclusively or exhaustively linked with the identity of the nation. ...The discourse of these mobilized majorities often has within it the idea that it could be itself turned into a minority until another minority disappears... [Predatory identities emerge] when they strive to close the gap between the majority and the purity of the nation as a whole.
>
> (Appadurai, 2006, pp. 51–53)

II The 'Other' in Nationalist Thought

Such analysis as mentioned earlier does provide some understanding of the 'fear of outsiders.' But it is not enough. These are part of a larger discourse and a larger phenomenon which needs to be understood. It was Prime Minister Nehru who was at the helm of affairs and provided a clue to this discourse. In the 1960s, the Assamese language was sought to be made the official language in Assam, and there were large-scale anti-Bengali riots in Assam, an exasperated Nehru found them to be a "new type of emotional fission of which every Indian would be ashamed"(Gopal, 1984, p. 175). He found the bloodshed "most ghastly and deplorable events in India since 1947" (Gopal, 1984, p. 175). Nehru then tried to understand the discourse of such hatred by saying "nationalism seems to be but a superficial layer cracking open at the slightest irritation. Democracy and nationalism should go together, for the essence of democracy was not merely to think of oneself or one's group but to work for the larger group or community which was the nation. But most Indians did not seem to have a common idea of nationalism but each one has a particular brand and events in Assam had brought the skeleton out of the mental cupboard. It is not a question of Bengali or Assamese. Each one of us is affected and affected in many ways." (Gopal, 1984, p. 176). He felt that the Assamese attitude was 'infantile,' with which 'one cannot compromise with this kind of folly.' Although he sympathized with the 'narrow loyalty' of the Assamese, which he attributed to a lack of development, but the displacement and migration of 50.000 Bengalis due to the riot made him feel that "such evacuation if continued would lead to a civil war in India. One has to get out of this small minds, India is bigger." (ibid)

What Nehru failed to understand why nationalism is a superficial layer' was already foreseen by both Tagore and Gandhi. Both rejected nationalism as a discourse and a model because these are inherently destructive and violent. Nations have always been concerned about 'us' as against 'them'. Nations are obsessed with 'self' and discriminate the 'other'. The construction of the national self has always been only vis-à-vis 'the other'. The basis of such a construction is differentiation. In other words, nation making is a coeval process of 'othering.' A nation cannot be constructed without a perceived other. The 'self' consists of people who share common cultural characteristics, and such commonalities could be measured only by contrasting against those who do not. Thus, the construction of nationhood is a narcissist practice while nation building is all about building walls around the 'self' and distancing from 'the other'. This obsession of 'nationalism' was what Tagore found to be the essence of 'Western-type nationalism,' which he deplored. Tagore wrote:

> (Racial) blindness is the fundamental disease of nationalism. Whether by fraud or by error, one (nation) has to prove itself to be the greatest and concurrently has to belittle others. This is the basic tenet of nationalism – the chief component of patriotism ... self interest is what national-ism stands upon. ...Even when there is direct conflict, the prosperity of one antagonises the others. The increased strength of one is a potential source of danger to the other.
>
> (Poddar, 1977, pp. 184–185)

Like Tagore, Gandhi, too, saw the potential of hate and violence in the Western concept of nationalism and did not want a replication of it in India. He asked,

> [I]s hatred essential for nationalism? You may not love but must you also hate ... [those who do] I do not blame them. They have to be pitted; they command my sympathy. But so long as they retain that attitude, so long as a large body of men and women retain that attitude the progress of this country, the progress of the world is retarded. ...We see the fatigue overcoming the western nations. We see that this song of hate has not benefitted humanity. Let it be the privilege of India to turn a new leaf and set a lesson to the world.
>
> (Habib, 2017, pp. 161–165)

The nationalist movements that arose in Asia and Africa were anti-colonial in character, and hence, hatred and hostility were brewing towards the white colonizers. Gandhi wanted Indian nationalism to be free of hatred for white men. He wanted a distinction between the evil and the evildoer. "It is not nationalism that is evil, it is the narrowness, selfishness, exclusiveness which is the bane of modern nations which is evil"(Habib, 2017, pp. 161–165). He asserted that hatred could kill the spirit of nationalism:

> Race hatred will kill the real national spirit. Let us understand what nationalism is. We want freedom for our country. We do not want suffering for other countries. We do not want the exploitation of other countries, we do not want degradation of other countries. For my part I don't want the freedom of India if it means the disappearance of Englishmen, if it means the extinction of Englishmen, I want the freedom of my country so that other countries may learn something from this free country of mine. I want freedom of my country so that the resources of my country might be utilized for the benefit of kicking just the cult of patriotism reaches us today that the individual has to die for the family, the family has to die for the village, the village for the district, the district for the province and the provinces for the whole nation, and when we indulge in provincialism I as a Gujarati say Gujarat first, Bengal and the rest of the Provinces next. There is no nationalism in it. On the contrary if I live in Gujarat and prepare Gujarat, I should prepare Gujarat so that the vast resources of Gujarat might be placed at the disposal of Bengal, nay the whole of India. That Gujarat may die for the whole of India. My hope therefore, of nationalism or my idea of nationalism is that my country may become free–free that if need be the whole of the country may die – so that human race may live. There is no reason here for race hatred. Let that be our nationalism.
>
> (Habib, 2017, pp. 161–165)

In his nationalism therefore lay the seed of internationalism. Gandhi felt it is impossible for anyone to be internationalist without being a nationalist:

> Internationalism is possible only when nationalism becomes a fact i.e. when people belonging to different countries have organized themselves and is able to act as one man. It is nationalism that is evil, it is the narrowness, selfishness, exclusiveness which is the bane of modern nations which is evil. Each wants to profit at expense of other's ruin.
>
> (Habib, 2017, pp. 161–165)

Gandhi hoped Indian nationalism would prove to be an exception. This is an exact echo of what Tagore said. The depravity and violence inherent in the concept of nationalism had become transparent to Tagore, who had denounced such a European type of nationalism. In fact, he deplored the fact that no trace of civilization in Europe could be found which could raise the nations above fierce conflicts, injustices and falsehoods. He reiterated this in course of his lectures on nationalism in Japan and America due to which he became unpopular in Japan. Through his lectures, he denounced nationalism with his entire wrath and fury and reposed his faith in humanism. He said,

> The nation with all its paraphernalia of power and prosperity, its flags and pious hymns, its blasphemous prayers in the churches and the literary mock thunders of its patriotic bragging cannot hide the fact that the nation is the greatest evil for the nation, the nation has thriven long upon mutilated humanity.
>
> (Tagore, 1917, pp. 29–30, 44)

The journey of nations begins with 'othering.' Originally 'nation' was a term used to differentiate one group of students coming from a region against the other in the European Universities in the late medieval period. The etymology of the term nation shows that the term originated from the Latin word '*nasci*' (to be born) and its original meaning was a group of people born in a the same place(Encyclopaedia of Social Science, 1968, p. 8). In another usage nation was used as a suffix term for differentiation. It meant a strange people (Encyclopaedia of Social Science, 1968, p. 8). Before 1884 the word *nacion* simply meant the aggregate inhabitants of a province a country or a kingdom and also a foreigner (Encyclopaedia of Social Science, 1968, p. 8). Nation with such a denotation was common to many parts of Europe. It was in this sense only the English colonialists in North America spoke of Sioux, Cherokee and other indigenous groups as '*nacions*.' Napoleon described the English as a 'nation' of shop keepers (Encyclopaedia of Social Science, 1968, p. 8). Nation hood therefore started off as a term of '*othering*.' A discourse which began with idea of 'othering' obviously has conflict and violence inherent in it. The discourse of nationalism has therefore always been self versus others. The Self is always created vis-à-vis others. In fact nationhood can be defined a unending process of othering. The self that is created in this discourse is homogenous, exclusive, narcissist, selfish and xenophobic. It is achieved only by 'othering' the others of the vicinity.

> "But the search for such homogeneity and exclusivity ends up as an exercise in peeling an onion as such pristine homogeneity proves elusive and such exclusivity impossible. Moreover, nation building is also a coeval process of majority building so as to ensure that the hegemony of a community is unchallenged. Hence, the creation of nations also requires constant shedding of people who do not fit the constructed identity or question the framework. This automatically involves minority persecution, ethnic cleansing, the denial of political rights to smaller groups and such forms of atrocities due to which exodus of the persecuted takes place. Displacement can take multiple forms: refugees, internal refugees, rejection, eviction, expulsion, asylum seekers and so on. It is ironical that the process then accelerates and emerges as a pattern because each of the minorities constructs a national identity and

> strives to build a majority for itself. As in the case of the Indian subcontinent the process eventually becomes a vicious cycles of peeling and shedding. In other words the process entails the formation of multiple national identities and the concomitant displacement and exodus of people who do not fit the frame-work of such an identity".
>
> (Nag, 2001, pp. 4753–4760)

The updating of the National Register of Citizens (NRC) in Assam is one such endeavour. In order to build its exclusive domain, the Assamese have identified an 'other' and has been trying to expel these 'other' group consistently. The current endeavour actually tries to exclude and expel a linguistic and religious minority group by cancelling their existing citizenship. This is unprecedented and unheard of anywhere else. People who are citizens by birth are subjected to a bureaucratic document verification process to annul their citizenship so that they could be rendered stateless and the host community attains unchallenged hegemony in the area. Such are the oppressions of the modern nation-making process. In this chapter, we try to see how there was a consistent othering process in Assam from the time the 'self' of the Assamese was being constructed in the nineteenth century. First, it targeted the Bengali Hindu migrants whom the Assamese leadership considered a stumbling block to their cultural and political hegemony and then shifted their attention to the Bengali Muslim migrants, whom, at one time, they favoured as their instrument to increase their linguistic strength against the Bengali Hindus. Thereafter, they targeted both, and since these groups could not be gotten rid of legally, they raised the bogey of 'illegal immigrants' as a mode of disowning the citizens. This has happened right from the 1930s,when all methods were attempted – violence, democratic movements, Gandhian *satyagraha*, the brutal concept of the 'D' voter, inhuman detention camps and constitutional mechanisms to the intervention of the Supreme Court, where the presiding judge who decided on NRC was himself an Assamese.

III Mode of Delegitimizing Citizens

The frontpages of the vernacular newspapers of 30 July 2018 in Assam carried two interesting visuals. One was a photograph of leaders distributing sweets among themselves, which was juxtaposed by the headline that a total of 4,0007,07 persons have been found to be illegal migrants to Assam. Obviously the celebration was about the prospect of getting rid of a mammoth 40 lakh people who were 'undesirable' in their state. Most of these non-citizens are Bengalis, both Hindu and Muslim. Such celebrations were witnessed in Assam earlier too one in 14th July 1947 and the other in 15 August 1985. On 15th August, the celebration was not for Independence Day but the signing of the Assam Accord in which it was agreed upon that those who entered Assam after March 31, 1971 would be detected and deported from Assam. On 14th July the result of the Sylhet Referendum was declared by which the district had been transferred to Pakistan. The transfer of Sylhet to Pakistan was hailed by the Assamese public opinion. The only daily newspaper of Assam, *The Assam Tribune*, hailed the transfer of Sylhet, 'the Assamese public seem to feel relieved of a burden' (21 July 1947). Rabindranath Aditya, a Congress leader from Sylhet said, 'The Assam leadership, too eager to get rid of Sylhet with a view to curve out a homogeneous province arranged little protection for the minorities of Sylhet in the free exercise of their united franchise. When the result of the referendum was declared, there was a subdued sense of relief in the Assam Valley as the majority of the votes cast were in favour of Pakistan.' (Aditya, 1970, p. 31). But the most blatant version of this jubilation was pronounced by Sri Akbar Hydari, the governor of Assam. Speaking on behalf of the provincial Congress cabinet, when the Assam Assembly met on 5 September 1947 for the first time after Independence, he said,

> the natives of Assam are now masters of their own house. They have a government which is both responsible and responsible to them. The Bengali no longer has the power, even if he had the will, to impose anything on the people of these hills and valleys which constitute Assam.
>
> (Choudhury)

The irony of history was that each of these events was followed by deep disappointment subsequently. The transfer of Sylhet was followed by a massive influx of refugees from the same district which replenished the Bengali population lost due to the transfer, causing the cessation of celebration. The Assam Accord was celebrated because it raised the hope of deportation of the suspected illegal immigrants from Bangladesh. The hope was further raised because there was a new government which was composed of people who had led the six-year-long foreign national movement. But after five years when there was no more than only a few thousand people could be actually deported, the hopes turned sour. Similarly, the first list of the NRC had raised the hope of deporting more than 40 lakhs of people, all of them Bengali-speaking Hindus and Muslims, but when the final draft reduced the number to a mere 19 lakhs, including also tribals and Hindi-speaking Indians, the celebration was transformed into complaints.

Similarly there was a 'visible' disappointment when the revised NRC list was published in which the number of people to be excluded and expelled from Assam came down from 40 lakh people had come down to 19 lakhs. This was because the expectation was much more – between 40 to 50 lakhs. There was suspicion of connivance, protests and a demand for a further revision of the NRC. The disappointment turned into anger when the

Bharatiya Janata Party (BJP) government legislated the Citizenship Amendment Act 2019 which would grant at least 6 lakh Bengali Hindu refugees from Pakistan and Bangladesh citizenship. Mass protests movements were witnessed, reminiscent of the Assam Movement days (1979–85) and people resolved to oppose its implementation tooth and nail.

These precursors show the celebration in Assam has a genealogy where the performance and the reasons had continuity. Even the mood of disappointment is organically connected to this genealogy. Indeed the publication of the final NRC report marked the end of a struggle that the Assamese had been fighting since the turn of the nineteenth century. It was a struggle to get rid of an increasing community of immigrants who were undesirable in Assam. The Assamese had to contend with these people within their territory since 1824 due to colonial territorial redistribution. The advent of British rule was a disruption in the historical continuity. A new bureaucracy-dominated administrative structure, a new revenue system in Assam, a new judicial system and a new educational system were introduced. The cumulative results of these changes were the gradual impoverishment of the Assamese peasants, the disappearance of the medieval gentry and the emergence of modern social classes. A number of Bengali functionaries had entered along with the British who carried out the actual function to effect the changes. The impoverished peasants who resented the new system saw the Bengalis functionaries, as the colonial collaborators and the new arbiters. The Assamese gentry, as well as the new petty bourgeois classes, blamed these Bengalis for taking away their jobs. It was not just an economic competition but cultural too. The Assamese not only contested the social dominance and cultural exhibitionism of the Bengalis, but they also viewed the Bengalis as conspirators in the persecution of the Assamese language when Bengali was introduced as the official language in Assam (1837) and the originator of the idea that Assamese was a dialect of Bengali. The transfer of three Bengal districts Sylhet, Cachar and Goalpara in 1874 to compensate the deficit of running a new province not only increased the number of Bengali speakers but also their dominance in the Assam legislature. The last straw was the colonial sponsorship of the immigration of farm settlers into the wasteland in Assam from the famine-stricken districts of Eastern Bengal. The initially reluctant trickle of landless Bengali Muslims soon grew into an unending stream.

IV Genealogy of Exclusionary Movement

The province of Assam was a huge deficit province, which did not generate enough revenue to cover its administration. The growing tea, coal and petroleum mining industries required the permanent presence of massive labour and white-collar workers in the state. This labour force came through immigration. This massive population had to be provided food for which Assam was not ready. Hence, the immigration of farm settlers became an absolute necessity to produce food crops and at the same time generate revenue for the government to run its administration. The Assamese gentry favoured the colonial scheme of importing farm labour from Bengal who could be settled in the 70.15% land that was lying waste. The Census Report showed that the immigration of farm settlers from East Bengal alone was 1751 in 1881, which increased to 17,250 in 1891 and 37,250 in 1901 (Goswami, 1976, pp. 12–24). In 1928, the British administrators put into effect the 'Colonisation Scheme', which opened up large areas of the Nowgong district and the Barpeta and Mangaldoi subdivisions for settlement by immigrants. It did not improve the financial condition of Assam. The total annual income of the state was Rs. 22,5,00,000, which was actually 12,5,00,000 less than even the Bombay Municipal Corporation (Times of India, 10 June1937). The province had very little income other than the royalty of oil and coal and huge expenditures. The flourishing tea industry benefitted the planters but the state gained very little. The only option was to increase the number of agriculturists who would not only generate substantial revenue but also increase agricultural productivity. With this aim in view, Saadulla adopted the 'Land Development Scheme' in 1938 which de-reserved the Professional Grazing Reserves and opened them up for settlement by immigrants. Thus, in just one year (1940–41), the Saadulla government settled Bengali Muslim immigrants on 150,000 *bighas* of land in the Brahmaputra Valley. Immigration had transformed the demography of this thinly populated province. The decadal increase due to immigration in Assam was208,000in 1901–11,575,000 during 1911–21, and 3,28,000 during 1921–31 (Zacharian, 1964). The total population of Assam including Cachar was 3,074, 670 in 1901, which increased to 8,028,856 in 1951 and to 26,6,55,598 in 2001.[2] The average density of population in the six districts of Brahmaputra Valley increased from 42per sq km in 1901 to102 per sq km in 1951 to 397 per sq km in 2011.

V The In-Humanitarian Resistance to Refugee Settlement

When the British withdrew after partitioning India into two nations, there was a massive influx of panic-stricken refugees who moved to either side of the partitioned nation. The migration of such displaced people into Assam was initially quite insignificant. By May 1949 the number of total refugees reaching Assam reached two and half lakhs, increasing to 2,74, 455. The Assam government tried for their rehabilitation by distributing them over a few districts. So 93,177 were settled in Cachar, 44,967 in Goalpara, 42871 in Kamrup, 18833 in Darrang, 13965 in Lakhimpur, 7541 in Sivasagar, 5990 in Khasi hills and 5072 in Garo hills (Census of India, 1951a, p. 357) amidst strong resentment from local people (Barooah, 2010, p. 386). Therefore, the Government of Assam refused to accommodate any more refugees in Assam on the plea of a scarcity of land, but actually, it feared it would increase the demographic strength of Bengali population in Assam. Even when distant provinces like Uttar Pradesh, Madhya Pradesh, Bihar and Andaman Island, besides West Bengal, were willing to share the burden of refugee settlement in their respective states, Assam refused. It drew the ire of Prime Minister Nehru, who accused the Assam chief minister of shirking a national responsibility (Barooah, 2010, p. 321).

The second wave of partition induced migrant or refugee influx took place in 1965 in the wake of Indo-Pak war. Thus, between 1971 and 1991, the rate of increase in the Hindu population was 83% – a 2%increase compared to Muslims. There was a decline in the Hindu population of Bangladesh, which came down from 22% in 1951 to 18.4% in 1961 and 13.5% in 1974. These two sets of figures are reflective of each other. It has also to be taken into account that while partition and the communal riots of 1950 in East Pakistan resulted in the migration of Hindu Bengalis to Assam, there was also a similar exodus of Muslims from Assam during the communal riots in 1950 in Assam. In Assam, from Goalpara, 60,000Muslims left; from Kamrup, 210,000, and from Darrang, 6000. Thus Muslims therefore were absent during the 1951 Census Survey. But they came back after the Nehru–Liaquat Ali Khan pact and were enumerated for the next Census. This accounts for the sudden rise of Muslims between 1961 and 1971. Between 1971 and 1991, the growth rate came down on account of out-migration of non-Assamese people due to anti-immigrant movement, language riots of 1972, foreign national movement between 1979 and 1985, the Nellie–Gohpur massacre, militancy and extremist violence. What is to be noted here that the propensity to leave Assam prevailed among the Hindus only as they could move to any other part of India whereas Muslims could not do so for fear of reprisal. This accounts for the decreasing trend among the Hindus.

The religion-wise percentage was 71.03% Hindus and 12.04 Muslims in 1901; It was 72.01% Hindus and24.68% Muslim in 1951, indicating a marginal increase in Hindus and a doubling of the Muslim population in a period of five decades. In 1971, the Census showed the population to be 72.51% Hindu and 24.68% Muslim. In 2001, the percentages were 64.89% Hindu (a decline) and 30.92% Muslim. This increase in their numerical strength made Muslims a very significant group in Assam. Initially, the Assamese leaders did not notice the increasing strength of the Muslims, but the colonial propaganda about this swarming population proved real when Assam was demanded in the proposed Islamic state of Pakistan in the Lahore Resolution (1940). A panic-stricken Assamese desperately wanted the expulsion of the immigrants to escape the possibility. It was seen as threat to Assamese identity and hegemony to which the only solution was the reduction in Bengali population in Assam, both Hindus and Muslims. The transfer of Sylhet to Pakistan in 1947 relieved the pressure to some extent but the return of Bengali as refugees from East Pakistan almost neutralized the situation. From 1946 to 1951 a total of 274,455 refugees entered Assam. There were 274,455 refugees in Assam between 1946 and 1951. By 1956, it rose to 3.90 lakhs and by 1961 to 7.26 lakhs . In Assam during 1971, about 0.3 million refugees, some of whom were suspected to have stayed back even after the formation of Bangladesh.

This was, however, not the only migratory inflow into Assam. There was another steady stream into the tea industry. The total labour force hardly exceeded 10,000 hands, while the requirement during the mid-nineteenth century was about 16,000 to 20,000 labour hands for the current cultivation alone (Government of Bengal, 1861, pp. 63–66, 69–72). To cover the deficit, indentured labour was introduced. Through this system from 1881 to 1947, a total of 24,3,70,000 persons were brought and settled in Assam as plantations labourers. The recruitment continued till 1950. By independence, this population had increase manifold in Assam. These were of a mixed population, mainly of tribal from the eastern and central provinces of India. However, there was no opposition to this inflow from the Assamese hosts as these immigrants posed no cultural or political threat. The hostility towards the Bengalis manifested in the form of frequent anti-Bengali riots notably in 1948, 1954, 1955 and 1960.[3]

VI Assamese Exceptionalism

The politics of demography and the demand for deportation of the immigrants had been the dominant themes of politics in Assam since the beginning of the twentieth century. There were vociferous demands from the Assamese to expel both the Hindu and Muslim Bengalis in Assam. Responding to the situation, Chief Minister Gopinath Bordoloi evicted a large number of Muslims and deported them to Pakistan after independence. But due to the Nehru–Liaquat Ali Pact (1950) they came back in 1951–52. Soon, Chief Minister Bordoloi began to see Bengali Muslims as a better bet as they were willing to assimilate to Assamese as well as act as Congress Vote bank as against the Bengali Hindus who 'considered themselves culturally superior and unwilling to assimilate.' His refusal to rehabilitate Bengali refugees in his state provoked strong criticism from Prime Minister Nehru who censured Bordoloi that the "prefer[ence]for Muslims of East Bengal to Hindus of East Bengal ... is a narrow minded policy" and shirking the responsibility of sharing the burden of partition. Simultaneously, under initiative of *Asom Jatiyo Maha sabha* and leaders like Ambika Giri Roychoudhury, these immigrants declared themselves as Assamese speakers, thereby inflating the demographic strength of the Assamese in the census of 1951. But a perpetual threat haunted the Assamese: that these immigrants might revert to their Bengali mother tongue at any time, reducing the Assamese Hindus into a minority again. In 1960, a bolder step was taken when the Assamese were sought to be imposed as the official language to consolidate the assimilation. But it backfired, leading to the balkanization of Assam into several states.

The flow of immigration of Bengali Muslims that had started from the turn of the century had not really stopped. But a migration which was inter-district and legal had now become illegal infiltration. Since the 1950s, there have been complaints about continuous Muslim infiltrators in Assam. The Intelligence Bureau reported that "the number of illegal immigrants into Assam from Pakistan over the course of the last 12 years has been very conservatively estimated about 250 thousand. Local unofficial estimates however put this figure even higher" (Gupta, 1984, pp. 201–211). The Government of Assam initially called for the introduction of a Permit System as early as July 1948. As nothing came of these demands the Government of India came out with The Immigrants (Expulsion from Assam) Act 1950 which tried to differentiate between Hindu refugees from Pakistan and deport only Muslim migrants who were seen as illegal infiltrators. Againstthe backdrop of the Chinese invasion, the government began to make a fresh security appraisal, where it found that "the fact that such a large number of immigrants succeeded in illegally crossing the frontier and settling down unnoticed would prove that the measures so far taken have not been effective".[4] It therefore launched the Prevention of Infiltration from Pakistan Scheme (PIP) to check and deport infiltrators from Assam. But deportation of illegal immigrants by the zealous B.P. Chaliha government had to be abandoned under the allegation of harassment and human rights abuse by Muslim leaders Fakhruddin Ali Ahmed and Moin-ul-Haque Chaudhury and organizations like Jamiat-ul-Ulama-e-Hind. It raised a debate about the threats posed to genuine citizens by illegal immigrants. The proposal for initiating the national registration of citizens as a means to tide over the vexed citizenship issue was first suggested in the PIP Scheme of 1965 (Datta, 2018). This scheme, which was drafted by Intelligence Bureau officials, proposed that a "National Registration System and the issue of Identity Cards should be adopted" (Gupta, 1984, pp. 201–211) for all the residents of Assam and the north-eastern region.

Since then, there been have many laws and measures adopted to deal with the vexed foreign national issue. Among these were the Foreigners Act 1948, The Foreigners Order 1948, Permits System, PIP (prevention of infiltration of Pakistanis), The Foreigners (Tribunal) order 1964, The Foreigners (Tribunal) Amendment order 2012, The Passport (Entry into India) Act 1920, The Citizenship Act 1955, The Citizenship (Registration of citizen & Issue of National Identity Cards) Rules 2003, The Citizenship Rules 2009, Foreigner Tribunal and illegal migrants (Determination Tribunal), Immigrants (Expulsion from Assam) Act 1950 and IMDT Act, a category of 'D' voters was used to detect, deport and intern the suspected infiltrators. There were even carnages (Nellie massacre, 1983) in which about 3000 Muslims were butchered. According to the government report, between 1951 and 1961, a total of 2,20,691 Pakistani infiltrators entered Assam of which 122,476 were detected and deported by June 1965 (Government of Assam, 2012 a, pp. 40–41). Between 1985 and July 2005 after the formation of Illegal Migration Detection Tribunal (IMDT) a total of 112,791 persons were referred to as foreign nationals, of which 12,846 were declared to be so and 1547 actually deported (Government of Assam, 2012, pp. 40–41). Between 1985 and July 2012, a total of 61,774 persons were declared D voters, of which 6590 persons were actually declared foreigners. Evidently, there were endeavours to detect and deport foreign nationals all throughout the period.

Following the detection of a massive increase in Muslim voters during a by-election in 1979 in Mangaldoi, the anti-Foreign National Movement was sparked, which ended in 1985 with the Assam Accord, which agreed to confer citizenship of India to all those immigrants who came to India up to 1971 with a caveat that those who entered between 1961 and 1971 would have to complete a term of ten years before the conferment of citizenship. There was no mention of NRC in the Assam Accord. Since neither the Assam Accord nor the *Asom Gana Parishad* could deport any significant number of foreign nationals the issue continued to generate passion and was used for political mobilizations.

By 1998, the foreigner issue again came to the centre stage of politics with a report sent to the president of India by the then governor of Assam, Lt. Gen S.K. Sinha, becoming public. Lt. Gen S.K. Sinha, who was a right-wing ideologue, propagated about a crore of illegal Muslims having infiltrated Assam with a grand design of Pakistan laying claim to the territory. Speculative claims were made that ranging from 30 lakhs to a crore of Bangladeshi (erstwhile East Pakistani) nationals were staying illegally in Assam who could easily reduce the indigenous Assamese into a minority soon. The rise of Muslim population to 30% and in the number of Muslim legislators in the Assam Assembly from 12 in 1952 to 24 in 1991 in a house of 126 only strengthened their conviction. It was propagated that

> (with the continuous increase in the Muslim population) it is only a question of time when the indigenous Assamese ethnic groups will be alien in their homeland... and the next step will be demand for referendum on merger with Bangladesh.

The real fear, however, was that if the Muslim legislators are united with the tribal, ex–tea garden, Nepali and Bengali Hindu MLAs, (Member of Legislative Assembly) they could easily threaten the political hegemony of the caste Hindu Assamese which had to be prevented. In fact, the commissioner of linguistic minorities reported that the Assamese speakers constituted only 48.81% in Assam.

VII New Modes of De-citizenization

The vexed foreign national issue had resurfaced at a tripartite meeting of All Assam Students Union (AASU) with the government in which it agreed to upgrade the NRC of 1951 for the first time in 2005. While debating the issue of citizenship, the then Assam chief minister Tarun Gogoi in the subsequent meetings in 2011 and 2013 wanted that the victims of partition Bengali Hindus case 'should be considered on humanitarian grounds.' But the process of updating of NRC by the Gogoi government in 2012 had to be halted due to violent protests from the Muslims of Dhubri and Goalpara. Riots had in the meantime broken out between the Muslims and Bodo tribals in Bodoland areas in 2012 and 2014.In 2012, a massive demonstration was organized at Guwahati to re-launch the anti-foreigner agitation. A new organisation called Assam Sanmilita Mahasangha, an umbrella organization of 'various indigenous and Tribal communities' led the new movement. The Mahasangha adopted a legal way by filing a petition in the Supreme Court of India to examine the constitutional position of the laws of citizenship in India and to upgrade the NRC prepared in 1951 for Assam. The judgment on this petition, delivered in December 2014, allowed the up-gradation of the NRC of 1951 to determine the contest between citizenship and illegal immigration.

There are vague ideas floating about the NRC of 1951. It was a by-product of the Census Act of 1948. This register of 1951 was prepared as a secret administrative document on the basis of the Census slipping by the Census enumerators, who were "unqualified or ill-qualified persons" (Roychoudhury, 1981, pp. 267–268). Moreover, it was not open to inspection. It was a casual attempt as it was prepared without any planning, training or any organization. The comments of the census superintendent, Assam about the persons who prepared this register are also very interesting:

> In filling up the sample verification forms, the tabulation officers sometimes experienced considerable difficulty in reading the names of persons and tracing their relationship to the head of the households as the National Register of Citizens was written by unqualified or ill-qualified persons.
>
> (Roychoudhury, 1981, pp. 267–268)

It had many shortcomings. As admitted by the then census superintendent himself, the names of the displaced were consciously not included in the Register. While the Census Report of 1951 admits that

> [a]n important innovation of this Census was the preparation of a National Register of Citizens in which all important census data was transcribed from the census slips with the exception of the Census questions No.6(displaced persons), No.8(bilingualism) and No.13(indigenous persons).
>
> (Roychoudhury, 1981, pp. 267–268)

The NRC, 1951, enumeration was a hurried one – having been completed between 9 February and 28 February 1951 (Roychoudhury, 1981, pp. 267–268). The register of an entire nation of citizens was prepared in an impossible span of mere 20 days. The enumerators, too, were grossly untrained (Roychoudhury, 1981, pp. 267–268). As is evident from the Census Report, the data entered into the NRC were copied into census slips contrary to the established procedure of the slips becoming the basis for the NRC (Roychoudhury, 1981, pp. 267–268). This was a gross irregularity. Its importance was also diluted in course of time, which is evident in that even the process of tallying the slips which formed the basis for the NRC was abandoned at the orders of the Registrar General of Census (Roychoudhury, 1981, pp. 267–268).As a result, even the courts refused to accept the NRC as a document that could be a basis for citizenship claims. The Guwahati High Court as early as 1970 held that the NRC, 1951 was inadmissible evidence according to the Evidence Act (Roychoudhury, 1981, pp. 267–268).

In other words, the authors of NRC were the enumerators who did the census work. Its task was not to track the genuine citizens but to enumerate the population structure of the country. Its basis was the information collected during this census enumeration. The enumerators had to complete the work of enumeration in only 20 days.

> If due to under-enumeration in an area or otherwise the name of a person was omitted in the census, then his name was automatically excluded from the NRC also. And if a person was accidentally not enlisted, he had no opportunity to get enlisted in the NRC subsequently. He could also not file objections. As the NRC was not publicly exhibited and was not a public document, a person could not even know if his name was at all included. The whole matter rested on the whims of the enumerators or their supervisors – a completely one-sided affair. No indication was given to the people of the terrible consequences which might overtake them at some future date if their names were not included in the National Register of Citizens, 1951.
>
> (Roychoudhury, 1981, pp. 267–268)

The qualification of the enumerators can be gauged from the fact that the place of birth of 558,833 persons living in Assam was shown as East Bengal in the Census of 1951, ignoring the fact that East Bengal had become East Pakistan in 1947. According to the census superintendent, an overwhelming majority of over 90%, if not more, of these were Muslims, which was inaccurate. This was because of the atmosphere of hostility against the immigrant Muslims from East Bengal. Again following the passing of the Immigrants (Expulsion from Assam) Act, 1950 by Parliament on 13 February 1950, (popularly known among immigrant Muslims as '*Mian Kheda Ain*') regularizing the ordinance promulgated in January 1950, those Muslims (52,600 families or about 1 lakh persons) Muslim who had been deported from Assam returned to India as a result of Nehru–Liaquat Pact. But due to the fear of expulsion again, these people returned to their birthplace in Assam in the 1951 Census which was completed in March. They also returned to Assamese as their mother tongue, increasing the number of Assamese speakers to a whopping 70%, which was ridiculed by Census Superintendent Vaghaiwala as a 'biological miracle' exposing the unreliability of census enumeration.

According to the Gauhati High Court, NRC cannot be accepted as evidence in a court of law under the census rules and for other reasons:

> [The] National Register of Citizens is a contemporaneous register prepared by the officers appointed under the provisions of the Census Act in course of census operations. If so, section 15 of the Census Act will make such record of census not open to inspection or admissible in evidence...and notwith1standing, anything to the contrary in the Indian Evidence Act, 1872, no entry in any such book, register, record or schedule shall be admissible as evidence in any civil proceeding whatsoever or in any criminal proceeding other than a prosecution under this Act or any other law 'or any Act or omission w which constitutes an offence under this Act. What is directly prohibited under section 15 of the Census Act cannot be let in by an indirect method through the agency of a private organisation.
>
> (Roychoudhury, 1981, pp. 267–268)

Unfortunately no counter petition was filed in the Supreme Court highlighting the inadmissibility of the NRC as the basis of citizenship.

VIII Enumerate to Eliminate

The enumeration of NRC was an arduous process in itself. It involved an expenditure of 1200 crores and about 50,000 employees who are mostly Assamese who, although trained, were not de-prejudiced. While the job was only to ascertain whether the person was a citizen of Assam before March 1971, all kinds of documents were sought in the name of legacy data. It included whether the person's or their forefathers' names were there in the 1952 Voters list, marriage certificates and birth certificates which were not in vogue in the 1950s and 1960s. Poor people were asked to move from place as far as 500 km to verify their data or submit their documents. There were accusations of bribe taking in the process. Women are the most affected. Most of the documents, be it land or personal data, are in the names of men. Often, they were married before reaching the voting age. Women found it difficult to prove their credentials. People were harassed to such an extent that a report was prepared and submitted to the National Human Rights Commission (NHRC). The United Nations Human Rights Commission and Amnesty International, Asian Legal Resource Centre, Hongkong had to take cognizance of the violations. Harsh Mandar, an activist, prepared a report independently and submitted to the Home Ministry as well as

NHRC. There was a climate of fear and insecurity that people not listed in the NRC would be deported to Bangladesh, detained in camps and tortured and perhaps declared stateless citizens. There were also campaigns that Hindus had nothing to fear, that Muslims will be deported and, alternately, that Muslims would be supported by Muslim countries whereas Hindus has no friends. It actually communalized the atmosphere and polarized the citizens, signalling an impending crisis. It was reported that

> the final draft was full of problems ranging from personal tragedies like a single member of a family being left out, to at places a whole community is left out. Those excluded include even persons like family members of a former President, veterans of Indian security forces, policemen, kith and kin of legislators to the poor who no paper to show...there are many cases in which direct descendants of those figuring in NRC 1951 have been left out of the final draft. The primary reasons behind this include clerical errors resulting in misspelt names, mismatched relationships and so on. Most of the people being very poor and living in areas regularly affected by floods have lost their documents.
>
> (The Telegraph, 31 August2018)

It was not just Bengali Muslims and Hindus who did not find mention in the draft. While the banned Uunited Liberation Front of Assam (ULFA) members who were in exile for last four decades and fighting a war against the Indian state found their names on the list tribal, like Garo, Hajong and Chakma who migrated to Assam as refugees due to persecution in East Pakistan, and even Assamese Hindu and Muslim without documents were unlisted, signifying the multifarious trajectories of incorrectness and impossibility of preparing an error-free NRC. The draft thus showed more than 40 lakh people as non-citizens.

IX Othering: Assam's Mode of Nation Making

The politics in Assam had a clear trajectory from the colonial period. It was an anti-Bengali and anti-immigrant movement in colonial Assam. It changed over to the Bongal Kheda movement after independence. In From 1971 to 1979, it was the anti-*bohiragoto* (outsider) movement, which was transformed into an anti-foreign national movement as the anti-*bohiragoto* movement was not tenable under the constitutional framework of the nation. In fact, the issue of the expulsion of immigrants has been described as the 'staple' of Assamese politics (Baruah, 2009). It has been substantiated by other Assamese scholars too. "Assamese violence against Bengali speakers was part of the political landscape of Assam until the late 1970's" (Saikia, 2012). In the 1980s, the rhetoric changed to anti-Bangladeshi and a religious flavour was introduced in the Assamese Agitation led by the AASU. The demand for the expulsion of so-called illegal Bangladeshi immigrants became the motivating slogan of the Assamese public (Saikia, 2012). The whole NRC upgradation idea was based on archaic, communal, chauvinist and exclusivist idea of the Assamese middle class. There were a significant group of working-class people, and others too, who does not share the optimism of the Assamese middle class about excluding people through NRC update (Gogoi, 2019). But the caste Hindu Assamese ignore such resistance and insist on the unanimity of the demand for the removal of undesirable people from their domain. The subtle difference from earlier agenda to the NRC movement was this: since substantial people could not be detected and deported as 'foreign nationals', a mechanism by which citizens could be branded as 'foreign nationals' and then seek their removal from the province of Assam. It would ensure the uncontested hegemony of the Assamese over the power structure and resources of the province.

Thus, with a stroke of pen, 40 lakh people were rendered stateless. For more than a century, the Assamese had struggled to cleanse their society of the immigrants of a certain ethnicity who were a perpetual cultural and political threat. What a century of campaign could not yield was achieved in two years of NRC upgradation. It was an effective ethnic cleansing accomplished through constitutional methods and without even a shred of violence. The visible happiness of the Assamese at the NRC verdict prompted the political parties to rush to make capital out of it. While the Congress took credit as the originator of the idea, the BJP showed '*himmat*' of actually cleansing Assam of Bangladeshi Muslim infiltrators, thereby fulfilling its election promise. In 2019, it has dangled the 'carrot' of Citizenship Amendment Act (CAA) to the displaced and panic-stricken Bengali Hindus who were not listed in the NRC, which would confer citizenship to them under the act. But this, too, has provoked unprecedented protest from the Assamese. Granting several lakhs of Bengali Hindus citizenship and residence in Assam would actually belie the hopes of Assamese of a Bengali-free Assam and prove the century-long movement of the Assamese completely futile and inconsequential. It is now the Assamese versus Assamese: Assamese BJP, who had to swallow the bitter bill of CAA, and Assamese nationalists, who are panicking to see their 100-year war be in vain. Even the NRC results were not implemented by a severely critiqued central government. The struggle of the Assamese to retain their cultural and political hegemony by disowning a section of citizens seems to be failing, and the leadership will be looking to invent another constitutional instrument or launch another movement to continue it.

Notes

1 The Anti-North Indian movement of the Shiv Sena/Maharashtra NavnirmanSangha in Mahararshtra cannot be compared with the anti-outsider movement of the North East because the Maharashtra movement is a nativist movement, happens once in a decade or so and is widely condemned by other parties and sections of people.

2 Computed from census-based table on 'Demographic composition: religion wise population of Assam' given in *White paper on Foreigners issue*, Home and Political Department, Government of Assam, October 20, 2012, pp. 40–41.
3 Jishnu Barua IAS (comp and ed), *A Brief Report on Linguistic, Communal and Ethnic Conflicts in Assam 1950–2013*. Chief Minister's Secretariat, Assam August, 2014.
4 Text of the PIP Scheme in Sekhar Gupta, *Assam A Valley Divided*, Vikas Publishing House, New Delhi, 1984. p. 201. Cited in Binayak Datta, 'The Unending Conundrum: The Story of Citizens/Foreigners between Politics and the Law in Assam' in http://pangsau.com, 31.05.2018.

References

Aditya, R. N. (1970). *From the Corridors of Memory*. Karimganj: Mirror. p. 31.

Appadurai, Arjun. (2006). *The Fear of Small Numbers: An Essay on the Geography of Anger*. Durham: Duke University Press. pp. 51–53.

Bakshi, Paramji. (2018). 'I, Dkhar,' in Gill, Preeti and Samrat Choudhary. (eds.), *Insider-outsider: Belonging and Unbelonging in North East India*. New Delhi: Amaryllis. pp. 135–136.

Barooah, Nirode K. (2010). *Gopinath Bordoloi, Assam Problem and Nehru's Centre*, Guwahati: Bhabani Publishers. p. 386.

Baruah, Sanjib. (2009). "Separatist Militants and Contentious Politics in Assam, India: The Limits of Counterinsurgency". *Asian Survey*, 49(6). November/ December. p. 953.

Census of India (1951a). Vol III, Assam Part I-A, p xxxi.as cited in Roychoudhury, Anil. "National Register of Citizens, 1951". (1981). *Economic and Political Weekly*, 16 (8).February. 21. pp. 267–268.

Census of India (1951b). Vol III, Assam Part I-A, p. xxxiii-xxxiv.as cited in Roychoudhury, Anil. "National Register of Citizens, 1951". (1981). *Economic and Political Weekly*. 16 (8). February. 21. pp. 267–268.

Census of India (1951c). Vol III. Assam Part I A. p. 365 as cited in Roychoudhury, Anil. "National Register of Citizens, 1951". (1981). *Economic and Political Weekly*. 16 (8). February. 21. pp. 267–268.

Census of India (Assam). (1951). Vol. XII. Part I A. p. 357.

Choudhury, Sujit. "A God Sent Opportunity,' in Seminar downloaded from https://www.india-seminar.com/2002/510/510%20sujit%20chaudhuri.htm, on December 2020.

Datta, Binayak. (2018). "The Unending Conundrum: The Story of Citizens/ Foreigners between Politics and the Law in Assam". Accessed on http://pangsau.com, at 31 May 2018.

Encyclopaedia of Social Sciences. Vol. II (b). (1968). London: McMillan. p. 8.

Extracts from the High Court ruling (ALR 1970, Assam and Nagaland 206 Second Appeal No 171 of 1967 as cited in Roychoudhury, Anil. "National Register of Citizens, 1951". (1981). *Economic and Political Weekly*. 16 (8). February. 21. pp. 267–268.

Mahatma Gandhi, "Is Hatred Essential for Nationalism?" in Habib, S. Irfan. (ed.) (2017). *Indian Nationalism: The Essential Writings*. New Delhi: Aleph. pp. 161–165.

Gill, Preeti and Samrat. (eds.). (2018). *Insider-outsider: Belonging and Unbelonging in North East India*. New Delhi: Amaryllis. p. x.

Gogoi, Suraj. (2019). "Psychology behind NRC mirrors narrow, dominating side of Assamese language, and its fragile nationalism, cultural identity" October 20. https://www.firstpost.com/india/psychology-behind-nrc-mirrors-narrow-dominating-side-of-assamese-language-and-its-fragile-nationalism-cultural-identity-7526031.html

Goswami, H. (1976). "Migration of Landless Labourers from East Bengal to Assam Valley 1881-1931" *Assam Economy Journal*, 2 (1). March, pp. 12–24.

Gupta, Sekhar. (1984). *Assam A Valley Divided*. New Delhi: Vikas Publishing House. pp. 201–211 as cited in Datta, Binayak. (2018). "The Unending Conundrum: The Story of Citizens/Foreigners between Politics and the Law in Assam". Accessed on http://pangsau.com at 31 May 2018.

Harrison, Selig. (1960). *India: The Most Dangerous Decades*. Princeton, NJ: Princeton University Press.

Jawaharlal Nehru as cited in Gopal, S. (1984). *Jawaharlal Nehru: A Biography*. Vol. III 1956-1964. Oxford and Delhi: Oxford University Press.

Nag, Sajal. (2001). "Nationhood and Displacement in Indian Subcontinent". *Economic and Political Weekly*, December22, pp. 4753–4760.

Roychoudhury, Anil, (Feb. 21, 1981). "National Register of Citizens, 1951". *Economic and Political Weekly*, 16(8): pp. 267–268.

Saikia, Yasmin. *Outlook India*, August 13, 2012, http://www.ooutlookindia.com/printarticles, aspx?282846

Selected from the Records of Government of Bengal. Vol. 37. (1861). Calcutta: Government of Bengal. pp. 63–66 and 69–72.

Tagore, Rabindranath. (1917). *Nationalism*. London, pp. 29–30 and 44.

Tagore, Rabindranath. "BirodhMulakAdarsha" in RabindraRachnavali, Vol X, P 594 as cited in Poddar, Arabindo. (1977). *Renaissance in Bengal: Search for Identity*. Shimla: IIAS. pp. 184–85.

The Telegraph, Guwahati, 31 August 2018. "Panel plea to UN on those left out of NRC". p. 1.

The Times of India. 10 June 1937 "Assam's Financial Outlook". p. 8.

Weiner, Myron. (1978). *Sons of the Soil: Migration and Ethnic Conflict in India*. Princeton, NJ: Princeton University Press.

White paper on Foreigners issue. (2012a). Home and Political Department, Government of Assam, October 20, pp. 40–41.

White paper on Foreigners issue. (2012b). Home and Political Department. Guwahati: Government of Assam, October 20. pp. 40–41.

Zacharian, M.C. (1964). *A Historical Study of Internal Migration in the Indian Subcontinent 1891-1931*. Bombay: Summarized.

Chapter 6

Legislating Anxiety

The History of Citizenship Conundrum in Post-colonial Assam

Binayak Dutta

I Introduction

Entanglement between displacement, citizenship and Assam is not a sudden recovery of the twenty-first century but a long-term politico-legal legacy in post-partition India since 1947. While interprovincial borders of colonial era became international boundaries, perceptions about population migration also underwent a change. Inter-provincial migration which was easy and mostly unrestricted became restricted by the legal regimes governing international population movement, which postcolonial India attempted to negotiate through a labyrinth of debates, legislations and subordinate legislations. Although there was no restriction on people from East Pakistan to Assam in the initial years after independence, gradually the provincial governments and the Government of India[1] began to discourage the migration of Muslims from Pakistan to India between 1948 and 1950.[2] In view of a rising discontent among Indians in general and refugees in particular about the inflow of Muslims into India from Pakistan.[3] Also, the East Pakistan political situation was very critical, and there was a steady exodus of Hindus who constituted 31 percent of the total population in 1947 and were reduced to 22 percent in 1951.[4] As people migrated, the entire subcontinent was in flux, especially in the east and the west of India bordering the two wings of Pakistan. One of the epicentres of intense activity in the east, although with difference was Assam which shared more than 885-km border with East Pakistan. Nehru, in his letter to the chief ministers on 1 April 1948 was quick to point out that "the exodus of non-Muslims from East Bengal continues. We are naturally as much bound to help these refugees as any from western Pakistan."[5] But despite utmost attempts from India, the conditions continued to deteriorate. By the next fortnight, the report was even grimmer. Writing back to the chief ministers, the prime minister was quick to inform that "conditions in East Bengal have deteriorated and over a million Hindus have come over during the past few months. The stream continues and we have to help those who come."[6]Hostilities between the displaced Hindu refugees, coming from Sind and East Bengal and the Muslim returnees from Pakistan had obviously grown and even the prime minister was unable to shake off the difference

DOI: 10.4324/9781003345152-10

between the Hindu refugees and the Muslims, who were popularly perceived as illegal and migrants and economic fortune seekers in partitioned India often articulated through demands of population transfer between the Hindus and Muslims from East and West Bengal, respectively.

II Burden of Partition: Legislating a Difficult Reality

As partition introduced the 'foreigners' dimension into politics the debate only became more intense and anxiety-ridden. The situation became critical as the initial trickle of people wanting to migrate to India from East Pakistan became a flood by 1949 as the political atmosphere in East Pakistan became increasingly hostile to the minority communities across the border. The hostile situation on the ground for the East Pakistani Hindu population was reflected in official correspondence between the ministers of the central government and other leaders of the Congress party, which were located in the provinces sharing a border with East Pakistan. Violence, violation and hostility took many forms which manifested themselves in the steady exodus of non-Muslims from East Pakistan to India. Although the central government were reluctant to admit the magnitude of the violence and intimidation faced by the Hindus in East Pakistan, they were forced to gradually acknowledge it. This difference could be perceived by 1949 when none other than Nehru himself, in a letter to B.C. Roy, the chief minister of West Bengal on 2 December 1949, he admitted that[7]

> [t]here was something elemental about this (the Punjab) and we have come to face the situation.
>
> In Eastern Pakistan the migration has been at a slower pace and rather gradual.

As the home minister, Sardar Patel also endorsed the difference between Punjab and Bengal. Patel was more evocative about the grim situation for the Hindus in East Pakistan when at Jaipur, in 1948, at a debate on the refugee situation and rehabilitation in the Subjects Committee at the Congress Session he pointed out that,

> the problem of East Bengal is difficult. There are about 15 million Hindus there. They are weak and soft. The people of the Punjab were different. They were strong, they could assert themselves and fight.
>
> The people of East Bengal are in a sad plight. Nobody wants to leave his own hearth and home without any reason. After all, in India they would have to starve. It is because of conditions in which they live there are bad that they migrate to India…[8]

Over the year, the situation only became worse. This increasing hostility faced by the non–Muslim League supporters in general and non-Muslims in particular in East Pakistan was at the core of public and political debates in the formative postcolonial years This debate informed the deliberations of the Constituent Assembly, a representative body of 385 members representing both the British Indian provinces and the Indian princely states.[9]

When the debates of the Constituent Assembly rolled into deliberations on provisions relating to citizenship in independent India, members, informed about the impact of partition on the demographic transformation of East Pakistan were positively inclined to make provisions for the religious minorities who were systematically displaced from their homes in East Pakistan and forced into 'refugee-hood' in India.[10] The distinction between 'displaced refugees' and 'immigrants' was one of the major thrust areas in the political positions and constitutional debates in the Constituent Assembly itself where members also deliberated on the future of non-Muslim 'displaced/refugees' migrating from East Bengal/East Pakistan to Assam. Rohini Kumar Choudhuri, a member representing a general seat from Assam championed the citizenship claims of the refugees coming to Assam, more so the partition victims. Rohini Kumar Chaudhuri who represented a general seat from Assam in the Constituent Assembly/provisional Parliament was aware of the difficulties posed by partition on the lives of the non-Muslims in East Pakistan and its impact on India in general and Assam in particular. It is significant that in pressing his amendments to the draft of Articles 5 and 6, he demanded citizenship for those persons who migrated from East Bengal to Assam

> because they found things impossible for them there....Can anyone imagine for a moment that there is no fear of disturbance in the minds of these East Bengal people who had come over to West Bengal and Assam?...Has that sense of security now after a period of two years been enhanced by the fact that Pakistan has been converted into a theocratic state?...The fear is latent in the minds of everybody. The moment any Hindu or a person of any minority community raises a protest against any action which is taken there, disturbances would immediately follow.... I want citizenship rights to this class of people who have originally belonged to Sylhet in the province of Assam, who long before the partition, have come to the Assam Valley as citizen 'of that province and are staying in the present province of Assam. ... I want to make it perfectly clear that I want citizenship rights for those people of East Bengal who had gone over to West Bengal or Assam out of fear of disturbance in the future or from the sense of insecurity and – also for those people who have come over from Sylhet, who at the time of coming had no fear of disturbance or anything of that kind, but who on account of fear of disturbances now have decided to live here.[11]

But even at that critical moment of his exposition on the future of citizenship in India and Assam, Choudhury did not lose sight of the obvious distinction between the refugee and the immigrants as he opposed the inclusion of Bengali Muslim immigrants into the new citizenship register, despite the severe ethnic tension that plagued provincial politics of Assam. For Choudhury, the only representative from Assam who spoke on citizenship rights, his intervention was significant in its representative character –on an amendment jointly tabled by him in his representative capacity as a representative of the Assamese Hindus, Mr. Dharanidhar Basumatari representing the Tribal people of Assam and Mr. Nibaran Chandra Laskar, representing the Bengali Scheduled Castes, also from Assam,[12] three important components of society in Assam. It was a spectacular joint front, unprecedented in the history of the times, especially in view of the anti-immigrant sentiments of the Assamese middle class in post-colonial Assam. The Congress ministry in Assam which came to office after the elections of 1946 had launched a vigorous anti-immigration drive and had also had to resort to forceful eviction drives and counter-measures against the civil disobedience that was launched by the Muslim League in Assam in March 1947,[13] a fact which resonated in the assertions of Choudhury. When the Constitution of India came into force in 1950, the sentiments of the Assembly clearly reflected itself in within the Constitutional framework accommodating the interests of the displaced/refugees in postcolonial India, though the term *refugee* did not find a mention in the bulky constitution that came to govern the nation state.

But between 1947 and 1950, as India was giving itself the Constitution, East Pakistan was in the throes of a violent conflagration which was singularly targeting the non-Muslim population. A memorandum submitted by the non-Muslim members of the Pakistan Constituent Assembly to Prime Minister Nurul Amin pointed out that

> [i]n February 1950, there was a repetition of the pattern of Calcutta killing in East Pakistan. Unfortunately, this was widespread. The atrocities which began in August 1949 all over East Pakistan continued almost for a period of 3 months.
>
> These incidents led to a fresh wave of migration and thousands of Hindus poured into West Bengal, Assam and Tripura.[14]

An obvious offshoot of this scenario across the border was the mass migration of minorities from East Pakistan to India. The Census Report for Assam, Manipur and Tripura, 1951 observed that

> the recent influx of Hindu refugees from Pakistan constitutes the biggest migration stream into Assam during the last decade. Following the Noakhali Riots, in October, 1946, and the Partition of India, there has been an almost steady and continuous exodus of the Hindus of Pakistan into Assam. According to the special Refugee Census taken by the Government of India of the displaced persons from East Pakistan in July 1949, there were 24,600 families of displaced persons in Assam or approximately 114,500 persons.[15]

The migration situation aggravated further as riots broke out in various other parts of East Pakistan in 1949 and 1950.[16] The Census Report 1951 observed that

> [s]oon after the 1949 Refugee Census occurred the incidences of Soneswar and Habiganj, the oppression of the Hajongs in Northern Mymensingh and the atrocities committed on the Santhals in Rajshahi, in East Dinajpur, etc. Then came the gruesome incidents over large areas of East Pakistan in February-March 1950, especially Dacca. These led to the inevitable result, viz, the desertion by hundreds and thousands of Hindus in East Pakistan of their hearths and homes to seek shelter in the neighbouring districts of West Bengal and Assam whichever was nearer...[17]

The number of displaced almost touched about half a million people by April 1950.But even in such a grave situation, while people belonging to the minority communities in East Pakistan poured into India, a large number of Muslim economic-opportunity seekers, who belonged to the majority, who otherwise had no political threat to their lives, took advantage of the political flux, also slipped into India. It was a scenario to which the Government of Assam drew the attention of the central government since 1948[18] and the Government of India was not prepared to overlook as it not only aggravated the economic pressures on partitioned India and Assam[19] but also created severe anxiety in the Indian official circles. In response to this anxiety, the postcolonial state for the first time decided to introduce emergent legislation to tackle the situation in the form of an ordinance to prohibit the entry of such Muslim migrants from East Pakistan into Assam and India. While the non-Muslim migrants were classified as 'displaced' or referred to as 'refugees' the latter were clearly identified as 'undesirable immigrants' in official discourse, including the Ordinance that the central government promulgated to overcome the grave scenario, pending the passage of a bill in the provisional Parliament to that effect.[20] The proposal was mooted by the police department, with the Deputy Inspector General, Assam writing to the chief secretary that

> information received from districts indicate that many Muslims from East Pakistan (Sylhet, Noakhali, Mymensingh Tipperah, Chittagong) have been daily coming to Assam for settling at Lanka, Hojai, Jamunamukh, Kampur, Silchar, Hailakandi, Karimganj and other places. It is time that some measures be adopted and the checking posts on our borders be instructed.
>
> I, therefore, request you kindly to see that an ordinance on the lines of the one (Ordinance No. XVII of 1948 the Influx from West Pakistan Control Ordinance) be promulgated to regulate such influx into Assam – especially during the emergency declared by the Governor General throughout the Indian Union.

The government of the day and many Congress leaders, including those from Assam, thought no different as they chose the legal course to "request the Governor-General to issue an ordinance,"[21] which was promulgated on 6 January 1950. Extant records indicate that there exists an extremely interesting connection between migration across the borders, socio-political anxiety both at the governmental and social levels and legislations of diverse kinds from early years relating to postcolonial Assam and the promulgation of this ordinance were just the beginning of many such legislative processes. And soon the provisional parliament met to debate and regularize this ordinance through an act. The government was forced to introduce the Undesirable Immigrants (Expulsion from Assam) Bill 1950 to the Parliament to " provide for the expulsion from Assam of undesirable immigrants",[22] as distinguished from "persons who on account of disturbances or disorder in Pakistan' or any other country have come to take refuge in Assam"[23] Shri Gopalaswami Ayyangar the central minister of transport and railways and the moved the bill and almost all the members speaking on the bill especially those from Assam, prominent being Shri Rohini Kumar Choudhury, Shri Surendranath Buragohain, Shri Dev Kanta Barooah, and Shri Kuladhar Chaliha rose to speak in its support. While the Bill, on becoming an act with the title Illegal Immigrants (Expulsion from Assam) Act, 1950 promulgated on the 1 March 1950, contributed to creating a legal foundation for a differentia between non-Muslim and Muslim migrants in Assam. On the grounds of crafting a difference in understanding the nature of migration on religious lines, it not only renewed focus on violence and its diverse manifestations on the non-Muslims in East Pakistan and its resultant insecurities and apprehensions, which were recognized as the primary cause for their displacement from home and hearth and migration to Assam and India, it also contributed to heightening communal tension and insecurities in the minds of the minorities in postcolonial Assam. Debates in the provisional parliament were extremely charged as Rohini Choudhuri, a senior Congress leader from Assam articulated the unique predicaments of the citizenship issue for the Bengali refugees from Sylhet while his colleague from Assam, Mr Surendranath Buragohain, took to the floor to assert the difference between the refugees and immigrants. Mr Deb Kanta Barooah's intervention, also from Assam, was even more categorical as he pointed out that

> although the dictionary meaning of the word 'immigrant' is anybody who comes from one country to another, in this particular case the word 'immigrant' means only Pakistani Muslim immigrants from Eastern Pakistan and does not include the refugees of whom a census was separately taken in Assam. We have learnt from Shri Rohini Kumar Choudhury that 1,20,000 displaced persons, who left East Bengal for fear of persecution have come to Assam. We must draw a line between these two types of people-People of Pakistani origin and nationality

> who owe no loyalty to our country and to our State, and people who for their love of India and patriotism have been persecuted in Pakistan and have taken shelter in Assam.[24]

These interventions from the debate led the Government of India to insert the provision to Section 2 of the act that asserted the distinction between persecuted displaced minority community person/refugee East Pakistan and illegal/undesirable migrants from East Pakistan who had 'subsequently come to reside in Assam'. Therefore, when the act came to be promulgated, the proviso to Section 2(b) read,

> Provided that nothing in this section shall apply to any person who on account of civil disturbances or the fear of such disturbances in any area now forming part of Pakistan has been displaced from or has left his place of residence in such area and who has been subsequently residing in Assam.

The passage of this act and its notification from 1 March 1950 and debate on the East Pakistan riots of 1950 were not a closure to debates on citizenship in postcolonial Assam. In fact, it continued to resonate in Parliament across the year. On 15 November 1950 when Nehru rose to speak on the President's address to Parliament and pointed to the refugee situation and assured that

> the hon. Member referred to the question of citizenship. There is no doubt, of course, that those displaced persons who have come to settle in India are bound to have their citizenship. If the law is inadequate in this respect, the law should be changed.[25]

This assertion had a serious impact on the citizenship question in Assam as well where it was far from becoming a settled issue, and it was evident that the state–both at the central and provincial levels – was grappling hard with it.

III Ethno-Linguistic Politics of Assam and Its Predicaments

But the settlement of migrants in Assam was not just a humanitarian or legal issue. It was deeply embedded in ethno-linguistic antagonisms as well which combined with pragmatic political considerations to directly impact communal apprehensions and tensions over the migration of people, their settlement and claims of citizenship. The continuous inflow of Bengali-speaking migrants from East Pakistan to Assam only helped to aggravate it. An immediate offshoot of this situation was the difference of opinion between the central and state governments over refugee rehabilitation in Assam. Conflicts arose over the Assam government's decision expressing its inability to part with any land for refugee rehabilitation. Nehru wrote to Bordoloi, the premier of Assam, that the decision of the Assam government was earning it a bad name[26] and threatened to curtail the central financial assistance to Assam if the government did not adopt a favourable attitude to rehabilitate East Pakistani refugees.[27]Bordoloi's reply to Nehru was firm and clear that it was not feasible for him to give more land to the refugees as the government of Assam had to accommodate the existing demand of land from local cultivators and "Assam was a purely agricultural economy, it was impossible for a popular government to ignore these facts in the face of continued industrial backwardness."[28]

It was clear that as the government of Assam gradually entrenched itself into power, the pressures of pragmatic electoral politics also coloured their positions on migration and citizenship. When Nehru drew the attention of Gopinath Bordoloi to allegations made against the Assam government by some of the members of his government, stating that some "[m]inisters have openly stated that they prefer Muslims of East Bengal to Hindus from East Bengal,"[29] Bordoloi countered the prime minister, a fellow Congress leader by informing him that

> [i]f one is to speak the truth, one has to admit that the Muslims of East Bengal, settled in the province, are becoming Members of the Congress in large numbers and are falling in line with the schemes the Government have undertaken to improve the lot of the common man in the establishment of rural panchayats and the working of village trading cooperatives. They have adopted the regional language of the province and are showing a desire to work together.[30]

On the ground, public reaction to the presence of refugees were extremely hostile. Riots broke out in Guwahati on 18 May 1948, which began as a clash between railway workers, believed to be communist sympathisers and local students but which acquired communal proportions. This was only the beginning of antagonisms and violent clashes between locals and refugees in different parts of Assam. Pressure groups and political parties like the Asom Jatiya Mahasabha led by Ambika Giri Roychoudhury began to make demands for dual citizenship. The situation became more critical over the issue of unchecked illegal immigration from East Pakistan to Assam. But this attempt to define citizenship in postcolonial Assam on the basis of an intelligible differentia proposed by postcolonial legislations could not be a success as the flow of refugees soon turned into an unstoppable deluge and apprehensions of the local people began to rise to unprecedented levels on the one hand and the immigrant Muslims also began to adopt innovative strategies of survival in postcolonial Assam in line with dominant Assamese aspirations and insecurities towards creating Assam as a homogenous Assamese province after independence on the other.[31] The decade of the 1950s was a benchmark of transforming the discourse of citizenship in

India in general and Assam in particular. If the passport system came to be introduced between India and Pakistan in October 1952, the Citizenship Act came into force in 1955. By 1957, the Foreigners Act, 1946 was amended to include the 'Pakistani' as a foreigner in 1957 and "detailed instructions were only thereafter issued by the Government of India in March, 1957 to all state governments including Assam to deport Pakistani nationals staying in India without proper authority or sanction."[32]

But despite these initial measures of discouragement to unrestricted migration from East Pakistan to India the number of refugees returned in 1961 Census was 628,000 as against 273,000 refugees in the Census of 1951. The matter became more difficult as the composition of the migrant population was mixed, belonging to both the minority and majority communities of East Pakistan, indicating therefore that all the migrants could not trace their uprooting to political persecution. This influx of refugees contributed to social tension in Assam as Assamese elite feared danger to their economic political and cultural life. The situation became more critical when the census superintendent observed in his report of 1961 that "after independence the Bengali Muslim immigrants into the Assam Valley have, almost to a man returned their mother tongue as Assamese whether they know the language or not."[33]This was alarming as these immigrants had also done the same in the colonial period as "what they want is land in the valley, and if knowledge of Assamese language helps them to become 'indigenous' they do not mind about their mother tongue."[34] The culture conscious Assamese elite who initially welcomed these Muslim immigrants subsequently began to be wary of them. As these immigrants became vote-banks of the party in power,[35] they became more assertive. In 1962, they flew the Pakistani flag with cries of Pakistan Zindabad in villages near Tezpur and Morajar area of the Nagaon district. In the backdrop of the Chinese invasion, the government began to make a fresh security appraisal and therefore came about the Foreigners (Tribunal) Order on 23 September 1964. Under this statutory order, four Foreigners Tribunals were set up and "as many as 35,080 persons were referred to these Tribunals till August, 1965. While these laws and schemes were deliberated upon, the numbers of Foreigner Tribunals under the Order of 1964 were raised from 4 to 9 with headquarters in Tezpur, Guwahati, Nowgong, Sibsagar, Goalpara, Dhubri, Barpeta and Jorhat."[36]

To further tighten the process, the Government of India through the Intelligence Bureau proposed the Prevention of Infiltration from Pakistan (PIP) scheme to check and deport infiltrators from Assam. The draft prepared by the Intelligence Bureau in its background note was categorical in stating that "the number of illegal immigrants into Assam from Pakistan over the course of the last 12 years has been very conservatively estimated about 250 thousand."[37]As the government of Shri B.P. Chaliha began to vigorously implement the scheme, politics over migration and settlement raised its head with cries of harassment by the Jamiat-ul-Ulama-e-Hind and opposition from two of the cabinet ministers of Assam. The Intelligence Bureau therefore observed, "The fact that such a large number of immigrants succeeded in illegally crossing the frontier and settling down unnoticed would prove that the measures so far taken have not been effective."[38] It is significant to note that the idea of national registration of citizens as a means to tide over the vexed citizenship issue was first articulated in the PIP scheme of 1965 which proposed that a "National Registration System and the issue of Identity Cards should be adopted"[39] for all the residents of Assam and the north-eastern region.

The birth of Bangladesh on the partition of Pakistan in 1971 made the situation more complex. It added the 'Bangladeshi' dimension to the 'foreigners' imbroglio. By the late 1970s, the issue of foreigners in electoral rolls had come to become a major issue in Assam politics. The Assam Anti-Foreigners Agitations were launched in 1978 and the All Assam Students Union, which led the movement in its memorandums submitted to the prime minister on 18 January and 2 February 1980 pointed out that "Assam will have to reckon with perhaps 50 lakh foreign nationals in 1981, and the Assamese in Assam shall become a minority."[40]This dominant Assamese apprehension over migration of people across the border and community antagonisms rooted in history came to dominate the discourse of the anti-immigrant movement in Assam. The agitations which came to a close with the signing of the Assam Accord in 1985 clearly brought out into the open Assamese apprehensions over the migration and settlement of Bengalis into Assam. The Accord signed between the Government of India, the Government of Assam and the All-Assam Students' Union highlighted

> profound sense of apprehensions regarding the continued influx of foreign nationals into Assam and the fear about adverse effects upon the political, social, cultural and economic life of the state.[41]

It is therefore in keeping with the mandate of the Assam Accord that the Government of India introduced the Citizenship (Amendment) Act 1985, which, the Home Minister of India categorically pointed out was in response to "the sentiment of the Assamese people."[42] But despite the amendment of 1985, the dominant Assamese anxiety over the question of the presence of foreigners of Bengali origin in Assam (refugees or otherwise) never really dissipated from Assamese popular imagination. The amendment of 1985 was strengthened in 1986 when the central government again brought another Citizenship (Amendment) Bill in 1986. While debates on this amendment were as animated and contested, there was no doubt that the realities of post-partition migration of minorities from East Pakistan (Bangladesh post-1971) continued to cloud the debate in parliament over the migration and citizenship of migrants from across the border. In course of the debate on the Amendment Bill, Shri Dinesh Goswami, the member of parliament (MP) from Guwahati not only made repeated references to the terms in the Assam Accord on the citizenship issue but also reminded both the treasury and the opposition members that

> it took the people of Assam six long years to make Government of India realize that a large number of people were clandestinely entering Assam and also the other neighbouring states from East Bengal ... the very existence of the State and the rights of the people – social, political and economic – were at stake ...[43]

But beyond the discussions on immigration, Goswami's speech was striking in view of the position that he took that "it has been a long standing demand from we, the people of Assam that mere birth should not be the criterion for grant of citizenship."[44] While nowhere in the Assam Accord was this position taken, it was evident that despite the signing of the Assam Accord and the passage of the Citizenship (Amendment) Act, 1985 inserting Section 6A into the Citizenship Act, 1955, the threat to Assam from across its eastern border, in the minds of the dominant Assamese middle-class leadership never really disappeared and the same apprehension resonated in 1986 as well. When in course of the same debate, Shri Gokul Saikia, the MP from Lakhimpur, demanded that "the citizenship act should be more stringent, severe punishment should be awarded to those who violate the provisions of this Act. If need be, even death punishment may be awarded,"[45] the anxiety of the representatives of Assam over migration and citizenship was hardly hidden from the other members of the house and the government of the day. Therefore, when the act of 1986 in section 2 (b) mandated that only those children whose at least one parent was an Indian citizen could be granted Indian citizenship henceforth, the act of 1986 was not only initiating a major change in the philosophy of Indian citizenship from *Jus soli* (citizenship according to birth) to *Jus sanguinis* (citizenship according to parentage), it was also responding to dominant Assamese middle-class anxiety. This was only the first step as in response to the demands of the Assamese members of parliament and undermining the objection of many others, the Government of India brought a further amendment to the act of 1955 in 2003 when through Section 3 of the Citizenship (Amendment) Act, 2004 it was provided that only those persons born of parents both of whom were Indian citizens or one being an Indian citizen and the other not being an illegal migrant, could be conferred Indian citizenship.[46] While this amendment of 2004 was passed without any debate on the major shift in the principle of citizenship in India, it could be surmised that there the process that was started in 1986 finally came to fruition in 2004 with the Bharatiya Janata Party government successfully piloting the Citizenship (Amendment) Bill 2003 and notifying it into an Act in January 2004, in order to partly assuage this anxiety of the dominant middle-class apprehensions in Assam.

By 2005, almost two decades after signing the Assam Accord, the Government of Assam again engaged the All Assam Students Union and the

Government of India in a Tripartite meeting which agreed to upgrade the National Register of Citizens of 1951.[47] Dominant Assamese apprehensions also found a place in the judicial pronouncements often reflected in the judgements of the High Court in Assam.[48] An interesting example of such judgements was in 2008 where it was observed that "large number of Bangladeshis present in the state of Assam ...have become the kingmakers,"[49] which found visibility in most newspapers in Assam and eastern India.[50] The ghost of partition and the apprehensions of the foreigners issue came back to haunt the politically sensitive elite who steadfastly argued that the foreigners issue had never really been buried for good.

But politics over migration and citizenship only became violent by 2012. In 2012, a massive demonstration was organized at Guwahati to relaunch the anti-foreigners agitation. Violent clashes between the Bodos and the Bengali-speaking Muslims broke out in Bodoland. The area was also a witness to large-scale violence again in May 2014, which also revolved around the 'Bangladeshi–foreigners' question. It is in this charged atmosphere the Assam Sanmilita Mahasangha filed a petition in the Supreme Court of India to examine the constitutional position of the laws of citizenship in India and to upgrade the National Register of Citizens prepared in 1951 for Assam in 2012, as highlighted at paragraph 18 of the Judgement, noting, "In the year 2012 and in 2014 largescale riots took place in Assam resulting in the deaths of a large number of persons. It is in this background that the present writ petitions have been filed." Between 2012 and 2016, the citizenship question in Assam has witnessed unprecedented churning. Although the Government of India instituted a pilot project on NRC in the districts of Dhubri and Goalpara in 2012, it had to be suspended after violent protests. But despite the initial hiccups, the process was revived on 5 December 2013 when the Registrar General of Citizen Registration issued a notification to update the national register of citizens 1951 in the state of Assam. The initiation and execution of the updation process of NRC took this anxiety and conflict to new levels with civil society organizations like Assam Sanmilita Mahasangha, Indigenous Tribal Forum and NDFB (Progressive) and political parties like Bharatiya Janata Party (BJP) and All India United Democratic Front (AIUDF) joining the process.[51]

The Supreme Court of India which had begun hearing of a bunch of writ petitions on the issue since August 2013 on a regular basis delivered its first judgement on 17 December 2014 which accorded utmost importance of the upgradation of the NRC as a mechanism for identification of and deletion of foreigners from Assam and directed that the upgraded National Register of Citizens (NRC) for Assam be published by the end of January 2016 on the basis of a prescribed time schedule. While the schedule was soon forgotten, the NRC including the register is far away from its completion despite publication and the final list by September 2019, at best, it was only a major turn in the irreconcilable conundrum between politics and law on the citizenship question.

IV The Coming of the BJP to Power in 2014: New Era in Citizenship Politics

Therefore, when elections to the Assam Legislative Assembly loomed large on the horizon in 2016, the people of this state were in the midst of the tumultuous exercise of NRC. Although the NRC was a major turn in the citizenship politics of Assam, the BJP was caught in a bind between its commitments to the cause of refugees, on one hand, and its support to the NRC updation in Assam, on the other. With the publication of the Assam NRC in September 2019, the state was left with over 19 lakh people excluded from the updated Register of which only 4 lakh 86 thousand persons were East Bengali Muslims and about 6 lakh 90 thousand persons were Bengali Hindus[52] which raised a hue and cry and local organizations which had earlier advocated for its speedy completion came out to condemn it and its cancellation. In this background, the BJP as the party in government both at the centre and the state in a rework of its strategy decided to undertake a national NRC but declared that "we will ensure implementation of the NRC in the entire country. We will remove every single infiltrator from the country except Buddhists, Hindus and Sikhs."[53] What compounded the problem was the complex issue of 'D' Voters and detainees in the six Detention Camps in Assam[54] which according to the Assam government affidavit in the Supreme Court dated 31 January 2019 was 938 of which approximately 35% were those who belonged to Bengali caste Hindus, Garos, Hajongs, Kochs, other Indigenous tribes and Dalit Hindus. As many as 31 children were lodged in these camps, and many inmates had died in the camp itself due to various reasons including suicide. The number of detainees rose to 1044 by November 2019. It is in pursuance of its electoral commitment the BJP Manifesto of 2019 promised for

> the enactment of the Citizenship Amendment Bill for the protection of individuals of religious minority communities from neighbouring countries escaping persecution. …Hindus, Jains, Buddhists, Sikhs and Christians escaping persecution from India's neighbouring countries will be given citizenship in India.[55]

Therefore, within six months of its return to power, the BJP-led National Democratic Alliance government presented the Citizenship (Amendment) Bill, 2019 on the 9th of December in the Lok Sabha and on 11 December 2019 to the Rajya Sabha and ensured its passage in both the Houses of Parliament. With the presidential assent on the 12 December 2019, the bill became an act with its publication in the Gazette of India, Extraordinary (No.71), Part II, S.1, dated the 12 December 2019. With the passage of this act, the government redeemed its pledge to the people of India wholly as those who were faced with the prospect of eviction and deportation from India belonging to the specified communities from the neighbouring countries, who had escaped to India to avoid persecution or the threat of persecution till 31 December 2014 were made eligible to be regularized as citizens subsequent to their application to the prescribed authority under the act and on fulfilment of the conditions for Indian citizenship as specified under section 5 of the Citizenship Act. It was declared by Section 2 of the Amendment Act that those belonging to the specified communities "shall not be treated as illegal migrant for the purpose of this Act."[56] For the north-eastern region, the act was especially sensitive to the sentiments of the indigenous communities as it addressed their concerns of being inundated by the migrants regularized by this Act as prospective citizens by exempting "the tribal area of Assam, Meghalaya, Mizoram or Tripura as included in the Sixth Schedule to the Constitution and the areas covered under 'the Inner Line' notified under the Bengal Eastern Frontier Regulation, 1873."[57]

V In Lieu of a Conclusion

The act is a major initiative to impact the citizenship conundrum of the region unleashed by the Assam Accord by proposing to resolve the lingering confusion between refugees and illegal immigrants. Citizenship had always been a contested site in Assam politics where partition took place along with Punjab and Bengal of India through a political process called a referendum in its southern non-Assamese, predominantly Bengali-speaking district of Sylhet. The rationale for a reference to the politics of referendum, even in passing, lay in relationship between the complex and multilayered history of communal and ethno-linguistic antagonism that dominated the politics of Assam since 1919 and the partition of Assam and its impact on the citizenship question in postcolonial India in particular. One of the most ominous effects of partition was the unending stream of migration of people across the borders, which, till 1947, was provincial and psychological but, after 1947, became international, legal and political which had to be accommodated in evolving legal frameworks on citizenship in India. Maximum churning on the citizenship question was on the question of migration of refugees and demographic transformation which was reflected through the political tumult on the ground and the manner in which these people came to be perceived in official debates and popular politics. This chapter attempts to weave a narrative on the citizenship question in Assam through a mixed reading of official debates and public reports about human mobility and migration across borders and perceptions about it and its troubled trajectory leading to the most serious attempts to close the conundrum since the time of Nehru. Although the attempts of the postcolonial government had been to move beyond the predicaments of the partition of India in 1947, it is something that we are yet to reconcile with it. The creation of Pakistan and the partition of India and Assam, partition continued to fester the lives of the people like a phantom through the predicaments of citizenship in North-East India. While partition of India may have been an event many years past for the other parts of the country, for the north-eastern region and its people, it is a live issue that we are still coming to terms with.

Notes

1 See interventions on the citizenship provision by Sardar Bhopinder Singh Mann in the Constituent Assembly Debate, dated 12 August 1948. For details on the introduction of the Permit System since 19 July 1948 in Feroz Meharuddin vs. Sub-Divisional Officer and Ors., AIR 1961 M.P. 110.
2 West Pakistan (Control) Ordinance, 1948 and the rules framed under the Ordinance introducing a system of permits see judgement in Feroz Meharuddin vs. Sub-Divisional Officer and Ors., AIR 1961 M.P. 110.
3 Durga Das, *Sardar Patel's Correspondence, 1945-50*, Vol-VI, pp. 262–263, Navajivan Publishing House, Ahmedabad, 1973.
4 Abul Barkat, et al., *Deprivation of Hindu Minority in Bangladesh: Living with Vested Property*, Pathak Samabesh, Dhaka, 2008, pp.61–66.
5 G. Parthasarathi, *Jawaharlal Nehru Letters to Chief Ministers*, Vol-I, OUP, Oxford/New Delhi, 1985, p. 100.
6 G. Parthasarathi, *Jawaharlal Nehru Letters to Chief Ministers*, Vol-I, OUP, Oxford/New Delhi, 1985, pp. 108–109.
7 P. K. Chakrabarti, *Marginal Men*, NayaUdyog, New Delhi, 1999, p. 21.
8 P. N. Chopra, *Sardar Patel: Muslims and Refugees*, Konarak Publishers, Delhi, 2004, p. 270.
9 B.B. Misra, *The Unification and Division of India*, OUP, Bombay, 1990, p. 364.
10 Although the initial term usedto indicate such people from East Bengal was *displaced*, subsequent subordinate legislations including manuals and reports in Assam indicate that the term *displaced* and *refugees* are coterminous. See '*Report of Statistical Survey of Displaced Persons from East Pakistan*', Department of Economics and Statistics, Government of Assam, 1958. p. 124.
11 *Constituent Assembly Debates* dated 12th August, 1949 see intervention by Rohini Kumar Chaudhuri, pp. 414–415.
12 *Constituent Assembly Debate* dated 12th August, 1949 see intervention by Rohini Kumar Chaudhuri, p. 413.
13 See details in File No. 119/46-Poll-I Home, National Archives of India.
14 *Jurists' Commission Report on the Recurrent Exodus of Minorities from East Pakistan and Disturbances in India*, New Delhi, 1965.
15 *Census of India*,1951, Vol.XII, Part I-A, pp. 356–357.
16 Binayak Dutta, Violent Parting: Recovering the History of Violence in Sylhet on Partition and After.(1947-50) in *The Heritage*, Vol-IV, Issue-1, 2013, pp. 20–36.
17 Census of India,1951, Vol.XII, Part I-A, pp. 356–357.
18 See Shri Gopalaswami's statement on the Undesirable Immigrants (Expulsion from Assam) Bill, 1950 in *Indian Parliamentary Debates*, 8 February 1950, Vol.-I, p. 315.
19 *Indian Parliamentary Debates*, 8 February 1950, Vol.-I, p. 315.
20 Home Confidential C 294/1948, National Archives of India.
21 *Indian Parliamentary Debates*, 8 February 1950, Vol.-I, pp. 313–314.
22 *Indian Parliamentary Debates*, 8 February 1950, Vol.-I, p. 313.
23 *Indian Parliamentary Debates*, 8 February 1950, Vol.-I, p. 315.
24 *Indian Parliamentary Debates*, 8 February 1950, Vol.-I, p. 329.

25 *Jawaharlal Nehru's Speeches*, Vol.Two, Publication Division, Government of India, Delhi, 1954, p. 10.
26 Nirode K. Barooah, *Gopinath Bordoloi, 'The Assam Problem' and Nehru's Centre*, Bhabani Print and Publications, Guwahati, 2010, p. 393.
27 Nirode K. Barooah, *Gopinath Bordoloi, 'The Assam Problem' and Nehru's Centre*, Bhabani Print and Publications, Guwahati, 2010, p. 394.
28 Nirode K. Barooah, *Gopinath Bordoloi, 'The Assam Problem' and Nehru's Centre*, Bhabani Print and Publications, Guwahati, 2010, pp. 394–395.
29 Nirode K. Barooah, *Gopinath Bordoloi, 'The Assam Problem' and Nehru's Centre*, Bhabani Print and Publications, Guwahati, 2010, p. 393.
30 Nirode K. Barooah, *Gopinath Bordoloi, 'The Assam Problem' and Nehru's Centre*, Bhabani Print and Publications, Guwahati, 2010, p. 396.
31 *Assam Legislative Assembly Proceedings*, 1947, p. 1481.
32 *White Paper on Foreigners Issue*, Government of Assam, 20 October 2012.
33 *Census of India* 1961, Vol III, Assam Part I-A, p. 204.
34 *Census of India* 1961, Vol III, Assam Part I-A, p. 203.
35 Nirode K. Barooah, *Gopinath Bordoloi, 'The Assam Problem' and Nehru's Centre*, Bhabani Print and Publications, Guwahati, 2010, p. 393.
36 Text of the PIP Scheme in Sekhar Gupta, *Assam A Valley Divided*, Vikas Publishing House, New Delhi, 1984. pp. 201–211.
37 Text of the PIP Scheme in Sekhar Gupta, *Assam A Valley Divided*, Vikas Publishing House, New Delhi, 1984. pp. 201–211.
38 Text of the PIP Scheme in Sekhar Gupta, *Assam A Valley Divided*, Vikas Publishing House, New Delhi, 1984. p. 201.
39 Ibid, p. 210.
40 Annexure 9(A) of the Government of Assam *White Paper on the Foreigners Issue* in Assam, p. 67.
41 Annexure 10 of the Government of Assam *White Paper on the Foreigners Issue* in Assam, p. 34.
42 Lok Sabha Debates, 20 November 1985.
43 Lok Sabha Debates, 10 November 1986.
44 Lok Sabha Debates, 10 November 1986.
45 Lok Sabha Debates, 10 November 1986.
46 The Gazette of India, 8 January 2004.
47 White Paper on Foreigners Issue, see p. 36, decision of 5 May 2005.
48 AIR 2005 SC 2920. And 2008(3) GLT 272 Mustt. Sarabari Begum vs State of Assam.
49 2008(3) G.L.T. 272 Mustt. Sarabari Begum vs State of Assam, para 208.
50 *The Indian Express*, Guwahati, July 30th 2008 with the headline, 'Bangla Infiltrators now Kingmakers in Assam: HC Judge.'
51 *The Telegraph*, 16 September 2012 'Groups oppose NRC Update'. BJP, AUDF in NRC tiff in The Telegraph, 21 April 2015.
52 *Pratidin* dated 12 September 2019.
53 Tweet by the BJP on 4 November 2019.
54 The Six Detention Camps in Assam are at Goalpara, Silchar, Tezpur, Kokrajhar, Jorhat and Dibrugarh.
55 *Bharatiya Janata Party Manifesto for General Elections, 2019*, p. 12.
56 *The Citizenship Act*, 1955, Section 2 (ii) 3 as inserted by the Act No.47 of 2019.
57 *The Citizenship (Amendment) Act*, 2019, Section 4,The Act No.47 of 2019.

Chapter 7

Citizenship in the Fabric of Hindu Nationalism in Assam

Bhupen Sarmah

I Introduction

Though the perceptible forms of communal mobilization in Assam virtually disappeared with partition and independence, the regionalist leadership now active in the political theater of the state has shown its proclivity towards the ideological construct of a Hindu nation. The narcissism immanent in the contemporary regionalist ideological constructions in the state does not essentialize any secular principle, and therefore, this can also be seen as pragmatism necessitated by the contemporary political economy with its ever-increasing tendency of centralization. In the present context of Indian politics imbued with the logic of governmentality that allows unabated shrinkage of political space for the constituent political units, the survival of the regional players of the economically-not-so-significant political units depends largely on their capacity to adjust with the regime that controls the nation state, whether secular or communal. The Asom Gana Parishad (AGP), the narcissistic outcome of the 'Asomiya' collective subjectivity reshaped by the protracted citizenship discourse in the regional society is one of the most palpable examples of such a political adjustment. Narrativizing the citizenship discourse in Assam in its present avatar, this chapter attempts to comprehend the historical factors that contributed to the construction of 'Asomiyajatiyatabad' embodied in the AGP and its response to the citizenship discourse remolded by Hindutva politics in the multiethnic regional society.

II Citizenship Discourse in Contemporary Assam

While the recent amendments in the citizenship laws, which have linked the idea of citizenship with religion, evoked nationwide contestations, the Assamese at large, being conscious of an 'Asomiya' cultural identity, became highly apprehensive. Besides being an assault on the secular fabric of the constitution, for an average Assamese, the amendments would jeopardize the 'Asomiya' identity, protection of which has been their primary concern for some time.

DOI: 10.4324/9781003345152-11

Undoubtedly, the citizenship discourse in Assam was shaped by the Assam Movement (1979–85), avowedly launched for the protection of the "Assamese national identity", essentializing citizenship for political mobilization. The movement was galvanized consciously directing and reshaping popular sentiment, especially against the "illegal" immigrants from Bangladesh, projecting all of them, irrespective of their religious identity, as an alarming threat to the 'Assamese national identity'. The commitments made by the state in the "Assam Accord" to resolve the impasse of illegal immigrants satisfied the leadership of the movement; the sanctity of the "Public Law Contract" was, however, quashed by a visible apathy of the state. The unresolved issue of illegal immigrants though played a crucial role in electoral politics for decades, it reappeared more vigorously with the idea of the "National Register of Citizens" (NRC), which was projected as a panacea of the protracted question. While the political project spearheaded by judicial activism was initiated without any well-conceived strategy to confront with the aftermath, the publication of the draft NRC substantially provoked the political regime at the center to immediately push the Citizenship Amendment Bill (CAB), linking citizenship with religion. The centrally sponsored move was defeated by the temporarily formed regional alliance, but interestingly, many of the regional forces that vehemently opposed the CAB remained with the Bharatiya Janata Party (BJP), despite the party in power seeking its mandate in the Lok Sabha elections in 2019 with a promise to make the CAB a reality. While the "Final NRC" that excluded nearly two million residents of Assam had largely been contested with a clandestine communal tone, hundreds of Foreigners Tribunals were promised to resolve the issue of citizenship for the excluded people, on one hand, and construction works of several detention camps were taken up for providing shelter to the people declared as "foreigners" by the Tribunals, until their deportation. The concomitant process has been the controversial amendments in the Citizenship Act. Therefore, in the specific context of Assam, the amended Citizenship Act was contested as it was perceived to be a move toward nullifying the essence of the Assam Accord while the NRC was initially accepted as a step towards implementation of the latter.

III Asomiya Nationalism as an Ideological Construct

Politics is, undoubtedly, ideology in praxis, but the concepts that correlate to constitute an ideology are often imprecise in meaning and subject to multiple (re)constructions and interpretations. As ordained by necessities of the practitioners, an ideology can, therefore, be reconstructed and projected as absolute and univocal. Understanding some of the ideas and concepts that emanated from the historical specificities of Assam is, therefore, crucial for analyzing the contemporary citizenship discourses in the regional society; as such, concepts and ideas are instrumental in shaping the ideology which has been significantly influencing the collective actions for long. Although it calls for much deeper and wider engagement than the scope permitted by the present chapter, the immediate reference point may be the academic debate in the *Economic and Political Weekly* that began "in the midst of an immense tide of popular passion and ominous flashes of Fascist threat against dissent and criticism" (Gohain 1985, p. xxii).

The debate started with Hiren Gohain's brief comments on the movement characterizing it as a counter-attack on the organized left by the ruling class when the former demonstrated a visible presence in the electoral politics of Assam (Gohain, 1980). This appeared as a "simple conspiracy theory" for Sanjib Kumar Baruah, who sought legitimacy of the movement as "the Assamese civil society in rebellion" under the leadership of the students (Baruah 1980). He asserted that the large-scale immigration into Assam within a relatively short period tangled Assam's nationality question. With an economic justification, Tilottama Misra characterized the movement as a resistance to the exploitation of an oppressed nationality (Misra, 1980), and the analysis that followed was framed by her theoretical interpretation of what can be called "internal colonialism" in the context of Assam vis-à-vis the extra-regional big business interests.

The debate veered back to the tangled nationality question in Assam with Amalendu Guha's polemical intervention (Guha, 1980). Guha defined the term *Asamiya* on the criteria of both language and territoriality, those amongst the "Assamese" (i.e., all who domiciled the present state of Assam) "who profess Asamiya to be their natural or acquired mother tongue". He argued that "Asamiya little nationalism'" began its journey in the 1850s through political mobilization by the Asomiya middle-class leadership initially on the language issue and to cover other issues later. Defining Little nationalism as "a spiritual sentiment that holds together a group of people claiming a common cultural-regional identity" aspiring for "a degree of autonomy within the larger nation-state", Guha depicted the trajectory of the Asomiya little nationalism since its inception till it resumed the "proto-fascist" method of political assertion during the movement. Essentially contesting Guha's characterization of the movement, Sanjib Kumar Baruah reiterated his earlier justification pointing out that "as a frontier people, the Assamese nationality is particularly vulnerable to threats to its rights as the 'basic population' of a territory, from exceptional immigration"; therefore, the fears and aspirations of the Assamese expressed through the movement were reasonable (Baruah, 1981). For Gail Omvedt also, the fears of being overrun expressed by the Asomiya through the movement had a material base; nonetheless, the fears were voiced by a petty bourgeoisie leadership with chauvinist tendencies in absence of left leadership (Omvedt, 1981).

The debate is worth reiterating for analyzing the present discourse on citizenship, although it ignored certain nuanced historical issues crucial for understanding the trajectory of the Asomiya nationalism or little/sub-nationalism. For instance, Guha's analysis of the origin of Asomiya little nationalism in the 1850s as political mobilization by the Asomiya middle class on language issue is not entirely flawless. Guha contradicts himself with his own definition of "Little nationalism", in which the idea of a nation state is crucial. Similarly, emphasis on the historical role of the "Asomiya middle class", the loosely structured concept commonly shared by most scholars, tends to camouflage the specific role played by the political leadership that is discernible at different historical juncture with different ideological constructs.

The concept of nationalism has widely been debated both in the context of Europe and its colonies. Avoiding the details, what can be accepted is that while nationalism in Europe surfaced essentializing cultural homogeneity for the formation of the nation states necessitated by the bourgeoisie revolution, nationalism in the colonies appeared much later in the form of struggle against colonial domination, for reclaiming sovereignty. In the specific context of India, being shaped by the politico-economic framework of colonialism, nationalism gradually emerged as a pan-Indian ideology imbued with the imagination of a nation state, a political conglomeration of the historically evolved cultural identities. For Partha Chatterjee, the advent of British rule, the 'Great Event' for India "terminated centuries of despotism, superstition and vegetative life and ushered in a new era of change – of 'destruction' as well as 'regeneration', destruction of antiquated tradition and the emergence of modern, secular and national forces" (Chatterjee, 1999, pp. 22–23). Notwithstanding its disputable secular and modern character, the core of the 'national forces' fostered by the 'Great Event' was constituted by the emerging 'ruling material force' (Marx and Engels, 1977, p. 47), for which, the Indian National Congress became the predominant political expression when it became a mass movement. Conceiving nationalism as the subjective manifestation of a political idea and a type of collective consciousness (Conversi, 2004, pp. 815–829), its instrumental role as an ideology cannot be overlooked. It is precisely for this instrumentalist role, almost all the cultural identities, including a multitude of ethnic, racial and religious categories across their class barriers, became integral part of the mainstream nationalist discourse. Subsequently, being the 'citizens' of India, their national identity (nationality) as "Indian" has been endorsed and objectified by the nation state.

The idea of "Asomiya nationality" was not an exception, and it was gradually brought under the pan-Indian nationalist discourse like many other such cultural identities, commonly comprehended as nationalities. Nevertheless, the depiction of the "Asomiya nationality" as a culturally cohesive and distinct subset of the "Assamese" has long been a serious political question. The so-called Assam Accord made the political equation between these two categories more complex than ever before. The state promised in the Accord constitutional, legislative and administrative safeguards to protect, preserve and promote the cultural, social, linguistic identity and heritage of the "Assamese" people. Since the Assamese language does not provide an equal term for "Assamese", its subsequent political interpretation consciously tagged it with indignity. Consequently, the concept "Asomiya/Assamese" became practically incomprehensible as well as indefinable and the resultant ambiguity has continuously been influencing the regional political theatre for decades. What is immanent in the contemporary imbroglio is that every "Asomiya" is an "Assamese" but not vice versa; and realization of the statist protection of the former, the assurance achieved through the protracted movement, is a historical necessity. Therefore, the nuanced conceptual difference between "Asomiya" and "Assamese" are crucial in the present context. While the former is deeply embedded in its history of political sociology, the latter is intrinsically linked with citizenship of the domiciled besides their preferred and professed cultural and linguistic identities. It is, therefore, imperative to relocate both the concepts in their own historical contexts for delineation of the nuanced difference as well as the congruities that contributed to the formation of a common political category against colonialism.

IV Asomiya Nationalism in Its Historicity

The history of nearly the first five decades of colonialism in Assam, since the annexation of the Ahom state in 1826 and then placing under the Bengal presidency till the creation of the province of Assam in 1874, is crucial not only for understanding the political-economy of colonialism but also for comprehending the political sociology of the Asomiya cultural and linguistic identity. As several empirical studies on the history of colonialism in Assam have demonstrated, expansion of administration alongside rapid investment of colonial capital especially in the upper valley of the Brahmaputra, the territory of Ahom state or Assam proper, necessitated a massive inflow of people from other parts of colonial India. While the conspicuous absences of a trading community in the non-monetized economy and English-educated people with professional proficiency were filled by the Marowari traders and English-educated Bengali Hindus settled in the emerging urban centers, the demand for manual labor force in the flourishing plantation sector was fulfilled largely by the immigrants from different parts of colonial India. Concomitantly, protection of the colonial interests in the valley required stringent measures of control over the surrounding hills executed through a process of gradual annexation and sociopolitical exclusion (Sarmah, 2018), the process that appeared as territorial expansion of the colonial state of Assam.

However, one of the most crucial outcomes of the colonial interventions during the first fifty years is the emergence of a small section of Asomiya intelligentsia after the adoption of the Bengali language in 1837 for administration and judiciary in Assam. This tiny section emanated mainly from the Hindu upper caste rural landed gentry instilled by the newly introduced ryotwari system. Back at home, this English-educated enlightened section grew up in Calcutta under the influences of the so-called Bengal renaissance, almost uncritically accepted the Bengali language instead of showing resentment against the denial of the justified position of the Assamese language in Assam proper. Nevertheless, they joined the American Baptist missionaries who relentlessly worked for establishing Assamese as distinct and separate language and consequently Asomiya as a separate cultural entity. Being preoccupied with social reforms, the primary concerns of this enlightened section were the plight of widows of upper caste Hindus, polygamy and widespread consumption of opium, and their endeavor to disseminate enlightened ideas and knowledge. With the backdrop of their upper caste Hindu aristocracy and having experienced the way Maniram Dewan was hanged publicly in February 1858 for his 'conspiracy' against colonialism, this enlightened section comprised mainly of the salaried employees, carefully distancing from the larger political issues raised by the peasantry.

Starting with the Phulaguri uprising in 1861, the organized militancy of the riots gradually expanded to other parts of the Brahmaputra Valley toward the end of the century. Nevertheless, by the time Assam became a Chief Commissioner's Province in February 1874, the amalgamation of Assam proper with the multitude of ethnic, racial and linguistic identities,[1] the numerical strength of the Assamese rickety intelligentsia substantially grew up with the spirit of a separate linguistic identity already boosted by restoration of Assamese to its rightful position in 1873. The size was swelled up by the increased number of employees and professionals together with the 'native' entrepreneurs that also included a few tea planters. However, their new professional and occupational engagement did not entirely detach them from their historical position, and therefore, they had also to respond to the issue of constant hike of land revenue, a concern common with the peasantry at large. In the wake of peasant rebellion, the position newly acquired by the rickety intelligentsia helped them engage the colonial administration for negotiation. The basic interests of this rickety intelligentsia are reflected well by the agenda and actions of different sabhas[2] they spearheaded during the last three decades of the nineteenth century when the common peasantry as a distinct class was active with its overtly anticolonial agenda. This small section of petit-bourgeoisie, professionals, traders and employees, despite their common concern for the growth and development of the Assamese language and social reforms, may be seen as what Gramsci termed as an "essential" social group (2007, pp. 6–7). Notwithstanding its enormous contributions in reshaping Asomiya as a distinct cultural and linguistic identity besides preparing the ground for the proliferation of a modern middle class, this category did not contribute much to the growth of any 'nationalist spirit' until the appearance of the Congress. While comprehending nationalism in the colonial context as politics against colonialism, the collective actions of the peasantry in contemporary Assam can only be regarded as the emerging nationalist spirit without dismissing the historical importance of the progressive and enlightened ideas propagated by the English-educated intelligentsia.

Although the formation of the National Congress in 1885 started attracting imagination of Assamese intelligentsia, the conformism it inherited debilitated visualization of the socio-economic as well as political future of Assam. Under the aegis of the educated gentry, the Assam Association that came into being in 1903 as the valley-based political organization remained primarily engaged with submission of petitions and memorials seeking more benefits from the colonial government and remained almost silent during the swadeshi movement as well as on the issue of formation of the Province of Eastern Bengal and Assam in 1906 (Mahanta, 2010, pp. 232–275; Dutta, 1969, pp. 41–45). However, deep engagement with the language question, now reconstructed as a conspiracy by the Bengali officials in Assam, the so-called Asomiya middle class, sharpened the existing societal divides between the Assamese and the Bengalis, which has still been influencing the political processes. At the same time, it welcomed the colonial project of peasantization inaugurated in the beginning of the last century backed by the logic of enhancement of both agricultural production and revenue. The obvious consequence is large-scale settlement of the hard-pressed tenants of East Bengal zamindars to make productive the water-logged, jungle-infested land of the Brahmaputra Valley, the wasteland in the colonial lexicon.

The tenants from East Bengal, with overwhelming majority of Muslims, favorably responded to the new colonial project to find the Brahmaputra Valley not only as their lebensraum but also as a land of plentiful opportunities. The political implications of massive immigration are expounded by many scholarly works (Kar, 1990; Guha, 2006; Barooah, 2010; Misra, 2017; Nag, 2017); however, it may be reiterated that the colonial language played a critical role in construction of a new set of social differences that constituted the core of political discourse gradually intensified by the growing numerical strength of the immigrants. The number of immigrant peasants scattered mainly in the western part of the Brahmaputra Valley in the first decade of the twentieth century was not more than the plantation labour brought to the tea estates of the eastern part. The Census Commissioner in 1911, however, characterized the immigration as a peaceful invasion of Assam by advancing hordes of Mymensinghia army. When the colonial project of peasantization through the settlement of immigrants continued, the unabated influx naturally caused apprehensions. The strange aggressive immigrants settled indiscriminately in the valley, besides occupying the village reserved land, forests, and the riverine *chars*, started procuring arable land of the autochthons. When alienation of autochthons' land and the growing strength of the culturally different immigrants appeared as a threat for the Assamese race,[3] C.S. Mulan, the census commissioner between 1921 and 1931 projected the influx as "conquest", "attack", "invasion" and so on.[4]

The colonial project of peasantization that continued with unabated influx not only created a fertile ground for communal polarization but also generated apprehensions amongst the plain tribes, especially the Bodos.

Formation of the Tribal League in 1933 after the demand of the Kachari Jubak Sammilani placed before the Simon Commission for reservation of seats in the provincial legislature for the plain tribes reflected the growing political aspirations of the valley-based myriad racial groups.[5] The short history of the Tribal League till it became a non-political entity in 1952 is crucial not only for the political struggle to protect tribal land but also for reshaping multitude of racial/ethnic identities that started gradually demystifying the perceived notion of assimilation of the valley based ethnocultural categories to form the so-called Asomiya nationality. Although the numerically strong but culturally and linguistically diverse laborers in the plantation sector had never been a serious concern of the cultural project of the Asomiya intelligentsia as they were not perceived to be a cultural threat, the immigrant Muslim peasants were expected to merge with the Asomiya cultural identity, and they favorably responded to it. The fear and apprehension of Bengali domination, however, continued and reappeared in the post-partition political theatre of the Brahmaputra Valley. Starting with little over twelve thousand in August 1947, while the number of Hindu Bengalis taking shelter in Assam as refugees constantly increased in the subsequent years after independence, the Asom Jatiya Mahasabha perceived it as a political design of the Bengalis for creation of a Brihattar Banga Samrajya. The riots in Assam in 1948 and 1950, characterized by the Calcutta press as "Bengali Kheda Andolon" were essentially to desist from running separate schools for Bengalis and to impose Assamese as a medium of instruction. Meanwhile, the government of Assam initiated steps to make Assamese as the medium of instruction in all the schools of Assam valley amidst steep opposition from the Bengali Hindus. The situation was worsened by West Bengal's claim over Goalpara district on linguistic consideration at the time of linguistic division of the states in the mid-1950s.

Consequent upon adoption of the principle of linguistic provinces for the Congress in 1920, the Assam Pradesh (Provincial) Congress Committee (APCC) emerged as the sole organized political movement with its defined territoriality to cover only the presumably Assamese-dominated areas, excluding the Surma Valley, that remained, as before, under the organizational command of the Bengal Provincial Congress. For its ideological expansion transcending all religious or socioeconomic fortifications and integrating the regional sentiment with the pan-Indian nationalist discourse, the primary concern of the APCC since its inception had been the issues specific to the regional society. For ensuring political integration of Assam with India, the leadership of the APCC precipitously opposed the All India Congress Committee for its position on the Cabinet Mission's proposal to group Assam with a predominantly Muslim zone in Eastern India. The same leadership was also instrumental in the political integration of the hill districts, which were hardly influenced by the pan-Indian nationalist discourse, with the nation state. The political consideration of the caste Hindu Asomiya elite leadership of the Congress was to retain the hills under its hegemonic political control without altering the colonial map of Assam. Amazingly, while the post-partition Hindu Bengali immigrants were treated as "refugees", the first attempt to push back and prevent the increasing number of Muslim immigrants was made through the Immigrants (Expulsion from Assam) Act, 1950 amidst communal riots. Nearly one lakh immigrants, who reportedly left Assam during the riots, however, came back following the agreement between India and Pakistan, the Nehru–Liaquat Pact, signed just one month after the enactment of the previous legislation. In the changed circumstances, when the political influences of the Assam Provincial Muslim League virtually disappeared after independence, the ruling Congress appeared in the guise of savior of the Muslim immigrants to monopolize the electoral dividends for the decades to come.

V Politics of Citizenship

The National Congress with its "regionalist ethos", the camouflaged political interests of the caste Hindu Asomiya elite, was successful in suppressing some of the localized political platforms that emerged in Assam in the wake of independence. However, it failed to keep its political territory undisturbed for long. Not only the Nagas but many other dominant communities also initiated their negotiations with the Indian state with their own imagination of greater autonomy and sovereignty. The militant form of political negotiations, often characterized as "insurgency", based on reconstructed history of the historically excluded communities resulted in the political disintegration of Assam that substantially reduced the political space of the Congress, on one hand, and total obliteration of the political hegemony of the caste Hindu Asomiya elite over the highlanders, on the other.

Nevertheless, with its irreproachable hegemony, the Congress continued its domination in the electoral politics of the Brahmaputra Valley till the Sixth Lok Sabha elections held in 1977, though the so-called Congress system was rejected by the people of India at large, at least for the time being. The electoral scenario of the Valley, too, however, had dramatically changed in a short while when the people rejected the Congress in the Legislative Assembly elections held in 1978. Nor did the Janata Party despite being in power at the center and having an alliance with the political forces, which grew with their demands for further disintegration of Assam on ethnic lines[6] could emerge as a clear alternative[7] to the Congress. Significant enough was the electoral victory of the Left parties[8] in a situation when the Congress, which always enjoyed mass support of the "immigrants", lost its power for the first time. Definitely it was formidable for the politically insignificant infant political platforms such as the Asom Jatiyatabadi Dal (AJD) and the Purbanchaliya Lok Parishad (PLP) which sought electoral mandate with the imagery of "jatiyotabad" (nationalism) constructed on the issue of foreign nationals in Assam, distancing themselves from all other existing political forces.

The reinvented jatiyotabad, although electorally despised by people, became more vigorous after the elections. Now it started political articulation of the officially reinforced question of foreign nationals[9] to make citizenship the most significant issue in electoral politics. As it was alleged, the police officials on instruction of the government of Assam hurriedly challenged the authenticity of citizenship of about 70,000 voters in the process of revision of the electoral rolls (ERs) before the by-election to the Mongaldoi LokSabha constituency that was to be held in December 1979. Subsequently, the All Assam Students Union (AASU), which remained almost silent on the issue after focusing the question of an unbridled influx of people from outside Assam in its twenty-four-point Charter of Demands formulated in 1974, was persuaded by some officers of the Border Police Organization for "filing objections against Bangladeshi voters, in the wake of the revision of ERs being done by the Election Commission" (Bhattacharyya, 2018, p. 121). Some senior police officials also supported the leadership of the PLP by providing information required for making the issue of foreign nationals a strong base for a popular movement (Bora, 2007, p. 22). For having a common platform to launch a broad-based movement on the issue of foreign national, the All Assam Gana Sangram Parishad (AAGSP) was formed in a meeting held on 27 August 1979 convened by the leadership of the Dibrugarh unit of AASU, as insisted by the PLP. The thinly attended meeting decided that a movement would be launched with the single issue of detection and deportation of foreign nationals on the basis of the NRC 1951.

However, the AAGSP soon became a much larger political platform and its deeper engagement with the rural society helped the movement to continue with the well-engineered pogroms. All the nationalist parties, except the BJP and the Janata Party, were projected as enemies. The political attacks, nonetheless, continued to be much sharper against the organized lefts, especially the Communist Party of India (Marxist) and its mass organizations, when the common Asomiya followers of the other parties had already shifted their political camp. Continuing the agitation with a reduced intensity, the AASU became active in the formation of a new regional political party during the post-1983 phase of the movement. Finally, the Assam Accord was signed on 15 August 1985, though its essence was not radically different from what was proposed in 1981 by the ruling Congress at the center as the solution to the problem of foreign nationals. The nucleus of the AASU leadership now ready for election politics with the image of a savior of the Asomiya national identity became more active in the formation of a new political party, uniting the PLP and the AJD. Although the PLP was initially unhappy with the accord; the lure of power in the changed circumstances compelled it to merge with the AGP formed just three months after signing of the Accord. The core of the leadership of the newly formed party, of course, was constituted by the leadership of the movement just retired from the AASU. Soon, many of them had to migrate from the university hostels to Dispur after capturing power through the Assembly elections in December 1985. Large-scale violence was triggered off by the Assembly elections in 1983 as the ERs allegedly contained a huge chunk of illegal voters, but the same ERs became uncontaminated in the changed circumstances when the reconstructed "Asomiya nationalism" assured its leadership easy access to power.

The accord that was instrumental for capturing power by the new leadership emerged through the movement, but it reinforced the political cleavages within the Assamese society already instilled by the prolonged violent movement which insinuated communalism. While the Muslim minority with its history of experiencing indiscriminate political harassment started political consolidation (Nath, 2019), other ethnic communities became apprehensive about their existence as distinct linguistic and cultural identities for use of the undefined term 'Assamese' in the Accord (Dewri, 2001). The six years of political mayhem created by the historic 'Asomiya nationalist movement' followed by the pandemonium of AGP rule (Sarmah, 2002) brought back the Congress to power, now to politically maneuver the difference. Implementation of the Assam Accord was not on the political agenda of the AGP, nor did the Congress which replaced the AGP in power could spare time for it. The immediate political priorities for the Congress were the growing popularity of the militancy under the aegis of the United Liberation Front of Assam (ULFA) that grew under the shadow of the Assam Movement and gained momentum during the period of the AGP in power, and the movement for separate state galvanized by the Bodo leadership. Besides the political engineering for damaging the basic spirit of the Assamese militancy reflected through ULFA, the ploy of the Congress leadership to politically disintegrate the Assamese society appeared in a form reimagining autonomy for the major ethnic communities of the Brahmaputra Valley.

Political negotiation with the violent movements of the Bodos that finally culminated on formation of the Bodoland Territorial Council (BTC) in 2003 under the Sixth Schedule to the Constitution was preceded by an ad hoc mechanism – the Bodoland Autonomous Council (BAC) constituted through a state legislation enacted in 1993, adding fuel to the fire. Concomitantly, three other autonomous councils were formed in 1995 reinforcing distinct cultural identities of the Rabha, the Mising and the Lalung (Tiwa). The number of such autonomous councils proliferated after a decade, again during the Congress rule in the state, reconstructing cultural distinctness of three other racial categories, namely the Deori, the Sonowal Kachari and the Thengal Kachari (Lalfakzuala and Sarmah, 2019). All these six communities, despite their nuanced cultural differences, were considered to be integral components of what has generally been comprehended as the broad 'Asomiya nationality'; nevertheless, they all occupied lower positions in the social hierarchy dominated by the upper caste Hindus. With such constructions, implementation of the Assam Accord was relegated to the back bench in everyday politics of the valley by both the AGP and the Congress, although the issue of foreign nationals was kept alive for electoral politics.

Amazingly, the issue of foreign nationals in Assam becomes a major concern mainly for the right-wing political parties only in the run-up to the elections. While the political leadership remained conspicuously indifferent to the question of deportation engaging Bangladesh in any negotiation, more than two lakh thirty thousand people in Assam were marked as ‘D’ voters (Doubtful voters) in 1998 debarring their right to vote, unless they prove their citizenship in the Foreigners’ Tribunal constituted for detection of foreigners. A large number of such cases referred to the Tribunals are yet to be resolved. The decision for updating the NRC 1951 was taken in 2005, but the Pilot Project for the exercise started exactly after five years. It was postponed due to violent resistance. While the BJP made its big claim to deport all Bangladeshis from Assam, of course with the promise to treat the Hindus as refugees, before the parliamentary elections held in 2014, the process for updating the NRC 1951 began with judicial activism. The apparently judicial initiative was welcomed by all political forces active in the Brahmaputra Valley across their ideological difference, as it was expected to resolve, at least, the question of detection of the illegal immigrants for the deportation process to be followed.

The mammoth exercise that continuously engaged a huge workforce for a long time came to an end with the final NRC published on 31 August 2019, confirming Indian citizenship to 3.11 crore people of Assam excluding 19.06 lakh applicants, whose citizenship has to be determined by the Foreigners’ Tribunals. Both the sanctity of the exercise and the accuracy of the outcome were, however, immediately questioned by different political parties as well as many other apparently nonpolitical organizations. The AASU expressed its resentment because of the phenomenal gap between the estimated numbers of illegal migrants stated by the central government from time to time and the total number of people excluded by the NRC. As pointed out by different organizations, the NRC excluded a large number of people from various tribal communities of the state, more prominently the Bengali Hindus. The total number of Hindu Bengalis excluded by the NRC is more than the total number of Muslims of East Bengal origin, as alleged.[10] The immediate reaction of the BJP was overtly communal. The president of the State Unit of the BJP alleged that claims of people having surnames like Biswas, Sarkar and Saha were intentionally rejected by the NRC authorities, and therefore, besides demanding an NRC for the country as a whole, he claimed that new laws would be brought, if necessary, to ensure the protection of Hindus.[11]

In the specific context, Assam therefore, the basic ethos of the Citizenship (Amendment) Bill, 2016 (CAB) introduced on the Lok Sabha on 19 July 2016 cannot be isolated from the whole process of NRC on one hand and the Assam Accord on the other (Roy, 2019). While the CAB was steeply contested by the people of the North East in general and Assam in particular for the fear that it would not only legitimize especially the Hindu immigrants who entered the region even after 25 March 1971 but would also open the new floodgates for infiltrators from Bangladesh, the discourse on the secular character of the constitution was not much visible in other parts of the country. The bill could not be placed in the Rajya Sabha mainly because of the political maneuver of the combined regionalist forces in the North East; the fragile issue-based alliance, however, soon became instrumental for the BJP in the subsequent Lok Sabha elections. While the Citizenship (Amendment) Act, 2019 became a political reality followed by nationwide contestations, the regionalist political leadership sharing power with the BJP in different states of the region preferred to remain silent. Nevertheless, spontaneous protest in Assam has been backed by the renewed anxiety of losing cultural and linguistic identity now aggravated by a fear of getting politically marginalized by the Bengali Hindus. Therefore, the sanctity of the Assam Accord, specifically its Clause 6, became a crucial issue. The BJP has tried to ameliorate its political position the North East by extenuating the historical political differences. The political engineering thus warranted exclusion of the states with Inner Line Permit (ILP) and the areas covered by the Sixth Schedule to the Constitution from the jurisdiction of the amended citizenship legislation. With that logic, Manipur has been brought under the ILP, the colonial device of exclusion framed in 1873 essentially required for fortification of the Brahmaputra Valley (Sarmah, 2018). It implies that, in the entire North East, only the plain districts of Assam and Tripura, excluding the areas covered the Sixth Schedule, will have to accommodate all those post-1971 Hindu immigrants now to be treated as citizens while the number of this new category of citizens may continuously increase. Appearing in the guise of savior, the government of India constituted a committee for working out the modality for constitutional safeguards for the "Assamese", essentialization of the historical differences between the "immigrant Muslims" and the indigenous people. The ruling BJP concomitantly announced its decision to create more autonomous councils for the ethnic communities demanding their inclusion in the category of Scheduled Tribes (Sarma and Hazarika, 2020).

VI Conclusion

The preceding discussion clearly delineates that the essential social category that came into being in the mid-nineteenth century, Brahmaputra Valley inherited a rational set of beliefs and practices from the so-called Bengal renaissance. The allegiance to colonialism demonstrated by this category was, therefore, not inimitable. In the given historical context, this category was incontrovertibly committed to reshape Asomiya as a distinct cultural and linguistic identity. However, the contemporary peasantry at large could overcome the dilemma of loyalty to and confrontation with colonialism.

Continuing the allegiance to colonial rule along with a commitment to further development of Asomiya linguistic identity, the emerging Asomiya middle class towards the end of the nineteenth century had sharpened the existing societal divides between the Asomiya and the Bengalis, implying Asomiya as a subset of Assamese. The emerging Asomiya middle class was, however, not averse to the colonial project of peasantization through the indiscriminate settlement of the strange aggressive immigrants, overwhelmingly Muslims, since beginning of the last century because the later consciously identified themselves with the Asomiya linguistic and cultural identity. Although communalization of resource distribution was inflicted upon the Brahmaputra Valley by the colonial administration, it could not outweigh the increasing influences of pan-Indian nationalism on the emerging Asomiya middle class. The nationalist ideology wrought by the Congress under the leadership of the Asomiya elites, however, compromised with the popular sentiment against the Bengali Hindus, rooted deeply in the language politics of Assam.

Although alienation of and right to autochthons' arable land in the predominantly agrarian economy of the Brahmaputra Valley has always been as a major political concern during the postcolonial phase, the question of citizenship of the immigrants had never influenced the electoral politics during the period of political hegemony enjoyed by the Congress. Although predominated by upper caste Hindu Asomiya, the Congress always projected itself as the savior of the immigrants, obviously for its electoral dividends. The political decline of the Congress by the end of 1970s, however, had brought new opportunities for the power seeking incipient regional political forces. In their imagination of a new form of identity politics, conscious remodeling of "Asomiya nationalism" required the numerically conspicuous immigrants of East Bengal/Bangladesh origin as the immediate reference point, essentializing citizenship for political mobilization of the common Hindu Assamese. Now the threat to "Asomiya identity" has been reconstructed, shifting political attention from language to citizenship. Since the immigrants are overwhelmingly Muslims, such a political maneuver naturally provided enormous opportunities for the BJP to demonstrate its solidarity with the reimagined "Asomiya nationalism", and the Assam Movement, besides all other political implications, created space for Hinduization of citizenship. While the so-called Accord helped the newly formed regional party to capture power in the state, the same irrevocable "Public Law Contract" became instrumental for the communalization of citizenship, a successful experimentation of Hindu nationalism in Assam to be replicated nationwide.

Notes

1 The province was newly structured mainly for convenience of colonial administration and it included five Assamese dominated districts of the Brahmaputra Valley, Goalpara where Bengali and Assamese cultures overlapped, the two Bengali dominated districts of Surma Valley, that is, Sylhet and Cacher, and all other hill districts. This administrative amalgamation with a sharp political/

cultural divide between the hills and the plains instilled by the Inner Line Regulations of 1873, juxtaposed the relatively smaller Assamese cultural/linguistic identity with the bigger Bengali cultural identity within a single administrative unit.

2 While the Jorhat Sarvajanik Sabha was formed in the middle of the 1880s, the Tezpur Ryot Sabha, the Nowgaong Ryot Sabha and the Upper Assam Association came into being in the 1880s. Mahanta (2010, pp. 213–223) provides a comprehensive analysis of these Sabhas/Associations.

3 For instance, Ambikagiri Raychoudhury formed the Asamiya Samrakshini Sabha in 1926 for the protection of the Assamese race.

4 For the hate campaign against the immigrants by Mulan, see 1931 Census Report, p. 51.

5 Although the Kachari Jubak Sammilani was formed in 1928 for representation before the Simon Commission, it reflected the political aspiration of the plain tribes, especially of the Bodos, and led to formation of the Tribal League in 1933. This was the beginning of the organized movement of the Bodos (Dewri 2001; Choudhury 2007; Pathak 2010).

6 The Janata Party had an alliance with the Plain Tribal Council of Assam (PTCA) formed in 1967 with the demand for Udayachal as a separate state for the plain tribes of Assam, and the Ujoni Asom Rajya Parishad (UARP) formed in 1970 with the demand for a separate state consisting of three upper Assam districts having concentration of the Ahoms.

7 Out of the 126 constituencies, the Janata Party could win 53 seats and the PTCA won 4 seats.

8 For the first time in the history of electoral politics in Assam, the Communist Party of India (Marxist) alone returned eleven candidates and the other Left forces such as the Communist Party of India, the Revolutionary Communist Party of India and the Socialist Unity Centre of India together returned another eleven seats.

9 In a conference of the state electoral officers held on 24 October 1978, the chief election commissioner stated that large inclusion of foreign nationals (in electoral rolls) in some states especially in the North-Eastern region was alarming and required drastic action (*The Assam Tribune*, 25 October 1978). Subsequently, the chief minister of Assam, who belonged to the Janata Party, announced in the State Assembly on 16 March 1978 that influx of foreign nationals was assuming alarming proportions (*The Assam Tribune*, 17 March 1979).

10 Without referring to any source, as the final NRC did not disclose anything about the people excluded, *Doinik Asom*, a widely circulated Assamese daily from Guwahati made the headline on 13 September 2019 stating that the NRC excluded 6.9 lakh Hindu Bengalis besides giving the ethnic community-wise breakup of the people excluded.

11 For immediate reactions to the final NRC expressed by different political parties, see the *Assam Tribune*, 1 September 2019.

References:

Barooah, Nirode K. (2010). *Gopinath Bardoloi, 'The Assam Problem' and Nehru's Centre*. Bhabani Print & Publications, Guwahati.

Baruah, Sanjib Kumar. (1980). Cudgel of Chauvinism or Tangled Nationality Question? *Economic and Political Weekly*, 15 (11), pp. 543–45.

Baruah, Sanjib Kumar. (1981). Little Nationalism Turned Chauvinist: A Comment. *Economic and Political Weekly*, 16 (15), pp. 676–81.

Bhattacharyya, Hiranya Kumar. (2018). *Operation Lebensraum: Illegal Migration from Bangladesh*. Bloomsbury, New Delhi.
Bora, Atul. (2007). *Abirata Sangram*. Ma Prokashak Goshthi, Guwahati.
Chatterjee, Partha. (1999). *The Partha Chatterjee Omnibus*. Oxford University Press, U.K.
Choudhury, Sujit. (2007). *The Bodos: Emergence and Assertion of an Ethnic Minority*. Indian Institute of Advance Studies, Shimla.
Dewri, Indibar. (2001). *Janagosthiya Samasya: Ateet Bartaman Bhabishyat*. Journal Emporium, Nalbari.
Conversi, Daniele. (2004). Can Nationalism Studies and Ethnic/Racial Studies be Brought Together? *Journal of Ethnic and Migration Studies*. 30 (4).
Dutta, K.N. (1969). *Landmarks of the Freedom Struggle in Assam*. Lawyer's Book Stall, Guwahati.
Gohain, Hiren. (1985). *Assam: A Burning Question*. Spectrum Publications, Guwahati.
Gohain, Hiren (1980). Cudgel of Chauvinism. *Economic and Political Weekly*. 15 (8).
Guha, Amalendu. (1980). Little Nationalism Turned Chauvinist: Assam's Anti-Foreigner Upsurge, 1979-80. *Economic and Political Weekly*, Special Number. (pp. 781–84).
Guha, Amalendu. 1991). *Medieval and Early Colonial Assam: Society Polity Economy*. KP Bagchi & Company, New Delhi.
Guha, Amalendu. (2006). *Planter Raj to Swaraj: Freedom Struggle & Electoral Politics in Assam*. Tulika Books, New Delhi.
Gramsci, Antonio. (2007). *Selections from the Prison Notebooks*. Lawrence and Wishart, London.
Kar, M. (1990). *Muslims in Assam Politics*. Omsons Publications, Delhi.
Lalfakzuala, Joseph K and Sarmah, Bhupen. (2019). The Constitution and Beyond: Negotiating Autonomy for the Plain Tribes of Assam. *Social Change and Development*, XVI.
Marshal, T.H. (1950). *Citizenship and Social Class: And Other Essays*. Cambridge University Press, New York.
Mahanta, Prafulla. (2010). *Asomiya Madhyabitta Shreneer Itihas*. Bhabani Print & Publications, Guwahati.
Marx, Karl and Engels, Frederick. (1977). *Selected Works*. 1. Progress Publishers, Moscow.
Mills, A.J. Moffat. (1984). *Report on the Province of Assam*. Publication Board Assam, Guwahati.
Misra, Tilottama. Assam: A Colonial Hinterland. *Economic and Political Weekly*, August 9, 1980.
Misra, U. (2017). *Burden of History: Assam and the Partition – Unresolved Issues*. Oxford University Press, New Delhi.
Nag, S. (2017). *Beleaguered Nation: The Making and Unmaking of the Assamese Nationality*. Manohar Publishers and Distributors, New Delhi.
Nath, Monoj Kumar. (2019). Muslim Politics in Assam: The Case of AIUDF. *Studies in Indian Politics*, 7(1), pp. 33–43.
Omvedt, Gail. (1981). Little Nationalism Turned Chauvinist: A Comment. *Economic and Political Weekly*. 16 (13).

Pathak, Suryasikha. (2010). Tribal Politics in the Assam: 1933-1947. *Economic and Political Weekly*. XLV (10).
Prabhakara, M. S. (2012). *Looking Back into the Future: Identity and Insurgency in Northeast India*. New Delhi, Routledge.
Roy, Anupama. (2019). The Citizenship (Amednment) Bill, 2016 and the Aporia of Citizenship. *Economic and Political Weekly*. LIV (49).
Sarmah, Bhupen. (2002). Asom Gana Parishad: Emergence and its Performance in Jana, Arun K. and Sarmah, Bhupen (ed.). *Class, Ideology and Political Parties in India*. South Asian Publishers Pvt. Ltd, New Delhi.
Sarmah, Bhupen. (2018). India's Northeast and the Enigma of the Nation-state. *Alternatives: Global, Local, Political*, 42 (3).
Sarma, Chandan Kumar and Hazarika, Obja Borah. (2020). Anti-CAA Protests and State Response in Assam: Identity Issues Challenge Hindutva-based Politics. *Economic and Political Weekly*, ISSN (Online) – 2349-8846, 55 (14).

Chapter 8

From 'Filthy Migrants'[1] to *Khilonjiya Musalmaan*

The Saga of Citizenship Question in Assam

Shofiul Alom Pathan

1 Introduction

What I vividly remember is that I was a student of the ninth standard at that time. We were gossiping and taunting each other before the beginning of a tutorial class during a humid summer afternoon. Causal jokes were being thrown at each other and one of my tutorial mates suddenly made a filthy joke about the Miya Muslim[2] *community in Assam while objectifying their typical dressing sense and visual attributes. Immediately, another friend within our bunch pointed out that I was a Muslim and one should refrain from making such a racial slur. Realizing the issue, the first guy got embarrassed, paused for a while and tried to make up on whatever slur he hurled at the community before. As a process of making it up and justifying his remark, he looked up to the other guy, saying, "That is fine; he is not a Miya Muslim". Then he turned towards me and asked for a validation: "Isn't it true?" Out of the awkwardness and disgust of such a mentality, I did not respond to him except to give him an ambiguous expression. I was too young to counter something theoretically or on empirical grounds about everyday discrimination and the bullying of Miya Muslim in Assam during those times.*

Two significant issues arise from this otherwise casual conversation amongst friends. First, bullying is deeply rooted in the historical and everyday stereotyping of Miya Muslims where they become synonymous with "illegal immigrants" and/or "doubtful Bangladeshis" and so on. In Assam, this phenomenon is related to the larger crisis of citizenship question in postcolonial Assam. Second, this simultaneously also highlights a politics of difference – where the "local" Muslims are of a "similar" kind and culturally an inseparable part of the imagination of a collective "indigenous" Assamese identity –unlike the Miya Muslims.

This chapter tries to interrogate three major concerns here. First, the chapter deals with locating Muslim identity questions against the backdrop of the larger Assamese society – particularly highlighting the Miya Muslim community. Second, the chapter attempts to highlight the Muslim citizenship question in Assam–an ongoing crisis with the inception of postcolonial

DOI: 10.4324/9781003345152-12

India. Third, keeping the citizenship issue at the heart of the analysis, the chapter tries to highlight the politics of difference – where a quasi-institutionalized binary of "indigenous" versus "migrant" Muslims operate – on the basis of cultural and linguistic identity. A significant and continuous aspect of the chapter resides in the narratives of different participants, including my own reflection, on cultural identity and the citizenship question. Being a Muslim Assamese, my own reflections through lived experience on Muslim identity and citizenship question in Assam have been an everyday yet intense issue that I consistently ponder– beyond and inclusive of its spatial and temporal boundaries. In this context, I have particularly attempted to use the idea of "reflexive ethnography" to talk about different situations, observations, conversations and narratives as part of my long-term ethnographic engagement with the topic over the years. Reflexive ethnography as an approach becomes crucial as it highlights the ways in which the research outcome is affected by the social location of the researcher and the process of doing research (Davies, 2002, pp. 4–5). This approach becomes crucial for an easy like this where the relation of the researcher and the participants is very close. Within the larger domain of ethnographic work, I have used semistructured interviews to understand and analyze the narratives of respondents related to citizenship crisis experience, including the present as well as historical context. Semistructured interviews require attention to the context of the interview and a relationship between the participants–beyond and inclusive of the themes of discussion (Davies, 2002, p. 95).

II Muslim Assamese and Assamese Identity: A Reflection

Muslim Assamese[3] is not a homogeneous category but rather an umbrella term that includes various types of Muslims in Assam, each having different histories of acceptance of Islam, migration and historical assimilation through marriages. Contrary to the dominant political narratives about monolithic Islam – that it spread through the power of the sword worldwide, South Asian Islam has always been distinct with the subcontinent's plural cultural and linguistic traditions. Sufism (*tawassuf*), a form of Islamic mysticism had been by and large one of the dominant ideologies when it came to preaching and propagation of Islamic religious values embedded in local culture (Metcalf, 2009, pp. xvii–xviii). In fact, in medieval Bengal (which includes present-day Bangladesh too), growth of Islam is attributed to a "creative adaptation" of Islamic theological preaching with local beliefs and practices in a gradual manner (Eaton, 2009, p. 217) Religious change in early medieval and medieval Bengal can't be detached from the larger socio-economic transformation and emergence of an agrarian economy and community itself. This gradual process of localizing Islam in vernacular writings and cosmologies resulted in a twin process of "Islamisation" and "Peasantisation" (Ibid, 2009, pp. 207–208).

Assam, which was once part of the undivided Bengal[4] during British colonialism, bears somewhat similar stories related to the first Muslim population in Assam. Several Sufi saints migrated to Assam during the medieval time. The acceptance of Islam through Sufi saints and captured Muslim soldiers from northern India marrying local women were some of the prominent factors of early Muslim Assamese population in Assam starting from 13th century CE. Many of them today are known as Goria and Moria Muslims depending on their history and occupation. They constitute a significant percentage of local Muslim population (Hussain, 2015, pp. 14–19). With every successive Muslim invasion of Assam, the Muslim population increased gradually due to the influence of preachers and captured soldiers, especially in lower Assam (Nath, 2021, pp. 17–19). Muslims of Barak Valley, who are Bengali speakers, are mostly converted from Hinduism during the Mughal era and Muslim rulers of Bengal (Hussain, 2015, p. 20). Miya Muslims living in Assam today are decedents of migrants from then East Bengal, particularly from Mymensingh, Rongpur and Pabna districts (Hussain, 1993, pp. 200–201). Miya Muslims migrated to Assam on influence of the British colonial government through some organized policies, which started since late 19th century. This migration intensified under the active support of colonial government as Muslim peasants were brought in for paddy cultivation to meet with the food shortage in Brahmaputra valley. A huge chunk of the Miya Muslim peasants were also brought by the colonial government for the cultivation of jute as a cash crop to earn more revenues (Nath, 2021, pp. 29–32). Some North Indian Muslims migrated to the state of Assam from mainly Indian state of Uttar Pradesh or Bihar in search of livelihood during the later stages of British colonialism and more after independence (Hussain, 1993, pp. 197–200). There also exist Muslim categories like Deshi, Juluha, Maimal and others that are considered to be part of the earlier Muslim population in Assam, although they are numerically not very high.

Assamese is not a static identity but, rather, an always evolving and dynamic one. Assam as a place and Assamese people over the years formed an identity that is based on "mixing, blending and sharing with multiple communities" (Saikia, 2017, p. 112). In this regard, Assam and Assamese identity has never been a homogeneous one[5]but a mix of several tribal, non-tribal groups who migrated to Assam in different periods of history. The tendency to homogenize and highlight the dominant Assamese caste Hindu practices as core "Assamese culture" is not only one-dimensional but also pushes several tribal and non-tribal communities – including the Muslims– at the margin[6] of social and political life in Assam.

I was born and raised in a small town located in the central part of Assam called Tezpur. Tezpur is also known as "cultural heartland" of Assam, a place from which hailed several prominent cultural icons. Jyoti Prasad Agarwala, one of the most celebrated cultural icons of modern Assamese society, was from Tezpur. A prominent litterateur, Congressman and a progressive Assamese nationalist; Agarwala showed how local nationalistic sentiments could very well go in parallel with Indian nationalism and internationalism without generating any kind of conflict (Guha, 1980, p. 1703). Agarwala wrote the famous poem called "AxomiyaDekarUkti" (Saikia, 2020). In the poem, Agarwala emphasizes the forming an Assamese cultural identity that is inclusive of all the ethnic groups – from tribal to nontribal, from the hill dwellers to the plains, inclusive of all the migrant groups which have immensely contributed to the building of the Assamese society. Here Agarwala identifies Miya Muslims by the term *Na-Axamiya* which means neo-Assamese. Negotiating different kinds of parochialism and chauvinism, he conceptualized the idea of a dynamic Assamese society on the basis of acceptance, assimilation and universal human values. However, contrastingly, this idea of assimilation of Miya Muslims seems to have little implication in general, as the peasant-origin Miya Muslims still find themselves culturally excluded from the mainstream Assamese society and partly even from other Muslim counterparts in the state. They are often stereotyped as "illegal immigrants" based on language and certain visual markers of identity (Pathan & Jha, 2022). This historical exclusion has resulted in a sense of cultural alienation among the peasant Muslims as they are often treated as "doubtful" or "culturally unfamiliar" bodies in many parts of Assam. When it comes to the question of formal citizenship, the majoritarian imagination is deeply rooted in upper caste middle-class imagination of an Assamese identity – which still carries an everyday notion that still millions of Miya Muslims are crossing the international border and coming to Assam in search of land and livelihood. However, no substantial academic work thus far could establish this notion empirically; rather, this notion seems to operate on politics of exclusion and cultural unfamiliarity about the Miya Muslims in Assam. It virtually has, in recent times, become a problem of cultural psychology rather than demography or legal issue. In one of the in-depth interviews (IDI) that I conducted for this chapter, one discussant, who belongs to Goria Muslim community narrated:

> See, I feel really sad regarding the fact that in the name of upgrading the NRC, many people had to commit suicide or go through a painful process of identity verification. It feels really sad to see all these harassment[s]. The Miya Muslims who are living in Assam for several generations must be considered as indigenous. My problem is with the people who are still coming daily to Assam in places like Dhubri etc. It goes for both Hindus and Muslim immigrants.[7]

It is explicit from such opinion that the dominant imagination among mainstream Assamese society still carries the notion that lakhs of illegal Muslim migrants are still crossing over from Bangladesh to Assam on an everyday basis to date. This idea is propagated and consumed on a daily basis through different generations since the inception of the Assam Movement (1979–85), the most prominent event related to citizenship crisis in postcolonial Assam. Even after the publication of final draft of National Register of Citizens (NRC) on 31 August 2019 – where only 19 lakhs people were excluded–the notion didn't change for the better. The NRC up gradation process was initiated by the Supreme Court in 2015.[8] Out of 19 lakh people excluded from the NRC final draft, only five lakhs were Miya Muslims and it excluded several thousands, if not lakhs, of local tribal and nontribal population (Ali, 2019).[9] There were allegation of several discrepancies at the local level while preparing the document. Although many welcomed it as a base document for a more correct NRC in future, the Hindu nationalist along with some Assamese nationalist hardliner argued that many Muslim names were illegally entered (PTI, 2019). Opinions like this makes the Muslim citizenship question in Assam beyond and above the rational, legal notion but more of an everyday cultural imagination that is systematically propagated among mainstream Assamese society through a discourse of doubt and exclusion (Azad et al., 2020).[10] In postcolonial Assam, often this process of exclusion is deeply rooted in the crisis of the citizenship question. Violence, in various forms like physical, cultural, psychological and structural forms, has occasionally surfaced related to any event or legislation concerning the citizenship question. Hence, it becomes imperative to look at how the historical question of citizenship in Assam is intrinsically connected to violence.

III Citizenship and History of Violence

In the prime-time discussions on national media or even at the regional/local level, Muslim citizenship and the upgradation process of NRC in Assam were discussed in tandem. However, this issue dates back to the NRC of 1951 and many subsequent political (often violent) developments thereafter. Post-1947, an Assamese middle class started to take shape, which began targeting the Bengali middle class and later the numerically prominent Miya Muslims. This targeting was of course implicitly based on the citizenship issue as they were considered as "outsiders" or "others" of an emerging Assamese middle-class nationalistic imagination. Amalendu Guha (1980) writes that it was post-1947 and shaking off Sylhet from India that the Assamese middle class emerged stronger with language or racial riots. Guha calls it "little nationalism", which degenerated into "chauvinism" and "minority-baiting", resulting in the formation of an aggressive linguistic nationalism. The same was noted by then census superintendent R P Vaghaiwala in 1951. Both, at all India and regional levels, nationalism was a phenomenon of the middle class to create their own domination in the markets (Guha, 1980, p. 1703). Assam was also not an exception,with nationalism developing at both the linguistic and the cultural frontier.

During the 1965 Indo-Pakistan war, a large number of Muslims, including known congressmen, were arrested and Muslims of Assam became victim of prejudice and discrimination. Muslims' loyalty was questioned, and it degenerated into a charged communal atmosphere in the state.

The Assamese bourgeoisie press created a war-like situation, and even on the floor of state assembly, some members continuously demanded the expulsion of "lakhs of Pakistanis" residing in Assam. These turmoils during 1960s resulted in a scheme called PIP (Prevention of Infiltration from Pakistan) in 1962. Under PIP, particularly many Muslims were harassed in the process of man hunting for "Pakistani" nationals. The Miya Muslim peasants became direct victims of PIP and only in Nagaon district from 1961 to 67 – a total of 71,081 persons were marked (detected) as "infiltrators" and out of them 66,917 were deported. The police used extra-legal instruments on Muslims and sometimes used force for the detection and deportation of Muslims. Most of the people deported were unorganized peasants without any agency in the state. The Assamese elites and middle class were silent on the atrocities by the Assam police on Muslims (Hussain, 1993, pp. 208–217). This phenomenon was not only limited to village or *char chapori* (river islands) areas where Muslim peasants reside but included many urban entrepreneur Muslims as well, who were also detained and deported. Some escaped out of fear to different districts of present-day Bangladesh. Many *Dhakkya* Muslims, that is Muslim traders who earlier hailed from pre-partition Dhaka, were detained and deported from Assam after the introduction of PIP in 1962. In the town areas of Tezpur, there are presently only a few Dhakkiya families. During one of my interviews with an older person, a Dhakkaiya Muslim man in his late 70s, narrated:

> There were many Dhakkiya, Chatgaya, Nuakhaliya people here in the town before. They were all involved in different trades ... they used bullock-carts, horse carts etc. for trading their goods and commodities. ... During 1962 during the India-China war, when we were young, most of these traders were deported to Dhaka. Police station, court, railway station were full of these people and there was chaos all round. Now, when I recall, it seems evident that the Muslim people were targeted as Pakistanis and they were chased out of the town. This manhunt continued for the next 2–3 years ...police personals used to pick up people from home during night and they were deported even without offering food & many Dhakaiya and Chatgaiya families simply left out of fear by donating all their properties in the name of the Mosque in town. These properties has remained as *waqf* properties till date.[11]

Miya Muslims similarly were particularly framed and targeted in Assam as "foreigners" or "illegal immigrants" from the time of independence. This phenomenon was not only limited to migrant Muslims as many Goria and Moria Muslim's houses were also raided in name of finding Pakistanis or foreigners.[12] However, a couple of decades later during the Assam Movement (1979–85), it reached a different proportion. A series of violent incidents were unleashed on the Miya Muslims, for example Nellie massacre being the biggest among them – drastically changed the scenario. The Nellie massacre is reported as one of the biggest incidents of collective violence in postcolonial India. The Nellie massacre happened in 1983. Nellie is the name of a place located in the heart of Assam with clusters of villages–hardly 70 km east of the capital city of Assam, Guwahati. In this massacre, the perpetrators, who primarily included people from the Tiwa tribe, Kochs, Hiras (Hindus of lower status) and others, almost 2000 people (numbers vary in different sources), were massacred within a span of a few hours, although the government and other the official sources claim the number to be less than 2000 (Kimura, 2013, pp. 68–69). Most of the killed bodies were women and children as they could not run faster than their perpetrators (Hazarika, 2000). Assam Movement was a display of agitation against all immigrant groups in Assam, but it got violently misdirected towards the poor Muslim peasants who migrated from erstwhile East Bengal. Many of the attackers' narratives later blamed that caste – Hindu, middle-class-centric leadership of Assam Movement – had manipulated them to participate in the massacre just to betray them at last (Kimura, 2013).

The communal elements associated with Assam Movement tried to portray Muslims as a threat by trying to associate them with Pakistan or Bangladesh. In fact, many of them labeled Muslims residing in Assam as foreigners indiscriminately. Several conspiracy theories emerged on the ground that Muslims will outnumber the Hindus in Assam. "Negative labeling, wild doubts and apprehensions" were expressed against the community both in implicit and explicit ways (Hussain, 1993, p. 196). This subtle communalization of an otherwise "ethnic" assertion was reflected in the form of the citizenship question, which was gradually followed up with several other events and legal provisions related to the citizenship question in Assam.

IV Complexities of Citizenship and Everyday Life: Insights from Field

After the turmoil of Assam Movement and its subsequent sustaining problem of citizenship crisis in Assam, several developments emerged with respect to the citizenship question in Assam. In fact, from the time of the Assam Movement, one new act titled the Illegal Migrants (Determination by Tribunals) Act, 1983 (IMDT) came into being. The act was introduced to detect and deport people who entered India illegally on or after March 25, 1971 *albeit* with some caution. Unlike the Foreigners Act 1946, which puts the burden of proof on the detected/suspected individual – the IMDThad put the burden of proof to declare someone as foreigners on the state authorities or the person who alleges someone to be a foreigner. Since the inception of the act, only 1,494"illegal immigrants" were deported from Assam till June 30, 2001 (Singh, 2019). IMDT, in popular opinion in Assam, got identified as a "shield" for foreigners as the majoritarian Assamese discourse registered its discontent with the act. The IMDT was scrapped by the Supreme Court of India in 2005 on the basis of a writ petition filed by the student leader Sarbananda Sonowal, who later on became the chief minister of the state. The court directed to close down all the tribunals constituted under the IMDT. However, at present, there exist 100 Foreigners Tribunals (FTs) that work primarily under the Foreigners Act, 1946. The burden of proof thereby as per the act (1946) got reverted back to the person or accused to appear before the tribunal and prove their credentials. The Foreigners (Tribunals) Order, 1964 was amended by the Ministry of Home Affairs which enables district magistrates in all States and Union Territories to set up tribunals. In Assam, the Border Police Organization, which is tasked with detecting foreigners, prepares and sends individual cases to these tribunals to decide whether an individual is foreigners or not (Singh &Karmakar, 2019). These are also known as "reference cases" in which a "suspected foreigner" gets a notice to appear before the tribunal.

The contemporary citizenship crisis worsened with the introductionof a category called Doubtful Voter (D voter) specific to Assam. During 1997, several thousand, if not lakhs of people, found themselves listed as D voters on the electoral list. In several of my visits to Barpeta district, many villagers narrated how they suddenly found their names listed as D voters while they went to cast their vote in an election – a trauma that has accompanied them since this encounter. D voter as a category was created by the Election Commission of India (ECI) under the advice and collaboration of the then Asom GanaParishad (AGP) government with the purpose of disenfranchising people who were thought to have illegally come from Bangladesh. As per statistics of 2017, there are 1,25,155D voters, where a significant majority of them are Muslims, Hindu Bengalis and Koch–Rajbongshis. This marking of "D" in front of their names are done in an arbitrary manner as it is alleged that the Border Police is given a task to mark approximately 10 to 20 people in every village, especially in a few districts of Western Assam (Siddique, 2019, p. 25). To talk about arbitrariness of marking someone as D voter, I personally interviewed a few people spread across several villages and districts in Western Assam. In many cases, it was apparent that while the father's name is included in the electoral roll, the name of his son(s) or daughter(s) has been marked as D. Such arbitrary framing of people as D voters denotes the pattern of a constructed discourse, where the perception is built on a narrative of lakhs and lakhs of "Bangladeshi Muslims" present in lower Assam. While conducting my interviews, I listened to real-life incidents of many uneducated, poor people, those who ended up in detention camps. They were tagged with being a D voter as they could not produce satisfactory proof of being a resident of Assam even though their parents, grandparents or relatives are Indian citizens. It seems evident from the pattern of targeting people as D voters that all these state apparatuses and processes target social groups that have historical connection with erstwhile

East Bengal. In this context, the Miya Muslims becomes the usual suspects of being a D voter and victim of arbitrary targeting. There are few instances of Deshi Muslims of lower Assam being markedas a D voter;[13] however, these numbers are exceptionally low among Goria, Moria and other local Muslim communities.[14]

The present-day crisis of citizenship among Muslims worsened after the initiation of the NRC process. People already grappling with D voter issue and reference cases found themselves stuck in immense suffering at both bureaucratic and a psychological level. Kamala Khatun, a 45-year-old woman from Sidhoni village of Barpeta district, narrated how she found her name as D voter even though her father's name appeared in the 1951 NRC list. She got notified by the border police and has been fighting a legal battle since the last 4 years. Meanwhile, she went to NRC hearing five times along with her family members but could not include her name in the NRC list as of now. A minor mistake of pronunciation in her name categorized her as D voter and despite showing all the documents she possessed, her name has still not been included in the list. Every day she lives through the trauma of being labeled as a foreigner and then lodged in a detention camp. During our conversation, she often trembled while narrating her uncertain future. The anxiety of ending up in detention is none less than an everyday trauma for her. She narrated how in every hearing she gets a similar kind of question, but every time, the case remains unresolved despite of assurances from the officials.With no financial fortune to rely on and affected by erosion frequently, locating newer sites of habitation, earning a living and keeping in touch with her lawyer for her citizenship updates have completely changed her life as a human being.

Historically, people belonging to Miya Muslim community, like Kamala Khatun, has lived in *char-chaporis* or nearby villages in the adjoining floodplains. They are landless, uneducated and suffer from frequent flood and erosion. Often due to illiteracy, migration in search of livelihood and lack of awareness about the long-term consequences, *char-chapori* villagers falls short in verifying whether their name appears on the electoral list. Moreover, they are least aware of the consequences of a misspelt name or address in the voter's list. Hence, while interrogating their land and other documents like voter lists, the role of tribunals and state officials becomes crucial and decisive. The officials, on the other, are largely unaware about the existential realities in the *char-chapori* areas, thereby, a minor mistake, which otherwise are unimportant in other walks of life turns out to be a major lapse in terms of deciding the citizenship status of the Miya Muslim community in Assam. On many an occasion, it has the probability to land a Miya Muslim in a detention camp due to a 'silly' mistake on the part of officials.

During another interview with Younus Ali, a 37-year-old sculptor from Kandapara village in Barpeta told me that he has now developed severe insomnia over the years on fear of ending up in detention camp. When he went to vote for the first time in 1997, it was marked D. He registered a legal complain thereafter through a lawyer. Ironically, the lawyer misplaced all his documents and expressed inability to pursue the case further, of course promising him with all possible help in future. Subsequently, he got hold of a second lawyer in Barpeta town and Younus produced voter lists from 1966 and 1970, photocopies of his documents, a ration card and a "foli copy" (certified copy) of the 1997 voter list to prove his citizenship. Recently, he appeared twice in an NRC hearing too where he submitted land documents, bank records along with copies of previous voter lists. His father's name is also included in the 1951 NRC list but, he along with his children, has not yet been granted voting rights. In the hearing, out of anxiety, he pronounced his mother's name slightly differently. Realizing the mistake, he tried to rectify it, and as he points out, the "judge" overruled it. He lost the hearing and the case too. He narrates:

> I walked out crying form the court. After so much of effort and having proofs of being citizen I can't vote. What I want is sheer justice. But will I ever get justice? ... I hear that many people are taken away to detention camps ...once I fainted as this anxiety haunts me ... nowadays, I can't remember anything. ... I hear many people are taken to detention camps in Kokrajhar.[15]

What I could understand by interacting with numbers of illiterate D voters during my fieldwork, people like Younus hardly knows the exact written form of their parents' names. Sometimes they are confused with the formal name that is registered in documents and that with which they are addressed in their localities. Even if they remember the written names correctly, the ambience of such hearings makes them awestruck, and they fumble. Many D voters and people with cases registered against their name narrated how the thought and process of attending the tribunal hearing is itself akin to symbolic violence for them as they tremble with fear and insult in the name of such hearings. The tribunal member, who has the responsibility of acting as an arbitrator of justice – rather dehumanizes these people by taking advantage of the power relation that exists between the defendant and plaintiff, along with the presence of border police. One of the prominent human right activist and lawyer from Guwahati, who deals with cases of D voters and declared foreigners, told in of our group discussion that the defendant is not even allowed to wear their slippers or shoes while entering the tribunal for hearing.[16]Such a level of dehumanization hardly has the possibility of fair judgment in which one is not treated as fellow humans due to their identity.

V Good Muslim and Bad Muslim: Politics of Difference and Muslim Citizenship Question

In Assam, the Muslim citizenship crisis does not have a linear narrative. Muslims in Assam is a heterogeneous category and the citizenship question also has varied dimensions and ramifications on them. While many Miya Muslims of lower Assam are arbitrarily put on trial regarding their citizenship, the Goria, Moria Muslims living in upper Assam do not have to undergo similar ordeals. There are very few cases of D voter or exclusion from the NRC among Muslims of upper Assam. Although schemes like the PIP once targeted Muslims across the state indiscriminately, in contemporary times a separate treatment by society and state machinery between the "local" and "migrant" Muslims is evident. Mahmood Mamdani's idea of "good Muslims" and "bad Muslims" is an interesting analogy to understand a situational binary of Muslims of Assam like this. Mamdani uses the terms *good Muslims/bad Muslims* as categories created by the United States along with the start of the "war on terror" post 9/11. Good Muslims are the ones who supported America's war on terror by not supporting the "bad Muslims" who were responsible for terrorism. By this logic, all Muslims are presumed to be "bad" unless they could prove themselves to be good (Mamdani, 2005). Mamdani here talks about political ideology rather than cultural identity of Muslims in a global context. However, in the context of Assam, the cultural identity seems to be the dominant marker in terms of distinguishing categories of Muslims. While an Assamese-speaking and culturally familiar Goria or Moria Muslim from upper Assam represents the ideal image of a "good Muslims", an East Bengal–origin, not-so-fluent-in-Assamese, working-class and culturally different Miya Muslims is projected as the "bad Muslim". However, to be a "good Muslim", one must always be validated by the dominant cultural institutions patronized by the Assamese nationalist intellectuals. Although the narratives on understanding communalism occasionally portray all Muslims as similar, by and large evidently a binary operates in everyday public life and popular opinion in Assam.

This notion of cultural difference is not just only a distinction but also historically deep rooted in the notions related to the politics on citizenship question of Muslims in Assam. By projecting the local Goria, Moria and other local Muslims as part of the "larger indigenous" community, the state and the public perception that it is able to generate through the media encourage the harassment of "other" Muslims, particularly Miya Muslims. This happens through arbitrarily marking D of voter, registering cases and number of NRC hearings, as *normal*. In February 2020, under the BJP-led government in Assam, Welfare of Minorities Minister Ranjit Dutta had convened a meeting which proposed a mechanism to identify the "indigenous" Muslim of Assam and work for their exclusive development. The indigenous as proposed by the state are Goria, Moria, Deshi and Jolha (a tea tribe community) Muslims (PTI, 2020). During my conversation, one of the state-level office bearers of Sadou Assam Goria-Moria-Deshi-JatiyaParishad (an organization that claims to represent the demands of indigenous Muslims in Assam) told me that they want to be recognized as individual Muslim "tribes", which the present government is keen to grant.[17]

In 2021, the Assam government constituted seven subcommittees to suggest measures for the overall development of the "indigenous" Muslim groups, as they are fewer in number and "underperform" on social and economic fronts. On 21 April 2022, the government clarified that it has accepted the "definition" of indigenous Muslims proposed by the sub-committees. Since the government knows the definition now, it very well knows "for whom they need to work and where they inhabit" (Kalita, 2022). As a result of this development, On 6 July, 2022 Assam government's cabinet decided to accept five Muslim sub groups – Goria, Moria, Syed, Deshi and Julha as 'indigenous' to the state's population. The population of the indigenous Muslims is slated to be 42 lakhs out of 1.06 crores of total Muslims of the state (Firaque and Agarwala, 2022). However, there is no separate census data available based on different Muslim ethnicities in Assam. This administrative categorization not only multiplies complications and divisions among Muslims in Assam but also attempts to unsettle very organic intra-community everyday relations among different ethnic and linguistic Muslim identities. Such categorization of certain groups as indigenous also overlooks the identity questions of Muslims of Barak Valley who speaks Bengali and their conversion process dates back to thirteenth century (Nath, 2021, pp. 22–23). It also excludes many small and old sub-group of Muslims like the *Datia, Dhulu, Tulu* and *Muchis* who are either converts from local population or migrated during medieval times (Nath, 2021, pp. 20–23). Moreover, it is administratively almost impossible to determine such a definition of the indigenous identity as many Muslim families today exhibit hybrid identities through intra- ethnic marriages. In fact, as mentioned earlier, the larger Assamese identity is itself a hybrid and dynamic category through various mix-ups of ethnic, linguistic and religious groups.

This politics of indigenous identity imposed on Muslims in Assam, patronized by the state serves two purposes–one is intra-religious communal polarization, and the other is a never-ending Muslim citizenship crisis through various mechanisms like D voter, the NRC and others. Since an outright scope of politics of religious polarization is a tricky task in Assam; this differentiation marks an easier way out for perpetuating the politics of Miya Muslims versus the "indigenous" population in the state. In doing so, the dehumanization of Miya Muslims in terms of citizenship and cultural identity is *normalized* as something organic to knowledge production in Assam. In this way, the four-decades-old discourse of "lakhs of illegal Bangladeshi Muslim" present in Assam is remanufactured and consumed in a never-ending manner.

VI Inferences

In a conventional sense, citizenship is understood as a subject matter of legislation or formal membership within a nation state. Contrastingly, in the context of Assam, the citizenship issue seems to have gone beyond the rational, legal discourse where virtually it seems to be a problem of cultural psychology rather than law. The politics of otherization and exclusion has successfully, over many generations seems to have taken the discourse beyond legal intervention by fighting imaginary "thousands of immigrants" entering Assam every day. This, coupled with the cultural and linguistic unfamiliarity among Eastern Assam, Western Assam and Barak Valley, makes the question of an Assamese nationalistic narrative complex and unique. People of Assam upper seems to have little knowledge about cultural and linguistic identity, borderlands, ethnicity and everyday life of Western Assam, the place worst hit by the citizenship crisis. Muslims of Western Assam is still perceived largely as "illegal immigrants" by their Eastern Assamese counterparts. Meanwhile, the "other" of Assamese nationalism keeping shifting between "Bengalis" and "Miya Muslims" depending on the context – whether it is linguistic or religious simultaneously.

Often a formal citizenship in a nation states grants social and political rights on paper to every member of the state. But it doesn't guarantee them a "substantive" citizenship as local practices determine citizenship discourse–many oppressed social groups are discriminated in several aspects–irrespective of their formal citizenship rights (Glenn, 2011, p. 3). Citizenship is not just a matter of formal equality, but it is also about belonging entirely to the nation, through recognition by other social groups or members (Ibid, p. 3). This reflection bears a particular significance in Assam, and linguistic, cultural and religious prejudices seem to have completely affected the citizenship experience in the state–where people are marked as D voters, sent to detention camps and so on. While executing these legal and administrative processes, it is difficult to not imagine any kind of bias. The conventional idea on citizenship is based on one culture in which citizenship belonging to other cultures are less accreted or treated as second-class citizens (Beaman, 2016, p. 852). If we put this into perspective, in the context of Assam, the citizenship question could be experienced better through an approach of understanding "cultural citizenship". Cultural citizenship focuses on bridging gap between the legal aspects of citizenship by bringing questions of recognition, symbolic presence, dignity, lifestyle and so on (Pakulski, 1997; Delanty, 2002; Stevenson, 2001). The approach to cultural citizenship bears a huge significance in understanding and recognizing the gap between legal and cultural citizenship question in Assam. Without this understanding, talking about a holistic idea of citizenship experience in postcolonial Assam and India seems incomplete.

Notes

1 The word filthy is used to lay emphasis on how a section of people in Assam dehumanise migrant identity, their body and everyday aesthetics identifying them as 'cultural polluter' i.e., a threat to the indigenous demography and culture. Further, they are also often stereotyped as 'illegal immigrants'. This chapter engages with some of these issues through a deeper introspection.

2 Prominent academician from Assam, Sanijb Baruah justifies and uses the word *Miya Muslim* rather than using other names like Bengali Muslims, Bengal origin Muslims and others. For details, see Baruah, Sanjib. (2020). *In the Name of the Nation: India and Its Northeast*. Stanford: Stanford University Press.
3 Drawing upon the work of Saikia (2017), I use "Muslim Assamese" to refer to multiple categories of Muslims who over several generations have become an integral part of Assam's cultural and political life (Saikia, 2017, pp. 111–134).
4 In 1874, Assam was made a separate province along with the two districts of Bengal- Sylhet and Cachar, under a chief commissioner. For details see Nath (2021).
5 By the term *homogeneous*, I refer to communities with only one predominant ethnic or linguistic identity.
6 Veena Das and Deborah Poole talks about different ideas of "margins" in modern state highlighting on the issue of law, territoriality, bio-politics etc. For our use of the term, I have used the word *margin* for how certain categories in Assam are pathologized through dominant kind of a knowledge production, pushing them at the bottom of social and political life. For details, see Das, Veena & Poole, Deborah. (2004). State and Its Margins: Comparative Ethnographies. In Das, Veena and Poole, Deborah (eds.). *Anthropology in the margins of the State*. New Delhi: Oxford University Press.
7 Interview taken at Nagaon on 11 June, 2021.
8 *Assam Sanmilita Mahasangha & Ors vs Union of India*. Writ Petition (Civil) No. 562 of 2012, Judgment dated 17 December, 2014.
9 Till the time of writing this chapter, these people have not lost their citizenship fully. But their citizenship status is under serious threat and they have to use various legal provisions to claim their citizenship rights.
10 Restricting or denying citizenship rights results in exclusion both in instrumental and non-instrumental manner. In the context of Assam, this exclusion regarding citizenship issue could be seen in several fronts including legal, executive and bureaucratic fronts. (India Exclusion Report 2020, pp. 189–211).
11 Interview taken on 12 July, 2019 in Tezpur town.
12 Interview of Musharaf Hussain (70), a Goria Muslim man from Lakhimpur (interview taken in Guwahati on 5 February 2020).
13 Interview with a Deshi Muslim respondent in Goalpara on 25 February, 021.
14 Interview with a Moria Muslim respondent in Tezpur on 27 February 2021.
15 Interview with Younus Ali conducted on 25 March 2021 in Barpeta.
16 Group discussion among community workers on Assam's citizenship issue; conducted on 24 October 2021 in Barpeta.
17 Interview conducted on 26 October 2021.

References

Ali, Zamser. (2019, September 17). Over 7 lakh Hindus among those Excluded from the NRC, Leaked Data Suggests. *Sabrang* https://sabrangindia.in/article/over-7-lakh-hindus-among-those-excluded-nrc-leaked-data-suggests

Azad, A. K., Bhat, M., & Mander, H. (2020). Citizenship and the Mass Production of Statelessness in Assam. *India Exclusion Report (2020)*.

Baruah, Sanjib. (2020).*In the Name of the Nation: India and Its Northeast*. Stanford: Stanford University Press.

Beaman, J. (2016). Citizenship as Cultural: Towards a Theory of Cultural Citizenship. *Sociology Compass*, *10*(10), 849–857.

Das, Veena & Poole, Deborah. (2004). State and Its Margins: Comparative Ethnographies. In Das, Veena and Poole, Deborah (eds.), *Anthropology in the Margins of the State*. New Delhi: Oxford University Press.

Davies, C. A. (2002). *Reflexive Ethnography: A Guide to Researching Selves and Others*. New York: Routledge.

Delanty, G. (2002). Two Conceptions of Cultural Citizenship: A Review of Recent Literature on Culture and Citizenship. *The Global Review of Ethnopolitics*, *1*(3), 60–66.

Eaton, R. M. (2009). Shrines, Cultivators, and Muslim Conversion in Punjab and Bengal, 1300–1700. *The Medieval History Journal*, *12*(2), 191–220.

Firaque, K & Agarwala, T. (2022, July 13). Assam's Muslims: Why Some Have Been Declared'Indigenous' and Some Left Out. The Indian Express. https://indianexpress.com/article/explained/explained-who-are-assam-indigenous-muslims-8022121/

Glenn, E.N. (2011). Constructing Citizenship: Exclusion, Subordination, and Resistance. *American Sociological Review*, *76*(1), 1–24.

Guha, A. (1980). Little Nationalism Turned Chauvinist: Assam's anti-Foreigner Upsurge, 1979–80. *Economic and Political Weekly*, 15 (41/43), 1699–1720.

Hazarika, S. (2000). *Rites of passage: Border crossings, imagined homelands, India's East and Bangladesh*. New Delhi: Penguin Books India.

Hussain, Ismail. (2015). *AxomorMusalmanorOitijyoaruXongskriti*. Guwahati: Banalata Publication.

Hussain, M. (1993). *The Assam Movement: Class, Ideology, and Identity*. New Delhi: Manak Publication.

Kalita, Prabin. (2022, April 22). Govt. has Accepted Definition of Native Muslims: Assam CM HimantaBiswaSarma. *The Times of India*. https://timesofindia.indiatimes.com/city/guwahati/govt-has-accepted-definition-of-native-muslims-himanta/articleshow/90990753.cms

Kimura, M. (2013). *The Nellie Massacre of 1983: Agency of Rioters*. New Delhi: SAGE Publications India.

Mamdani, M. (2005). *Good Muslim, Bad Muslim: Islam, the USA, and the Global War against Terror*. New York: Three Leaves Press.

Metcalf, B. D. (Ed.). (2009). *Islam in South Asia in practice* (Vol. 33). Princeton: Princeton University Press.

Nath, Monoj Kumar (2021). *The Muslim Question in Assam and Northeast India*. Oxon and New York: Routledge.

Pakulski, J. (1997). Cultural citizenship. *Citizenship Studies*, 1(1), 73–86

Pathan, S. A., & Jha, M. (2022). Miya Muslims of Assam: Identity, Visuality and the Construction of "Doubtful Citizens". *Journal of Muslim Minority Affairs*, 1–10. https://doi.org/10.1080/13602004.2022.2051947

PTI. (2019, September 9). NRC list has errors, claims RSS as majority excluded are Hindus. *The Print* https://theprint.in/india/nrc-list-has-errors-claims-rss-as-majority-excluded-are-hindus/289084/

PTI. (2020, February 10). Assam Plans Survey to Identify Indigenous Muslim Population. *The Hindu*. https://www.thehindu.com/news/national/assam-plans-survey-to-identify-indigenous-muslim-population/article30780667.ece

Saikia, A. (2020, January 1). The Art of Resistance: 'AxomiyaDekarUkti' by Jyoti Prasad Agarwala is about Assam then and now. *Scroll.in*. https://scroll.in/article/948208/the-art-of-resistance-axomiya-dekar-ukti-by-jyoti-prasad-agarwala-is-about-assam-then-and-now

Saikia, Y. (2017). The Muslims of Assam: Present/Absent history. In *Northeast India: A Place of Relations* (pp. 111–134). New Delhi: Cambridge University Press.
Siddique, N. (2019). Discourse of Doubt: Understanding the Crisis of Citizenship in Assam. *Economic & Political Weekly*, *54*(10), 25–30.
Singh, R. Soibam. (2019, November 24). What are the Laws in Place to Tackle Illegal non-Citizens? *The Hindu*. https://www.thehindu.com/news/national/what-are-the-laws-in-place-to-tackle-illegal-non-citizens/article30063702.ece
Singh, V. and Karmakar, R. (2019, June 5). Why Does Assam Need more Foreigner's Tribunals? *The Hindu*. https://www.thehindu.com/news/national/other-states/why-does-assam-need-more-foreigners-tribunals/article27951416.ece
Stevenson, N. (2001). Culture and Citizenship: an Introduction. In N. Stevenson (Eds.), *Culture and Citizenship* (pp. 1–10). London: Sage Publications.

IV

Tracing Lived Experiences

The Curious Case of West Bengal

Chapter 9

Disaggregating the "Anti-immigrant Consensus"

Party–Community Relations and the Politics of Citizenship in Contemporary West Bengal

Himadri Chatterjee

1 Politics at the Site of Protest

The poster shown in Figure 9.1 was a much-admired piece of campaign art during a demonstration organized by the Joint Action Committee for Bengali Refugees (JACBR) and the Association for the Refugees in India (AFRI) in Esplanade, Kolkata, in September 2014. The poster depicts a gigantic snake with a pronounced, full set of teeth chewing and swallowing two half-clad male bodies dripping blood. Two sections of text in the poster describe the political import of the scene without ambiguity, as is to be expected from this genre of visual art. The snake represents the Citizenship Amendment Act of 2003 (CAA 2003) which introduced the phrase "illegal immigrant" in Indian legal parlance. This act predated and laid the foundation for the CAA 2019 which triggered a vibrant popular movement against the Bharatiya Janata Party (BJP) regime. The two male bodies being swallowed by the snake in the poster represent the future of refugees in India. The image seemed to approximate the Indian reticulated python. Each of the swirling markings on the body of the snake was adorned with the symbols of political parties spanning the entire ideological spectrum of the electoral field in the country at the time. The tricoloured hand of the Indian National Congress (INC); the red star, hammer and sickle of the Communist Party of India (Marxist) (CPIM); twin grass flowers of All India Trinamool Congress (AITMC); and the saffron lotus of the BJP were all depicted on the body of the snake. The snake represents the *anti-immigrant consensus* as defined by Namasudra refugee activists. This chapter seeks to disaggregate this conceptualization and understand its political and historical import.

Throughout this chapter, we refer repeatedly to this poster. It is a window into the site of protest where public opinion is presented, arguably at its most articulate and mobilized form. This chapter is an exploratory study of Matua Namasudra activists associated primarily with JACBR and periodically associated with the AFRI. While this chapter engages with these two organizations, there are more than 60 such organizations which exist at the block and village levels in Nadia, North 24 parganas and South 24 Parganas. These three districts are home to the largest proportion of the Matua

DOI: 10.4324/9781003345152-14

Figure 9.1 Field photograph

Courtesy: Author (Himadri Chatterjee)

Namasudra population in West Bengal, and over the last two decades, this population has become increasingly more politically mobilized on the question of formal legal citizenship which resonates with demands for both religious recognition and access to various policies of affirmative action. The proliferation of such local activist committees in rural and mufassil West Bengal for addressing social, cultural and political issues is a testament to the vibrancy and creativity of grassroots politics in the state. Studies regarding Matua Namasudras have focused mainly on the fortunes of the Matua Mahasangha (MM), the central spiritual organization of the community as the primary representative, mobilizer and mediator (Sinharoy, 2016). These studies use the political fortunes of the MM as a barometer to measure the political pressure that the Dalit communities of West Bengal may bring to bear upon the state and mainstream political parties at important junctures (Guha, 2019). This chapter seeks to qualify this centralizing narrative through a description of the micro-anatomy of Matua mobilizations which maintain a critical distance from most political parties while the MM office bearers have sought power through party membership. In describing this process, we also seek to present a genealogy of anti-immigrant politics in the state which arrests the progress of citizenship negotiations being led by the Namasudra community.

The snake in the poster in Figure 9.1 is an amalgamation of various political parties and a legal instrument of exclusion that blurs ideological and institutional boundaries. The poster represents a frustration that social movements often express regarding ambiguous signalling by party leaders. This tension has been noted by several scholars in the context of the anti-corruption movement of 2011. The non-party structure of the anti-corruption movement had made it easy to categorize it as a civil society movement (Sheth, 2018). The middle-class status of the significant activists associated with the movement at various levels substantiated that identification (Sitapati, 2011). The movement was widely seen as a signpost of deepening and widening participatory democratic politics in India (Sarker, 2018). Astute observers of Indian politics commented upon the double-edged nature of the multiple possibilities opened up by the outpouring of popular anger against an increasingly alienated and non-responsive group of senior party bosses (Menon & Nigam, 2011). While some scholars pointed out radical democratic possibilities of that moment, others, like Partha Chatterjee, were more sceptical of the limited understanding of corruption and increasingly anti-political activism that characterized the field (Pillai & Joshy, 2012).

In the year of the anti-corruption movement, another group of activists were also trying to take their issues to the national stage. Several small block-level committees of Namasudra refugees from West Bengal had come to be consolidated under the umbrella organization called JACBR. They were aiming to translate the momentum of the highly visible and impactful march organized by Matua Namasudra refugees in Kolkata in 2010 at the national level. The impact that the Matuas were beginning to have on state-level electoral calculations was remarkable. It was argued at the time that electoral mobilization in West Bengal was becoming less dependent on political parties and more so on community identities (Sinharoy, 2012). This trend was seen as a major departure from earlier models of mobilization and political mediation in the state. Studies of mobilization patterns in the Left Front era had demonstrated that political parties could function as the primary anchor of political subjectivity in rural West Bengal (Bhattacharya, 2001) (Bhattacharya, 2009) (Dasgupta, 2009). In the case of the Namasudra refugees however, there seemed to be a greater emphasis on their caste based spiritual organization. JACBR called for a hunger strike at Delhi's Jantar Mantar in late November of 2011. The demonstration and hunger strike started on 28 November and continued till 1 December. This protest, however, did not generate as much national attention as the leadership of the organization had expected. Competing with the other popular movements at the time, especially the Right to Food movement which had parallel programmes and events at Jantar Mantar in those days, was not possible for this small coalition of village-level activist committees. After a few meetings with representatives from all the political parties depicted in the poster with which we started this chapter and a few that are not, the demonstration and hunger strike had to be called off for a meagre promise of more meetings (Chatterjee, 2018). Not surprisingly, many of the activists who were active and present in the formative years of the movement from 2004 to 2012 became increasingly disillusioned with the process of negotiating with political parties while also building the network precisely to mediate between the party and the community. This skill and the limited effectiveness of their engagement make them a particularly telling example to study in the context of non-party politics from below.

II The "Party Sceptic"

National attention for the Namasudra community arrived three years after the 2011 hunger strike. The BJP picked up the issue of citizenship and combined it with the older discourse on illegal immigration. The high-voltage campaign hammering home the difference between Hindu asylum seekers and Muslim "infiltrators" altered the nature of political expression in West Bengal, perhaps permanently. From 2014 to 2021, the BJP's campaign in West Bengal focused on religious polarization on the basis of the citizenship issue. The foundations of this discourse had been laid by the earlier BJP-led National Democratic Alliance government under the leadership of Atal Bihari Vajpayee. The CAA 2003 had shifted Indian citizenship law towards the principles of blood and descent. As an extension of this shift, a new clause was added to the citizenship matrix, defining the category of "illegal immigrant". This had created new instruments of marginalization and polarization, producing residual categories of the population excluded from formal and social citizenship (Roy, 2010, pp. 135–160). The Namasudra population of West Bengal had begun mobilizing against the amendment demanding special accommodation within the law or a full repeal since 2004. That movement finally consolidated in 2010 in a highly impactful march in Kolkata six years later. During the last two decades, the Matua Namasudra population has been involved in a two-fold negotiation with the political and legal system of this country in search of formal membership in the nation state. They have had to simultaneously manage two registers of negotiation. First, the community has engaged in a complicated ideological and social struggle for inclusion into Hindu society as a formerly ritually excluded community. Secondly, there has been a protracted struggle against arbitrary cut-off dates, ever narrowing windows of naturalization and increasingly stringent regimes of documentation that stand in the way of legal citizenship registration (Sinharoy, 2019). The Namasudra community, already extremely significant in provincial politics since before independence, became even more decisive in the political discourse in West Bengal. The electoral clout of the community has been much discussed in media throughout the 2014, 2016, 2019 and 2021 election cycles.

The Namasudra community, and specifically the Matuas among them, have had several experienced leaders given their impressive electoral successes both before and after the partition of Bengal. The community has had elected representatives from every political party that has successfully controlled the West Bengal legislative assembly. In the post-partition period, beginning with Pramatha Ranjan Thakur, who was elected as a Member of Legislative Assembly on a ticket from the INC in 1962, the community has had continuous representation in the assembly including significant stretches of representation in successive cabinets. Kanti Biswas was elected on a CPIM ticket and remained the education minister of West Bengal for almost two decades. Haripada Biswas of All India Forward Bloc successfully played the dual role of community representative and an influential member of the legislative assembly for a decade. In recent times, the first family of the Matua community has been significantly successful in both national- and state-level elections. Manjul Krishna Thakur, the younger son of P. R. Thakur, became an MLA on an AITMC ticket in 2011. His elder brother, once considered closer to the Left Front, won the member of parliament (MP) seat from the Bongaon constituency on an AITMC ticket in 2014. After his sudden demise in October that same year, his wife, Mamata Bala Thakur, was elected to the same seat in the 2015 by-election, once again on an AITMC ticket. In recent times, there has been a pronounced shift towards the BJP in the community and within the Thakur family. Manjul Krishna Thakur had abandoned the AITMC and his post as the minister of refugee rehabilitation in the Government of West Bengal in January 2015 and joined the BJP along with his sons Subrata Thakur and Shantanu Thakur. He announced the decision to quit the AITMC after the party leadership decided to nominate Mamata Bala Thakur to the MP seat earlier held by her husband and Manjul Thakur's elder brother. His younger son Shantanu Thakur would go on to win the Bongaon MP seat on a BJP ticket in 2019. His elder son Subrata Thakur has also recently won the MLA seat from Gaighata in 2021 on a BJP ticket. Despite this long litany of elected leaders who graced assembly seats and ministerial chairs, the community found itself without a dependable voice for proposing a durable solution to their legal exclusion from formal citizenship and this lack was keenly felt in the last three years of national protests against the CAA and the NRC. The Thakur family and the MM have been seen as the focal point of mobilization and organization within the Matua Namasudra community. The Thakur family are the inheritors of the divine legitimacy of Shri Harichand Thakur, the prophet and God in the Matua tradition. However, as the electoral competition for Matua support has increased among political parties, the community has also grown circumspect of their political gains in real terms. The touchstone of political gain for the community is the legal acceptance of their full and unconditional citizenship. In that direction, not much gain has been made even though the current regime at the central government has promised that the CAA 2019 was designed precisely to help communities like the Matua Namasudras. A section of activists from the Matua community has remained sceptical of the claim (Biswas, 2018). Regardless, due to the failure of the central government in providing any concrete directions for implementing the act in Eastern India, there is significant ground for doubting their good faith. The experiences of this movement have made it harder for politically active members of the community to hold on to their strategic suspension of disbelief while negotiating with party leaders.

It should come as no surprise then that the poster at the beginning of this chapter was at the centre of a fascinating conversation between activists and spiritual leaders from the Matua Namasudra community at the time of the demonstration. The poster had been given its own exhibition corner in a protest site. It was hung at a well-lit corner of the white-and-pink tent erected to shelter protesters from the sun. It was surrounded by several groups of Dhoti clad men with *dankas* (drums played during religious rituals) and *nishan* (red flags carried in obeisance to the divine). When asked what the poster stood for, one older man replied quickly and unambiguously, "Every political party has stabbed us Bangali refugees in the back. None of them will ever help us unless we force them to. These gluttons only want to gobble up our votes" (K. Biswas, Personal Communication, 15 September 2014). Biswas had arrived at the protest site along with his own Matua *Dal*. Most villages with a significant Matua Namasudra population in West Bengal have multiple *Dal* or teams that observe kirtan festivals, community feasts and other religious rituals together. They are the building blocks of the spiritual community of this sect and caste group. The *Dal* is usually led by a *Gosain* who is considered the spiritual elder of the group based on both the performance of devotion and the accumulation of social and mobilizational influence. The leader of a *Dal* is called *Dalapati*. Mr. Biswas, therefore, represented not only his individual understanding of political parties but also the collective frustration of the spiritual community. This was underlined by the fact that the image in the poster was also a work of collective imagination executed by a very young artist.

Biswas's claim resonates with earlier expressions of non-party forms of participatory democratic politics. It was also a very concise expression that flagged a multitude of ideas concerning the process of representation of community demands by the political parties at the level of legislation. Over the last two decades, representation has become an increasingly thorny question for the Matua community. There have been two significant registers in the contest over the representation of Namasudra identity: the first is electoral, and the second is cultural. The limitations of scholarly investigations into both registers have been pointed out that new evidence has come to light. In the process, descriptions and understandings of Dalit politics have gained heterogeneity (Das, 2015). Dalapatis across several protest sites claim that the community's spiritual elders and their local followers have become *party sceptic*. It is a double-edged claim, distancing the Dalapati from the party while anchoring him in politics.

Scepticism about the effectiveness of political parties and their integrity in fulfilling promises is a fairly common feature of politics in the sub-continent. Mistrust of political parties is also specifically intense among Dalit political activists. B. R. Ambedkar had questioned the effectiveness of political parties with large non-brahmin constituencies in serving the needs and aspirations of untouchable communities in his criticism of the Justice party (Nagaraj, 2010, pp. 27–34). Autonomous Dalit organizations in Maharashtra have demonstrated similar mistrust for political parties in the 1970s and 1980s. Such mistrust often stemmed from fears of subsumption, co-optation and internal fragmentation of the Dalit organizations under ideological and practical political pressures exerted by various electoral political forces (Omvedt, 1993, pp. 55–82). The apathy and mistrust towards political parties demonstrated by the Namasudra refugee activists can therefore be easily ideologically categorized under the same tendency. However, that would require the importing of an ideological and analytical artefact from the context of Tamil Nadu and Maharashtra without localizing its specific contours and history. Such an importing of argument and concept runs the risk of historically determining a single essential nature or strategy for the Dalit movement traceable to the 1940s. This chapter takes the path of situating this mistrust within the context of the development of refugee politics in West Bengal over the last four decades. The primary reason for doing so is the complex field of opinions that exist under the broad category of anti-party politics within the universe of Namasudra refugee activism.

Let us return once again to the site of protest we had started our discussion with and disaggregate the anti-party sentiments further. As we sat and discussed the poster several other voices and understandings emerged to add to, correct and even challenge the views expressed by Biswas. Anirban Halder, one of the organizers of the protest demonstration and a former vice-president of the MM, added in a tone of dark humour:

> How do you think Namas are going to force anyone to do anything? We cannot even get our own community to follow wisdom. Or maybe I should say there is too much wisdom in our people for their own good! (Personal Communication, 15 September 2014)

Following a significantly Gandhian impulse, he argued for "social activism" divorced from "vote-seeking" politics. There was a sharp edge to the use of the shortened form of the name of the community which is often used in a pejorative tone. Some members of the community, however, believe the shortened form to be the original term used to designate the group in antiquity since they prefer to trace their origins back to the sage 'Namas'. Halder delivered three powerful observations from the perspective of an activist and community organizer who was in touch with but also distinct from the 'Bhaktas' (devotees) and 'Gosain' who form the core of the spiritual community. First, he questioned the actual capacity and effectivity of the community in terms of sustained agitation which may force the hand of the government of the day to deliver a positive solution. This challenge is particularly significant because there is a popular and persistent idea of Namasudras as peerless protesters and agitators, especially in the context of their 19th-century history of localized caste-based mobilizations (Bandopadhyay, 2011). Second, he was pointing out the disarray in which the community found itself following displacement. This is a point now well accepted in the studies of Dalit politics in Bengal. Partition and the resulting migration severely affected the political and organizational capacity of the Namasudra community and sapped their pre-partition political eminence (Bandyopadhyay, 2009). Third, the comment about "too much wisdom" contained some vitriol for the decision-makers in the various community organizations closely allied with electoral interests. Both of these voices in the community were then highly sceptical of the political parties as a vehicle for their group interest. Their difference lies in the spiritual leader's assumption of unity of the community against party-aligned actors and the non-party activist's understanding of internal fragmentation.

The question facing community organizers and activists was therefore to find a different method for negotiating with political parties. The main organizer of the event was Sukritiranjan Biswas – a veteran of the first hunger strike of 2004, organized under the banner of the MM, immediately after the passage of the CAA 2003. He was the founder, president and convenor of the JACBR; former chair of the West Bengal unit of the Republican Party of India; and a vice-president of MM for several consecutive terms. He admired the poster but was circumspect about keeping the piece of art too close to the main stage in the protest site. "We have to speak to everyone. We know they have all been equally negligent of the issue. But unless you have your own party, you have to talk to all of them." (Biswas, Personal Communication, 15 September 2014). This response represents the broad consensus among community organizers and activists from the Namasudra community till 2019. Sukritiranjan Biswas was making two significant arguments about the community's relationship with political parties. On one hand, he was pointing at the necessity of being somewhat ideologically agnostic while trying to represent community interests to policymakers. Second, there was a permanently deferred ideal of "your own party" against which the current condition of negotiation was constantly pitted, measured and found wanting. All three types of actors agree that there has been a significant failure in the part of all mainstream parties in handling the issue of Namasudra citizenship.

Qualifying his strategy of staying open to all political parties, Sukritiranjan Biswas was quick to add "political parties do not take your issues. One must remember, they make their own issues" (Personal communication, September 2014). This adds several layers of complexity in political communication between the political parties and a community. First, this points to the possibility that the political party, while taking up an issue may transform it. Second, an issue which has been made electorally relevant by community organizations or committees of activists may become part of the agenda for various political parties. The way he begins the second part of that statement is indicative of a certain emphasis "mone rakhte hobe" (one must remember) signifies a lesson. He makes it into a historically demonstrable principle that has become now a rule of thumb. Since he was speaking to veterans of the movement, the historical lesson was already part of the community's collective memory. He was attempting to separate the political will to continue expressing the "issue" in the community's own frame, if such a unified frame were to be found, from the convoluted history of "betrayals" that he has detailed in pamphlets published since 2004. The danger of the second possibility is something another Dalapati noted while talking about the involvement of the BJP in the citizenship struggle of the Matuas – "We have now become part of the Assam equation. We had asked for an accommodation within the existing law or a reversal of the law. Now we have been given a new law altogether. It is neither here nor there". It may be argued that the community had in fact gotten their wish fulfilled in the form of a special accommodation for "persecuted" minorities written newly into the citizenship law through the CAA 2019. But the first part of the section demonstrates the gap between the party's framing of the issue and the community's framing of the issue. The demand for legal citizenship had been converted into a competitive political agenda upsetting delicate demographic, cultural, regional and electoral balances. The Namasudra mobilization became pitted against the Assamese nationalists and Bengali Muslims in a way that segregated them from their social milieu.

As the legislation of CAA 2003 and 2019 was led by the BJP which has always been vocal about their views to further the Hindu nationalist cause (Verma, 2020) (Chatterjee, 2019b), they have also been significant in the state and national dialogue on migration and citizenship (Chatterjee, 2019a) in the Bengal borderlands for nearly two decades. Namasudra scepticism about party politics, however, has developed over the last 50 years of negotiations with various actors. In the next section, we explore a brief genealogical sketch of these negotiations and the various tensions underlying them.

III The Making of the Anti-Immigrant Consensus

Let us begin from 1979. The year of the Marichjhapi incident. This confrontation lives on in the popular history and memory of the Namasudra community as one of the foundational moments of the scepticism about negotiating with political parties across the ideological spectrum. The event has been the subject of several academic investigations (Chatterjee, 1992; Mallick, 1999; Jalais, 2005). Most scholars agree that the fledgling Left Front government had used police force to violently evict several thousand refugees from an island in the Sunderban forest reserves. The official count of casualties was two. First-hand accounts and contemporary reportage claim that number to be nearer a thousand or more. Taking stock of the growing literature concerning the memory of the confrontation, first-hand accounts, documentation and collected reportage is beyond the scope of this chapter. However, it is useful to briefly note the historical development of the issues. Bengali refugees unwillingly dispersed far away from West Bengal, in the deciduous forest regions of Central India had migrated back to look for a homeland more suited to their cultural and economic skills. The migration was not accidental. It was part of anti-dispersal mobilization by the Left parties and the subsequent trust generated among refugees that the "friendly" Left Front government will make a policy accommodation to take back the refugees who found the Dandakaranya Development Project areas arid and impossible to inhabit. As Mallick has demonstrated, there was a reversal in the policy of the Left Front after coming to power (1999). The reversal left the refugees without political support and soon faced with overwhelming state repression.

The resulting break between the Namsudra refugees and the left was not immediately visible in the electoral field. Leaders like Kanti Biswas remained within the fold of the Left Front. Parties like the CPI and the Revolutionary Socialist Party, which had taken a pro-refugee stand during the colonization and evictions from Marichjhapi also became long-term partners within the Left Front. Across North 24 Parganas, South 24 Parganas and Nadia, strongholds of the Namasudra refugee population, the electoral power of the Left Front waxed bright over the next three decades. Perhaps for this reason, it was also easy to undermine and nearly erase the memory of the moment from the public conscience.

Looking at the absence of significant fall-out from another political vantage point may help us frame this forgetting better. On 14 September of that year, the revised voter lists were notified for the upcoming Loksabha elections of 1980. In West Bengal, Barkat Gani Khan Chaudhury, a popular representative of the landed Muslim gentry and one of the stalwarts of Congress (I) at the national level had gone on war footing. Reportedly, he had written to the Election Commission of India demanding review of voter's lists. He had complained that false voters had been enumerated in the lists – primarily migrants from Bangladesh and refugees from the Dandakaranya project. In response, the Republican Party of India (RPI) had taken the path of resisting Goni Khan on his own turf by forging an electoral alliance with the Bolshevik Party, the CPI(ML), Uttarkhand Party, Forward Bloc (Subhashist) and Gorkha League. Many of these parties are now defunct in West Bengal like the Uttarkhand Party and Bolshevik Party. Others, like the Gorkha League and the Forward Bloc (S), have merged into larger organizations that carry on their legacy. The RPI itself has gone through a series of unit dissolutions and splits since the early 80s. It is interesting to note the RPI's framing of demands. They demanded "[n]on-Muslim immigrants from Bangladesh will have to be accorded the right to citizenship" (Republican, 1979, p. 1). Gani Khan's reservations concerning the possible electoral clout of recent migrants can be seen as part of the growing anti-migrant sentiments in post-liberation war public discourse in

West Bengal. Scholars like Schendel (2005, pp. 210–212) and Datta (2013, pp. 128–137) have observed that the initial outpouring of moral support and unity articulated by West Bengalis for the Bengali nationalist forces was concentrated in urban areas and also quite short-lived. In districts where agricultural production was severely affected by the massive scale of refugee influx, the rural social and political forces became arrayed against the refugees. Later in the war, as refugees began pouring into the city of Calcutta even the urban civil society became more reserved in their support. This incident demonstrates the unpredictability of social forces arrayed against migration. The spatial location of the refugee and the nature and structure of the local economy has a telling effect on political positioning. Gani Khan as a popular leader of the landed Muslim peasantry in the border districts of West Bengal felt a threat not only to his electoral clout but also to the economic structure of his local constituency. Even though anti-migrant policies would later go on to become a mainstay of Hindu nationalist mobilizations, we can safely say that such was not entirely the case in West Bengal till the late 1970s and early 1980s.

RPI had cobbled together a significant coalition against the formidable leader of Congress (I). Its significance lay in the sheer political and ideological breadth of the coalition. It brought together ethno-nationalists, Ambedkarites, militant nationalists and Marxist-Leninists. This moment shows us the historically contingent and local character of the citizenship question. It will be difficult to imagine a Muslim leader from Congress arguing for the shrinking and tightening of the bounds of citizenship today. It will be equally implausible to expect pro-migration politics from the ethno-nationalist parties of northern Bengal. This rainbow coalition was united by their mutual dislike for the Congress (I). Negotiations with the Left Front may have been made difficult by the Marchjhapi evictions. By the mid-1970s, the Dalit Panther organization was beginning to split between its Marxist and Ambedkarite blocs. The RPI leadership in Maharashtra was a close witness to this episode. The dislike for Marxist-Leninist activists especially was high among the Panther Ambedkarites in Maharashtra who would later find space in RPI and Congress. The Naxalites were seen as infiltrators in the organization and were allied to the Dhasal group which was opposed to the Dhale group (Omvedt, 1993, pp. 65–67). However, the West Bengal Unit of the party decided to ally with the ML for local- and state-level issues despite their differences on the national stage which demonstrates the weight of local and state-level considerations.

The forces arrayed against the migrants at the time give us a clue as to why the Left Front's electoral fortunes continued to be bright after the confrontation at Marichjhapi. For the Namasudra refugee population already settled in West Bengal, the primary opposition to the Left Front, Congress (I) seemed to have been unacceptable with its stand against "fake voters" with "fake fathers" and illegal settlers migrating from Dandakaranya. In fact it seems that the Congress opposition in West Bengal marked the

CPI(M) as not just pro-refugee but also pro-immigration, so much so that they accused the Left Front of stalling the registration of local voters while assisting migrants from Bangladesh and Dandakaranya to get on the electoral rolls. Two important observations can be made on the basis of this instance. First, the political distinction between Muslim and non-Muslim refugees predates the rise of the BJP in the region and it is embedded the local economy and spatial distribution of communities. Second, political actors take a complex set of elements into account comprising local, regional and national ambitions and negotiations. The second observation is probably particularly true for states with international borders, even more so for regions with fluid borders.

The INC in West Bengal continued to mobilize public opinion for the comprehensive revision of electoral rolls even as new faces took up the mantle of leadership. Abdul Mannan, the then leader of opposition in the West Bengal legislative assembly, had commented in 2016 that current chief minister Mamata Bandyopadhyay was the architect of the centralization of the process of naturalization and citizenship application in the mid-1980s. As a significant young leader of the INC, Mamata Bandyopadhyay had written to the then home minister Buta Singh in 1986, demanding that the process be centralized in order to control its alleged misuse by the state government. (Ananda Bajar Patrika, 2016, p. 6) Congress at this time was busy wrapping up the refugee rehabilitation department and had set up a monitoring committee for refugee colony regularisation at the central level. This committee was in conflict with the state government at the time (Estimates Committee, 1989, pp. 43–47). The process of providing refugees with land for housing had stalled for a number of years raising questions for other parliamentary committees and earning their opprobrium. Two INC leaders of this monitoring committee would go on to become important figures in their respective state's politics. Mamata Bandyopadhyay will go on to split the INC in West Bengal, found the AITMC and finally become the CM. Bhubaneswar Kalita would go on to join the BJP to pursue sharper anti-immigrant politics while assisting the religious transformation of linguistic and ethnic nationalist politics in Assam. This strand of anti-immigrant politics evolved from its electoral expression to its infrastructural and policy-oriented expression over a decade. Mamata Bandyopadhyay's current pro-refugee stance demonstrates the contingent nature of migration as an electoral and policy issue. The same actor may take opposing stands on the policy politics and electoral politics of migration.

The existence of cross-border migration has been a matter of political concern for the left as well. Anxieties regarding immigration gained legitimacy when Jyoti Basu, the longest-standing chief minister of the Left Front, offered a contested reading of the phenomena in the 1990s, underlining that a shift in the nature of migration had taken place in 1979 (Basu, 1992, p 4). Jyoti Basu claimed that of the number of immigrants apprehended and returned from the border in 1977 and 1992, 68,472 were Hindu and

1,64,132 were Muslim. The article argued that this demographic signalled that this was going to be a far more long-term problem than was originally envisaged. What used to be connected to partition migration was now increasingly seen as a continuous process of economic migration and therefore there was a need for reframing policy. The choice of the year of break is twice significant. It was the first year of his chief ministership, and it was also the year of the greatest accusation to be levelled against his regime. The article served to address exigencies related to both trajectories of significance. He pointed out the lackadaisical approach taken by the central government in relation to immigration control even after his repeated letters and requests since 1985. The statistics were also arrayed to imply that since 1979 all has not been well with the migration scenario in West Bengal and that untoward events may happen unless a vigilant state government stood in the way. His charge against the central government and the Bangladesh government also carried significant weight. His arguments were aimed against the central governments of both countries. He indirectly blamed the Bangladesh government for their inaction on the migration issue. He criticised the Indian government more directly for its inaction on the various cases of interstate transfer of suspect migrant populations to West Bengal from erstwhile rehabilitation states like Assam and Orissa. The migration crisis was accompanied by a diplomatic crisis because of Bangladesh's inability to develop a bilateral understanding of immigration. Basu's insistence that the issue required both national and international attention was also a testament to his growing national ambitions which would end with the bid for prime ministership in 1996. The attempt was aborted by his own party which he later characterized as a historic blunder. This period of diplomatic impasse and increasing anti-immigrant sentiments resulted finally in operation push back (EPW, 1992, p. 2391). This problem continued into the early 2000s.

On 1 February 2003, border security forces of India and Bangladesh came to a confrontation while trying to push back 239 people across the Indo-Bangladesh border in south and north Bengal (Telegraph, 2003).'Push back' designated the forcible transfer of population across the border between West Bengal and Bangladesh when suspected immigrants were arrested and compelled to cross the international border without the knowledge of the security forces on the other border (Ramachandran, 2002, pp. 311–332). In this particular incident, the activities of the two border forces coincided:

> The BSF jawans stopped 213 alleged Bangladeshis when the BDR was trying to herd them into India at Satgachi in Cooch Behar district. Conversely, the BDR personnel prevented 26 Bangladesh nationals, who had been picked up in Delhi and taken to the border by the BSF today, from crossing over at Phulbari in Nadia district.
>
> (Telegraph, 2003)

The situation calmed when on 7 February, the Bangladesh government accepted 213 people back into their territory. (Mitra, 2003)

On 15 February 2003, the then foreign minister of Bangladesh Mohd Morshed Khan met Atal Behari Vajpayee (Baruah, 2003). The Bangladesh foreign minister made three important points: (a) the use of force at the border to enforce 'push-ins' needed to be dealt with bilaterally, (b) Asia's 'common market' had to be taken as the foundation for contemporary egalitarian growth and (c) the wide imbalance in trade between the two countries had created "illegal movement of people and illegal trade" which were "linked" phenomena (Baruah, 2003). On the same day, the West Bengal government had asked the police to intensify vigil in the "districts along the border with Bangladesh" (Bhattacharya, 2003). The police force was deployed across the border districts at this time to 'supplement' the efforts of the Border Security Force. Newspapers reported border skirmishes and arrests of which the most significant was the incident of 13 February 2003 when the BDR "tried to push in about 200 persons at Hilli" in north Bengal (Bhattacharya, 2003). By this time, the idea of infiltration had gained enough national currency to have brought in the state government's cooperation. A newspaper report of the time read:

> Apparently, the Bhattacharjee Government has decided to supplement the BSF's efforts after the failed attempts of the Bangladesh Rifles (BDR) to push Bangladeshi nationals into India came to light following the stand off at Saatgachi, in Coochbehar along the North Bengal border, over a group of gypsies.
>
> (Bhattacharya, 2003)

The state government's policy on this particular issue was one of cooperation with the central government decision of governing the Indo-Bangladesh border. In the meeting information on 'infiltration' was reportedly exchanged. They were formulated with inputs from the chief ministers of Tripura and West Bengal compiled over 'several months' and sent to the prime minister's office to be then shared with the Bangladesh foreign minister (Bhattacharya, 2003)

The article presented a three-part argument supporting the 'concern' felt by the chief minister. First was alleged evidence of Inter-Services Intelligence "taking advantage of the infiltration to send in agents". Second were the "Bangladeshi crime lords based in Kolkata" who were apparently "flush with funds and contacts" and had relocated to India, specifically West Bengal, in order to escape their homeland authorities. Thirdly the report states that infiltration had been "rapidly changing the demographic profile in many parts of the State" (Bhattacharya, 2003) That the Left Front government of the time not only went along with but supported the creation of this hyper-securitized environment is testament to the blurring of ideological and practical political lines between the central and state regimes.

The INC's legacy of anti-immigrant electoral politics was taken forward by Mamata Bandyopadhyay and the AITMC in the early 2000s. An interesting document was circulating among activists from JACBR and AFRI in the North 24 Parganas in 2011. The document was a photocopy of what seemed to be a covering letter to an extensive survey of illegal immigrants and false voters allegedly signed by the Trinamool Congress leader Jyotipriyo Mallick which was addressed to the election commission. According to several activists, in 2006 Trinamool Congress had approached the 'Chief Election Commissioner's' office with detailed lists of names of persons whom the party activists believed to be infiltrators. The Bongaon, North 24 Parganas legislative assembly committee of the AITMC was rumored to have written to the central observer from the Election Commission forwarding a list of names from the 85th legislative assembly constituency who they thought were infiltrators (Chatterjee, 2012, p. 187). Another letter shared by local activists was allegedly sent to the chief election commissioner under the authority of the then secretary of the Pradesh Committee, Mr. Jyotipriyo Mallick. Along with the letter was enclosed a list of names stating names of persons who apparently had "fake/false fathers/anuprabeshkaries" (Chatterjee, 2012, p. 188). The veracity of the photocopies themselves remains unconfirmed. However, their political impact in the locality was intense. The letter specifically marked out that the list covered the Gaighata area, which housed several government-sponsored refugee rehabilitation colonies. The demographic anxieties noted in 2003 had become instrumental in the political practices at the district and local levels.

Even after breaking away from the NDA and in spite of their stringent anti-BJP rhetoric the legacy of AITMC's anti-immigrant politics in its early years is still visible in the politics of the state. The Namasudra community voted in six BJP candidates from within their fold in districts where they hold significant electoral dominance in the 2021 assembly elections. The cracks in the negotiation between the AITMC and the MM were visible in their public posturing and in a sudden loss of capacity to coordinate activities at the state level. An important instance of this loss of communication and coordination was on display on 10 December 2019. The then food minister and influential AITMC district boss, Jyotipriyo Mallick, had organized a demonstration at Esplanade in Kolkata. The protest was against the discriminatory nature of the CAA 2019 which had been passed by the LokSabha on 8 December. Jyotipriyo Mallick had announced the event as a united demonstration staged by the MM and the AITMC. At the time of the sit-in, however, Mamatabala Thakur, the sanghadhipati of the AITMC faction of the MM did not appear to grace the stage. Some activists and then a few of the journalists present at the venue began inquiring for her, and the minister was at first reticent about the absence. Finally after a few phone calls and some cajoling, it was announced that due to her ill health she had been delayed, but she would appear on stage before the end of the event.

Meanwhile, a few influential dalapatis and two vice presidents of the AITMC faction of the MM who were present at the event began calling Mamatabala Thakur on phone to inquire about her health. Quite suddenly a rumour emerged that Thakur had refused to come to the venue as she had apparently not been consulted before calling for the demonstration and as such MM had nothing to do with the protest or the line being taken by the AITMC on the issue. Several Dalapatis and activists close to the MM leadership began leaving the venue. The minister attempted to do some damage control by announcing that Thakur had taken ill and could not attend the meeting. By this time, a few journalists had also apparently gotten in touch with Thakur, who reportedly confirmed on the phone that neither the protest nor the particular political angle being represented had the sanction of the MM (Das, 2019). A day after the primary opposition to the CAA 2019 in West Bengal put up this show of disarray the bill was passed by the upper house and was soon finalized as an act. The fact that AITMC was not able to mobilize either the central leadership of the MM or even individual dalapatis shows the rift that existed between the AITMC and the Matua population. It is very possible that Mallick's involvement made the situation worse as he was seen as the main architect of the illegal immigrant detection survey and complaints to the ECI backed by the AITMC in 2005–6.

Activists from Nikhil Bharat Bangali Udbastu Samiti (NIBBUS), JACBR and AFRI were also present at the venue. Most of them decided to stay on at the site of the protest as they had an autonomous understanding of the bill and the issues and were eager to express their difference from the centralizing attitude of the MM. On their request, a few of the dalapatis returned with their ritual red flags and drums to maintain a thin veneer of cultural representation of the Matua community. Interestingly, at this time both AFRI and NIBBUS were widely considered to be BJP-aligned organizations. In spite of their alignment with the opposition their decision to stay on at the AITMC protest site is a poignant example of the precarity of the autonomous organizational space that is built on micro-transgressions of party discipline and electoral alignments.

The refugee activists I encountered at the protest site in 2014 had asserted that there was a fundamental equivalence between all parties when it came to the issue of Namasudra refugees. All parties were equally adept at wooing them for votes while betraying their cause. The preceding discussion helps historicize this understanding at the level of state politics where most of the electorally dominant parties have had a history of taking anti-immigrant policy and legislative stances at important and delicate junctures. The ability to take anti-immigrant postures without damaging electoral prospects stabilized the consensus. The BJP has been the most fortunate beneficiary of this consensus. They were able to pass the CAA 2003 without any significant opposition from the other political parties and their representatives from West Bengal precisely because these parties were already primed to accept hardline solutions to border security and immigration controls.

As the record shows, there was hardly any resistance from the INC, the CPI, the CPI(M) or the AITMC when the bill was discussed in the Home Affairs Standing Committee (Rajya Sabha, 2003). This bill brought in sweeping changes to the provision for citizenship by birth to a question of descent and additionally wrote an eminently over-extendable definition of the term illegal immigrant into the citizenship law. The previous discussion also throws up a set of conceptual issues which we discuss in the concluding section.

IV Scaling Negotiation

The earlier discussion shows us that there are issues of both horizontal and vertical scaling that constraints Namasudra refugee politics in West Bengal. Horizontally, there are significant differences in demand formulation and imaginations of solutions across party, community and autonomous organizations. These differences are intensified by local economic competition happening along community lines. They also vary by districts which are regions within regions. For example, the issue of immigration mobilizes opinions that are polar opposites in southern and northern Bengal. Vertically, the position of organizations and political actors is determined by national ambition and access to the central government. If we look closely at the case of Gani Khan, it will be quite clear that the INC had inherited a concern about immigration that stemmed from concerns with the local economy and micro-regional electoral clout. Due to his access to the central government, he was able to project it as a national issue. This was inherited as a legacy by Mamata Bandyopadhyay who went on to use her position first in the INC and then as an ally of the NDA government to intervene in the immigration discourse with both electoral dominance and national security in mind. In both cases, the projection of a local issue to the national level of political discourse was key to its future shape. The CPI(M), on the other hand, drove the issue at both international and national scales of negotiation with regards to both visa administration at the Bangladesh border and the propensity of other Indian states to deport refugee families back to West Bengal without proper discussion or policy decisions at the national level. This push by the CPI(M) had also come at their highest point of national political ambition. The RPI and later organizations like the AFRI and the JACBR remained arrested at the local level of agitation and opinion building and have not been particularly successful in communicating the nuances of the issue at a national scale. However, in the case of the RPI we can also see a willingness for strategic flexibility where the organization was able to bring together diverse political actors; some of whom were considered opponents by the national leadership of the party. At the most abstract and vertically highest scale the negotiation about immigration concerns diplomatic communication and national policy on border control and security. At a local level, it is coloured by economic and electoral concerns. It would seem that the issue is arrested by its disaggregation across these various scales.

The autonomous organizations find it extremely difficult to keep any viable control over the negotiations because of (a) their highly localized capacity for mobilization, (b) the capacity of political parties to co-opt larger community religious organizations and (c) the inaccessibility of the central government except through national parties. These organizations can therefore only effectively negotiate at the level of the state government. The state government as we can see is engaged in its own negotiations and competition with the parties in power at the centre. Oftentimes, the negotiation between the ruling regime at the state level, and the Namasudra activists is over-determined by a set of national and international factors that are placed entirely outside the reach of the local activists. The larger community organizations like the MM are trying to address this problem of multiple scales of negotiation by focusing primarily on the highest or central authority. However, such a negotiation cannot happen without a revision of the demands and solutions on the part of the community religious organizations. This Gordian knot of multiscale negotiations preserves the anti-immigrant consensus flagged by the Namasudra activists, buttressing their suspicion of political parties. Simultaneously, this architecture of the negotiation decreases institutional channels for finding durable solutions.

References

Ananda Bajar Patrika. (2016, 02 18). Bangladeshi tash khellen Mamata. Anandabajar Patrika, p. 6.

Bandyopadhyay, S. (2009). Partition and the Ruptures in Dalit Identity Politics in Bengal. *Asian Studies Review, 33*(4), 455–467.

Bandopadhyay, S. (2011). *Caste Protest and Identity in Colonial India: The Namasudras of Bengal, 1842-1947*. Oxford University Press

Baruah, A. (2003, February 16) "Illegal immigration on both sides", *The Hindu*, http://www.hindu.com/thehindu/2003/02/16/stories/2003021605050800.htm (accessed 7th June 2012).

Basu, J. (1992, 10 11). Onuprobesh somoshyar prokrito samadhan proyojon. Ganashakti, p. 4.

Bhattacharya, D. (2001). "'Civic Community' and its Margins: School Teachers in Rural West Bengal". *Economic and Political Weekly, 36*(8), 673–683.

Bhattacharya, D. (2009). "Of Control and Factions: The Changing Party-Society in Rural West Bengal". *Economic and Political Weekly, 44*(9), 59–69.

Bhattacharya, M. (2003, February 16). "Bengal police to intensify vigil against infiltration from Bangladesh". *The Hindu*, http://www.hindu.com/thehindu/2003/02/16/stories/2003021605000800.htm (accessed on 7th June 2012).

Biswas, S. (2018). *Nagorikotto Ain, NRC ebon UdbastuManusherSomosya O Tar Samadhan*. Chianobboi Prakashani.

Chatterjee, H. (2012). Refugee Afterlife in West Bengal: A Study of The Camp and The Colony, *Unpublished M.Phil dissertation*, Jawaharlal Nehru University

Chatterjee, H. (2018). "Partitioned Urbanity: A Refugee Village Bordering Kolkata". *Economic and Political Weekly, 53*(12), 93–100.

Chatterjee, H. (2019a). "Why Scheduled Caste Refugees of Bengal Are Resisting CAA and NRC", *The Wire*, https://thewire.in/rights/scheduled-caste-refugees-bengal-caa-protest (accessed on 23rd June 2022).

Chatterjee, H. (2019b). "বজিপেরি হনি্দু উদ্বাস্তু প্রমে একটি ব্রাহ্মণ্যবাদী রাষ্ট্রীয় মথি্যাচার", *The Indian Express: Bangla*, https://bengali.indianexpress.com/opinion/caa-hindu-refugee-bjp-dual-standard-173519/ (accessed on 23rd June 2022).

Chatterjee, N. (1992). Midnight's Unwanted Children: East Bengali Refugees and the politics of Rehabilitation, *Unpublished thesis*, Brown University.

Chatterjee, P. (2004). *The Politics of the Governed: Reflections on Popular Politics in Most of the World*. Permanent Black.

Das, J. (2019). "Trinomuli Matua Shibire Antorkoloho?" *Indian Express*. http://164.100.47.5/rs/book2/reports/home_aff/107threport.htm (accessed on 25th January 2022).

Das, K. (2015). "Subaltern Historiography to Dalit Historiography: Tracing Heterogeneity in Dalit 'Subalternity'". *Economic and Political Weekly*, *L*(7), 60–65.

Dasgupta, R. (2009). "The CPI(M) Machinery in West Bengal: Two Village Narratives from Kochbihar and Malda". *Economic and Political Weekly*, *44*(9), 70–81.

Datta, A. (2013). *Refugees and Borders in South Asia: The Great Exodus of 1971*, Routledge, London & New York, pp. 128–137.

EPW. (1992). "Operation Pushback". *Economic and Political Weekly*, 45(27). 2391–2392.

Estimates Committee. (1989). *Rehabilitation of Migrants From East Bengal*. New Delhi: Government of India.

Guha, A. (2019). "Is There a Second Wave of Dalit Upsurge in West Bengal?" *Economic and Political Weekly Engage*, *54*(2), https://www.epw.in/engage/article/is-there-a-second-wave-of-dalit-upsurge-in-west-bengal (accessed on 30th August 2022)

Jalais, A. (2005). "Dwelling on Marichjhapi: When Tigers Became Citizens and Refugees Tiger Food". *Economic and Political Weekly*, *40*(17), 1757–1762.

Mallick, R. (1999). "Refugee Resettlement in Forest Reserves: West Bengal Policy Reversal and Marichjhapi Massacre". *The Journal of Asian Studies*, *58*(1), 104–125.

Menon, N. & Nigam, A. (2011). "Anti-Corruption Movement and the Left". *Economic and Political Weekly*, *46* (37), 16–18.

Mitra,S.(2003,February17)."FrontierFracas:ImmigrantsontheBorder",*IndiaToday*, https://www.indiatoday.in/magazine/neighbours/story/20030217-bangladesh-takes-213-immigrants-back-india-needs-to-decide-what-to-do-with-16-mn-others-793450-2003-02-17 (accessed on 25th January 2022).

Nagaraj D. R. (2010). *The Flaming Feet: A Study of the Dalit Movement in India*. Permanent Black, pp. 27–34.

Omvedt, G. (1993). *Reinventing Revolution: New Social Movements and the Socialist Tradition in India*. M. E. Sharpe.

Pillai, M.B. & Joshy, P. M. (2012). "Old Elite are Co-opted, Subdued or Oppressed?: The politics of Anti-corruption Crusade in India in Perspective". *Indian Journal of Public Administration*, *58*(1), 1–14

Rajya Sabha (2003). 107th report, http://164.100.47.5/rs/book2/reports/home_aff/107threport.htm (accessed on 25th January 2022).

Ramachandran, S. (2002). "Operation Pushback: Sangh Paribar, State, Slums". *Singapore Journal of Tropical Geography*, 23(3), 311–332.

Republican (1979, September 20). *Votar Talika Sombondhe Congress (I) erGatro-daho*. Republican Party of India.

Roy, A. (2010). *Mapping Citizenship in India*. Oxford University Press.

Sarker, K. (2018). "Social Movements in India: From Institutional Politics to Participatory Democracy". *Journal of Politics and Governance*, 7(2), 5–19.

Schendel, W. (2005). *The Bengal Borderland: Beyond State and Nation in South Asia*. Anthem.

Sheth, D.L. (2018). "Civil Society and Non-party Political Formations". In P. deSouza (ed.), *At Home with Democracy* (pp. 71–86). Palgrave Macmillan.

Sinharoy, P. (2012). "A New Politics of Caste". *Economic and Political Weekly*, 47(34), 26–27.

Sinharoy, P. (2016). "Building up the Harichand-Guruchand Movement: The Politics of the MatuaMahasangha". In Uday Chandra, Geir Heierstad and Kenneth Bo Nielsen (eds.), *The Politics of Caste in West Bengal* (pp. 147–168). Routledge.

Sinharoy, P. (2019). "To Be a Hindu Citizen: Politics of Dalit Migrants in Contemporary West Bengal". *South Asia: Journal of South Asian Studies*, 42(2), 359–374.

Sitapati, V. (2011). "What Anna Hazare's Movement and India's New Middle Classes Say about Each Other". *Economic and Political Weekly*, 46(30), 39–44.

Telegraph (2003, February 1). "Border Forces Push Back And Forth". *The Telegraph*, http://www.telegraphindia.com/1030201/asp/nation/story_1628751.asp (accessed 7th June 2012).

Verma M. (2020). "India Has Long Granted Citizenship to Refugees; CAA Is Just a Step towards a Hindu Rashtra". *The Caravan*, https://caravanmagazine.in/politics/india-has-long-granted-citizenship-persecuted-refugees-caa-step-towards-hindu-rashtra (accessed on 23rd June 2022).

Chapter 10

Muslims between Citizenship and Media Bias

Insights from Anti-CAA Protest Sites

Mohammad Reyaz, Kaifia Ancer Laskar and Furquan Ameen

I Introduction

The Citizenship Amendment Act (CAA), 2019, and the proposal for the controversial National Population Register (NPR), leading to the National Register of Citizens (NRC) witnessed countrywide protests, particularly by Muslims. Driven by the survival instinct of now or never, Muslims feared losing citizenship like many did in Assam after the state-wide NRC process. Reyaz (2021a) notes instances of inhabitants of Assam such as the Assamese Muslims, Hindus with North Indian origin, ethnic Koch Rajbongshi also being "declared illegal immigrants" by the Foreigners Tribunals. Stories of long-drawn-out legal hassles and harassment of the marginalized during the Assam's NRC process furthered the fear and desolation among protestors. The pent-up anxieties found expression in sit-ins at protest sites across India after the brutal police crackdown on the students of Jamia Millia Islamia. The protests, primarily led by women, also brought to the fore their assertion of religious identity while simultaneously pressing for civic and legal rights as equal citizens who were not willing to accept second-class citizenship. But the February 2020 targeted violence against protesters on multiple sites – particularly in north-east Delhi and the state crackdown in Uttar Pradesh – appeared to be aimed at teaching a lesson or two to the Muslims and showing them their place in India.

The coverage of the protests (Alam, 2019) and the subsequent violence (Ahmad, 2020; India Today, 2019) has further deepened the general distrust Muslims held against the media, who perceive the fourth estate as prejudiced and an organ of the ruling dispensation. In contrast, our ethnography revealed how protestors utilized new media as an alternative channel of communication to reach out to their target audience.

II Sociopsychological Factors and Moral Outrage

After the electoral victory in 2014, the Bharatiya Janata Party (henceforth BJP) provoked debates and enacted laws that were largely seen as a part of its ideological baggage, aimed at vilification of Muslims. The included laws

DOI: 10.4324/9781003345152-15

on Triple Talaq (Agnes, 2018), uniform civil code, alleged conspiracies on 'Love Jihad' (Shah, 2021), alleged cow smuggling and slaughter (Deol, 2021), and the CAA – which ensured citizenship to non-Muslims from three neighbouring Muslim countries. The threat of a nationwide NRC made the country's Muslim citizenry cautious of the nefarious motive of disenfranchisement if they failed to prove their citizenship through legacy documents – which women are often not entitled to (Deka, 2020). The protests, mostly led by women, also brought to the fore the assertion of religious identity while simultaneously also pressing for their civic and legal rights as equal citizens. Malhotra (2021) posits that women's bodies have remained the sites of contestation in the Indian subcontinent since partition. Given the history of partition, natural disasters and social fabric, demanding proof of citizenship based on legacy documents would be a harrowing journey for the disadvantaged, religious minorities, women and sexual minorities (Saha, 2021). Women have mostly remained excluded from holding entitlements to land or lineage, with erroneous insertions and spelling mistakes in property deeds, birth certificates and educational records. Many women have been left out of the final list of NRC in Assam, being unable to produce the "legacy documents" deemed necessary for citizenship (Singh, 2019; Saha, 2021). Owing to these motivations, the women in Delhi's Shaheen Bagh and Kolkata's Park Circus portrayed the firm determination of their fight for their children's future. Much like the earlier women-led movements, the anti-CAA protests staged across India faced brutal crackdowns by the state but on a higher scale.

This is what drove the Delhi protests in the winter of 2019, spearheaded by Muslim students and women congregating at Shaheen Bagh. There has been some research on the anti-CAA protests (Ahmed, 2022; Bhatia, 2021; Bhushan, 2021; Gupta, 2021; Mustafa, 2020; Ohm, 2021; Salam, 2021), but none were able to explain how such a movement evolved. Building upon ethnographic studies of protest sites of Delhi and Kolkata, this chapter looks at the way Muslims resist or negotiate their identities and assert their democratic rights as citizens. It further looks at the media's attitude towards Muslims in general and the protestors in particular, and how the new media provides alternative spaces of expression and dissent. Co-author Furquan Ameen recorded his first-hand observation from the CAA protests in Delhi at Shaheen Bagh, Jamia and other places, and subsequent violence in northeast Delhi in February 2020. The CAA protests in Kolkata at Park Circus, Metiabruz and Ekbalpur were observed and analyzed by Mohammad Reyaz and Kaifia Ancer Laskar. The ethnographic methodology also adopted in-depth interviews of select female participants who were either organizers or took up active roles in the protests and even faced trolling or cyberbullying.

III Individual Discontent into Collective Mobilization

Muslims have remained the victims of otherization and persecution in post-partition India, for reasons that have been naturalized in the popular majoritarian consciousness (Pandey, 1999; Anand, 2005; Reyaz, 2017; Reyaz, 2019). Ohm (2021) argues that the orchestrated violence to silence Muslims in 2002 (Gujarat) and 2020 (Delhi) has a lot to do with the consolidation of the majority's trust in the able leadership of the ruling government in teaching Muslims a lesson.

From the demolition of Babri Masjid in 1992 through the Gujarat pogrom in 2002 to the recent enactment of the CAA (Malhotra, 2021), use of the media and violence and targeting of dissident voices from the minority community, Hindutva politics has gained prominence and a strong foothold in the country. This has been achieved mainly by dehumanizing, othering and labelling Muslims and other minorities as anti-nationals and secondary citizens (Dayal, 2011). The protests were a result of emotional discontent arising out of the aforementioned factors.

Jasper (1998) describes the role of emotions as means and ends to protests. Drawing on his theories of emotional discontent, anger and fear are the two most common precursors for the mobilization of protests. CAA as a discriminatory law triggered the dormant fear among the Muslims and the marginalized, along with an outburst of anger against the crackdown on students of Jamia Millia Islamia (Siddiqui, 2020). When the famous *Daadiyan (*grandmothers) of Shaheen Bagh were repeatedly asked by the media as to why they protested at such an old age, they responded, "[T]his is for our children, our next generation" (Upadhyay, 2020). Asmat Jamil, the architect of the Park Circus protest, echoed on similar lines.

The protest outside Delhi's Jamia Millia Islamia could have been any other student protest in the country if not for the high handedness of the government. On Friday, December 13, 2019, two days after the enactment of the CAA, protestors had gathered outside the university campus for a protest march to the Parliament. The Delhi police resorted to tear gas and lathi charge to disperse the crowd (Ameen, 2019b). On Sunday, December 15, 2019 (Express News Service, 2020), in another protest, students and local residents of Jamia Nagar had gathered outside the college, but by late afternoon, things became grim. A brutal crackdown ensued wherein policemen and paramilitary forces donning riot gear stormed the university campus with tear gas shelling and lathi charge. Staff members and students, including female students, inside libraries and mosques were mercilessly beaten, wounded were picked up and detained at the local police station (PTI, 2019). Students who were inside the libraries preparing for their examinations were caught like sitting ducks. The police and the paramilitary forces went inside and ruthlessly assaulted the students, many had fractured limbs, and one of them lost sight in one eye (Ravi, 2020).

A similar action was taken by the Uttar Pradesh police in the Aligarh Muslim University where the students had gathered in solidarity to protest against the police crackdown in Jamia. The brutal crackdown in another "minority institution" was seen as an attack on Muslims (The Wire Staff, 2019). Scenes of violence in the form of videos and pictures accompanied by desperate audio messages of students pleading for help went viral across Facebook, Instagram and WhatsApp groups. Even before the mainstream media could understand what was happening inside these universities, the frantic SOS calls had already flooded the new media #SOSJamia #CAA2019 (PTI, 2019).

Responding to the violent crackdown on students and rumours of similar action in the Muslim neighbourhood, locals came out and occupied the road on the southern edge of the Jamia Nagar's Shaheen Bagh locality. A day after, on December 16, 2019, students and locals had also gathered on the main road dividing the main campus of Jamia.

Many have tried to unravel what brought *Shaheen Bagh ki Auratein* (the women of Shaheen Bagh) on the roads that would eventually emerge as a historical opposition to the Narendra Modi–led government's amendments to the citizenship laws. Shaheen Bagh soon turned into an epicentre of protest where resilient Muslim women and youth set a template for scores of similar anti-CAA protest sites across the country (Ameen, 2020a). Shaheen Bagh became a metaphor of resistance against the hegemonic forces. The protestors resorted to non-violent means, chanting the national anthem and echoing slogans given out during India's freedom struggle against the British. The physicality and resolve of the women of Shaheen Bagh and other such protest sites spurred the imagination of an "imagined community" (Anderson, 2006), irrespective of religious and political leanings. What prompted these women was not restricted to their existential crisis but a resolution to stand up against the wrong done against their children (metaphorically) at Jamia Millia Islamia. Jamia fanned the aspiration of the dwellers of the locality of Shaheen Bagh for a better future for their children who were pursuing or dreamt of education in the institution. It seems that the images of police brutality shattered those dreams which left no other way for them but to vent out their emotions through their body. Similar studies (Bhushan, 2021; Gupta, 2021) chronicling the trajectory of these protests into a movement give credit to the Muslim women for standing up for something that was not related to the usual signifiers of oppression associated with them in the mainstream discourse, for example Triple Talaq, the issue of veil or polygamy. The anti-CAA protests transformed into sites of struggle to safeguard their existence by clinging to both nationalistic symbols and religious assertion.

IV The *Dadis* and Mothers of Shaheen Bagh

Sometime in January, almost a month into the protests, co-author Furquan Ameen met Kahkashan, a young mother of two who had come out to protest and helped manage the stage at the protest site. She said that it was the brutality on students of Jamia that motivated them. "When they can blind an eye of a student sitting inside the library, they can also attack these women sitting in their homes. Ask anyone why they are here and they'll tell you it is for their children," said Kahkashan. She further added, "[I]f they hadn't entered the library and brutalized the kids, I think, you wouldn't have seen so many women out here today".

Over the period of the protests, Ameen also spoke to the famed *Dadis* (grandmothers) of Shaheen Bagh on several occasions, and they maintained that they were forced out on the road amid severe winter, as they could not bear students being brutally beaten up. Similarly, when three of the *Daadis* appeared on NDTV's prime-time show in January 2020 (Upadhyay, 2020) and were asked for the reason behind their protest, they emphasized that other than the police brutality on students they wanted to ensure that the "black laws" (CAA) are repealed for the protection of their future generations. "We are here for our children. We don't fear death," said Asma Khatoon, the oldest *Daadi* in the gathering.

By early March, despite the desolation after the violence in north-east Delhi, where more than 50 persons were killed, Shaheen Bagh's women remained determined to continue the protest, even with reduced numbers as the government restricted the number of participants in any gathering to 50 as the scare of the COVID-19 pandemic grew. Khatoon and other *dadis* told Ameen that they were not scared of the virus but were anxious about the ill motives of the state towards Muslims. They categorically emphasized their determination and grit to stand their ground. "*Bandook chala doge tab bhi nahi hatenge*" (Even if they fire on us, we will not leave [the protest]), said a 90-year-old Khatoon. This sentiment resonated with many in the locality who either lived in Jamia Nagar or were directly or indirectly linked to the university.

V Park Circus, "Kolkata's Shaheen Bagh"

After Assam, West Bengal is a state that would be severely affected in case NRC is implemented in the future as a sizable population of the state is of East Bengal origin, and a vast majority of them are Hindus (Ghosh, 2019). Still, Bengal did not see the kind of anti-CAA momentum in the early days of the protest. Probably because, like Assam, the BJP was successful in convincing the majority of Hindus of East Bengal origin that they would eventually be allowed a backdoor entry through the CAA, even if they fail to produce legacy documents (Reyaz, 2021a). However, there were some token protests by "usual suspects": left-leaning groups, university teachers and student unions. Students, teachers and staff of Jadavpur University, Presidency University and Aliah University, among others organized several such protests.

For a change, however, these protests witnessed a sizeable number of Muslims, many participating for the first time, like in Delhi. But Kolkata had no sustained dharna like Shaheen Bagh till the first week of January. On January 7, 2020, Asmat Jamil, now deceased, a female resident from central Kolkata who ran a social organization Azzumar, along with some of her supporters, sat on dharna at Park Circus maidan (Ghatak, 2020). She was joined by a city-based activist, Uzma Alam; a research scholar, Nousheen Baba Khan; and a few others. It soon came to be referred to as "Kolkata's Shaheen Bagh". In weeks to follow, like other parts of the country, several such big and small *dharnas* began in Rajabazar, Ekbalpur, Metiabruz and Zakaria Street, among others, all Muslim-dominated pockets of the city.

Noor Mehvish, a hijab-wearing college student who hardly went to public gatherings earlier, became one of the important people in organizing the protest in her Metiabruz locality. Talking to Mohammad Reyaz, she said, "[T]his movement has shown the world that hijab is not a sign of oppression. Muslim women are claiming and fighting for their rights and against the discrimination they face."

Mehvish Khan, another college graduate, was one of the prominent faces of the Ekbalpur protest. She viewed the protest as an empowering process that helped her to work for female education. While she found support in family, she also faced discouraging comments from her relatives: "*do chaar kitaab parh li ho toh dimag kharab hogaya*" (reading a book or two has ruined your mind). But this only strengthened her resolve.

Not everyone was new to protests. Nousheen Baba Khan, a research scholar at a university in Kolkata, did participate in a few protests as a student. But it was the anti-CAA protests which brought her to the larger public sphere. She expressed her anguish over people compromising reason and debate with divisive narratives. "The day before I hit the street, I had only one longing in mind, I needed to make sure that people joined this historic movement in large numbers," she said. However, her activism has never been a smooth ride as she often gets targeted and vilified. But she remains undeterred. "*Family hai isiliye main raaste par hoon*" (I am here on the road because I have a family), she explained.

The involvement of these women experiencing such a form of physicality for the first time brought uniqueness to the anti-CAA protests across India. Years of bottled-up angst against the domination and exclusion they witnessed in their societies fuelled their participation. For Muslim women, who were experiencing political engagements in public sphere, these protests opened new avenues of expression and assertion. Watching protestors from a distance, we were amazed at the energy the participants displayed as they chanted, "*Hum kya chahte? Azadi!*" (What do we need? Freedom!) or "*Apna haq leke rahenge*" (We shall take our rights) or "*Hum kagaz nahi dikhayenge*" (We will not show our documents).

VI The Social Fabric of Protesters

Initially, as the protest spread and started getting the attention of activists, politicians and regular folks of all hues and colours, a raging debate emerged regarding the character of the protest. Whether this was a secular protest or was it largely limited to the Muslim community? The debate started with some protesters chanting slogans with religious overtones such as '*Allahu Akbar*', '*Tera mera rishta kya? La ilahaillallah*' and more. Many left-liberals and intellectuals, most prominently Congress leader Shashi Tharoor, claimed that such chants manifested "religious fundamentalism" and "extremist" position of the protesters (Khan, 2020). Tharoor later tweeted that "the phrase '*tera mera rishta la ilaha illallah*' tends to isolate the community from others whose *rishta* is to India," adding, "You can't fight Hindutva communalism by promoting Muslim communalism" (Amin & Mushtaq, 2019). Many Muslims, however, disagreed, and called out their "Islamophobia of selective solidarity" (Amin & Mushtaq, 2019), stressing that they expected them to be "allies (and) not patrons" (Khan, 2020).

Nonetheless, as the debate raged, organizers on most protest sites took caution to throw out or at least sideline those who had "communal" intentions to allay the concerns of non-Muslims who came to express their solidarity. Sharjeel Imam, for example, played a crucial role in the initial days of the Shaheen Bagh protest (Reyaz, 2020). He was eventually sidelined and even pushed off the stages at Shaheen Bagh and Jamia by other protestors who found his statements uncomfortable. One of his speeches was later misconstrued as a call for breaking the country and was used to implicate and incarcerate him (Venkatesan, 2021). Around the same time, Sikh farmers from Punjab came to Shaheen Bagh to extend their support and organize daily *langar* (community kitchen) for the protesters. The New Year and Republic Day celebrations at Shaheen Bagh also garnered a lot of attention as it set the tempo for similar celebrations at other sites. At Kolkata's Ekbalpur, a blood donation camp was organized to mark the day, while a day earlier drawing competitions were also organized for children.

Despite the attempts to make the protest appear "secular", the majority of the protesters – except in a few prominent protest sites – remained Muslims. Reports from different parts of the country (Ameen, 2020a; Bakshi, 2021), as well as our observations in Delhi and Kolkata, suggest that these protest sites had turned into a pilgrimage for the secular and liberal-minded people, irrespective of their affiliations. While the major political parties visibly stayed away from the protests, the local workers from the community, however, provided support irrespective of their political and ideological affiliations. For instance, Ishrat Jahan, a former councillor from the Congress party and Tahir Hussain, an incumbent Aam Aadmi Party (AAP) councillor, among others provided support to some of the *dharnas* in north-east Delhi. The two were later imprisoned under the draconian Unlawful Activities (Prevention) Act and other charges for allegedly inciting violence during the 2020 Delhi pogrom (Ahmad, 2020; Iyer, 2021). Shaheen Bagh, too, witnessed politicians and activists holding varied ideologies extend their support. In Kolkata as well, there were allegations that the protests, including in Park Circus, were hijacked by the state administration led by Trinamool Congress (TMC). It is undeniable that unlike Delhi or Uttar Pradesh, protestors in West Bengal did not have to face a hostile state administration, but it is also true that the chief minister of West Bengal did not visit the protest site herself. She, however, did lead several anti-CAA protests in the state and made it clear that she will not allow the implementation of CAA in her state (Chatterji, 2020).

VII Role of the New Media

Multiple studies have shown that mainstream media is largely biased against Muslims and has helped in stereotyping and reiterating negativity to the point of vilifying and othering them (Laskar & Reyaz, 2021). The coverage of anti-CAA protests was no different (Alam, 2019), except by The Telegraph and NDTV to an extent. Almost daily, news channels held discussions where Muslims and the protests were associated with *jihad*, conspiracy by 'foreign elements', *tukde tukde* (divisive) gangs and others (Grewal et al., 2020). The anti-CAA protest was primarily against the BJP-led government's attempt to disenfranchise Muslims, but it was also manifested against the Delhi-based media – often referred to as the national media. However, online media platforms, such as The Quint, The Wire, Scroll, News Laundry and others, offered a balanced coverage of the protests.

Challenged by a barrage of misinformation and misleading shows and articles by mainstream media, the protesters relied on new media to access authentic information. Social media was primarily used for mobilization and dissemination of information related to campaigns and protest gatherings. In fact, protest organizers often used WhatsApp and Telegram groups for their on-the-go discussions. One of the prominent examples was a WhatsApp group called 'Jamia Coordination Committee', a group of Jamia students and alumni who had come together to organize and agitate. The group organized events and shaped the larger campaign, and even facilitated media reach out. Members of the group, however, became victims of the state witch-hunt with many receiving legal notices and were interrogated. Records of the same WhatsApp group conversations were used to frame them. President of the Jamia Alumni Association Shifa-Ur-Rehman, students Meeran Haider, Asif Iqbal Tanha and Safoora Zargar were accused of inciting violence in Delhi and sent to jail (Tanha and Zargar are out on bail as of October 2021).

Facebook pages and groups, YouTube channels, Instagram and Twitter handles had become popular during the period for those looking for information independent of mainstream media and, at times, to track updates on daily events. Social media accounts such as the Facebook group 'India Against Citizenship Amendment Act (CAA) & NRC', with 244,000 members (IACAA & NRC, n.d.), had emerged as key virtual spaces for collating and disseminating information related to the protests.

With multiple protest sites and rapid developments, mainstream media houses struggled to cover or authenticate news in real time. Influencers and independent journalists, who adopted new media tools, filled this void by verifying and sharing information through their social media accounts. Many protestors, activists and journalists often went 'live' on social media platforms from the protest sites to reach a wider audience. For example, Saahil Murli Menghani, a former News18 journalist, and several individual accounts such as Sawhneyyyyy (Instagram handle) and Purani Dilli Waalo ki Baatein (Instagram handle) amplified efforts on the ground.

Shaheen Bagh organizers had set up their own social media accounts for direct public interaction and, more important, to dispel rumours and misinformation about the protest. Similarly, other protest sites had also set up their accounts. Community news portal TwoCircles.net relayed 'live' broadcasts on YouTube from Shaheen Bagh and uploaded recordings from Park Circus (YouTube channel of TCN, n.d.), especially in the initial days. Other portals, such as Maktoob, an independent community-led digital news initiative, gained prominence during this period. Maktoob famously accessed and published the closed-circuit TV (CCTV) videos from December 15, the day students were beaten up inside Jamia's campus and library. The videos captured the brutality of the personnel, who not only assaulted students but destroyed university resources. Similarly, in Kolkata, ETV Bharat Urdu and hyperlocal online media such as News Tag India, Halaat-e-Bangal, JKV News and JKB News, among others, had become very popular among protesters.

What happened after the violence inside the Jamia campus is a prime example of the use of new media. After the crackdown in Jamia Millia Islamia, several students were picked up and kept in illegal detention in police stations. A call for an 'emergency protest' was given by the Jawaharlal Nehru University (JNU) Students' Union and promoted by the young citizenry of Delhi chiefly using social media posts, text and audio messages. Within a few hours, lawyers and activists were outside police stations demanding answers while hundreds, wrapped in woollens on that chilly winter night, had gathered outside the Delhi police headquarters seeking the release of the detained students. Similarly, civil society groups and individual activists such as the Delhi-based lawyers' collectives called the Indian Civil Liberties Union (ICLU) used social media to respond to SOS messages in case of police summons, detentions or arrests during and after the protests. Forums of artists on Instagram like the 'Creatives Against CAA' (Instagram handle) and other graphic and comic spaces also helped spread awareness about protests and countered state propaganda. Reyaz (2021b, p. 57) has argued,

> Internet and social media have provided an alternative 'third space' of communication, and have given them voices that they hitherto were denied in the traditional media. ... [The]new media is helping Muslims engage with the larger society by giving them an alternative platform to assert their identity.

VIII Aftermath of the Dissent

Following the incidents in Jamia and AMU, a wave of protests gripped the country. The protests in Uttar Pradesh, however, took a grim turn as the state resorted to brute force to discourage the spread of protests. On December 19, responding to different calls to protest across the state, protestors had gathered in prominent cities. While it was claimed that the protest in the state capital Lucknow turned violent, state police had resorted to using force in several other places where peaceful rallies were organized. In a matter of days, during the police action, about twenty people were killed, more than a thousand were arrested and hundreds were put in detention (Rashid, 2019). One region that witnessed the most suppression by the State was western Uttar Pradesh, where, as widely reported, the police resorted to door-to-door crackdown that terrorized Muslims who dared to protest (India Today, 2019). Despite the state action, the protests in Uttar Pradesh took root at least in major cities such as Lucknow, Kanpur, and Allahabad, among others. Shaheen Bagh remained the inspiration for all even as the state administration created obstacles on multiple occasions such as switching off the lights at Lucknow's Hussainabad clock tower and putting up banners with photographs of protestors accused of inciting violence.

In Delhi, protests initially limited to Jamia and Shaheen Bagh had spread to more areas after a few weeks. More than 15 sit-in protests had taken root in Delhi alone, with at least six concentrated around north-east Delhi's Seelampur-Mustafabad area, home to a large migrant population mostly from neighbouring Uttar Pradesh. Delhi assembly elections were just round the corner as well with polling scheduled in early February. Electorally, the east and northeast Delhi has remained a focus of the BJP where prominent leaders like Yogi Adityanath, Amit Shah and J. P. Nadda had convened meetings or election rallies in the area. These stages were used by the BJP leaders to rile up sentiments against anti-CAA protestors. In Karawal Nagar, Adityanath said that Congress leaders and Delhi chief minister Arvind Kejriwal had the habit to "feed Biryani over incidents like Shaheen Bagh, it is not a BJP habit" (Hindustan Times, 2020). In Babarpur, another neighbourhood in north-east Delhi, Shah had said that people should "press the (voting) button [with such anger] that the current is felt at Shaheen Bagh" (Ameen, 2020b). In the same election season, union minister Anurag Thakur lead a crowd of BJP supporters into chants of "*Desh ke gaddaron ko, goli-maro salon ko*" (shoot the traitors of the country) which later became an infamous slogan used by the right to target protesters (Krishnan, 2020).

In February 2020, Aam Aadmi Party came back to power in Delhi with the party winning all Muslim-dominated seats (First Post, 2020). Soon after Kejriwal took the oath as Delhi chief minister, north-east Delhi descended into communal mayhem. For more than a week, February 23 onwards, marauding Hindu mobs went around killing and assaulting people on the streets of northeast Delhi. More than 50 were killed, about two-thirds of them Muslims, and scores of houses, mosques and shops, largely belonging to Muslims, were destroyed and subject to arson (Delhi Minorities Commission, 2020). Independent fact-finding committees and the Delhi Minorities Commission (2020) established that it was targeted violence against Muslims which, everyone concurred, started soon after the provocation of a few BJP leaders, primarily Kapil Mishra (The Wire, 2020). Mishra, a local BJP leader known for his provocative statements, and his supporters had gathered near a protest site in Jafrabad and warned the police to take action against the protestors. In the presence of Delhi police officers, Mishra publicly threatened and gave an ultimatum to clear the roads (The Wire, 2020). The violence started in different pockets of the area the same evening. By the next day, violence had spread, especially in and around areas where sit-in protests were ongoing.

Late at night on February 24, co-author Ameen was reporting from the Jafrabad–Maujpur intersection where the protestors were still on the road. Many other protest sites remained inaccessible even as reports of continued violence kept pouring in, despite a heavy deployment of police personnel. About a kilometre away from the protest site, the spot where Mishra gave his ultimatum, were small groups of young men – donning saffron stoles, armed with rods and sticks, and a few with helmets – raised slogans, as hundreds of police in riot gears stood by the stretch of road strewn with stones and charred vehicles. The men shouted slogans of '*Bharat Mata ki Jai*' and '*Jai Shree Ram*'. As a motorcade of Delhi police made its way across the crowd the slogans changed to "*Yeh andar ki baathai, police hamare saath hai*" (this is an inside talk, police are with us) implying that the Delhi policemen deployed were on their side. They opposed the protesters sitting there and on the other end, protestors blamed Mishra for the violence. Several locals told Ameen that "the protest was on for two months but there were no incidents of violence. It all started after Mishra's provocation".

Ameen interviewed more than 100 people including protestors, those who were displaced by the subsequent violence and took refuge in different mosques and relief centres, attended funerals of riot victims, and met those who lost their businesses or got injured while escaping rioters. It was clear from the conversations that the anti-CAA protestors and the sit-in sites were the targets of those indulging in violence. In multiple interviews, people alleged involvement by the police in the violence or blamed them for ignoring their SOS calls. Shopkeepers of a tyre-market – largely owned by Muslims from Old Delhi – in Gokulpuri located right next to two police stations, claimed that their shops were set on fire on separate occasions over three days. Similarly, residents of Ganga Vihar, also a neighbourhood that had a sit-in protest, claimed that the police ignored their plea to intervene despite violent clashes. Yet in the next few months, as the country went into a nation-wide lockdown due to the pandemic, a witch-hunt had started where young Muslim men and women were picked up from north-east Delhi neighbourhoods and Jamia Nagar for their alleged involvement in the violence. Most remain behind bars, as of October 2021 although Delhi police have been criticized for their skewed investigation. A Delhi court even slapped a fine of Rs. 25,000 on the Delhi police and called its investigation "callous and farcical" (PTI, 2021).

IX Conclusion: Assertion of Collective Rights

While the incident in Jamia, and subsequently in Aligarh Muslim University, was a trigger behind these protests, it was also to vent an underlying insecurity of living as a Muslim in India. After the lynching of Mohammad Akhlaq, if we have to pick up a watershed moment in recent history, countless incidents of attacks on Muslims continue to be reported (Doto,2021; Statistica, 2020). Such blatant targeting has only increased over the years. Protests against the changes in the citizenship laws were only seen as a culmination of those anxieties. In one corner of the protest site in Shaheen Bagh, as well as Jamia, volunteers had erected a replica of a detention centre. This was a reference to what was happening to Muslims in Assam and what triggered frantic calls to "keep their documents in order" among the community residing in other states lest they too are rendered stateless (Ameen, 2019a, 2021; Siddiqui, 2020). One of the end products of the Assam movement, which started in the late 1970s as an anti-immigrant protest, were detention camps constructed to house declared foreigners (Ameen, 2020a). Saha (2021) states, "the foreigners were primary Muslims of East Bengal origin who had been living in Assam for generations". Over the years, the process of NRC, conducted under the supervision of the Supreme Court, was increasingly seen as a process to target Muslims (Saha, 2021). From the stages of Shaheen Bagh and other protest sites, and the conversations with women participants, it was clear that the NRC process in Assam and the detention camps fuelled the imagination of Muslims in India.

These anti-CAA protest sites gained strength from Muslim youth, irrespective of their gender, class, and political leanings, creating an imagined community. It was probably for the first time that Muslims in India were mobilized at this scale after independence creating a "virtual ummah" (el-Nawawy & Khamis, 2009) of sorts, connected by social media and a common cause. Siddiqui (2020), Reyaz (2017, 2021a, 2021b) and others have noted how the new generation of Muslims have increasingly become assertive and are not afraid of their past or shy away from expressing themselves. This assertive young generation helped sustain the movement for weeks despite hostile administration in many places, most notably in New Delhi. This can be substantiated by the now iconic photograph from December 15, 2019, which showed five girls, including three in hijabs, standing up to the police atrocities (Ashraf, 2019). This image, along with another of four girls raising slogans at Jamia campus (Sarkar, 2020), helped monumentalize what was then a nascent movement and caught the imagination of anti-CAA protesters.

The anti-CAA protests at Shaheen Bagh and Park Circus evolved as a shock and surprise to the harbingers of neoliberal flags who mostly took it upon themselves the responsibility to speak for the subaltern. These protests have shown that Muslim women are as keen on claiming their homeland like anyone else. According to *Narmada Bachao Andolan* activist Medha Patkar, women-led movements sustain longer as they do not give up (Bhowmick, 2020). Reports stated that despite health issues some of the ailing female protestors registered their presence at these protest sites. Two of the protestors, including Asmat Jamil mentioned earlier, who were part of the Park Circus protest despite their severe comorbidities, passed away during and after the protest. Engulfed within several intersectionalities, Muslim females are also at the receiving end. There have been reports of cybercrime, rape threats towards some of the protestors (Bhandari, 2021; Farooqui, 2021).

The women converged from sections with strict gender norms to participate in the protests which symbolized intersections of religion, class and gender (Matta, 2020a, 2020b). The perception of these congregations of Muslim women and their body politics in both onsite and online presence "to foster trans-local connection and sustain the movement" (Bhatia, 2021, p. 13) invigorated even the Indian secular-liberal elites to mingle with them (Malhotra, 2021). The prevailing fear of becoming stateless forced the Muslim citizenry, embodied in the women-led anti-CAA protests at various sites in India, to assert their identity and voice in claiming their political dignity at par with non-Muslims. The Muslim woman's body that always remained shadowed under their "emancipator-benevolent" men or the government and women's organizations have unsettled the ruling class by their sudden ability to act autonomously (Malhotra, 2021). We observed that with the anti-CAA protest, the Muslim males also supported the women in voicing their opinion in all possible means. What was also significant in these protests was its identification and celebration as "women-led" in media and academia, unlike any other protest in India. This was a protest for a cause which affected both men and women, yet women were at the forefront. Men often limited themselves to the margins, indulging in backroom work like putting up the tent, arranging food, managing the crowd, logistics or even standing guard against repressive means. Kumar (2020) and Kotak (2020) have also presented similar observations from different protest sites. Hence, contrary to the dominant discourse around the oppressive Muslim males, the anti-CAA protest sites also unravelled the counter-narrative of such a dominant discourse.

References

Agnes, F. (2018, January9). The triple talaq bill and BJP's selective concern for Muslim women. *The Wire*. https://thewire.in/gender/muslim-triple-talaq-bill/

Ahmad, I. (2020, March28). Violence after violence: The politics of narratives over the Delhi pogrom. *The Polis Project*. https://www.thepolisproject.com/read/violence-after-violence-the-politics-of-narratives-over-the-delhi-pogrom/

Ahmed, N. (2022). *Nothing Will Be Forgotten: From Jamia to Shaheen Bagh*. New Delhi: Left Word.

Alam, M. (2019, December29). CAA: The peaceful protests by Muslims that no one is talking about. *The Wire*. https://thewre.in/rights/caa-peaceful-protests-muslims/

Ameen, F. (2019a, September17). The NRC alarm: What Muslims across the country fear and why. *The Telegraph*. https://www.telegraphindia.com/india/the-nrc-alarm-what-muslims-across-the-country-fear-and-why/cid/1705638/

Ameen, F. (2019b, September 29). *The NRC alarm: What Muslims across the country fear and why*. Retrieved from The Telegraph: https://www.telegraphindia.com/india/the-nrc-alarm-what-muslims-across-the-country-fear-and-why/cid/1705638

Ameen, F. (2020a, January15). Shaheen Bagh inspires many protests across the country. *The Telegraph*. https://www.telegraphindia.com/india/shaheen-bagh-inspires-many-protests-across-the-country/cid/1736089

Ameen, F. (2020b, January 28). *Amit Shah baits Kejriwal with Shaheen Bagh*. Retrieved from The Telegraph: https://www.telegraphindia.com/delhi/delhi-assembly-elections-2020-amit-shah-tries-to-instigate-elicit-repsonse-from-arvind-kejriwal-on-shaheen-bagh/cid/1740315

Ameen, F. (2021, March 25). 'Stress on Hindu identity': BJP hate campaign in poll-bound Assam. *Al Jazeera*. https://www.aljazeera.com/news/2021/3/25/stress-on-hindu-identity-bjp-hate-campaign-in-poll-bound-assam/

Amin, M., & Mushtaq, S. (2019, December 31). To invoke Allah or to not: Secular Islamophobia and the protesting Indian Muslim. *The Caravan*. https://caravanmagazine.in/politics/to-invoke-allah-or-to-not-secular-islamophobia-and-the-protesting-indian-muslim

Anand, D. (2005). The violence of security: Hindu nationalism and the politics of representing 'the Muslim' as a danger. *The Round Table*, 94(379): 203–215.

Anderson, B. (2006). *Imagined Communities: Reflections on the Origin and Spread of Nationalism*. London: Verso Books.

Ashraf, S.F. (2019, December 17). Meet the face of the Jamia students'protest. *Rediff.com*. https://www.rediff.com/news/interview/meet-the-face-of-the-jamia-students-protest/20191217.htm

Bakshi, A. (2020, January 10). The old guard: Meet the elderly protesters of Zakir Nagar and Shaheen Bagh. *Mint*. https://www.livemint.com/mint-lounge/features/the-old-guard-meet-the-elderly-protesters-of-zakir-nagar-and-shaheen-bagh-11578659942897.html

Bhandari, H. (2021, August 19). Probe in 'Sulli deals' case hits legal hurdle. *The Hindu*. https://www.thehindu.com/news/cities/Delhi/probe-in-sulli-deals-case-hits-legal-hurdle/article35987910.ece/

Bhatia, K.V. (2021). The revolution will wear burqas: Feminist body politics and online activism in India. *Social Movement Studies*. https://doi.org/10.1080/14742837.2021.1944850

Bhowmick, N. (2020, January15). Women don't give up. Why female protesters are at the forefront of India's resistance movement. *Time*. https://time.com/5765702/india-protests-women/

Bhushan, B. (2021). Citizens, infiltrators, and others: The nature of protests against the citizenship amendment act. *South Atlantic Quarterly*, 120(1): 201–208. https://doi.org/10.1215/00382876-8795854

Chatterji, S. (2020, August 9). Mamata Banerjee is back to the streets over the citizenship law. Here is her plan. *Hindustan Times*. https://www.hindustantimes.com/india-news/why-mamata-banerjee-took-part-in-citizenship-law-protests-and-how-it-will-benefit-her-party/story-osC9mBF30IdmeqN7eCLIWK.html/

CreativeAgainstCAA. Instagram Account. Accessed on 23 August 2021. https://www.instagram.com/creativesagainstcaa/

Dayal, P. (2011, April 23). Modi wanted Muslims to be taught a lesson: Gujrat Cop. *The Times of India*. https://timesofindia.indiatimes.com/india/modi-wanted-muslims-to-be-taught-a-lesson-gujarat-cop/articleshow/8061738.cms

Deka, K. (2020, January 10). Expert view: Does India need CAA, NPR, NRC? *India Today*. https://www.indiatoday.in/india/story/expert-view-does-india-need-caa-npr-nrc-1635665-2020-01-10

Delhi Minorities Commission. (2020). *Report of the Fact-Finding Committee on the North-East Delhi Riots of February 2020*. Delhi: https://archive.org/details/dmc-delhi-riot-fact-report-2020.

Deol, K. (2021, July 7). Cow protection was a sensitive subject in India even when the Constitution was being framed. *Scroll*. https://scroll.in/article/998735/cow-protection-was-a-sensitive-subject-in-india-even-when-the-constitution-was-being-framed

DOTO (Documentation of the Oppressed) (n.d.). Accessed on 23 August 2021, http://dotodatabase.com/

El-Nawawy, M., & Khamis, S. (2009). The "Virtual Umma": Collective Identities in Cyberspace. In *Islam Dot Com* (pp. 113–163). Palgrave Macmillan, New York. https://link.springer.com/chapter/10.1057/9780230622661_5

Express News Service. (2020, February 17). *Jamia confirms video from library, says didn't release it*. Retrieved from The Indian Express: https://indianexpress.com/article/cities/delhi/jamia-confirms-video-from-library-says-didnt-release-it-6271517

Farooqui, S. (2021, July 16). Sulli deals': Muslim women in India being put up for sale. *Inter Press Service*. Accessed on 23 August 2021.https://www.ipsnews.net/2021/07/sulli-deals-muslim-women-india-put-sale/

First Post. (2020, February 12). Five Muslim candidates, all from AAP, emerge victorious in Delhi Assembly polls; 3 seats dominated by minority community post highest turnout. *First Post*. https://www.firstpost.com/politics/five-muslim-candidates-all-from-aap-emerge-victorious-in-delhi-assembly-polls-3-seats-dominated-by-minority-community-post-highest-turnout-8034091.html

Ghatak, A. (2020, January 15). At Kolkata's park circus, another women's sit-in protest keeps the struggle going. *The Wire*. https://thewire.in/rights/kolkata-park-circus-anti-caa-protest-women

Ghosh, A. (2019, December). Explained: Why west Bengal is in crosshairs of Citizenship Amendment Bill and NRC. *The Indian Express*. https://indianexpress.com/article/explained/why-west-bengal-is-in-crosshairs-of-cab-nrc-6160684/

Grewal, K., Sharma, U., Jha, F., & Deol, T. (2020, January 28). Sudhir Chaudhary & Deepak Chaurasia visit 'DilliKa Kashmir' — ShaheenBagh turns on them. *The Print*. https://theprint.in/plugged-in/sudhir-chaudhary-deepak-chaurasia-visit-dilli-ka-kashmir-shaheen-bagh-turns-on-them/355417/

Gupta, U.D. (2021). Chilli powder and resistance: Mirch Masala, ShaheenBagh, and the politics of space. *Jindal Global Law Review*, 12: 157–169. https://link.springer.com/article/10.1007/s41020-021-00143-8

Hindustan Times, (2020, September 9). EC sends notice to Yogi Adityanath for his 'Biryani for ShaheenBagh' remark. *Hindustan Times*. https://www.hindustantimes.com/india-news/yogi-adityanath-gets-ec-notice-over-his-kejriwal-feeding-biryani-to-shaheen-bagh-protesters-statement-at-delhi-s-poll-rally/story-dsDTqn87sWsD45AhNpFz2K.html/

IACAA& NRC. (n.d.). Facebook group: India against Citizenship Amendment Act (CAA) & NRC. Accessed on 23 August 2021. https://www.facebook.com/groups/1832157863618527

India Today. (2019, December 28). Rioters shocked into silence: UP CM justifies crackdown, says violent protesters will cry under Yogi govt. *India Today*. https://www.indiatoday.in/india/story/yogi-govt-rioters-shocked-up-cm-police-crackdown-violent-properties-seized-1632116-2019-12-28

Iyer, A.S. (2021, July 24). 'Driven, tolerant and warm': Who is Ishrat Jahan, Beyond being a UAPA accused? *The Quint*. https://www.thequint.com/news/india/ishrat-jahan-uapa-accused-congress-councillor-delhi-riots-2020

Jasper, J.M. (1998, September). The emotions of protest: Affective and reactive emotions in and around social movements. In *Sociological forum*, 13(3): 397–424. Kluwer Academic Publishers-Plenum Publishers. https://link.springer.com/article/10.1023/A:1022175308081/

Khan, F. (2020, January 15). Indian liberals missed the mark yet again by protesting 'la ilahaillallah' in CAA debate. *The Print*. https://theprint.in/opinion/indian-liberals-miss-mark-again-by-protesting-la-ilaha-illallah-in-caa-debate/349740/

Kotak, Y. (2020, January 30). Man behind the success of Mumbai Cental's Shaheen Bagh. *Hindustan Times*. https://www.hindustantimes.com/mumbai-news/men-behind-the-success-of-women-at-mumbai-central-s-shaheen-bagh/story-seQyRSX5dirUG1NKYV2CdM.html/

Krishnan, R. (2020, January 27).Days before Budget, minister Anurag Thakur chants '*deshkegaddaronko, golimaarosaalonko*'. *The Print*. https://theprint.in/india/days-before-budget-minister-anurag-thakur-chants-desh-ke-gaddaron-ko-goli-maaro-saalon-ko/355124/

Kumar, A. (2020, February 20). Women playing prominent role in anti- CAA, NR protests. *The Hindu*. https://www.thehindu.com/news/national/other-states/women-playing-prominent-role-in-anti-caa-nrc-protests/article30777618.ece/

Laskar, K.A., & Reyaz, M.(2021). Mapping the fake news infodemic amidst the COVID-19 pandemic: A study of Indian fact-checking websites. *Journal of Arab & Muslim Media Research*, 14(1), 93–116. https://doi.org/10.1386/jammr_00026_1

Malhotra, A. (2021, March 4). State, Patriarchy, and Muslim Women in India: A Historical Perspective on the Anti-CAA Protests. 14(4). 21st Century Global Dynamics. Accessed on 23 August 2021, https://globalejournal.org/global-e/march-2021/state-patriarchy-and-muslim-women-india-historical-perspective-anti-caa

Matta, A. (2020a, February 8). For women at protests, challenging NRC-CAA starts with defying sexism at home. *The Swaddle*. https://theswaddle.com/how-women-are-fighting-the-resistance-at-home-to-get-out-to-protest/

Matta, A. (2020b, February 15). Anti-NRC-CAA protests have left women more empowered, confident at home. *The Swaddle*. https://theswaddle.com/how-do-anti-nrc-caa-protests-affect-womens-lives/

Mustafa, S. (2020). *Shaheen Bagh and the Idea of India*. New Delhi: Speaking Tiger Books.

Ohm, B. (2021). Media against communication: Media/violence and conditionalities of Muslim silencing in Northern India. *Media, Culture & Society*, 43(4): 750–763. https://journals.sagepub.com/doi/abs/10.1177/0163443721994531/

Pandey, G. (1999). Can a Muslim be an Indian? *Comparative Studies in Society and History*, 41(4): 608–629.

PTI. (2019, December 16). *'Asked to leave campus with hands raised': Jamia students on police action*. Retrieved from The Hindustan Times: https://www.hindustantimes.com/india-news/jamia-protest-asked-to-vacate-campus-with-our-hands-raised-jamia-students-on-police-action/story-LarSwu4T0XZGDYGIta85hL.html

PTI (2021, July 14). Delhi riots: Court calls police probe 'callous', imposes Rs 25,000 fine. *Business Standard*. https://www.business-standard.com/article/current-affairs/delhi-riots-court-calls-police-probe-callous-imposes-rs-25-000-fine-121071400649_1.html

Rashid, O. (2019, December 26). Anti-CAA protests: 1,113 arrests, 5,558 preventive detentions, 19 dead in UP. *The Hindu*. https://www.thehindu.com/news/national/anti-caa-protests-1113-arrests-5558-preventive-detentions-19-dead-in-up/article30402858.ece/

Ravi, S. (2020, February 17). *Jamia viral video: student partially blinded in violence was in same room*. Retrieved from The Hindu: https://www.thehindu.com/news/cities/Delhi/student-partially-blinded-in-jamia-violence-was-in-same-room-as-viral-video/article61630318.ece

Reyaz, M. (2017). New found Muslim assertiveness in Bengal and the rise of Hindutva. *Café Dissensus: Special Issue* on *Muslim Life in West Bengal*, Issue 37 (July). ISSN: 2373-177X. https://cafedissensus.com/2017/07/15/new-found-muslim-assertiveness-in-bengal-and-the-rise-of-hindutva/

Reyaz, M. (2019). Hindutva's reach out to Muslims in 2014 elections: A historical analysis. In *The Algebra of Warfare-Welfare: A Long View of India's 2014 Elections*, edited by Irfan Ahmad & Pralay Kanungo, pp. 242–270. New Delhi: Oxford University Press.

Reyaz, M. (2020, January 26). Are You with Sharjeel Imam (& Sharjeel Usmani)? Or against them? *Beyond Headlines*.https://beyondheadlines.in/2020/01/are-you-with-sharjeel-imam/

Reyaz, M. (2021a, August 21). No land's people is an important document on Assam's NRC mess. *Outlook Magazine*. https://www.outlookindia.com/magazine/story/books-no-lands-people-is-an-important-document-on-assams-nrc-mess/304793

Reyaz, M. (2021b). New media, identity and minorities: The role of Internet in mainstreaming of Muslims in India. In *Inhabiting Cyberspace in India: Theory, Perspectives, and Challenges*, edited by Simi Malhotra, Kanika Sharma, & Sakshi Dogra, pp. 57–68. Singapore: Springer. https://doi.org/10.1007/978-981-15-9934-7_6

Saha, A. (2021). *No Land's People: The Untold Story of Assam's NRC Crisis*. New Delhi: HarperCollins.

Salam, Z.U. (2021). *ShaheenBagh: From a Protest to a Movement*. New Delhi: Bloomsbury India.

Sarkar, P. (2020, January 5). These three Jamia Millia girls have become the face of CAA protests. *She the People*. Accessed on 23 August 2021. https://www.shethepeople.tv/news/three-girls-jamia-millia-protest/

Sawhneyyyyy. (n.d.). Instagram account. Accessed on 23 August 2021. https://www.instagram.com/stories/highlights/17843125318888155/

Shah, A.P. (2021, January 31). 'Love Jihad' ordinance is symbolic of social fabric being aggressively changed: Justice A.P. Shah. *The Wire*. https://thewire.in/law/love-jihad-ordinance-communal-rhetoric-divisive-justice-ap-shah

Siddiqui, F.A. (2020, January 3). The demagogue and his labyrinth-four writers respond to India's Citizenship Amendment Act. *The Baffler*. https://thebaffler.com/logical-revolts/the-demagogue-and-his-labyrinth

Singh, A. (2019, November 29). Women 'Worst Victims' of NRC: Gendered and discriminatory nature of the register revealed. *The Citizen*. Accessed on 23 August 2021. https://www.thecitizen.in/index.php/en/NewsDetail/index/7/17924/Women-Worst-Victims-of-NRC-Gendered-and-Discriminatory-Nature-of-the-Register-Revealed

Statistica.com. (2020, October 21). Incidents of hate crimes across India in from September 2015 to December 2019, by identity of victims. Accessed on 20 August 2021. https://www.statista.com/statistics/980033/identity-of-hate-crime-victims-india/

The Wire Staff. (2019, December 24). *'More Brutal Than Even Jamia': AMU Fact Finding Report Accuses UP Police of Violence, Islamophobia*. Retrieved from The Wire: https://thewire.in/government/amu-caa-protests-up-police

The Wire. (2020, July16). 'Delhi Riots Began with Kapil Mishra's speech, yet no case against him': Minority commission report. *The Wire*. https://thewire.in/communalism/delhi-riots-kapil-mishra-minority-commission-report

Upadhyay, S. (2020, January 2). CAA protests: In biting cold, 'Dadis'of Delhi's Shaheen Bagh protest citizenship law. *NDTV*. https://www.ndtv.com/india-news/caa-protests-shaheen-bagh-protest-in-winter-dadis-of-shaheen-bagh-delhi-protest-citizenship-act-2157818

Venkatesan, V. (2021, October22). Police case 'Sketchy' but judge cites Sharjeel Imam's tone, tenor, thoughts to Deny Bail. *The Wire*. https://thewire.in/law/despite-calling-evidence-sketchy-delhi-court-denies-bail-to-sharjeel-imam

YouTube channel of TCN. (n.d.). Accessed on 23 August 2021. https://www.youtube.com/user/twocirclesTV/videos?view=2&live_view=503

Chapter 11

'Rights', 'Lived Worlds' and Citizenship

The Case of Kolkata's Muslims

Anasua Chatterjee

1 Introduction

The question of Muslim citizenship has vexed India since independence. The Indian nation-state had come into being after the partition of erstwhile British India into India and Pakistan on the grounds of religious differences between Hindus and Muslims. Even though India had adopted a 'civic-liberal' model of citizenship, and was officially accommodative of Hindus and Muslims alike, historians have pointed out that independent India witnessed a process of mainstreaming which involved the construction of an essentially 'Hindu' core, that, with time, came to constitute the unambiguous 'natural soul of the nation' (Pandey, 1999). This 'core' was placed in opposition to the 'others', the minorities, predominantly the Muslims, who became an unwelcome and often mistrusted collectivity in the new nation (ibid.).This marked the beginning of a steady process of Muslim minoritization (Gupta, 1995) which has had far-reaching consequences on Muslim citizenship in the country in subsequent years (Hasan, 1997).

Nearly six decades later the Sachar Committee Report[1] (2006) amply demonstrated the gaps in Muslim citizenship by showing how Muslims as a socio-religious group fell behind all others in nearly every index of socio-economic development. Besides, several historical, sociological and anthropological studies have also highlighted the prejudice, stigma, discrimination and communal persecution that Indian Muslims routinely encounter which prevent them from becoming, in practice, 'full members' (Marshall, 1950, p. 8) of the political community.[2] In recent times, the verdict on the *Ramjanmabhoomi* issue, the criminalization of triple *talaq*, the passage of the Citizenship Amendment Act (CAA)[3] by the parliament has, among others, provided renewed context to the debates around Muslim citizenship in India.

Ethnographic in orientation, this chapter attempts to understand Muslim experiences of citizenship in Kolkata by locating 'lived' accounts of citizenship in the city. I draw from alternative perspectives presented by the literature on 'informality' and citizenship in the South Asian context to explore the many ways in which a vast majority of the Muslims in Kolkata experience, articulate, and, claim citizenship in their everyday lives.

DOI: 10.4324/9781003345152-16

II 'Right-Based' versus 'Lived' Citizenship

Conventional theories of citizenship drawn from Western experiences have generally interpreted citizenship as a legal status which outlines the 'rights' and 'duties' held by citizens vis-à-vis the state (Marshall, 1950). These perspectives have tended to put more emphasis on the evolution of formal citizenship rights without paying much attention to the ways in which the legal 'rights' of citizenship are actualized in lived contexts. They, therefore, often prove to be inadequate in grasping fully, experiences drawn from non-Western contexts which display very different trajectories of state formation than those of the West. Within the highly diverse post-colonial societies, for example, socially marginalized groups often find that the promise of equal status enshrined in constitutionally granted citizenship rights is not automatically 'given' but rather needs to be wrested in the face of entrenched structures of social exclusion (Chatterjee, 2004; Holston, 2008). Again, in many of these societies, poorer sections of the population have increasingly come within the ambit of the developmental state whose support is indispensable to their survival. Few among them possess the means to access the state through 'formal' channels and instead do so by forging connections with intermediaries who act as go-betweens between the citizens and the state. These sites of mediation and fuzziness that often lie beyond the scope of legality ultimately constitute the 'lived', 'informal' dimensions of citizenship in such societies (Fuller and Benei, 2001; Berenschot and Klinken, 2018).

Indian Muslims, on finding themselves suddenly transformed into a minority[4] in the aftermath of Partition, had initially tended to frame their political concerns through the language of identity focusing predominantly on minority-related issues such as Urdu and Personal Law (Ahmed, 2009). It was only during the 1980s, with the mobilization of backward Muslim groups at the grassroots level that shifts from 'identity' to concerns of development and increased participation were identified in Muslim political demands (Jodhka, 2007). The publication of the Sachar Report had led many Muslim groups to use the language of community to voice concerns over social exclusion and continued developmental deficit. However, while these shifts marked Muslim politics at the national and the state level, another mode of claiming citizenship is increasingly becoming apparent among poorer Muslims who were employing their own initiative and resources to carve out a respectable life for themselves without necessarily requiring a 'leader' to speak on their behalf (Hansen, 2000). Often attributed as a 'plebian turn' (ibid) these processes represent a new space where citizenship is being negotiated by ordinary Muslims of India. In the recent years, the proliferation of political Hindutva across the country has led to newer anxieties which have further affected Muslim politics at all levels.

This chapter is based on fieldwork among Muslim groups in Kolkata who, despite being categorized as minority (Sengupta, 2017), constitute nearly a fifth of the city's population (Census 2011). Kolkata's Muslims are, however, an extremely diverse collectivity who differ in terms of sect, caste, and linguistic affiliations besides displaying considerable differences in wealth, social class, educational attainment, and occupational status (Bose, 1968). Internal diversity further accounts for the differences in experiences of exclusion and perceptions of disprivilege, which vary by actual social locations of Muslim groups. This, in turn, is reflected in their particular understandings of citizenship. Among the poorer sections in particular, the vocabulary of right-based citizenship remains distant and unfamiliar, whose complex legalities they can barely grasp. Instead, negotiating with the local administration for accessing state benefits assumed immediate relevance in their everyday lives. Drawing on observations from Park Circus, one of the many 'Muslim' neighbourhoods[5] of Kolkata and the site of the recent anti-CAA protests in the city, this chapter highlights how 'lived-worlds' (Ortner, 1995) produce situated accounts of citizenship. The chapter, however, foregrounds these accounts within the backdrop of the contemporary citizenship debate in the country and argues that escalating anxieties over access to the state could play an important role in re-structuring the modes of articulating citizenship in such contexts. In this regard, collective perceptions of threat can be found to create, even if temporarily, a common language of citizenship among the diverse Muslim groups, thereby instituting newer imaginaries of inclusive citizenship.

III The Muslim as 'Other': Trajectories of Muslim Marginalization in Kolkata

Partition was a defining moment which shaped the subsequent experiences of Muslims who stayed on in the Indian part of the subcontinent. Kolkata's Muslims, who had for long been a vibrant part of the city's social fabric suddenly found themselves reduced to a powerless and vulnerable 'minority' with very little control over their destinies in the new nation (Chatterji, 2007). Most significantly, all Muslims, irrespective of their ethnic, sectarian, cultural and socio-economic differences were classed as simply 'Muslims', an external corporate attribution that focused primarily on their religious community membership over all other competing claims to identity.

The immediate aftermath of Partition saw a trail of social processes that worked to push Muslims to the margins of the city. The numerous instances of persecution and intimidation that regularly happened in Calcutta at the time meant that Muslims lived in constant fear of their lives and property in the state (Das, 1993). While Muslims adopted strategies for survival that varied according to their socio-economic standing (Chatterji, 2007, pp. 171–81), they also realized that in order to ensure 'safety' they needed to constantly proclaim their allegiance to the Indian state which, in practice, often meant either 'assimilating' and accepting their subordinate status or 'leaving' the country (ibid: 172; Hasan, 1997, p. 148).

It turned out that for the ordinary Muslims who stayed back, the decision involved accepting greater losses than their more influential counterparts. While for the latter the decision mainly involved making a few strategic political choices, for the former it entailed a number of compromises at the level of everyday social existence. For the most part, the repercussions were visible in the significant contraction of symbolic (public) and physical space so far available to Muslims in the city. Controls were imposed over decibel limits of *azaan*, over routes taken by Muharram processions, and, over the sale and consumption on beef in the city. Public rituals like cow sacrifice during Bakr-Id often brought violent communal retributions in their wake, and in quite a few cases, dominant Hindu groups were able to successfully challenge Muslim rights to bury their dead in the city's many graveyards (Chatterji, 2007). Many Islamic institutions and symbols, such as the Calcutta Madrasah and the Islamia College, were almost effectively 'erased' from public memory, and over the years, Muslims steadily lost control over many of their religio-social spaces evident in the state of disrepair of the many mosques and burial grounds in the city (Sengupta, 2017, pp. 446–49). In these, and several other ways, Muslims were coerced into gradually giving up their claims to public spaces in the city, evermore as a way to show Muslims their 'true place' in the new social order.

Another trend complementing this process was the gradual re-ordering of physical spaces, which produced discrete ghetto-like (Bose, 1968; Chatterji, 2007) neighbourhoods for the city's Muslims. The terrible memories of communal riots in the years preceding Partition and the 'demonization' of Muslim personalities in narratives of East Bengali refugees fleeing persecution in East Pakistan (Chatterjee, n.d.) had already instituted Muslims as aggressive, communally oriented and inward-looking whose ways of life were essentially 'alien' to the gentle-mannered Hindu *bhadralok*. They, therefore, had to be kept apart and confined to designated spaces, so that social interaction could be curtailed and fears of contamination,[6] both ritual and moral, minimized. This resulted in a steady process of unmixing of populations as Muslims and Hindus got 'sorted out [into] clear-cut blocks of communities' (Chatterji, 2007, p. 182) explicitly marked out, both socially and geographically, from each other. As Hindu neighbourhoods became progressively 'cleansed' of their Muslim inhabitants, Muslims huddled together in densely populated 'pockets' in search of shelter and security which a preponderance of numbers could provide. Overcrowded, congested, and lacking in comparable civic amenities, these highly heterogeneous and often stigmatized Muslim spaces, which were a far cry from their colonial counterparts,[7] soon came to possess an air of a ghetto (ibid.). Carrying entrenched negative ascriptions, these neighbourhoods would define, and limit, life chances of Muslims many of whom had but little option than to organize their lives within them.

Kolkata has been generally considered to be a safer space for Muslims in comparison to other cities in India such as Ahmedabad and Mumbai owing to the relative absence of communal disturbances and the professedly 'secular' inclination of the ruling regimes since the Left Front. Yet segments of the community constitute some of the most deprived social groups in the city (Siddiqui, 2004; Seabrook and Siddiqui, 2011). The reality of marginalization reflects in their poor economic status, their low educational attainment, their limited access to organized sector employment, and most endemically, in the everyday tribulations of discrimination, fear and stigma that are consequences of carrying a 'spoilt' identity (Goffman, 1963). The Muslim neighbourhoods formed after Partition have only grown bigger and denser with time as increasing numbers of Muslims come in the search of security and a familiar milieu. In a way, they both reflect and are constitutive of the predominant arcs of prejudice and discrimination faced by Muslims in Kolkata.

The neighbourhood of Park Circus, on which this study is based, is one such Muslim neighbourhood in central Kolkata. Originally home to educated, politically influential, and upwardly mobile Muslims (McPherson, 1974), the neighbourhood's demographic composition has altered over the years, paralleling the general fate of Muslims in the city. At present, Muslims comprise nearly three-quarters of Park Circus's population, with the larger section drawn from poor and lower-middle class backgrounds, primarily engaged in making a living by negotiating the unpredictable informal economy of the city. Unlike the small section of the affluent and the middle classes, their lives are far more circumscribed by the immediacy of the ghetto which lends them a negative spatial identity, a bad address, which they find difficult to shed in the course of their interactions with the wider urban.[8] The section that follows describes some of the ways in which Muslims, especially ordinary Muslims, frame the issues of exclusion and rights in their everyday lives in the neighbourhood.

IV Informality and Citizenship: Experiences of Ordinary Muslims of Kolkata

The diversity of Park Circus's population makes it rather difficult to identify common political concerns that hold equal relevance for all its Muslim residents. While there is an overall familiarity with the larger discourse of Muslim social exclusion in the country, perceptions of marginalization are 'situated' and tend to be shaped by actual experiences of discrimination and prejudice faced by Muslims. In comparison to the poorer sections, the upper and middle classes among Muslims are far more conscious of the shifts in political discourse concerning the community at the national level. A wide range of factors, external and internal, shape their political views and they do not seem to be very keenly invested in the local political affairs of the neighbourhood. The latter remains the realm of poor and ordinary Muslims whose negotiations with the local-level administration comprise the everyday political life of the neighbourhood.

For ordinary Muslims of Park Circus, the primary concerns of everyday life include issues such as access to basic civic amenities, affordable health-care and education, the ability to lead stable and dignified lives with a regular income, for all of which they rely heavily on the support provided by the developmental state. Access to the state and its institutions thus becomes vital to their survival. However, few among them have the necessary skills to negotiate the complicated bureaucratic structures of the state on their own and have to depend on the assistance of locally 'big men' (Harriss, 2005) to secure these ends. Such assistance comes at a price, usually of reciprocal obligations, which may include a number of gestures such as enlisting in a political party, paying the party subscription, attending the occasional rally, and maintaining 'good relations' with locally important figures. Active participation in the day-to-day processes of local politics thus becomes a reality poor Muslims can ill afford to avoid and they would only stand to lose if they do not maintain regular connections with the local sites of power.[9]

The strong tradition of party-based networks of patronage in Bengal has meant that local-level political party representatives play an important role in matters of resource delivery to the slum dwellers. Proximity to a party leader usually implies benefits such as assured access to state resources, prior induction to welfare schemes, easy securing of institutional support, and so on. However, given their stature and nature of commitments, party leaders are not always available for providing everyday support to the slum dwellers. A more prominent figure in this regard is the 'social worker' who acts as a broker between the people and the local administration and plays an important role in facilitating locals' access to state services.[10] Their characteristic enterprise, along with their abilities to improvise situationally (Gudavarthy, 2012, p. 160) and 'get work done' through strategic contacts (Corbridge et al., 2005), have made social workers an increasingly popular figure within local politics. Such popularity, however, does not suggest a total shift away from the politics of patronage, which perhaps still remains the single most important way of ensuring electoral support. It rather leads to a curious hybrid at the level of everyday politics where 'personal loyalty' derived from clientelistic patronage (Piliavsky, 2014) sits together with multiple forms of issue-based political strategizing on part of common people to be on the right side of power and therefore secure state benefits.[11]

The interactions of ordinary Muslims with the state therefore display a 'mediated' character (Berenschot et al., 2017, p. 13) in the sense that as 'citizens' they tend to rely more on mediation by politically or socially relevant figures, than concerted 'civic' action, in order to gain access to state resources. In other words, forms of 'civic' engagement do not appear either effective or attractive in these contexts. In recent years, the proliferation of the developmental state seems to have made traditional clientelistic relations less asymmetric, if not less pervasive and new modes of political strategizing, involving increasing levels of participation of local Muslims has become visible in the neighbourhood in the last decade or so (Chatterjee, 2019). Ordinary Muslims in Park Circus often seem entirely nonchalant about discourses linking their fate to the broader trajectory of Muslim marginality in the country even though they have, on occasions – depending upon the proximity and intensity of the incident – taken to the streets to voice their concerns.[12] However, given the compelling realities of their lives, they seem to be mainly interested in wresting benefits from the everyday state without being overtly engrossed with concerns of identity.

V Threat and Reconfiguration of 'Situated' Accounts of Citizenship

Political perceptions and participation among this section of the neighbourhood's Muslims seemed to show an ostensible shift during the anti-CAA protests that unfolded across the country in 2019 and early 2020. Park Circus, in particular, became the site of a massive anti-CAA protest that took place in a park adjacent to the neighbourhood. Identified as Kolkata's 'Shaheen Bagh' – in reference to similarities with the anti-CAA protests at New Delhi's namesake venue – the protests were by no means a neighbourhood-level mobilization even though large numbers of women (and men) from the neighbourhood participated. By looking into local narratives, I argue that escalating anxieties over a proposed test of citizenship played an important role in producing alternative framings of 'rights' and belonging.[13]

The continuous sit-in at Park Circus began in early January 2020 when a Muslim homemaker organized around sixty-odd women to agitate against the CAA and the proposed National Register of Citizens (NRC) which seemingly threatened to disenfranchise Muslims in the near future. Despite the severe January chill, the women managed to hold out for long enough to be eventually able to secure necessary permissions for putting up sheds and other facilities and continue protests. Soon, civil society activists, members of the Muslim intelligentsia, students, Dalit representatives, and other supporters joined the protests. Each evening saw estimated crowds of twenty to twenty-five thousand, with the atmosphere turning particularly intense on Republic Day when nearly a hundred thousand protesters gathered at the site.[14] On an average day, large numbers of Muslim women, often in tow with children, occupied the central pagoda-like structure in the *maidan*. Surrounded by Muslim men, members of the press and itinerant onlookers, they held ground led by sloganeering 'leaders' – usually educated, middle-class, often younger women – who took turns to keep up their morale. As the protest matured, national-level politicians, student leaders, leaders of the opposition and representatives of Shaheen Bagh came in to offer support.

Despite the apparent fair-like festivity of the milieu with floodlights and roadside hawkers and vehicles choking up the busy seven-point crossing, the seriousness of its intent could not be missed. Neither could be the very novel ways employed to voice the demands of the protestors. While the larger part of the crowd was composed of Muslims– evident from their outward religious identifications – posters at the entrance displayed solidarity with student movements in Delhi and Aligarh and urged visitors to keep aside their religious identities once they entered the arena. The arena in question was configured predominantly as a 'citizen' space that stood for equal belonging and recognition away from hyphenated perceptions of incomplete membership. Large cut-outs of Babasaheb Ambedkar, who drafted India's constitution, and those of Swami Vivekananda, Ishwar Chandra Vidyasagar, and Raja Rammohan Roy, Bengali icons of reform and education, filled the grounds alongside soaring tricolours around the main protest site. The apparent 'Muslim-ness' of the protest seemed to coexist in a compelling mix with narratives of equality, 'rights' and awareness. As a sustained leadership began to emerge mostly from within sections of Muslim civil society, there were calls for book donations, performances, reading hours – including dedicated hours for familiarizing the 'masses' with the constitution – in order to 'educate' them and draw attention to the 'uncalled-for acts' which held pervasive effects on their futures. Above all, the protests were cast as a 'people's initiative' which did not explicitly fall under any political banner. The primary purpose lay in 'defending [the secular spirit of] the constitution' despite the immediate focus on the specific predicament of the Muslims.

The past year had witnessed a series of events that had, evidently, raised doubts among many Muslims regarding their actual status in the country. The abrogation of Article 370 in Kashmir, the verdict on the *Ramjanmabhoomi* issue and the criminalization of triple *talaq* were perceived by large sections of Muslims as attacks on crucial symbols of Muslim political identity in India. The pro-Hindu outcome over Ram Mandir, had, for example, fanned up dormant Muslim sentiments around the Babri Masjid issue while the criminalizing triple *talaq* had dented, according to many, the sanctity of the *shariya* which bound Muslim religious practice. Nonetheless, despite the countrywide reactions they drew, the sentiments stirred up by these developments, continued to remain dormant if not distant, and did not result in a full-blown campaign disrupting Muslim everyday life in Park Circus.

The CAA and the impending NRC, in contrast, appeared to have very grave and immediate consequences on Muslim lives. On the one hand, they represented a culmination of processes potentially capable of turning a considerable section of Muslims into the quintessential 'outsider/migrant' who would then not have equal claims of membership in society (Roy, 2010, p. 12). On the other hand, the question of surviving a 'test' of citizenship through 'documents' in the near future via a process evidently biased against them produced considerable anxiety regarding a looming future of de-legitimization and detention among many Muslims who could not perhaps produce the 'required' citizenship documents. This latter fact seemed to call out to large sections of even the poor and ordinary Muslims who saw in it a pressing threat to their very survival in the city.

The narratives from the women at the site variously upheld the idioms of rights (*adhikar*), constitution (*samvidhan*), and injustice (*zulm*) as key elements to frame the issue. They questioned the undue significance being attached to documents (*kagaz*) for establishing citizenship (*nagarikata*). While many of them are unsure of their documentation status, their roots go far back in the region, long enough to consider themselves as legitimate inhabitants without having to undergo a trial for proving belonging. In the absence of any original constitutional merit, they perceived it as a 'wrong' collectively imposed on them. Also interesting were the parallels drawn between their own plight and those belonging to other communities, including a section of Hindu refugees who would not, as pointed out, be spared the travails of 'proving' their citizenship. While it appeared to be a problem for everyone, there seemed to be a clear recognition that, at the moment it was Muslims, especially ordinary and poor Muslims who did not have the necessary legal knowhow or the 'right connections' for making relevant claims, whose futures were gravely at stake. It was perhaps the looming immediacy of a threatened future (Massumi, 2010) over which they had little control that pushed many among this segment of Park Circus's Muslims to join the protests in large numbers even if that came at the cost of disrupting their already precarious everyday lives. Thus, while mobilization of poorer sections in India has not usually been of the 'right-claiming' variety given the demographic limits of civil society (Chatterjee, 2004, p. 66) – here the narrative quickly picked up on the language of 'rights' since the 'impending withdrawal of citizenship', and therefore the 'rights' that came with it, seemed to immediately put lives and livelihoods at stake for the Muslims.

Here, several points arise which are perhaps of value with regard to citizenship in post-colonial democracies like India. The massive participation of large numbers of poor and lower-class Muslims in a protest directly critiquing the government despite dependencies on the developmental state raises questions regarding the place of a rights-based approach in such contexts. While citizenship rights are not entirely irrelevant and poorer social groups have occasionally been found to invoke the discourse of rights (Gibbings, 2017), their scope seems to be rather limited. The realization of rights often rests on the cooperation of political intermediaries as well as on personal initiative and resourcefulness which define the practice of claim-making in these societies. We have seen that the everyday political behaviour of ordinary Muslims of Park Circus typically followed such clientelistic and post-clientelistic persuasions. During the Park Circus protests, there was definitely a concerted attempt on part of civil society activists, both Muslims and otherwise, to encourage a rights-based discourse in engaging with the state but that perhaps does not fully explain why such large numbers of ordinary Muslims responded to the call. While the significance of religious community in shaping citizenship rights in India has been widely debated, it is worth noting that for many poor Muslims, 'community' instead of carrying a sense of pre-modern attachment often becomes a site for extending clientelistic bargains. Laurens Bakker, for instance, points out that community-based organizations also operate at the level of political society, mobilizing followers to prove their capacity for collective action, including that of delivering or withdrawing large numbers of votes depending on reciprocal promises made by politicians (Bakker, 2017). For large sections of Muslims from the nearby slums, the protests were of utmost significance because the very basis of clientelistic bargains was potentially being taken away and 'community' – in this case, community-based mobilization – ultimately provided a platform for negotiating more effectively with the state.

This does not necessarily imply that the reality of Muslim marginalization is completely alien to poorer Muslims. Community-based discrimination is a reality they experience every day in the course of their lives in stigmatised urban spaces, in the many prejudices of social encounters with dominant groups, and in the multiple strategies of managing identity they are forced to employ to secure livelihoods in the city. The gathering narrative of Muslim exclusion across the country, the numerous stories of lynching, intimidation and arson have only added to their sense of fear and insecurity. As a result, the narrative of 'threat' and the discourse of 'rights' for demanding equality seem to hold strong appeals for them. This has perhaps been responsible for a temporary bridge in the usual languages of citizenship employed by the different segments of protesters at Park Circus, one defined by middle-class, right-based civil society engagements, the other by ordinary, less-educated, strategic bargains directed at securing resources from the developmental state. But whether poor and ordinary Muslims have really internalized a right-based approach towards articulating citizenship remains to be seen and will depend, to a large extent, on their ability to overcome the compelling constraints of their everyday lives.

VI Conclusion

The nation-wide anti-CAA protests met with a rather abrupt end in mid-March 2020 in the face of the COVID-19 pandemic that gripped the world, setting new protocols of social behaviour and physical distancing in its wake. The pandemic's consequences have been especially hard on socially marginalized groups, such as refugees, slum dwellers, and migrant labourers whose insecurities have spiralled during the pandemic period. Across India, ordinary Muslims in particular, were reported to have experienced new forms of social prejudice, public aversion, and general apathy as socially dominant groups often displayed anxiety around Muslims in an already crises-ridden milieu.[15] At the same time, there were calls for carrying on with the anti-CAA protests symbolically and even virtually on part of many activists and civil society actors involved with it. However, it remains to be seen whether the common language of citizenship that emerged in the context of the protests endures over the long run or fades out as differently located Muslims try to come to grips with the new realities of their everyday lives unleashed by the pandemic.

What requires an appraisal is the fact that despite their many limitations, the anti-CAA protests perhaps represent an important 'act of citizenship' bringing together multiple actors, so far marginalized, as claimants of rights in newly emerging sites which can potentially change our very understanding of the political, and of citizenship (Isin, 2009, p. 370). It also draws our attention to the processual dimensions of citizenship where citizenship is 'viewed as a series of expanding circles which are pushed forward by the momentum of conflict and struggle' [over rights] (Turner, 1986, p. xii). While it is still too early to comment on the effect of the protests over the impending NRC and the futures of Muslims in general, they have shown, if not anything else, that the ideal of inclusive citizenship is not just an end but, rather, a continuing process of achieving the ad infinitum that underlines its significance (Hoffman, 2004, p. 13).

The case of Park Circus's Muslims is but one instance of many similar Muslim experiences in Kolkata. Their large-scale participation in the protests brought to the fore the many anxieties and fears that seem to have, over the years, become an endemic part of their everyday lives. While, it is true that experiences of marginalization have not been the same for all Muslims, the shift in narrative that potentially turns a section of Muslims from the 'other-within' to the 'outsider/migrant' seems to have unsettled the very basis of their abilities to make a claim as citizens of the country. The multiple languages, modalities, and framings through which diverse Muslim groups have articulated their anxieties about 'rights' and belonging underscore the complexities of citizenship both as an ideal and as a process in contemporary India.

Notes

1 The Sachar Committee was instituted by the United Progressive Alliance (UPA) government to look into the levels of socio-economic attainment by religious community membership in the country. It tabled its Report in 2006.

2 The literature on the subject is too vast to be appraised here. Of particular significance are Mukulika Banerjee's *Muslim Portraits* (2008), Deepak Mehta and Roma Chatterjee (2001), Rowena Robinson (2005) and Dipankar Gupta's (2011) studies on communal riots and ethnic violence, Christopher Jaffrelot's edited volume (2012) on Muslims in Indian cities among others.

3 The Citizenship (Amendment) Act, 2019 available at http://egazette.nic.in/WriteReadData/2019/214646.pdf. Accessed on 12th May 2020.

4 Becoming a minority does not merely follow from smallness numbers but rather from a sense of vulnerability, and of feeling discriminated against in a nation-state (Seth and Mahajan, 1999, p. 8).

5 The terms 'Muslim neighbourhood' is often used to imply social and spatial stigma and exclusion rather than numerical predominance of Muslims in a locality (Jaffrelot et al., 2012; Chatterjee, 2017).
6 Hindu fears of ritual pollution over beef and leatherwork are significant here (See Sennett, 1994; Steiner, 2004 [1956]).
7 Colonial Muslim neighbourhoods in Kolkata were not communally constituted but were composed of distinct 'sub-communal groups' among Muslims (McPherson, 1974, p. ii).
8 For an elaboration on the consequences of confinement of differently located Muslim groups in Park Circus, see Chatterjee, 2017, Ch. 6.
9 For details on political participation of ordinary Muslims in Park Circus see Chatterjee, 2019, pp. 234–39.
10 These intermediaries have been variously identified in anthropological literature as 'dalals', 'nayanetas', 'political entrepreneurs' and, in urban contexts, as 'urban specialists' (Bailey, 1969; Hansen and Verkaaik, 2009; Jodhka, 2010).
11 These methods have been referred to as post-clientelism within anthropological literature on the state (Manor, 2013).
12 The agitations over alleged state complicity in the persecution and eventual murder of Rizwanur Rahman, a local Muslim youth, who married the daughter of a wealthy Kolkata-based Hindu businessman is an example.
13 The term belonging is used to describe an 'emotional attachment' and a 'aboutfeeling 'at home" (Yuval-Davis et al., 2018, p. 230) that is dynamic in nature.
14 Data sourced from estimates given in article by Suhrid Shankar Chattopadhyay available at https://frontline.thehindu.com/the-nation/article30800912.ece. Accessed on 23rd May 29 2020.
15 In mid-March 2020 a religious gathering of the Talibaghi Jamaat was identified as a 'super-spreader' of the novel corona virus, an incident which resulted in the collective blaming of the community. While the event led to outrage among both Muslims and non-Muslims, it was predominantly Muslims who then began to be accused of deliberately spreading the virus as part of a social media hashtag 'coronajihad'. For details see article https://www.hindustantimes.com/india-news/jamaat-brought-collective-shame-and-islamophobia-muslims-say/story-ermZoPYGGZ8HBMNeErSnvM.html. Accessed on 1st May, 2022.

References

Ahmed, H. (2009). Muslims as a Political Community. *Seminar* (602), pp. 54–59.

Bailey, F. G. (1969). *Stratagems and Spoils: A Social Anthropology of Politics*. New York: Schocken Books.

Bakker, L. (2017). Militias, Security and Citizenship in Indonesia. In: W. Berenschot, H. S. Nordholt, and L. Baker (eds.), *Citizenship and Democratization in Southeast Asia* (pp. 125–154). Leiden: Brill.

Berenschot, W. and G. Klinken. (2018). Informality and Citizenship: The Everyday State in Indonesia. *Journal of Citizenship Studies* 22(2), pp. 95–111.

Berenschot, W. et al. (eds.) (2017). *Citizenship and Democratization in Southeast Asia*. Leiden: Brill.

Bose, N. K. (1968). *Calcutta 1964: A Social Survey*. Bombay: Lalvani Publishing House.

Chatterjee, A. (2017). *Margins of Citizenship: Muslim Experiences in Urban India*. New Delhi and London: Routledge.

Chatterjee, A. (2019). Negotiating a Better Life: Emerging Trends in the Politics of Ordinary and Poor Muslims in Kolkata. *Journal of South Asian Development* 14(2), pp. 223–243.

Chatterjee, N. (n.d.). *Interrogating Victimhood: East Bengali Refugee Narratives of Communal Violence* From: http://www.swadhinata.org.uk/document/chatterjeeEastBengal%20Refugee.pdf on May 15, 2012.

Chatterjee, P. (2004). *The Politics of the Governed: Reflections on Popular Politics in Most of the World*. New York: Columbia University Press.

Chatterji, J. (2007). *The Spoils of Partition: Bengal and India, 1947-1967*. New Delhi: Cambridge University Press.

Corbridge, S.et al. (2005). *Seeing the State: Governance and Governmentality in India*. Cambridge: Cambridge University Press.

Das, S. (1993). *Communal Riots in Bengal: 1905-1947*. New Delhi: Oxford University Press.

Fuller, C. J. and V. Benei (eds.) (2001). *The Everyday State and Society in Modern India*. London: Hurst and Company.

Gibbings, S. L. (2017). Sosialisasi, Street Vendors and Citizenship in Yogyakarta In: W. Berenschot, H. S. Nordholt and L. Baker (eds.), *Citizenship and Democratization in Southeast Asia* (pp. 96–122). Leiden: Brill.

Goffman, E. (1963). *Stigma: Notes on the Management of a Spoilt Identity*. Harmondsworth: Penguin Books.

Gudavarthy, A. (2012). Introduction: Why interrogate political society? In A. Gudavarthy (ed.), *Re-framing Democracy and Agency in India: Interrogating Political Society* (pp. 1–10). London: Anthem Press.

Gupta, D. (1995). Secularization and Minoritization-Limits of Heroic Thought. *The Economic and Political Weekly* 30(35), pp. 2203–2207.

Gupta, D. (2011). *Justice Before Reconciliation*. New Delhi: Routledge.

Hansen, T. B. (2000). Predicaments of Secularism: Muslim Identities and Politics in Mumbai. *Journal of Royal Anthropological Institute* 6(2), pp. 255–272.

Hansen, T. B. and O. Verkaaik (2009). Urban Charisma: On Everyday Mythologies in the City. *Critique of Anthropology* 29(5), pp. 5–26.

Harriss, J. (2005). Political Participation, Representation and the Urban Poor: Findings from a Research in Delhi. *Economic and Political Weekly* 40(11), pp. 1041–1054.

Hasan, M. (1997). *Legacy of a divided nation: India's Muslims since Independence*. New Delhi: Oxford University Press.

Hoffman, J. (2004). *Citizenship Beyond the State*. London: Sage: Publications.

Holston, J. (2008). *Insurgent Citizenship: Disjunctions of Democracy and Modernity in Brazil*. Princeton: Princeton University Press.

Isin, E. F. (2009). Citizenship in Flux: The Figure of the Activist Citizen. *Subjectivity* 29, pp. 367–388.

Jaffrelot, C. et al. (eds.) (2012). *Muslims in India's Cities: Trajectories of Marginalization*. New Delhi: Harper Collins.

Jodhka, S. S. (2007). Perceptions and Receptions. *Economic and Political Weekly* 42(29), pp. 2996–2999.

Jodhka, S. S. (2010). Engaging With Caste: Academic Discourses, Identity Politics and State Policy, Working Paper Series 2(2), IIDS, New Delhi and UNICEF.

Manor, J. (2013). Post-clientelist Initiatives. In K. Stokke and O. Tornquist (eds.), *Democratization in the Global South* (pp. 243–253). London: Palgrave Macmillan.

Marshall, T. H. (1950). *Citizenship and Social Class and Other Essays*. New York: Cambridge University Press.

Massumi, B. (2010). The Future Birth of the Affective Fact: The Political Ontology of Threat. In M. Gregg and G. J. Seigworth (eds.), *The Affect Theory Reader* (pp. 52–70). Durham and London: Duke University Press.

McPherson, K. (1974). *The Muslim Microcosm: Calcutta 1918-1935*. Wiesbaden: Franz Steiner Verlac.

Mehta, D. & Chatterji, R. (2001). Boundaries, Names, Alterities: A Case Study of a "Communal Riot" in Dharavi, Bombay. In V. Das, A. Kleinman, M. Lock, M. Ramphele & P. Reynolds (Ed.), *Remaking a World: Violence, Social Suffering, and Recovery* (pp. 201–249). Berkeley: University of California Press.

Ortner, S. (1995). Resistance and the Problem of Ethnographic Refusal. *Comparative Studies in Society and History* 37(1), pp. 173–193.

Pandey, G. (1999). Can a Muslim be an Indian? *Comparative Studies in Society and History* (41), pp. 608–629.

Piliavsky, A. (ed). (2014). *Patronage as Politics in South Asia*. New Delhi: Cambridge University Press.

Robinson, R. (2005). *Tremors of Violence: Muslim Survivors of Ethnic Strife in Western India*. New Delhi: Sage Publications.

Roy, A. (2010). *Mapping Citizenship in India*. New Delhi: Oxford University Press.

Sachar Committee Report (SCR) (2006). A Report on the Social, Economic and Educational Status of the Muslim Community of India. Available at http://www.minorityaffairs.gov.in/sites/default/files/sachar_comm.pdf. Accessed 29th May 2020.

Seabrook, J. and I. A. Siddiqui. (2011). *People Without History: India's Muslim Ghettos*. New Delhi: Navayana Publishing.

Sengupta, A. (2017). Becoming a Minority Community: Calcutta's Muslims after Partition. In T. Sarkar and S. Bandyopadhyay (eds.), *Calcutta: The Stormy Decades* (pp. 434–458). New Delhi: Social Science Press.

Sennett, R. (1994). *Flesh and Stone: The Body and the City in Western Civilization*. New York: W. W. Norton and Company.

Seth, D. L. and G. Mahajan (eds.) (1999). *Minority Identities and the Nation-State*. New Delhi: Oxford University Press.

Siddiqui, M. K. A. (eds.) (2004). *Marginal Muslim Communities in Calcutta*. New Delhi: IOS.

Steiner, F. (2004[1956]). *Taboo*. London: Routledge.

Turner, B. (1986). *Citizenship and Capitalism: The Debate over Reformism*. London: Allen and Unwin.

Yuval-Davis, N., Wemyss, G., and Cassidy, K. (2018). Everyday Bordering, Belonging and the Reorientation of British Immigration Legislation. *Sociology* 52(2), pp. 228–244.

V

The Citizenship Question

Borders and Border Crossings

Chapter 12

'To Be or Not to Be'

Tibetans and the Question of Citizenship

Jigme Yeshe Lama

1 Introduction

'To be or not to be', these lines from Shakespeare's Hamlet can be used to define Tibetans and their relationship to citizenship. The title of this chapter has been borrowed from two sources, the first being Shakespeare's *Hamlet* and the second from an article written by the erudite Fiona McConnell that dealt with the issue of citizenship among Tibetans in India. That article was written for the website tibetanpoliticalreview.org, which is no longer available. Fiona McConnell's pioneering work has focused on the Tibetans in exile, on their issues of identity and statehood. While the chapter borrows from McConnell's work, it tries to understand the issue of Tibetans and citizenship through Shakespeare's line in Hamlet as for them citizenship has always raised questions, one that is linked to identity and statehood.

The idea for this chapter arose from a question: Whether it is true that Tibetans in exile don't want to acquire citizenship? Hopefully it will provide some answers to this query but as with all questions and issues, there is no straightforward answer. Like all realities, the issue of Tibetans and citizenship is complex, having several layers that need to be excavated. On this basis, the chapter is divided into three sections. The first deals with the "not to be" part, where the argument is how Tibetans are citizens of the Tibetan Government in exile (TGiE) and hence do not acquire citizenship in their host countries. The second section looks into the "to be" part, investigating why a few Tibetans acquired and a number of them aspire for citizenship of India but more of the Western countries. Finally, the last section elaborates how within the Tibetans, a creamy layer has citizenship(s), making them transnational citizens.

The Tibetans were forced into exile when the newly formed People's Republic of China (PRC) under the leadership of Mao Zedong and the Chinese communists decided to invade Tibet. In 1950, they made it clear that they would liberate Tibet from foreign imperialists and the feudal reactionaries and integrate it with the motherland. Without getting caught in the political rhetoric, the "liberation of Tibet" needs to be analysed from the activities of the newly created postcolonial Chinese nation state and its

DOI: 10.4324/9781003345152-18

project of nation state building. Tibet assumed importance as the high Himalayan region was the periphery that had to be secured for China. The communists feared the region would be used as a backdoor to its inner heartlands, an issue present since the days of the Great Game between Imperial China, British Raj in India and the Russians. Hence, Tibet had to be placed under the direct control of Beijing, which would be done by imposing a carrot-and-stick policy. The 'stick' took the form of a military campaign launched in eastern Tibet in 1950 by the People's Liberation Army (PLA) while the 'carrot' was through coaxing the Tibetan government under the Dalai Lama to enter into negotiations with the Chinese Communist Party (CCP). This strategy worked, and the Tibetan government signed the Seventeen Point Agreement with China that paved the way for the peaceful liberation of Tibet. Initially, the Chinese communists implemented their 'united front' policy towards the Tibetans. Under this, the Chinese delayed 'democratic reforms' in the Tibetan society and initiated a process to co-opt the Tibetan ruling elites. It failed as the Chinese communists had imposed their 'democratic reforms' that entailed collectivisation and an attack on local culture in eastern and north-eastern Tibet.

Tibetans call these regions Kham and Amdo. While these regions were populated by ethnic Tibetans, they were never under the direct authority of Lhasa and the Dalai Lama's government. Still, as devout Buddhists, their faith towards the Dalai Lamas were unshakeable. The current Dalai Lama himself hails from Taktser, Amdo, which is north - eastern Tibet. Such bonds were not understood by the Chinese communists who were the offspring of the modern nation state. For them, primordial religious and cultural connections were not the foundation of a state. Thus, they brought their harsh reforms to these regions, which led to an armed uprising from the local population. The Tibetan uprising against the Chinese can also be seen as a rejection of citizenship brought by the Chinese nation state for Tibetans. The PRC saw Tibetans as one among 55 nationalities that constituted China. Prior to the arrival of the Chinese state, the Tibetans were either subjects of the Dalai Lama's government or of the various other sovereigns present in the plateau. For instance, parts of Amdo and Kham were under the rule of the Chinese warlords, affiliated with the Kuomintang government. However, the local Tibetans were treated as subjects of a frontier region where the reach of the state was less. The coming of the Chinese nation state brought the notion of citizenship among Tibetans. For the first time in their collective memory, Tibetans residing in all parts of the plateau came under the single sovereignty of the PRC. The process of including Tibetans in communist China evoked armed resistance from the Tibetans.

Initially the uprisings were local in nature, concentrated mostly in Kham and Amdo (Eastern Tibet) which were brutally crushed. The survivors fled to Lhasa, where the Chinese presence had already brewed popular discontent. It finally percolated to a massive uprising on 10 March 1959, which was suppressed by the Chinese, leading to the fleeing of the Dalai Lama.

The Dalai Lama, with his people, sought refuge in India, which agreed to provide assistance to the Tibetans. Along with India, the Tibetans sought refuge in Bhutan and Nepal. India provided land and other material resources through which 39 major and minor Tibetan settlements were established. At present out of the 128,944 Tibetan refugees worldwide, about 94,203 are currently based in India. Successive Indian governments have facilitated the preservation and promotion of the distinctive culture, tradition and identity of the Tibetans by establishing separate schools for the Tibetan children and allowing the functioning of the Tibetan government in exile (CTA) to manage their affairs (Choedon, 2018). As Choedon (2018) mentions, the uniqueness of the Tibetan refugees is that they sought refuge not only for personal safety but also for the preservation and protection of their culture and religion which was under attack in their homeland (Choedon, 2018). Hence, the issue of identity preservation for the Tibetans is important. Under the stewardship of the CTA, the Tibetans are seen to be emerging as one of the most successful refugee communities in the world as they have been properly rehabilitated and resettled. It is precisely due to the presence of the CTA, an exile government that the Tibetans are seen to be not aspiring for citizenship of their host countries.

II The "Not to Be" – CTA and The Creation of Tibetan Citizens in Exile

The CTA, based in Dharamsala, in the Indian state of Himachal Pradesh claims legitimacy through terming itself as a continuation of the traditional government established by the Fifth Dalai Lama in Lhasa in1642. Till 2011, the current 14th Dalai Lama was the spiritual and temporal leader of the Tibetans. However, the same year he devolved his power to an elected individual or the *Sikyong*, Lobsang Sangay, a Harvard law graduate. Proper elections are held every five years in the Tibetan community to elect a political leader as well as members of the Tibetan Parliament. The CTA operates as a fully- fledged government within the sovereign space of another state and is made of the three organs of the government, with 7 government departments performing a number of functions for its diaspora (McConnell, 2013, p. 970). Regular elections among exiled Tibetans and the further devolution of power by the Dalai Lama has aided in the creation of the Tibetan citizen in exile. Tibetans in India and the west are seen to be exercising their right to adult franchise, which coupled with other democratic entitlements increases the process of citizenship among them.

In this, the CTA is seen to be playing a highly important role in constructing and managing identity categories, political membership and rights as well as having further essentialised identity labels to further their political goals (McConnell, 2013, p. 968). The territory less CTA is seen to be involved in the construction of the identity of a Tibetan citizen. This is institutionalised through the bureaucratic administration of the pseudo-passbook

– the "Green Book" or the *Rangzen Lagdeb* through which the CTA is seen to be taking voluntary taxes from the Tibetan citizens. Furthermore, the establishments of the quasi embassies of the CTA in different parts of the world are much involved in the granting of the "Green Book" to Tibetans (McConnell, 2013, p. 972). These quasi embassies are located in other countries as well as in the settlement camps, where a settlement officer; a bureaucrat is delegated by the CTA, who looks after the activities of the camp as well as acts as an important medium between the Tibetan citizens in exile and the CTA.

Along with the "Green Book", we see an institutionalisation of Tibetan citizenship through the rights and duties enshrined in the Charter of the Tibetans in Exile, which had been adopted in 1991 and whereby

> Tibetan citizenship is granted to all Tibetans born within the territory of Tibet and those born in other countries who are eligible to be citizens of Tibet. Any person whose biological mother or biological father is of Tibetan descent has the right to become a citizen of Tibet. (McConnell, 2013, p. 975)

Hence, through these "everyday practices" of the CTA, we see the emergence of Tibetan citizenship, which are a part of the ongoing process of nation state building. The practice of citizenship by exile Tibetans also emerges with the direct elections for president (*Sikyong*) of the CTA and the deputies/members of the Assembly of the Tibetan People's Deputies (ATPD), which is a unicameral legislature. The 1991 charter also provided for the creation of local assemblies in Tibetan settlements, which manage local issues as well as critically scrutinise the work of officials who were sent from Dharamsala. These local assemblies, elected for a tenure of three years, address the issues of the residents in a democratic way and hold assembly sessions in which settlement officers are generally held accountable. There has also been a steady participation of Tibetans in the elections especially from the younger generation, who have voted as well as contested in the elections. Reflected in the last constituted 16th Tibetan Parliament in Exile (2016–2021), nine members of parliament (MPs) were younger than age of 35. The growth of institutionalised democracy in exile is also an important indication of a conventional shift in a state's population from one based on subjects and duties to one grounded in citizenship and the language of rights and duties (McConnell, 2013, p. 975).

Tibetans in exile are citizens of the CTA with their citizenship linked to the idea of 'rights' and 'services' provided by the exiled dispensation to them. An important service provided by the CTA is in the form of education. The Department of Education is one of the seven main departments of the executive organ of the CTA. It currently oversees 73 Tibetan schools – excluding the pre-primary sections and private schools – in India and Nepal under different autonomous administrative bodies. There are around

24,000 students and 2,200 staff members in these schools. The autonomous school administrative bodies include Central Tibetan Schools Administration (28 schools), Tibetan Children's Villages (18 schools), Tibetan Homes Foundation (3 schools), Sambhota Tibetan Schools Society (12 schools), and Snow Lion Foundation (12 schools) (Tibet.net). These schools are heavily subsidised by the exiled government with the Department of Education also providing scholarships to meritorious students to pursue their higher education. The same department of the CTA also administers the Tibetan Scholarship Program sponsored by the Bureau of Educational and Cultural Affairs of the US State Department through which it offers scholarships to Tibetans to study abroad (Tibet.net). Interestingly, the Tibetans who are recipients of this scholarship after completion have to serve in various capacities in the CTA. This can be termed as reflecting the 'duties' performed by citizens.

The CTA also runs the 'Delek Hospital', based in Dharamsala, which has 45 beds divided into general and tuberculosis wards (Department of Health). However, it is an autonomous institution, run by its own Board of Directors. It also oversees the healthcare of 19 Tibetan settlements in Himachal Pradesh. The hospital is seen to be helping the underprivileged and the under-resourced and has also provided many medical services to Tibetan settlement camps in other parts of India. The CTA has also established 7 hospitals, 5 primary health centre and 38 clinics located in all the refugee settlements in India and Nepal with 174 medical staff and 68 administrative staff working under it (Tibet.net). It is seen to be providing the basic rights to the Tibetans in exile, who are transformed into citizens in this project of state building. For the CTA, the maintenance of Tibetans as refugees should be seen as an action, an act of integrity in defence of faith (Bruno, 2019, p. 71). Creating a 'refugee citizen' by the Tibetan government in exile is necessary for its survival as well as for the future of the Tibetan state.

Constructing citizenship is an ongoing process for exiled Tibetans, as they have encountered significant cultural challenges and limitations in their efforts to accommodate such a modern western model. There has been difficulty in translating and interpreting the concept of citizen in both Tibetan language and Tibetan cultural and political contexts (McConnell, 2013, p. 975). This is denoted by the fact that the Tibetan meaning for *citizen* is "*miser*", which was also used to denote a "subject" in pre-1951 Tibet that was more or less a feudal system, where land and resources were owned by the ecclesiastical state, the aristocracy and also the monastics. There was the extraction of "free services to be provided to the aristocrats" or the "*ulag*", which consisted of labour, resources and transportation. The Chinese nationalist authorities controlling eastern Tibet used to extract the same from local Tibetans. This gross oppression prevalent in pre-1951 Tibet was cited as the reason for the Chinese communists to "liberate" the Tibetan regions. It remains an important mode of gaining legitimacy for the Chinese, which is evoked from time to time. While such narratives have been contested, what remains is the idea of an ongoing transition from subjecthood to citizenship for the Tibetans. This is a top-down process in exile, with the Tibetan elites, especially the Dalai Lama, stressing the need for democratisation and providing rights to the Tibetan citizens in exile. Interestingly, during the initial period of exile, the Tibetans were seen to be resisting this process and embracing their subjecthood. This was also seen recently in 2011, when the Dalai Lama devolved power to an elected head, which was resisted by the Tibetans.

Divinity associated with the Dalai Lama is a key reason for exiled Tibetans to oppose his decision to retire from political duties. Pre-1951 Tibet was a theocratic state, with the Dalai Lama, a reincarnated monk having temporal and spiritual powers. Through traditional and religious legitimacy mixed with charisma, 14 Dalai Lamas have ruled over Tibet. The modern atheist Chinese state also values the institution of the Dalai Lama, as understood through their attempts to control and continue the institution. Religious devotion and faith in the Tibetan population towards their monks and monasteries are a reason for them to not hanker for more rights. Rights and democratisation are the key values associated with the project of citizenship. Also, citizenship provided by the CTA is unequal as the monks are seen to be enjoying more electoral rights.

Nonetheless, the Tibetans in exile are categorised as citizens by the CTA, which can be termed an identification regime adopted by the Tibetan state. As elaborated earlier citizenship is brought through certain institutional and bureaucratic practices in the form of legal discourses through which exile Tibetan citizenship is constructed and through identity documents through which this is materialised (McConnell, 2013, p. 974). The presence of a Tibetan citizenship in exile is seen to be generating a Tibetan nationalism, which actively encourages the Tibetans to remain as stateless refugees within India, making it an affirmation of their patriotic commitment to Tibetan nationalism. This is the most common reason for refusing Indian citizenship by Tibetans as it is deemed as contradicting the CTA as well as harming Tibetan nationalism that aspires for a return to their homeland Tibet. This can be understood as due to the conflict arising out of the post-colonial creation of identities among Tibetans, whereby the Tibetan nation and nationalism remain primal and a major barometer for measuring loyalty.

Taking up citizenship of another nation would mean a weakening of this nationalism. This sharp duality is seen to have emerged due to their exilehood and their desire to secure the Tibetan identity. It is precisely this reason that led to many Tibetans leaving Bhutan in 1974 as there was a conflict of identities. The Tibetan refugees had arrived after the 1958 law, the National Law of Bhutan, had been passed. They could only acquire citizenship through a submission to the king, but there seemed no pressing reason (Ahmad, 2013, p. 160). The Tibetans believed that they would be in exile for a short period and hence there was no need to take citizenship in Bhutan (Ahmad, 2013, p. 161). Even after this, we see the Bhutanese government offering citizenship to the Tibetans, with most Tibetans rejecting this offer as citizenship of Bhutan would mean giving allegiance to the royalty and integration into Bhutan. This rejection led to the monarchy charging the Tibetans with "creating a state within a state", and hence, all the 4000 Tibetans who did not accept Bhutanese subjectship would be deported to Chinese-occupied Tibet unless there were countries willing to receive them (Ahmad, 2013, p. 163). This led to almost all Tibetans leaving Bhutan, mostly for India, who were rehabilitated in new settlements near Dehradun and in Karnataka. What is clear from the preceding example is how the acquiring of citizenship is seen to be contradicting the Tibetan national identity that prevents Tibetans from becoming citizens of another country.

In recent times, the CTA's stand is neutral, leaving the decision regarding citizenship as a personal choice and being a fundamental right of the individuals (Choedon, 2018). Earlier no formal restrictions were imposed by the CTA on Tibetans seeking Indian citizenship, yet according to Yeshi Choedon, they have actively discouraged Tibetans from taking this step. On the other hand, the famous poet and Free Tibet activist Tenzin Tsundue has opposed Tibetans acquiring citizenship. In an interview, he states how many Tibetans wouldn't apply for Indian citizenship as their dream is to go back to Tibet is more important than getting Indian citizenship (Sahay, 2018). Hence a degree of societal pressure is seen towards acquiring citizenship by Tibetans. It is also witnessed that Tibetans having Indian citizenship is of advantage to the individual but disadvantageous to the community.

This came about with Tibetans getting a reprieve from a number of issues such as in 2012, a civil petition had been filed in the high court of Himachal Pradesh alleging that Tibetans in Dharamsala were squatting on protected forest land. However, the petition also mentioned that along with the Tibetans, a large number of Indian citizens had also encroached forestlands. The court eventually gave eviction orders to the encroachers to move by 31 March 2013. Over 1,000 dwellings were owned by Indian citizens, while there were 218 Tibetan families. However, the Tibetan houses were not touched as the state government ordered an indefinite stay on the eviction, overruling the courts and confirming that it was the Tibetans' status as foreigners and not citizens that saved them. It was the non-legal status of Tibetans as guests that gave them the reprieve. Also, if the CTA couldn't protect its own people, it would have raised doubts about the legitimacy of the exiled government. Thus, the Tibetan administration itself had the most to lose should Tibetans claim Indian citizenship (Bruno, 2019, pp. 107–108). Still, we do see Tibetans applying for citizenship in recent times and there are many who are holders of Indian citizenship since the early periods. This leads to the second section which will try to address the "To be" part of the question, which emphasises why Tibetans have and are planning to take citizenship in India and other countries.

III The "To Be" – Tibetans and Their Aspirations for Citizenship in India and the West

There has been a steady rise in the number of Tibetans applying and acquiring citizenship in India. In 2018, about 1400 Tibetans from Dharamsala applied for Indian citizenship (Sahay, 2018). In 2016–17, there were 60 Tibetans who surrendered their RCs with the police for Indian citizenship, with 47 males and 13 females who were applying for Indian passports. Thus, we see that majority of the Tibetans acquire Indian citizenship to gain a passport, making travelling abroad easier for them. This need has emerged since the Tibetans have risen as one of the most successful refugee communities in the world as they have been properly rehabilitated and resettled. Their success is seen through the Second Tibetan Demographic Survey of 2009, which revealed a general literacy rate of 79.4 per cent and an effective literacy rate of 82.4 per cent among the exile community, which, however, does not translate into full employment (Choedon, 2018). The survey revealed over 17 per cent of the total workforce population being unemployed or underemployed (Choedon, 2018). The CTA is unable to absorb the burgeoning educated youth, while the latter are seen to be not following the footsteps of their parents and avoiding sweater selling or other businesses (Choedon, 2018).

This has led to many Tibetan settlement camps (*shichaks*), giving a weary outlook as the younger generation have mostly left for higher education or better employment opportunities. Furthermore, the status of statelessness disqualifies the Tibetan youths from jobs in India. They are not allowed to own businesses or obtain a license to engage in business activities nor entitled to secure bank loans. Another major challenge relates to acquiring travel documents for going abroad. For this purpose, the Tibetans can acquire an IC (Identification Certificate) issued by the Indian government, which however is filled with many bureaucratic hassles. Due to these practical problems of earning a livelihood, getting admission in Indian universities or colleges as well as the difficulties in travelling abroad on an IC, the issue of Tibetans acquiring Indian citizenship has gained currency in recent years (Choedon, 2018). Gaining Indian citizenship is thus linked to personal convenience and material benefits, which the CTA is unable to provide. However as mentioned earlier, there are societal pressures on those who have adopted Indian citizenship as it is tantamount to giving up hope for a Free Tibet (Choedon, 2018).

Furthermore, the Indian government is seen to be putting bureaucratic hurdles for Tibetan applicants, such as having to leave their settlements and forfeit refugee documents (Thakur, 2017). A report in the *Washington Post* mentions about how Tibetans in India were discouraged from taking Indian citizenship by the CTA and other social elites, which was done through word-of-mouth campaigns. A Tibetan-language circular from the CTA urges passport applicants to "take a long-term view rather than considering short-term advantages" (Thakur, 2017). There is a strong argument that acquiring Indian citizenship will dilute the Tibetan movement, which is not a convincing argument as a number of Tibetans who are Indian citizens continue to propagate the Tibetan cause. For instance, Lhagyari Namgyal Dolkar and Mr. Lobsang Wangyal are seen to be sincerely serving the Tibetan movement. These two examples are important as the former, Ms. Namgyal Dolkar's family traces its line from the earlier kings of Tibet, the *Tsenpo* rulers of the 7th century CE and is currently serving as an elected member of ATPD or the Tibetan Parliament in exile. She is also the president of the Gu Chu Sum organisation constituted by former political prisoners in Tibet and which champions their rights. On the other hand, Lobsang Wangyal is the editor of a prominent online news portal TibetSun.com and the founder of the Miss Tibet pageantry, which is a unique platform that has provided a degree of global attention to the Tibetan issue. These individuals have taken up Indian citizenship but are seen to be still serving the Tibetan cause, without any dilution of their identity.

What is interesting is how a degree of double standard seen among certain Tibetan elites, as well as the CTA, by encouraging Tibetans living in other countries, especially those in the West, to take up the citizenship of their host countries and labelling them as Tibetan ambassadors to distant lands (Choedon, 2018). Such an argument is not seen to be present for Tibetans aspiring for Indian citizenship. This might be due to the fact that the CTA is seen to be indulging in a highly modernist state-building project in its exile base in India, which requires a sizeable community that can be placed under its citizenhood. The relevance of the exile government remains when there are a large number of Tibetans in exile in India and is seen to be displaying loyalty to the CTA by remaining as stateless refugees. The Tibet support groups in India are seen to be arguing against taking Indian citizenship, as elaborated by N K Trikha, national convenor of Core Group for Tibetan Cause, a pan-India group which advocates Tibet's independence from Chinese rule, who said, "Acquiring Indian citizenship will knock the bottom out of their reason for living in exile with a determination to return to their motherland or see her become free at some point in time." He said that by taking any other country's citizenship in search of greener pastures, the exiled community would lose its sovereign identity as Tibetans for a few "mundane" advantages (The Pioneer, 2015).

Thus, the formation of a Tibetan national identity, which has its foundation in India, is seen to be not in favour of the Tibetans in exile taking up Indian citizenship. What is to be understood is this national identity is a construct of the CTA and a section of Tibetan elites, which is seen to be garnering a degree of legitimacy from the Tibetan population. Interestingly, in a few cases, some Tibetans have opted for Indian citizenship as a form of dissent against the CTA and the ruling order based in Dharamsala. Like any community, the Tibetans in exile have numerous fissures and divisions among them, many of which have their roots in pre-1951 Tibet, when the

Dalai Lama and the Lhasa authorities did not have direct authority over large parts of the Tibetan plateau. These regions had their own self-governing mechanisms which expressed their sovereignty and independence from Lhasa as well as from Beijing. However, after being forced into exile we see the Dalai Lama and the CTA emerging as a binding force that attempted to unite all Tibetans. This was done through a democratic project that included creating a citizenship, whereby the erstwhile independent voices were to be eventually assimilated.

Such a project is seen to be still ongoing, with the remnants of the earlier streaks of independence exhibited by a few seen within a couple of settlement camps in India or from groups who are not fully compliant with the exile establishment based in Dharamsala. Hence, the members of these groups have been more enthusiastic towards acquiring citizenship of India or other countries. This was seen in 2017–18, when a large number of Tibetans from the Bir Tibetan settlement camp in Himachal Pradesh applied for Indian citizenship. Bir as a settlement has its own dynamics, like any other settlement camp in India, with it being populated by Tibetans from eastern Tibet or the Kham region, who have mostly resisted tendencies of centralization, especially from the Lhasa government. In exile, this resistance is seen with them embracing Indian citizenship or of other countries. A somewhat similar case can be seen with the followers of the controversial deity Dorje Shugden, whose propagation has been censured by the current Dalai Lama. Ironically, the deity which is a primary protector of the Geluk or Yellow Hat school in Tibetan Buddhism to which the Dalai Lama belongs was an important tool of consolidating power inside Tibet prior to 1951. It still played an influential role during the early years of exile. The followers of the deity are seen to be practicing a degree of sectarianism against the other Tibetan schools, which was the main criticism outlined by the Dalai Lama against them. A majority of the followers are seen to be socially ostracised by the larger Tibetan community, thus leading them to opt for citizenship of other countries. In a way, the social boycott faced by the followers of the deity can be understood as a denial of citizenship in the exiled Tibetan state.

IV Conclusion

There has been a steady rise of Tibetans in the western countries, with them settled in North America and followed by a few European countries like Switzerland, France and Germany. A large number of them have acquired citizenship, with the CTA and the western governments facilitating this process. The Canadian government, for instance, in 2010, facilitated immigration of 1000 Tibetan refugees from the three Tibetan settlements located in Arunachal Pradesh that would be carried out within the next five years. This immigration policy is seen to be worked out with the Indian government and the CTA (Bisht, 2010). Under this program in 2013, the first batch of Tibetans from Arunachal reached Canada in July 2013 (Wangyal, 2013). As these settlement camps located in India's remote northeastern state are backward and materially poor, the CTA and the Canadian government decided to resettle them in Canada.

Most of the Tibetans settled in the West have acquired citizenship of their host countries or are in process of acquiring one. In many ways these Tibetans are seen to be challenging the rising influence of China in their respective countries as seen with Tibetan students and their supporters rallying against the Confucian centres established by the Chinese authorities on foreign campuses. Their presence and the demands that the Tibetan citizens in the Western countries have rattled the Chinese authorities as seen in the case of Ms. Chemi Lhamo, a Canadian citizen of Tibetan origin who had been elected as the president of the University of Toronto's Scarborough campus. This had led to her receiving strong hate mails and inflammatory messages, which, according to the Chinese consulate in Toronto, was "an entirely spontaneous action of those Chinese students based on objective facts and patriotic enthusiasm," (CBC News, 2019). Thus, the presence of a transnational Tibetan population holding citizenship of their respective host countries and enjoying rights is seen as denting the image of China. In 2019, the CTA demographic survey revealed how more than half of the population shown by survey to have moved from India to Western countries (Wangyal, 2019). According to the CTA, the large-scale immigration of Tibetans from India is of concern as it will lead to a weakening of identity and the national movement. Many did not participate in the survey as they felt they were citizens of another country (Wangyal, 2019). On the other hand, demands for more representation in ATPD from outside India were seen in the 2020–21 elections in exile. Currently, the ATPD has two seats representing each the communities in North America and Europe and one from Australasia and Asia (excluding India, Nepal and Bhutan; Tibetan Parliament in Exile, 2021).

Finally, with regard to acquiring citizenship among Tibetans, we witness how for a few, it's easier to obtain citizenship of other countries, while for a majority, it is an uphill task. This can be understood in terms of the Tibetan body and its relative worth, clearly defined through the notion of sacrality linked to Tibetan Buddhism, whereby the Tibetan reincarnates or the tulkus find it easier to obtain citizenship in a foreign country, with many in the possession of dual citizenship. The 17th Karmapa, Orgyen Trinley Dorje, who is head of the Karma Kagyu school in 2018, acquired citizenship of Dominica. The passport of Dominica allowed the Karmapa visa-free entry into many Commonwealth countries (Mohan, 2018). The ease of mobility is a major reason why the Karmapa sought a Dominican passport. The present Karmapa has been seen as a potential successor to the Dalai Lama. The attraction and commercialisation of Tibetan Buddhism, which is currently packaged as a new-age spirituality, lead to much demand for its proponents. The monks and reincarnated lamas, who are seen to be globetrotting figures riding the post-modern consumerist vehicle, gain easy access over international borders. These Tibetan Buddhist teachers are transnational and have done much to propagate Tibetan Buddhism, which remains an endearing identity attached to Tibet.

In conclusion, the identity of a Tibetan as a citizen affiliated to the state building project of the CTA is seen to be the hegemonic narrative constructed due to exile-hood. Like citizenship in most postcolonial states and societies, the Tibetan case is one where new identity formations have taken place, ones absent earlier. The current CTA and the earlier ruling elites of the exile Tibetan community are seen to be adopting the language of citizenship as a way of modernising and thus creating the foundations of a nation state. This is still an ongoing process, with both the exile state and its former subjects undertaking several practices to complete citizenship. However as elaborated in the chapter, a significant number of Tibetans are either acquiring citizenship of countries in the West or India, to which the CTA and other Tibetans have given mixed responses, which is discussed above. Finally for Tibetans acquiring citizenship, it is still a question they have to grapple with, as they are seen to be pushed into contemporary projects of identity formation determining their future.

References

Ahmad, O. (2013). *The Kingdom at the Centre of the World: Journeys into Bhutan*. New Delhi: Aleph Books.

Bruno, Greg. (2019). *Blessings from Beijing – Inside China's War on Tibet in Exile*. New Delhi: Speaking Tiger.

CBC News. (2019, February 15). "China Denies Role in Backlash against Tibetan Student's Election at U of T". *CBC*. Accessed on March 3, 2021. Retrieved from https://www.cbc.ca/news/canada/toronto/china-denies-role-in-backlash-against-tibetan-student-s-election-at-u-of-t-1.5021226

Choedon, Yeshi. (2018, February 23). "The Unintended Consequences of India's Policy on Citizenship for Tibetan Refugees". *Idsa.in*. Accessed on March 3, 2021. Retrieved from https://idsa.in/policybrief/unintended-consequences-of-india-lpolicy-on-citizenship-for-tibetan-refugees-ychoedon-230218

Department of Education. Tibet.net. Accessed on March 3, 2021. Retrieved from https://www.sherig.org/

Department of Health – Delek Hospital. *Tibetanhealth.org*. Accessed on March 3, 2021. Retrieved from https://tibetanhealth.org/delek-hospital-dharamsala/

McConnell, F. (2013). "Citizens and Refugees: Constructing and Negotiating Tibetan Identities in Exile". *Annals of the Association of American Geographers*, 103(4), 967–983. https://doi.org/10.1080/00045608.2011.628245.

Mohan, L. (2018, December 8). "Karmapa now a Dominican Citizen". *Tribune News Service*. Accessed on July 31, 2021. Retrieved from https://www.tribuneindia.com/news/archive/himachal/karmapa-now-a-dominican-citizen-695631

Sahay, T. (2018) "The Dream to go Back to Tibet is more important than Getting Indian Citizenship": Tenzin Tsundue. *The Manipal Journal*. Accessed on March 3, 2021. Retrieved from https://themanipaljournal.com/2018/09/17/the-dream-to-go-back-to-tibet-is-more-important-than-getting-indian-citizenship-tenzin-tsundue/

Thakur, Naresh K. (2017, June 26). "Government Sets Conditions for Tibetans to Get Passports, Says Move Out of Settlements, Forgo Benefits". *Hindustan Times*. Accessed on March 3, 2021. Retrieved from https://www.hindustantimes.com/india-news/govt-riders-for-tibetans-to-get-passports-move-out-of-colonies-forgo-benefits/story-jBsKDOitUKmDACZ1DP2jFK.html

The Pioneer. (2015, January 19). "Tibetans in Exile Divided Over Right to Vote". *Dailypioneer.com*. Accessed on March 3, 2021. Retrieved fromhttps://www.dailypioneer.com/2015/sports/tibetans-in-exile-divided-over-right-to-vote.html

Tibetan Parliament in Exile. 2021. "Composition". *Tibetan Parliament in Exile*. Accessed on July 31, 2021. Retrieved from https://tibetanparliament.org/about-tpie/composition/

Wangyal, Lobsang. (2013, April 1). "First batch of Tibetans from Arunachal to Canada likely in July". *Tibetsun.com*. Accessed on March 3, 2021. Retrieved from https://www.tibetsun.com/news/2013/04/01/first-batch-of-tibetans-from-arunachal-to-canada-likely-in-july

Wangyal, Lobsang. (2019, December 18). "Demographic Survey Shows Exile Tibetan Exodus to the West". *Tibetsun.com*. Accessed on July 31, 2021. Retrieved from https://www.tibetsun.com/news/2019/12/18/demographic-survey-shows-exile-tibetan-exodus-to-west

Chapter 13

Citizenship Dilemmas of the Nepalis(ese) of Darjeeling Hills and Beyond

Biswanath Saha

13.1 Introduction

History teaches us that the state system we experience today had been evolving for ages. From being small-scale sovereignties with ambiguous frontiers, in the pre-modern era, to the hard-fenced politically bounded spaces, in the modern era, it remains the reality of the state system today (Scott 2009). The seeds of the modern state system lie in the Treaty of Westphalia, 1648, which heralded the initiation of political borders, with replacing the existing frontiers, apart from a host of other attributes. With its initiation, automatically, the question of *otherization* came into existence, as the creation of borders divided the people into different political spaces. This *otherization* necessitates states identify the 'nationalist core' – the citizens, and the 'others' – who are 'doubtful' and do not constitute the 'nationalist core' (Pandey 1999). However, the question of citizenship remained ambivalent in the initial days of state formation, as mere becoming a subject of a state does not necessarily qualify an individual to become a *citizen*. Citizenship roughly transcribes as a full and equal member of a state having certain rights. According to Timothy Marshall, while subjects hardly possess politico-legal rights, citizens do enjoy civil, political and social rights (Marshall 1950).

Interestingly, the story of the Eastern Himalayan state making also resembles the processes discussed earlier. In the pre-colonial settings, there were several Kingdoms and principalities, having ambiguous frontiers, in the said region. The arrival of the British replaced the existing frontiers in their colonies in the Eastern Himalayas with hard political borders. Additionally, their arrival also encouraged a heavy influx of Nepalis(ese)[1] migration in the region for various reasons. Henceforth, what happened to the citizenship question of the Nepalis(ese), after their migration, is the scope of this chapter. This chapter also traces out the formation of the Eastern Himalayan[2] states – Sikkim and Bhutan, and the formation of *Drukpa* identity. Alongside, it also seeks to analyse the interrelationships between identity preservation of the *Drukpas* and the citizenship anxiety of the Nepalis(ese) in the Eastern Himalayas as a whole. The issue becomes topical when one notices that more

DOI: 10.4324/9781003345152-19

than one lakh Nepalis in Assam were delisted from the National Register of Citizens (NRC), as they failed to become part of the 'nationalist core' (Pandey 1999) with the enactment of Citizenship Amendment Act, 2016 (CAA).

But, before that, a brief historical sketch of the Eastern Himalayas would set the tone meaningfully.

13.2 A Brief History of the Eastern Himalayas

State-making projects in Sikkim, as well as in Bhutan, were initiated by the Tibetan Buddhists tradition since the seventeenth century. It is argued that a section of Drukpa Lamas from Tibet came to the Eastern Himalayas in order to preach and 'convert' (Sinha 1975) people into Buddhism. Eventually, they enthroned Phuntso Namgyal as the ruler of Sikkim in 1614 (Subba 1992). It should be clarified that the presence of Tibetan Lamas in the Eastern Himalayas could be noticed from the eighth century. But their existence became influential only after the initiation of state-making project, with the establishment of *Dharmaraja* in 1642, that increased the Bhutia population considerably (Subba 1985a; Sinha 1975, 1973). The *Dharmarajas* are chosen from the collection of monks with the process of reincarnation, popularly known as the *Shabdrung* system. Similar was the case with Bhutan, which also followed the *Shabdrung* system to choose the *Dharmaraja* (Phuntsho 2013; Aris 1979). The *Shabdrung* system had two components – 'spiritual and temporal' (Joseph 1997; Aris 1979). The spiritual head was known as *Dharmaraja* while *Deb Raja* was heading the temporal affairs. The former is also known as *Chogyal* – the abbreviated form of '*Chos*' (dharma) and the '*rGyalpo*' (ruler; Sinha 1975, 11).

When the Drukpa Lamas came to Sikkim from Tibet in the seventeenth century, they had witnessed only two ethnic groups – Lepchas and the Limbus (Sinha 1975), although Lepchas are regarded as the earliest settlers in Sikkim (Subba 1985a). Likewise, there were four major ethnic groups in Bhutan, namely the Ngalongs, Sharchops, Khengs, and the Nepalis(ese), apart from a small number of Adivasis, Birmis, Brokpas, Doyas, and Toktop (Joseph 1997). Relevantly, the Drukpa Lamas, who came to the Eastern Himalayas, were the ones who were ousted by their Gelugpa counterparts in Tibet (Joseph 1997; Dixit 1992a; Rose 1977). Since then, Sikkim and Bhutan had been trying to maintain their identity of being Drukpa[3] states (Subba 1985a; Sinha 1975, 1973; Phuntsho 2013). The following quote suggests that

> dominant political and religious ideologies linked to the Dalai Lama's Gelugpa sect did not leave much space for dissent, and the antecedents of many of today's populations in the Himalayan regions of Nepal, India, and Bhutan that skirt Tibet's southern borders were adherents of other sects (primarily Nyingmapa and Sakyapa but also Kaguyapa and Bonpo) who fled religious persecution in Tibet . . .
>
> (Shneiderman 2010, 299)

On the other, it is well known that the frontiers of Darjeeling hills had frequently been annexed by various Himalayan Kingdoms in its historical past and finally the British formed a district called Darjeeling in the 1860s (Dasgupta 1999; Subba 1992, 1985b). The British had acquired the Darjeeling hills from Sikkim in 1835 as a '*deed of grant*' because of its 'cool climatic' condition conducive for the British officials (Aitchison 1892, I:164), potentiality of becoming a tea estate (Datta 1991; Subba 1992), apart from its 'geopolitical' importance (Dasgupta 1999). Taking these into account, the next section briefly sketches the colonial rationale of encouraging migration in the Eastern Himalayas.

13.3 Colonial Migration in the Eastern Himalayas

The literature suggests that the geopolitical interests of the British over the Eastern Himalayas had been around Kalimpong–Lhasa Road, the plantation economy and the recruitment of personnel in the British Gorkha Army. Thereby, this section attempts to analyse these issues.

By the late eighteenth century, a majority of the Himalayan Kingdoms were wrested by the Gorkhali rulers. The annexation of 'Kathmandu valley' (Joseph 1997) in 1769 and its subsequent consolidation by the shah rulers had invariably challenged the authority of the British over the Eastern Himalayas. One of the foremost challenges to the British, throughout the nineteenth century, had been establishing a trading network, in the Eastern Himalayas, to which the Gorkha rulers in Nepal seemed to be the bone of contention. The old trade route to Tibet, which passed through Nepal, remained dysfunctional after the Gorkha upheaval in the late eighteenth century (Joseph 1997; Sinha 1975). However, there was an alternate trade route, the 'Royal Road to Lhasa' (Bhanja 1993) or the 'Kalimpong–Lhasa Road' (Dasgupta 1999), that passed through the Chumbi Valley. Interestingly, this trade route was under the tutelage of Sikkim which was under the patronage of the *Drukpa* Buddhists (Dasgupta 1999). On the other, Chumbi Valley was believed to be the territory of Tibet within the meaning of the 1890 Anglo-Chinese Convention (Aitchison 1892) and had proximity to Bhutan. Hence, Bhutan was also under the watchful eye of the British. So, to find an alternative to the old trade route passing through Nepal, the British had to mould their geopolitics over the Eastern Himalayas to maintain control over the Kalimpong–Lhasa Road. To actualize this, the British had used the tactics of demographically disbalancing the *Drukpas* by encouraging the Hinduized Nepalis(ese). It was more so because the British had the belief, as written by Risley (1894), that there was an apparent religious crosscurrent between the Hinduized Nepalis(ese) and the Mahayana Buddhists.

Relevantly, being geopolitically anxious to securitize the frontiers of British India from Chinese mobilization into Tibet, the British bargained in the 1890 Convention with China 'to clearly define and permanently settle certain matters connected with the boundary between Sikkim and Tibet' (Aitchison 1892, I:170). Article II of this Convention instated for the first time the status of Sikkim as the 'protectorate' (Aitchison 1892, I:171) of British India. Earlier, the British assumed sufficient suzerainty over Sikkim through the provision of Article III of the *1817 Titaliya Treaty* (Aitchison 1892, I:162) without categorizing it as a protectorate. Moreover, dissatisfied with repeated kidnappings and abduction of British subjects in Sikkim, the former forced the latter to sign the *Treaty of Tumloong*1861 that eventually patronized a heavy influx of 'British subjects' into Sikkim (Aitchison 1892; Risley 1894). As Article VIII of the Treaty of Tumloong 1861 allowed mobility of people from surrounding areas, the growth of the Nepalis(ese) population altered the existing ethnic divide in Sikkim (Aitchison 1892, I:167). On the other, Bhutan, as well as Sikkim, practised the *Shabdrung* system of incarnations to choose the head of the state. One of the rationales of this system was to protect the *Drukpa* identities of these states. To preserve its *Drukpa* identity, Bhutan fought as many as five wars with Tibet and the Mongols (Aris 1979). Concomitantly, for its sustenance, Bhutan used to raid the Dooars to get the required resources (Kar 2012). Perhaps, 'the Dooars was an area to be explored, controlled and conquered' for the Bhutanese who preferred to live at a certain altitude (Sinha 1991, 128). To avoid repeated kidnappings, 'plunder', taking British subjects hostage and the like in Bhutan, as was the case in Sikkim, the British signed the 1865 Sinchula Treaty with Bhutan (Aitchison 1892, I:189–92). The British had assumed considerable suzerainty over Bhutan in matters relating to foreign affairs through the Article VIII of the Sinchula Treaty (Aitchison 1892, I:189–92). This treaty had also forced Bhutan to open its frontiers for free mobility of people, as well as ceding the territories in the east, named Dooars, to the British. British adopted the policy, as same as was with Sikkim, of opening up the frontiers of Bhutan to encourage the migration of subjects from the surrounding areas. In hindsight, it seems that the British interest of outplaying the Buddhists' influence in the Eastern Himalayas by encouraging the influx of Hinduized Nepalis(ese) was getting satisfied automatically.

Relevantly, the influx of these Hinduized Nepalis(ese) was also encouraged as it fulfilled the British aspiration of having personnel recruited in the British Gorkha Army. During the first half of the nineteenth century, the British were recruiting personnel directly from Gorkha Kingdom, and with this Gorkha Army, the British even fought wars with the Gorkhali rulers (e.g. the Anglo-Gorkha War 1814–16). The mercenary calibre of the Gorkha personnel led the Gorkhali ruler to prohibit subjects to be recruited into the Gorkha Army. So, as an alternative to this, the British encouraged the migration of the Gorkhas into the Himalayan hill stations like Darjeeling, Shillong, Dehradun and others so that they could be recruited directly from here (Subba 1992; Dasgupta 1999). One of the recruiting stations is Ghoom, in Darjeeling, which is still being referred to as 'Old Gorkha station'

(Dasgupta 1999). Apart from this, migration of people from the surrounding areas was also encouraged so that they could be employed in the flourishing tea industry in the Eastern Himalayas. As the Nepalis(ese) are regarded as well versed in undergoing sedentary cultivation, and their ability to speak *khaskura* language; thereby, their migration was tactfully encouraged by the British.

While this section deals with migration in the Eastern Himalayas during the colonial period, the next section discusses the interrelationship between migration in postcolonial with Drukpa identity.

13.4 Postcolonial Migration in the Eastern Himalayas and the Drukpa Identity

As discussed earlier, colonial interest over the Eastern Himalayas was largely shaped by the Kalimpong–Lhasa trade route, plantation economy as well as recruitment of personnel in the British Army. Interestingly, all these interests had directly manifested in encouraging migration in the Eastern Himalayas. Noticeably, immediately after India's independence in 1947, the loosely defined frontiers of the colonial era became well demarcated political boundaries. As these loose frontiers were getting politically defined through hard fencing, several political boundaries across the Eastern Himalayan states were having territorial overlaps as the borders have been lying virtually open. Border treaties of India with Nepal, Bhutan and Sikkim were negotiated in such a way that they could not restrict the mobility of people across these states. The Indo-Bhutan Treaty 1949, Indo-Nepal Treaty 1950 and the Indo-Sikkim Treaty 1950 patronised unhindered migration of people across borders. In other words, these treaties somewhat facilitated the continuation of the pre-colonial migration in the postcolonial period in the Eastern Himalayas as well. Hence, the rationale for laying the borders open, along with encouraging migration into the Eastern Himalayas in the postcolonial period, is analysed in this section. Alongside, this section also seeks to analyse the conflictual relation of growing number of people in Sikkim and Bhutan with the Drukpa identity.

13.4.1 Statelessness of the Nepalis(ese) in Drukpa Sikkim

After Independence, with the change in political establishment and ushering in of democratic set-up in India, a section of people in Sikkim formed the Sikkim State Congress (SSC) to demand reforms (Datta-Ray 1984; Phadnis 1980). Since its inception, the SSC had started demanding the replacement of monarchy with 'democracy' (Datta-Ray 1984; Phadnis 1980; Sidhu 2018) desertion of feudalism (Chakrabarti 2012), close association with India (Sinha 1975), and even 'accession' of Sikkim with the Indian Union (Phadnis 1980; Verghese 2004). It is also argued that the reformist movement in Sikkim had actually started since 1949 and the Sikkimese Nepalis(ese) pioneered this cause under the leadership of Chandra Das Rai, also a Sikkimese Nepalis(ese) (Datta-Ray 1984). But political organisations like the National Party (NP) did not welcome either the idea of 'democracy' or 'accession' to India (Phadnis 1980). As a result, differences between the members of these political organisations emerged and ultimately the members with diverging viewpoints came together to form Sikkim National Congress (SNC) in May 1960 under the leadership of Kazi Lhendup Dorji (Phadnis 1980, 1239).

Additionally, India entered into a new Indo-Sikkim Treaty in 1950, which reaffirmed the status of Sikkim as a 'protectorate' of India, in lieu of ever-increasing Chinese shadow over Tibet (Datta-Ray 1984). Conversely, demands for democratic reforms in Sikkim was given a partial hearing, as the Chogyal felt disturbed by the 'accession' demand of the Nepalis(ese) (Verghese 2004). In terms of adult franchise, each Sikkimese Nepalis(ese) was assigned one vote, but the impact of one vote for each Lepcha and Bhutia would extrapolate to six votes in the count. The Chogyal argued that as the Lepcha-Bhutias were minority communities in the state, providing them a level playing field against the majority Nepalis(ese) was necessary. This lopsided arrangement, according to the Chogyal, would guarantee a balanced right of franchise to the minorities. This resulted in the movement demanding one person one vote, although it was denied (Datta-Ray 1984). The demand by the Nepalis(ese) brought some reform measures in the form of equal rent pay for all in 1956 which was said to be an initiation of *ethnic parity* by the Chogyal in Sikkim. Earlier the Nepalis(ese) used to pay higher rent compared to the Lepcha-Bhutias (Chakrabarti 2010).

These reformist agendas were carried forward in the Chogyal-led Sikkim by the SNC since its establishment in 1960. However, these reformist forces became apprehensive of India's intentions, as the security agency of India, Research & Analysis Wing (R&AW), encouraged (Sidhu 2018) them to push their reformist demands in 1973 (Datta-Ray 1984) which ultimately led to the signing of May 8, 1973, agreement (Sinha 1975; Gupta 1975). The 1973 agreement empowered India to indirectly override Sikkim's internal administration (Verghese 2004, 249). Alongside, the May agreement also ensured adult suffrage on the basis of 'one person one vote', which was denied in 1950s, so that a legislature can be established under 'constitutional monarchy' (Datta-Ray 1984). It was also guaranteed that proportional representation of the Bhutia-Lepchas (BL) and the Nepalis(ese) could be followed to continue with the Chogyal-initiated ethnic parity (Verghese 2004). As a follow-up measure, total 32 seats were decided for the upcoming assembly. Out of these, 15 seats were reserved for BL and another 15 seats for the Nepalis(ese); dedicating one seat each to the Scheduled Castes and the Sangha[4] (Phadnis 1980; Sinha 1975).

Meanwhile, Sikkim Congress came into existence when Janata Congress and National Congress decided to merge with Kazi Lhendup Dorji as their president. In the first assembly election, Sikkim Congress won 31 seats out of a total 32, and immediately after, the first assembly meeting was called for (Phadnis 1980; Sidhu 2018). Kazi was under the influence of the R&AW (Sidhu 2018), and henceforth, the Constitution of Sikkim came into existence on July 5, 1974, headed by an Indian political executive. Immediately after, the Government of India asked the Sikkim assembly 'to fulfil the promise of association with India' (Verghese 2004, 250). Furthermore, with the passing of the 36th Constitutional Amendment Act in 1974, Sikkim become an 'associate state' of India with representations in both Houses of the Parliament (Datta-Ray 1984; Duff 2015). Consequently, a referendum was staged on April 14, 1975, to decide the 'merger' issue. The electoral roll for the referendum was based on the voters' list prepared for the Assembly election of 1974 through the Sikkim Subjects' Regulation 1961. This regulation treated only those as *Sikkimese* subjects who had been living in Sikkim at least for 15 years from the commencement of the regulation (Kar 2012). In other words, 1946 was taken as the cut-off year. With the frames of this regulation, the Sikkimese subjects took part in the referendum, where Sikkim's merger with India received a resounding mandate. Thereafter, the 'associated status' of Sikkim was declared null and void only to formally accede Sikkim as the 22nd state of India in 1975 (Phadnis 1980, 1243).

Here, it is important to note that the merger with Sikkim was conditioned by the granting of Indian citizenship to the Sikkimese Nepalis(ese), their proportional representation in the Sikkimese Assembly, along with the recognition of Nepali language in the Constitution of India. Therefore, the Government of India declared the Sikkim Citizenship Order, 1975 under the aegis of the Indian Citizenship Act 1955. The order professed, 'every person who immediately before the 26th day of April 1975 was a Sikkim subject under the Sikkim Subjects' Regulation 1961, shall be deemed to have become a citizen of India on that day' (Sikkim Government Gazette 1975). In other words, 1946 was deemed as one of the criteria for considering anyone as Sikkimese Subject (Sikkim Government Gazette 1989) that ultimately left scores, who migrated to Sikkim in the intermittent period – after 1946 but before merger – *stateless*. All round, protests erupted against this regulation in Sikkim. As a protest, Sikkim Sangram Parishad (SSP), headed by Narabahadur Bhandari, one of the prominent figures in the politics of post-merger Sikkim, demanded either to bring an amendment to the Sikkim Citizenship Order 1975 by taking 1970 as the cut-off year, or to take the merger year, that is 1975, for considering Indian citizenship of the Sikkimese (Kar 2012, 28–29). Following such pressures, the Government of India in 1989, through the Notification number 26030/69/88-IC.I, amended the Sikkim Citizenship Order 1975 and inserted the following:

> Provided that any person whose names was eligible to be entered in the registrar maintained under the said regulation but was not so entered because of any genuine omission shall also be deemed to have become a citizen of India on that day if so determined by the Central Government.
> ("Sikkim Government Gazette" 1989)

Thereby, it is apparent from the above discussion that as the Nepalis(ese) had been the latest settlers in Sikkim at the temporal scale, they had to face discrimination in terms of franchise, land ownership, differential taxation and more. Hence, they took the recourse of reformist demands, since the 1950s, which were later on tactfully dealt with by the Indian state to merge the *Drukpa*-ruled Sikkim with India. Such a merger is still etched in the mind of the *Drukpa* Bhutias. However, even after the merger, the Nepalis of Sikkim had to struggle hard to get their citizenship in India.

While this sub-section analysed the migration of Nepalis(ese) into Sikkim and its subsequent ramifications, the next sub-section analyses the Nepalis(ese) migration into Bhutan, another important state in the Eastern Himalayan jigsaw.

13.4.2 Nepalis(ese) Migration into Drukpa Bhutan

It has already been argued that the initiation of state-making in Bhutan, much like Sikkim, had been the efforts of the *Drukpa* Lamas from early seventeenth century. Since then, these states had been hellbent on preserving their *Drukpa* identities (Sinha 1991; Dixit 1992a; Rose 1977; Sinha 1975). Later on, the colonial encounter in Bhutan encouraged a centralized monarch with the enthronement of Ugyen Wangchuk in 1907 as there were rampant internal conflicts amongst the clergies and the *Penlops* in Bhutan (Joseph 1997). This monarchical arrangement kept continuing in Bhutan without much alteration till the late 1940s. Meanwhile, India achieved Independence in 1947 and upheld Bhutan's sovereignty status, however, at the cost of signing a new treaty in 1949. This treaty had re-necessitated Bhutan to be guided by India in a matter of its defence and external affairs (Phuntsho 2013).

India signed this treaty with Bhutan in the wake of Chinese activities in the Eastern Himalayas (Chengappa and Krishnan 2017), and this treaty, perhaps, provided a shield to Bhutan from external aggression 'as far as the international politics' in the Eastern Himalayas was concerned (Phuntsho 2013). At the same time, the Indian state aspired to have representation in its Assembly from the princely states, and thereby, this scope was extended to Bhutan as well (Phuntsho 2013) on the same line as offered earlier to Sikkim. But Bhutan had categorically written to the *Cabinet Mission* in Simla on May 7, 1946, to maintain its *Drukpa* identity, that the sociocultural heritage of Bhutan hardly had any resemblance to India; rather, it had commonalities with Tibet and China (Chawla 2019). In this struggle of preserving the *Drukpa* identity, Nepalis(ese) of Bhutan were the 'sufferers' (Dixit 1992a), in similar ways as was the case with the Sikkimese Nepalis(ese). For this, Bhutan did not even allow any constitution to be drafted; rather, the sermons of the Chogyal based on the *Drig Lam Namzha* (Shabdrung's code) became the philosophical guardian of the state. It is also exasperating that the Bhutanese Nepalis(ese) could only become the 'subjects' of *Drukpa* Bhutan but failed to secure their 'citizenship'. Even, cultivation and ownership right over land for the Nepalis(ese) were restricted to south Bhutan only (Rose 1977, 111).

Intrigued by such ill-treatments to the Nepalis(ese) in Bhutan, a political organization named Bhutan State Congress (BSC) came into existence in Bhutan in 1952 to carry forward reformists demands like desertion of feudalism, bringing democracy along with providing civil rights to the Nepalis(ese) and even maintaining closer ties with India (Joseph 1997; Sinha 1991). Thereby, to carry forward the struggle of the Nepalis(ese) to demand 'democracy' and human rights in Bhutan, political organisations like Bhutan People's Party (1990), the Bhutan National Democratic Party (1992) and the Druk National Congress (1994) also came into existence (Joseph 1997). Argumentatively, the BSC was following the footsteps of the Sikkim State Congress in demanding sociopolitical reforms (Rose 1977, 110–11) and as a measure for such reformist demands, the Bhutanese Nepalese were provided citizenship in 1958 (Dixit 1992a).

On the other hand, Jigme Dorji Wangchuck, the third king, opened the door for modernization in Bhutan, which was deemed as a potential threat to the *Drukpa* identity by the traditional folks in the state. Under his reign from 1952 to 1972, Wangchuk had introduced Five Year Plans since 1961, established national assembly and abolished landlordism, among others (Joseph 1997; Rose 1977). The implementation of these reforms was entrusted to Palden Dorji, whose roots were at the Kalimpong-based clan called 'Dorji'. He was assassinated in 1964 by the Bhutanese authorities on the pretext that he had developed the aspiration of his Kingdomship (Dixit 1992a). There was hardly any ethnic conflict between the northern *Drukpas* and the *Lhatshampas* – the southern Nepalis(ese), before his assassination. South Bhutan so far did not directly come under the administration of *Drukpa* Bhutanese except during the time of tax payment. Mostly, south Bhutan was the responsibility of the Dorjis from Kalimpong-based clan, and hence, *Drukpas* hardly assumed any direct administration of the south. But, soon after his assassination, *Lhatshampas* came directly under the *Drukpas*. In this renewed environment also, ethnic harmony between the *Drukpas* and the *Lhatshampas* was observed (Aris 1979). During the 1970s and early 1980s, even restriction over Nepalis(ese) mobility within the state was relaxed, barring the earlier *de facto* restrictions to move and settle within south Bhutan only. Moreover, inter-ethnic marriages between these ethnicities were also allowed with cash incentives (Rizal 2004, 153) concomitantly declaring the Nepali festival of *Dasain* as the national holiday of Bhutan in 1980. Apart from these, Nepali also became the medium of instructions in Bhutan, besides Dzongkha and English (Dixit 1992a).

With the pronouncement of the Sixth Five Year Plan in 1987, the entire ethnopolitics in Bhutan suddenly got derailed. Erstwhile ethnic harmony all of a sudden seemed to have transformed into the goal of preserving the minority *Drukpa* identity with strict implementation of the *Drig Lam*

Namzha and with the census exercise in 1988 to identify Butanese citizens (Hutt 1993). Needless to mention, Nepalis(ese) had been uncomfortable with accepting the *Drig Lam Namzha* rather they were happy with their own rituals. Ethnoculturally, in fact, the Nepalis(ese) of Bhutan would connect to the Nepalese of Nepal than that of the northern *Drukpas*. There was complete unanimity amongst the *Drukpas* that the *Lhatshampas* needed to be completely assimilated within the Drukpa Bhutanese core without any 'compromise' (Sinha 1994, 182). Hence, the *Lhatshampas'* fate started fast approaching towards the gallow. As Bhutanese Nepalis(ese) were against the *Drig Lam Namzha*, modernisation ceased to be the threat to *Drukpa* identity and the Nepali-speaking *Lhatshampas* became the new crosscurrent (Joseph 1997). The Bhutanese authorities wanted to weed out the '*Lhatshampa* problem' as their growing presence in Bhutan became the main concern towards protecting the *Drukpa* identity (Sinha 1994).

The threat perception of *Drukpa* Bhutan was so entrenched that they used to take reference of the Nepalis(ese) ethnopolitics in Sikkim. They argued that the erstwhile *Drukpa*-ruled monarchial state first collapsed under the democratic wave led by the Sikkimese Nepalis(ese) and that, later on, it fell prey to Indian interests to become the 22nd state of India in 1975 (Sinha 1975; Datta-Ray 1984). Hence, Bhutanese became apprehensive over Nepalis(ese) presence in Bhutan and started calling the *Drukpas* as "endangered species" that ought to be preserved. To them, the greatest threat to the *Drukpa* identity had been posed by the continuous migration from surrounding areas into Bhutan, the Chogyal said in the early 1990s. Even, the Bhutanese authorities officially argued, unless there is a check over the migration into Bhutan, the *Drukpa* state will loose its identity soon and become another 'Nepali state' much like what happened to Sikkim. However, Kanak Mani Dixit, a commentator on the Himalayan politics and the founding editor of *Himal Southasian*, was of the opinion that there was hardly any evidence that the Bhutanese Nepalis(ese) were planning to overthrow the monarch (Dixit 1992a).

As the status of Nepalis(ese) in Bhutan was considerably short of that of citizens (Rose 1977), they became awfully concerned about their citizenship in the wake of census enumeration from 1988 onwards (Sinha 1995). The earlier attempt to identify Bhutanese citizens according to the 1958 law included places of birth, *thram* (documents of land ownership), and naturalisation of five years, among others. Later on, citizenship certificates were provided to the Bhutanese through the census of 1970 and a cadastral survey of 1972 (Ahmed 2019; Sinha 1991). The next census of 1980 proved to be one of the most important in Bhutanese history in matters relating to citizenship. This census paved the way for the enactment of the 1985 Citizenship Act (Dixit 1992b) that retrospectively declared all the earlier existing citizenship criteria as 'null and void' and took the 1958 National Law as the cut-off year. Earlier, tax receipts, registered house number, *thram*, and so on were accepted to delineate citizens and others in Bhutan, but the retrospective cancellation of such documents left the Nepalese completely exasperated (Hutt 2005, 2003; Rizal 2004). With these measures, Bhutan expelled more than a lakh Nepalese from Bhutan during the early 1990s. The hidden agenda of the *Drukpa* Bhutanese about the *Lhatshampas* has been aptly put,

> In Thinmphu, it is commonly believed that the *Lhatshampas* had designs to change the Bhutanese political and ethnic scenario within the next 25 years by altering the citizenship laws and opening up Bhutan to a flow of alien Nepalese. This, it is alleged, would have made it easier to extend Nepal's hegemony to Sikkim, Darjeeling, and the *Dooars* in West Bengal, and ultimately to Bhutan.
>
> (Sinha 1994, 182)

13.5 Citizenship Anxiety of the Nepalis of India

It is widely known in the academic domain that the Darjeeling hill dwellers had been struggling hard to usher in their ethnic aspirations since 1907. In this century-old struggle, the Darjeeling hills have witnessed the demand for politico-administrative set-ups, recognition of Nepali language as well as the creation of Gorkhaland. Of late, we have also seen the crystallization of all-round claim for tribal status, demand for land rights as well as nascent citizenship anxiety in the Darjeeling hills. This section seeks to contemporaries the notions related to citizenship of the Nepalis of Darjeeling hills in particular and India in general.

At the outset, it should be made clear that the citizenship anxiety among the Nepalis in India did not became an issue only after the emergence of the National Register of Citizens (NRC) in Assam. It has its roots in the Darjeeling hill politics well before in 1950 with the signing of the Indo-Nepal Treaty of Peace and Friendship, and particularly the Article VII of the treaty. This issue further got prominence in 1988 when Subash Ghising publicly burned copies of the treaty (Sarkar 2013), as Article VII necessarily creates confusion over the citizenship of Nepalis of Darjeeling. Article VII of the treaty facilitates unhindered mobility of citizens of both India and Nepal in each other's territories, along with providing legal rights over property ownership, thus, generating a doubtfulness (Saha and Chakraborty 2019b) over *Nepalis* and *Nepalese*[5] (Subba 1992). Henceforth, Darjeeling hills become land for anybody and everybody, as hardly any *land-patta* is needed to settle in Darjeeling hills. Thereby, as a sequel to it, the hill intelligentsia had been urging the Indian state to either modify the 1950 Indo-Nepal Treaty or abrogate Article VII of the same treaty (Saha and Chakraborty 2019a).

Such citizenship anxiety of the Nepalis of Darjeeling hills became a potent issue only in the late 1980s because they have already witnessed the 'ousting' of their ethnic brethren from Bhutan in the early 1990s with the strict implementation of 1985 Bhutan Citizenship Act through census enumeration in 1988 onwards. Concomitantly, the Nepali-speaking people in the North-East

India also had to face push-back measures (Misra 1986) during the latter half of the 1980s. Such incidents towards the Nepalis of India were the outcome of the political developments in Sikkim and Bhutan. As discussed earlier that the Nepalis, who migrated late as compared to their other counterparts in the Eastern Himalayas in the historical time scale, first, became the political elites bypassing other ethnies – Lepchas, Bhutias and Limbus, among others, in Sikkim. Second, the Indian state by using the Nepali card subsequently 'annexed' (Datta-Ray 1984) the then sovereign Sikkim.

These political developments prompted other territories in the Eastern Himalayas to become apprehensive about Nepalis(ese)'s presence in their territories, and concomitantly, they had to bear the wrath of 'ethnic cleansing' in Bhutan (Hutt 2005) and backlash in North-East India. This entire episode of the merger of Sikkim, with concomitant maltreatment, as well as the subsequent expulsion of Bhutanese Nepalis(ese), gave reasons to the Darjeeling Nepalis to renew their demand for Gorkhaland in the late 1980s. Activists argue that the proposed separate state comprising the Darjeeling hills would provide them better security and a territorial identity. Although the citizenship notification No. 26011/6/88-IC.I. on August 23, 1988, clarified the status of the Darjeeling hill dwellers by recognizing the 'Gorkhas' as Indian citizens, but the absence of proof of inhabitancy still haunts them (Subba 1992). This fear of security got reignited when they learnt that more than one lakh Nepalis in Assam failed to find their names in the final list of NRC in the absence of proof of inhabitancy. The citizenship anxiety became institutional when a sitting minister of West Bengal, Gautam Deb, gave a statement in 2019, "if NRC is implemented in the Darjeeling hills, the hills will become empty" (Pradhan 2019).

This absence of proof of inhabitancy becomes another conundrum for the Darjeeling hills politics. As discussed earlier, rationale for the British to encourage migration in and around Darjeeling hills were centred on plantations, the recruitment of personnel in the British Gorkha Army and minimising the influence of Tibetan Buddhism. Later on, the Nepalis of Darjeeling hills were encouraged to become *mandals*, the collector of rent from the raiyats and under-raiyats, by the British for the capacity of the Nepalis to work long. By virtue of being *mandals*, the Nepalis of Darjeeling hills had accumulated a considerable portion of land to become the *de facto* landowners (Sarkar 2010), meaning, thereby, that there is hardly any land-ownership documents in the Darjeeling hills. However, the land transaction are happening through local deeds without any official registration. Henceforth, the issue of land-patta gained momentum in the absence of documents of land inhabitancy in the recent times.

Pertaining to this, the politics over the demand of tribal status deserves special mention. One can notice that the decade of the 2000s opened up new grounds for various ethnic communities in the Darjeeling hills to get recognised as Scheduled Tribes (Middleton and Shneiderman 2008). Earlier, during the late 1980s, the Indian state was willing to extend the 6th Schedule provision to the Darjeeling hills. However, the Darjeeling 'hill intelligentsia' and the political organisations subsequently discarded the Sixth Schedule provision by saying that the tribal majority provisions cannot be implemented in non-tribal majority areas (Sarkar 2013; Saha 2016). After realising the importance of this constitutional arrangement, which can provide them considerable autonomy, often understood as the first step towards attaining a separate state, there is an all-round demand for recognition as STs in the Darjeeling hills. To them, this arrangement can provide security over the land of inhabitancy, which, in return, can become one of the indomitable documents to ensure citizenship status.

13.6 Conclusion

To sum up, it is already argued that the British had negotiated treaties with its neighbouring states in such a manner that it could encourage migration, and then, they could be recruited in the British Gorkha Regiment, plantation economy, apart from aiming at waning down the influence of Mahayana Buddhists in the Eastern Himalayas in order to take possession of the Kalimpong–Lhasa trade route. Interestingly, post-colonial India also renegotiated the treaties like the Indo-Nepal Treaty, 1950; Indo-Sikkim Treaty, 1950; and the Indo-Bhutan Treaty, 1949 which made the borders virtually open. These treaties provided an *alibi* for unhindered mobility of people in each other's territories. In other words, it was a kind of tacit continuation of colonial geo-politics of migration in the post-colonial period.

Consequently, when the Nepalis(ese) population started increasing in Sikkim as well as in Bhutan, by virtue of open borders, they started pursuing the demand for sociopolitical reforms since the 1950s. Their demands included removal of feudalism, granting land rights, representation of the Nepalis(ese) in the House of Electorates, introduction of 'democracy' and even 'merger' with India. Taking this democratic reform movement as an *alibi*, the Indian state seemed to have played a role in actualizing the merger of Sikkim in 1975 with co-option of the Nepalis(ese) ethnopolitics. Thereby, Sikkim lost its *Drukpa* identity to become an Indian state, which led the *Drukpa* Bhutanese to feel apprehensive about Nepalese presence in their territory. A fear perception starts afflicting the minds of Bhutanese that the Indian state by playing the Nepalese card would possibly impose a merger of another *Drukpa* state – Bhutan into India, as was evident in case of Sikkim. Thereby, in order to weed out this anxiety, Bhutan expelled scores of Nepalese from Bhutan during the first half of the 1990s. Moreover, Nepalis were also ousted from North-East India in the late 1980s. The external and internal pushes, resultantly, forced the Nepalis of Darjeeling to demand for a separate state in the name of Gorkhaland in the 1980s so that their security and citizenship status in India could be assured.

Related to this, the politics over tribal status and the demand for *land-patta* deserve credence. The contemporary all-round demand for ST status in the Darjeeling hills has a direct relation with land rights. As every ethnic community has claims for land rights in the Darjeeling hills, the demand for tribal status is the outcome of a 'trinity' consciousness. First, tribal status guarantees constitutional benefits; secondly, as the majority of the hill dwellers do not have land documents, getting tribal status at least may provide some sort of security in the absence of legal *land-patta*. Finally, it paves the way for attaining the 6th Schedule status, which is a formidable step towards full-fledged statehood. As Lepcha-Bhutias had been included as STs way back in the 1950s, their lands of inhabitancy, in a way, have already been secured. On the other, in the absence of land ownership document as well as ST status, the Nepalis are nowadays utilizing every possible manoeuvrings to prove their historical attachment to the land they have been inhabiting.

Finally, it can be argued that there is a nascent citizenship anxiety among the Nepalis of India in general and the Darjeeling hills in particular. To minimize this anxiety, which is also rooted in land-ownership documents, there is an all-round claim for ST recognition, along with the demand for *land-patta*, in the Darjeeling hills. Although there are hardly any guidelines from the Indian state over the required documents to get enlisted in the NRC through the CAA, the experience of Assam suggests that *land-patta* may certainly help in enlisting in the proposed NRC roll, as it is an important proof of inhabitancy. On the other hand, getting recognized as ST necessarily provides security against uprooting from the land of inhabitancy, so, it may ease out the anxiety of being non-citizens.

Notes

1 This chapter will use the terminologies like Nepalis, Nepalese and Nepalis(ese) with different connotations. *Nepalis* refers to the Indian Nepalis, whereas *Nepalese* signify, following Subba (1992), the people of Nepali origin in the other sovereigns. However, the terminology *Nepalis(ese)* is used when there is no clarity of the origin of Nepalis.

2 In common parlance, regional division of the Eastern Himalayas also consist of the Poorvanchal Himalayas. But this work will restrict itself to Nepal, Sikkim, Bhutan and Darjeeling Himalayas as part of its conceptualisation of the Eastern Himalayas.

3 There are different lineages in the Tibetan Buddhism like Gelugpa, Nyingmapa, Sakyapa, Kagyupa and Bonpo. Drukpa is a sect within the Kagyupa lineage of Tibetan Buddhism.

4 *Sangha* is basically a collection of monks in a given monastery.

5 Please see footnote 1.

References

Ahmed, Omair. 2019. "The Forgotten 'NRC' in Bhutan." *The Wire*, September 25, 2019. https://thewire.in/rights/the-forgotten-nrc-in-bhutan

Aitchison, C. U. 1892. *A Collection of Treaties, Engagements and Sanads Relating to India and Neighbouring Countries*. Vol. I. Calcutta: Government of India Central Printing Office.

Aris, Michael. 1979. *Bhutan: The Early History of a Himalayan Kingdom*. Warminister: Aris & Philips Ltd.
Bhanja, K. C. 1993. *History of Darjeeling and the Sikkim Himalaya*. New Delhi: Gyan Publishing House.
Chakrabarti, Anjan. 2010. "A Critical Review of Agrarian Reforms in Sikkim." *Economic and Political Weekly* 45 (5): 23–26.
Chakrabarti, Anjan. 2012. "Migration and Marginalisation in the 'Himalayan Kingdom' of Sikkim." *Journal of Exclusion Studies* 2 (1): 1–6.
Chawla, Swati. 2019. "How Bhutan Came to Not Be a Part of India." *The Wire*, February 8, 2019. https://thewire.in/south-asia/how-bhutan-came-to-not-be-a-part-of-india
Chengappa, Raj, and Ananth Krishnan. 2017. "India-China Standoff: All You Need to Know about Doklam Dispute." *India Today*, July 17, 2017. https://www.indiatoday.in/magazine/cover-story/story/20170717-india-china-bhutan-border-dispute-doklam-beijing-siliguri-corridor-1022690-2017-07-07
Dasgupta, Atis. 1999. "Ethnic Problems and Movements for Autonomy in Darjeeling." *Social Scientist* 27 (11): 47–68. https://doi.org/10.2307/3518047
Datta, Prabhat. 1991. "The Gorkhaland Agitation in West Bengal." *The Indian Journal of Political Science* 52 (2): 225–41.
Datta-Ray, Sunanda K. 1984. *Smash And Grab: Annexation of Sikkim*. New Delhi: Vikas Publishing House Pvt. Ltd.
Dixit, Kanak Mani. 1992a. "The Dragon Bites Its Tail – Part I." *Himal Southasian*, October 16, 1992. https://www.himalmag.com/the-dragon-bites-its-tail-part-i-bhutan-nepal-lhotshampa-kanak-dixit-1992/
Dixit, Kanak Mani. 1992b. "The Dragon Bites Its Tail – Part II." *Himal Southasian*, October 17, 1992. https://www.himalmag.com/the-dragon-bites-its-tail-part-ii-bhutan-nepal-lhotshampa-kanak-dixit-1992/
Duff, Andrew. 2015. *Sikkim: Requiem for Himalayan Kingdom*. Gurgaon: Random House India.
Gupta, Ranjan. 1975. "Sikkim: The Merger with India." *Asian Survey* 15 (9): 786–98.
Hutt, Michael. 1993. "Refugees from Shangri-La." *Index on Censorship* 4 (September): 9–14. https://doi.org/10.1080/03064229308535539.
Hutt, Michael. 2003. *Unbecoming Citizens: Culture, Nationhood, and the Flight of Refugees from Bhutan*. New Delhi: Oxford University Press.
Hutt, Michael. 2005. "The Bhutanese Refugees: Between Verification, Repatriation and Royal Realpolitik." *Peace and Democracy in South Asia* 1 (1): 44–56.
Joseph, C. Mathew. 1997. "Ethnic Conflict in Bhutan: Political and Economic Dimensions." PhD Dissertation, Jawaharlal Nehru University, New Delhi.
Kar, Debiprasad. 2012. *The Gorkhaland Movement: A Cladenstine Invasion*. Siliguri: N.L. Publisher.
Marshall, T. H. 1950. *Citizenship and Social Class*. Cambridge: Cambridge University Press.
Middleton, Townsend, and Sara Shneiderman. 2008. "Reservations, Federalism and the Politics of Recognition in Nepal." *Economic and Political Weekly* 43 (19): 39–45.
Misra, Baniprasanna. 1986. "Behind Gorkhaland Agitation." *Mainstream* 25 (7): 15–20.
Pandey, Gyanendra. 1999. "Can a Muslim Be an Indian?" *Comparative Study on Society and History* 41 (4): 608–629.

Phadnis, Urmila. 1980. "Ethnic Dimensions of Sikkimese Politics: The 1979 Elections." *Asian Survey* 20 (12): 1236–52.

Phuntsho, Karma. 2013. *The History of Bhutan*. Noida: Random House India.

Pradhan, Upendra Mani. 2019. "The 'outsider' Fiasco: Revisiting the History of Darjeeling." *Eastmojo*, September 26, 2019. https://www.eastmojo.com/news/2019/09/26/the-outsider-fiasco-revisiting-the-history-of-darjeeling/

Risley, H. H. 1894. *The Gazetteer of Sikhim*. First. Calcutta: The Bengal Secretariat Press.

Rizal, Dhurba. 2004. "The Unknown Refugee Crisis: Expulsion of the Ethnic Lhotsampa from Bhutan." *Asian Ethnicity* 5 (2): 151–77. https://doi.org/10.1080/1463136042000221861

Rose, Leo E. 1977. *The Politics of Bhutan*. Ithaca and London: Cornell University Press. https://doi.org/10.5771/0506-7286-1980-2-171

Saha, Biswanath. 2016. "Gorkhaland Movement: Responses of the State." Unpublished MPhil Dissertation, Institute of Development Studies Kolkata, University of Calcutta.

Saha, Biswanath, and Gorky Chakraborty. 2019a. "The Paradox of Autonomy in the Darjeeling Hills: A Perception Based Analysis on Autonomy Aspirations." *Social Change and Development* XVI (1): 16–32. https://www.okd.in/downloads/jr_19_january/2.BiswanathSaha.pdf

Saha, Biswanath. 2019b. "Stoking a Fire in the Hills." *The Telegraph*, July 25, 2019. https://epaper.telegraphindia.com//printtextviews.php?id=282962&boxid=141525399&type=img

Sarkar, Swatahsiddha. 2010. "The Land Question and Ethnicity in the Darjeeling Hills." *Journal of Rural Social Sciences* 25 (2): 81–121.

Sarkar, Swatahsiddha. 2013. *Gorkhaland Movement: Ethnic Conflict and State Response*. New Delhi: Concept Publishing Company.

Scott, James C. 2009. *The Art of Not Being Governed: An Anarchist History of Upland Southeast Asia*. London: Yale University Press.

Shneiderman, Sara. 2010. "Are the Central Himalayas in Zomia? Some Scholarly and Political Considerations across Time and Space." *Journal of Global History* 5 (2): 289–312.

Sidhu, G. B. S. 2018. *Sikkim: Dawn of Democracy: The Truth Behind the Merger with India*. Gurgaon: Penguin.

"Sikkim Government Gazette." 1975. http://sikkimarchives.gov.in/gazettes/gaz1975.pdf

Sidhu, G. B. S. "Sikkim Government Gazette." 1989. http://sikkimarchives.gov.in/gazettes/Gazette1989.pdf

Sinha, A. C. 1973. "The Feudal Polity and Political Development in Sikkim." *Indian Anthropologist* 3 (2): 71–87.

Sinha, A. C. 1975. *Politics of Sikkim: A Sociological Study*. Faridabad: Thomson Press (India) Limited.

Sinha, A. C. 1991. *Bhutan: Ethnnic Identity and National Dilemma*. New Delhi: Reliance Publishing House.

Sinha, A. C. 1994. "Bhutan in 1993: Continuing Ethnic Stalemate." *Asian Survey* 34 (2): 181–84.

Sinha, A. C. 1995. "Bhutan in 1994: Will the Ethnic Conflict Be Resolved?" *Asian Survey* 35 (2): 166–70.

Subba, Tanka Bahadur. 1985a. "The Lepchas: From Legends to the Present Day." *Religion and Society* XXXII (2): 61–70.

Subba, Tanka Bahadur. 1985b. *The Quiet Hills: A Study of the Agrarian Relations in Hill Darjeeling*. Delhi: Published for the Christian Institute for the Study of Religion and Society, Bangalore, by the I.S.P.C.K.

Subba, Tanka Bahadur. 1992. *Ethnicity, State and Development: A Case Study of the Gorkhaland Movement in Darjeeling*. New Delhi: Vikas Publishing House Pvt. Ltd.

Verghese, B. G. 2004. *India's Northeast Resurgent: Ethnicity, Governance, Development*. Revised Ed. New Delhi: Konark Publishers.

Chapter 14

Border and Belonging

Historicizing the Question of Indigeneity and Citizenship in Manipur

Pum Khan Pau

1 Introduction

The passing of the Citizenship Amendment Bill (CAB) in the Lok Sabha on 9 December 2019 had its ripples in many parts of India including the North East. When protests against the CAB were organized in several parts of the North East, Manipur seemed to be jubilant not because of the CAB, but because of the announcement of the Union Home Minister for the implementation of the Inner Line Permit (ILP) in Manipur. An order issued in the name of the governor by Sunanda Thokchom on that very day declared 10 December 2019 as 'Holiday' for all government offices and educational institutions, including public-sector undertakings/corporations/autonomous bodies under the government of Manipur as a mark of celebration of the ILP. Like all other North-Eastern states, the people of Manipur did protest against the CAB. But the news on the implementation of the ILP seemed to have effectively subsided the voices of protests against CAB. It may be mentioned that the ILP was a long-drawn-out demand of the Joint Committee on Inner Line Permit System (JCILPS), which also spearheaded the passing of three controversial bills[1] by the State Legislative Assembly on 31 August 2015 that resulted to the killing of nine tribal protesters. Unlike the plain people, the ILP was not received quite well by the hill people who were quite apprehensive of the misuse of such legislation to fulfil the 'hidden motive' of the valley-based Meitei people who used to label the hill tribes as 'outsider', 'foreigner' or 'migrant'. In Manipur, the Meiteis form 66 per cent of the total population and occupy 10 per cent of the territory. In such a situation, therefore, the ILP was seen by the hill people who occupy 90 per cent of the territory as a tool that could possibly be used against the interest of the hill tribes.

Recent issues such as the three bills and the ILP not only brought misunderstanding among the hills–valley populations, but they also provoke one to rethink the discourse of 'citizenship' vis-à-vis 'indigeneity' in Manipur. One of the keys to understanding 'indigeneity' is to examine the historical processes of border making because border is ultimately what decides or dictates one's belonging territorially. Border is a territorial 'container' of

DOI: 10.4324/9781003345152-20

people and therefore one's citizenship or belonging is measured in relation to border. Therefore, in order to understand the problem of indigeneity in Manipur, it is imperative to examine the historical process of border making in the Indo-Burma frontier in the nineteenth and twentieth centuries. In a globalized world today, John Agnew rightly says: 'We are living in a world that is increasingly global and local and decreasingly national'. He further adds, 'The universality of claims to equal freedom and the inherent rights attached to one's status as a human rather than as specific nationality strongly suggest that borders should be in question if they pose a barrier to movement of people searching for a better life or seeking to escape from persecution or hide behind them unspeakable crimes of one sort or another' (Agnew, 2008, p. 182). Before moving forward, it is important to discuss briefly how the term *indigeneity* has been understood in a local and global context.

II A brief introduction to 'indigenous' or 'tribal people'

Sociologists in India face the challenge of defining who is indigenous and who is not? Apart from the colonial usage of *tribe*, a term such as *adivasi*, the Indian language term for the indigenous people has been employed by social workers, missionaries and political activists (Xaxa, 1999, p. 3590). According to Andre Beteille, 'the designation of any given population in a region as "indigenous" acquires substance when there are other populations in the same region that can reasonably be described as settlers or aliens' (1998, p. 188). He further adds that 'physical or racial, habitat, language or dialect, and even religion are not sufficient to use as marker of tribalism'; however, 'the idea of indigenous people must have some basis in the territory inhabited by them in the past and the present' (ibid., p. 190). Perhaps, it is best to see indigeneity through the lens of the International Labour Organization (ILO) definition. In its revised convention (No. 169) in 1989, the ILO refers to indigenous and tribal populations as

> (a) tribal peoples in independent countries whose social, cultural and economic conditions distinguish them from other sections of the national community, and whose status is regulated wholly or partially by their own customs or traditions or by special laws or regulations;
>
> (b) peoples in independent countries who are regarded as indigenous on account of their descent from the populations which inhabited the country, or a geographical region to which the country belongs, at the time of conquest or colonisation or the establishment of present state boundaries and who, irrespective of their legal status, retain some or all of their own social, economic, cultural and political institutions. (Indigenous and Tribal Population Convention, 1989
>
> (No. 169, Part I, Article I)[2]

Based on the ILO definition of *indigeneity*, Virginias Xaxa proposed three aspects which are central to the conceptualization of the indigenous people. First, the indigenous are those people who lived in the country to which they belong before colonization or conquest by people from outside the country or the geographical region. Second, they have become marginalized as an aftermath of conquest and colonization by the people from outside the region. Third, such people govern their life more in terms of their own social, economic and the cultural institution than the laws applicable to the society or the country at large (Xaxa, 1999, p. 3590). Following Xaxa's three proposals, I would like to probe to what extent the hill tribes of Manipur are indigenous in the territory in which they live today and argue against the policy of 'marginalization' and 'othering' of these tribes by dominant community through unravelling the historical processes of border making. Since the focus of this chapter is largely on the Zo (Kuki-Chin) people, it gives particular reference to border making in south and southeast of Manipur.

III 'Ill-defined' Manipur border?

Throughout history, it has been recorded that Manipur's border with Burma kept on changing because of the dispute over the possession of the Kabaw Valley. Many wars had been fought by the two powers over this issue before the advent of the British. Following the victory of the British over the Burmese in the first Anglo-Burmese War (1824–26), in which Gambhir Singh of Manipur and his Manipur Levy also played a significant role, the issue of the Kabaw Valley dispute came under the sole monopoly of the British. In 1833, the British concluded a treaty with Manipur to solve the western boundary followed by another one in 1834, where Captain Grant and Captain Robert Pemberton were ordered to proceed to the Kabaw Valley to make it over to the Burmese Commissioners and a compensation of Rs 6000 given to the Raja of Manipur as a compensation annually. Completely shocked by the transfer of the Kabaw Valley to Burma against his will, Gambhir Singh died in January 1834. The Treaty recommended the necessity to station a British officer in Manipur for '[t]he preservation of a friendly intercourse, and as a medium of communication with the Manipur Government, and as occasion may require, with the Burmese Authorities on that frontier, and more specially to prevent border feuds and disturbances' (Mackenzie [1884] 2001, pp. 151–2). One great concern in this treaty in terms of border making is the drawing of Pemberton's 'imaginary line'. In fact, Pemberton's brief in 1834 was to point out to the Burmese Commissioner the northern and southern boundaries of the Kabaw Valley. However, curiously enough, no clear instruction was given to him about the southern border of Manipur and worse of all, he had never surveyed the region in question. What Pemberton found out ultimately was that the Numsailung (Namsaweng in Burmese and *Tuipu* in

Chin/Zo) River was the southern border of the Kabaw Valley albeit he did not have any idea where its source originated. Therefore, by drawing an imaginary line of boundary in southern Manipur, which he never visited or surveyed, Pemberton unilaterally committed one of the greatest mistakes of his career. The Agreement of 1834 thus says: 'On the south, a line extending from the eastern foot of the same hills (Muring) at the point where the river called by the Burmans Nansaweng and by the Muneepoorees Numsailung enters the plain up to its sources, and across the hills due west down to the Kathe Khyoung (Muneepooree River)'.[3] The problem is that in 1834 the British had vague knowledge about the position of the hills on either side of the Kabaw Valley and the rivers in it. Pemberton did not go down there to determine it for himself as the agreement was signed on the banks of the Chindwin River (Ibid.).[4] Thus in his *Report of the Eastern Frontier of India*, he admitted that the southern frontier of Manipur was 'very irregular and ill defined' (Pemberton, [1835] 2000, p. 21). The Treaty of 1834 which mentioned 'part of the Sootie (Sukte) tribe at present live in Manipur and part in Burmese or independent territory' (Mackenzie, [1884] 2001, p. 172) was due to Pemberton's misunderstanding of the frontier area which he had never visited or surveyed. Thus, when the boundary was to be demarcated it was found that the Namsailung/Namsaweng River referred to in 1834 was actually what the Chin/Zo called *Tuipu* and the Burmans *Nanpalaw*. From there the boundary was supposed to go up the Manipur River to a certain point, and then west to the Lushai and Cachar border, thus giving a large enclave on the east of the Manipur River to Manipur that became known as 'Pemberton's Enclave'.[5] The truth is that the hill tracts on the east and west of the Manipur River had never been under the control of Burma or Manipur as clearly admitted by colonial officers. In 1856 the Political Agent of Manipur, Colonel McCulloch, remarked 'the south-eastern portion of Manipur territory had never been explored and that the Manipur authorities had never tried to bring the tribes inhabiting it into subjection' (Mackenzie, [1884] 2001, pp. 174–5). In his *Account of the Valley of Manipur*, McCulloch further stated, 'To the North-East and South, the boundary is not well defined, and would much depend upon the extent to which the Munnipore Government might spread its influence amongst the hill tribes in those directions' ([1859] 1980, p. 1). That the Raja of Manipur had little influence beyond the valley is clearly reflected in the location of his frontier posts,[6] which essentially marks the limit of his influence and territory. This may be clearly proved by what another political agent, Colonel Mowbray Thomson, said in his report of 1872: 'The whole tribe seems to be practically independent and not to have been effected at all by the Treaty of 1834 . . . for all practical purposes this tribe should be considered as independent, and liable to punishment from either power [Manipur or Burmese] it raids' (Mackenzie, [1884] 2001, pp. 173–4).

IV Kam Hau and his dominance

As mentioned earlier, after the establishment of their political agency in Manipur, the British began to slowly explore the extent of Manipur's authority towards its southern frontier. From this exploration, they came to encounter the power and dominance of the Sukte rulers of northern Chin Hills, which actually extended beyond the so-called Pemberton's Enclave. Therefore, in order to understand the problem of Manipur's southern frontier a brief introduction of the rise of the Sukte under its powerful chief Kam Hau would be helpful.

In 1810, a powerful Sukte *Ukpi* (paramount ruler/chief) Khan Thuam of Mualbem in northern Chin Hills allowed his eldest son, Kam Hau, to establish his own realm of domain from Tedim. Kam Hau successfully fought against other tribes/clans and thereby established Tedim as his capital (Committee 1996, 48). At the time of his father's death in 1848, Kam Hau had already emerged as a powerful *Ukpi* (paramount ruler/chief) like his father and extracted a separate tract of control from his father's realm, which the British referred to as the Kamhau tract. Like his father, Kam Hau's sway extended over the entire region east of the Manipur River (locally known as Meitei Guun in the Chin Hills), comprising over 135 villages (ibid., p. 44). 'Although by right of custom Kam Hau of Tedim was subordinate to his brother Za Pau, who inherited his father Khan Thuam's chiefship at Mualbem, Carey and Tuck wrote, 'he nevertheless ruled his villages so absolutely that the Sokte tribe became known as two separate communities' (Carey & Tuck, [1896] 1932, p. 119). KamHau was, in fact, not only able to consolidate his father's territorial conquests but for the first time succeeded in uniting the entire tribes of the northern Chin Hills, except the Sizangs. Thus, on the ground prepared by his father, Kam Hau firmly established a powerful chiefdom in the northern hills. A recent scholar aptly remarks:

> What is remarkable is that the Kamhaus took the lead of the Sukte tribes to war and peace. It was Kam Hau who led his tribesmen to victories over those alien tribes and made himself known to his victims as a dreadful name. He was the real figure which made the Tedims (Sukte, Sihzang, Guite and Kamhau) reknown to the Chin Hills frontier as Kamhaus .
>
> (Khai, 1995, p. 30)

Since then the name 'Kamhau' itself became a 'terror' to Manipur, the Lushai hills and Burma (Carey & Tuck, [1896] 1932, p. 120).[7] Of the Kamhau–Sukte power, Sir Alexander Mackenzie rightly observed in 1883:

> The Manipuris consider this tribe to be a much more formidable one than the Lushai. They are a constant source of trouble to them, and

> have at times rendered the southern portion of Manipur uninhabitable. . . . The Lushais hold the Sookties in great dread, and are falling back before them. They are well supplied with fire-arms, supposed to be procured from Burma, whence they also obtain their ammunition. They have never had any dealings whatever with the British government.
> ([1884] 2001, p. 163)

As Abraham I. Pershits rightly says the status of a chief mainly stems from 'tribute relations' (1979), and his popularity largely depends on the magnitude of his power, the rise and popularity of Kam Hau naturally came at the cost of several villages. He thus was able to carve out a separate administrative tract from the existing Sukte tract and added many more villages to it. As a result, the term *Kamhau People* or *Kamhaus*, after the name of the chief, began to appear in colonial terminology to refer to the people who belonged to the Kamhau tract, in particular, and represent the northern hill peoples, in general. The Sukte and the Kamhaus should not, therefore, be construed as different people. The term *Sukte* appeared to be more popular during the early decades of the nineteenth century, particularly during the reign of Khan Thuam, whereas the Kamhaus later emerged as the dominant power after the rise of Kam Hau in the 1840s.

The impact of Kam Hau's power was strongly felt by Manipur. The continuous raids and depredations carried out by Kam Hau people and his subordinates in southern Manipur prompted Colonel William McCulloch, the Political Agent of Manipur, to form 'sepoy village' near Moirang as a defensive measure (Mackenzie, [1884] 2001, pp. 157–64). In the 1850s when even more serious raids occurred, an exasperated Chandrakirti Singh, the Raja of Manipur, decided upon strong military action against Kam Hau in January 1857, which, however, ended in a defeat and 'disgraceful flight of the Manipur troops' from the hands of the combined Kamhau–Sukte–Sizang people (ibid.). Thus, the failure of the Raja to defeat the Kamhaus clearly explains the fact that the latter's influence extended up to the valley of the former's kingdom. Actually, what the colonial rulers often refer to 'Manipur's southern frontier problem' is nothing but a contest for supremacy by two rulers: Raja Chandrakirti Singh of Manipur and the Sukte chief Kam Hau. Although Manipur also suffered from occasional Lushai depredations, her concern was more with the Kam Hau's menace (ibid., p. 163).

V Frontier posts and Memorial stone

This section examines the actual extent of Manipur's southern border and the events that occurred beyond its border during the Lushai Expedition in 1871–72. Matters in the Indo-Burma frontier had been seriously taken into consideration by the British in the late 1860s. The series of attacks on the Tea gardens in Cachar, a British protectorate, by the Lushais prompted the British to launch a series of military campaigns in the hills. One such major operation was conducted in 1869 which, however, ended without any substantial result. A bigger and more concerted military campaign, better known as the Lushai Expedition, was launched against the Lushai in 1871–72 from Cachar and Chittagong, respectively. To assist the Cachar Column on its left flank, a contingent from Manipur, which was a British protectorate, was drafted by Brigadier-General G. Bourchier, commanding officer of the Cachar Column, with the sole objective to 'restrain' the Kamhau-Sukte people. The Manipur Contingent was led by Major-General N. W. Nuthall and two Meitei majors. Accordingly, the officiating political agent of Manipur, Major-General W. F. Nuthall, discussed the matter with Raja Chandrakirti Singh and decided to increase the strength of the existing posts along the southern frontier and add a few more to them. The selection of posts was largely with special consideration on easy communication, mutual support, and rapid concentration and control of supply.[8] The main objective of the establishment of the southern frontier posts by Manipur was to defend themselves from Kamhau-Sukte as the latter had successfully pressed northwards and established their dominance in the hills south of Moirang in the nineteenth century. Brigadier-General Bourchier's instruction to Nuthall was to station his force at Tseklapi (also spelt Jolpi), the headquarters of the southernmost frontier posts, and not move beyond that without further instruction. He wrote to Nuthall on 23 November 1871: 'It was never my intention that the Officer commanding should be tied down to Moirung, but that it should be moved to the south of the Munnipoor valley, but not further than the point marked Tseklapi in your map (spelt Yolepee by Colonel McCulloch), and which is about the southern frontier of Munnipoor'.[9] However, against his brief, Nuthall moved beyond Tseklapi and encamped at Chivu. After the conclusion of the expedition, the contingent withdrew from Chivu camp and moved to Situl Subhum, nine miles from their camp on 6 March 1872. The following day when Go Khaw Thang (erroneously written as Kokatung), chief of Mualpi and his followers passed through Situl Subhum, they were treacherously enticed and captured by the Manipuri majors.[10] What is important to note is at Chivu Nuthall erected a 2½ feet high, 2 feet wide, and about 4 inches thick stone to commemorate his so-called victory over four Lushai chiefs and 112 villages.[11] A rough translation of the inscription on the stone goes:

> In 1793 of the era Sakabda, in the month of Wakching, two Manipuri Majors, Balaram Sing and Tangal Sing, with 130 officers and 2000 men, accompanied by General Nuthall, conquered 112 villages, including Poiboi, Lenkam, & c., and took possession of this salt well, placing there the footprints of the Rajah Chunder Kirtee Sing Maharajah.[12]

The fact is, the Manipur–Lushai Treaty, which was signed during the Lushai Expedition, was not about a conclusion of war where the winner dictates terms against the victim. According to the Lushai chiefs, as clearly written in the treaty, it was to 'swear according to our custom that *mutual friendship* (emphasis mine) shall always be maintained by us towards the British Government and the Maharajah of Munnipoor'.[13] This treaty completely invalidates the term 'conquered' used in the inscription, which actually reflects Meitei's own interpretation of the Lushai Expedition for its vested interest. Furthermore, the act of the Meitei majors and Nuthall was neither approved by the British nor recognised by the Kamhau people. John W. Edgar, civil officer of the Cachar Column and Brigadier-General Bourchier, the commanding officer dubbed the capture of Go Khaw Thang and his follower by Nuthall and the Manipur Contingent as a 'treacherous act'. There is no doubt that Nuthall was working at the behest of the Raja of Manipur and the commemoration stone erected by him was aimed to appease the latter. Taking serious note of the Manipuris' infringement on its territory, the Kamhaus prepared to launch military campaigns against Manipur, which greatly alarmed the new political agent Colonel Mowbray Thomson, who left no stone unturned to avoid another confrontation by trying to patch up peace between them, to which he somehow managed to achieve in 1873 (Pau, 2020), albeit it was short-lived. It is not surprising that Manipur had been always looking for an opportunity to avenge their defeat at the hands of the Kamhaus in 1857 and the influence exerted by the chief Kam Hau and his subordinates in the southern frontier of Manipur was a cause for serious concern. However, to interpret the success of the British over the Lushai in the Lushai Expedition and laid claim over their temporary camp at Chivu, which was beyond their original border, is a great mistake on the part of the Raja of Manipur. Because the standard measurement of a ruler's power and influence before the adoption of modern cartography is 'tribute relation' but not based on the number of 'memorial stone' erected. Memorial stone without the exaction of any tribute from the so-called defeated people is meaningless. Therefore, mere claim of a particular place without exacting tribute/taxes from the inhabitants does not make any sense in terms of 'control' or 'conquest'.

VI Boundary demarcation

In the early 1890s when the British successfully penetrated into the Chin Hills, the question of solving its border issue with Manipur became one of Bertram Carey's prior concerns given such prevailing circumstances discussed above. In 1892, Bertram Carey, the political officer of the Chin Hills, strongly felt that 'the reality of the boundary is urgent'[14] and proposed to the chief commissioner of Burma that 'the Manipur border will presumably be fixed at a distance of 80 miles north of Tiddim in the latitude of Howbi Peak'. He also suggested keeping one assistant political officer at Lenacot (Sialmong) who would control the northern tribes such as Guite, Zou and Thados[15]? Burma and Assam agreed that the Boundary Commission should begin the work in March 1893.[16] On 21 October 1893, the Government of India instructed: 'The Commissioners [of Burma and Assam] should have full power and a free hand to settle and demarcate the boundary once for all. If unfortunately, they cannot agree, the decision will rest with the Government of India'.[17] But the delimitation of the Chin Hills–Manipur boundary was postponed till 1894 due to the 'Sizang-Sukte Rebellion' which was discussed in the previous chapter.

It was only on 27 January 1894 that members of the Boundary Commission from Manipur and Burma assembled at Tinzin, a Burman village on the left bank of the Tinzinchaung (Tuisa River). Members representing Burma included B. S. Carey, Political Officer, Chin Hills, Captain F. B. Longe, R. E. Survey of India and 12 followers, Lieutenant W. H. Dent, 2nd Battalion (P.W.O.), Yorkshire Regiment, Intelligence Officer, and two surveyors, Lieutenant B. Trydell and fifty rifles of 1st Burma Rifles as escort, Sergeant James, and one hospital assistant. Representatives of Manipur were A. Porteous, political agent of Manipur; Captain M. A. Kerr, Lieutenant H. Baillie and 100 rifles; the 43rd Gurkhas as escort; and one hospital assistant. According to Lieutenant W. H. Dent, the Kamhau Chief Hau Cin Khup and two young followers also accompanied Carey.[18]

On 28 January 1894, the Boundary Commission begun the exploration from *Tuisa* (Tinzinchaung), instead of *Tuipu* (Nanphalaw, which was claimed by Manipur as Numsailung), as it entered the Kabaw Valley in latitude 23° 49′ 30″ from the hills on its west up along the course of this stream in a general north-westerly direction to one of its sources called the Khengzoidung where the first pillar was placed, and the last one was on the source of *Tuimong* river. Altogether eight pillars were erected from east to west. The boundary pillars were slabs of stone facing north and south. 'M' (for Manipur) is cut on the north and 'C.H.' (for Chin Hills) on the south, and underneath these letters, the figure represents the number of the pillar, which commences to be numbered from east and works west. On 1 March 1894, Bertram Carey and Alexander Porteous signed the agreement at Tuikui camp on top of the Lunglen hills. The northern latitude of the line at any point is at Lunglen hills 24° 0′ 42″ while the extreme southern point is 23° 49′ 30″ where *Tuisa* enters Burma.

According to W. H. Dent, the reason why Tuisa was chosen, instead of Tuipu, was because of the government's instruction, which said that 'the line was to be in the latitude of Pemberton's line and drawn so as to exclude Lenacot from Manipur'.[19] They followed a river line instead of a range of hills because the latter are 'so ill-defined in that neighbourhood'.

VII Reconfigured frontier

The big question regarding the boundary demarcation is, since, Carey himself said that except during the time of Colonel McCulloch, Manipur was never able to control its southern tribes, who often raided the plains and defied the state, then why did he allow Manipur to claim a vast tract of land on its southern hills? There is no doubt that there was a tug-of-war between Bertram Carey of Chin Hills and A. Porteaus of Manipur on the question of the boundary line. It may be noted that the political agent of Manipur, who was working on behalf of the infant Raja, wished to secure all that Pemberton had given to the state in 1834 and to annex the fringe of villages on the right bank of the river and on the border of the Manipur plain. Unfortunately, he had been wrongly led to believe that there were 91 villages (only half of which actually existed on paper) on the right bank of the river from which Manipur could derive a comfortable income and that left bank of the river, in addition to the pine forest, which do exist, was capable of producing vegetable and mineral resources in the future.[20] That the political agent of Manipur was working at the behest of the Raja of Manipur is undoubtedly confirmed by J. Clerk, who remarked: 'The Political Agent is dependent on the will and pleasure of the Maharaja for everything. His every word and movement is known to the Maharaja. He is in fact a British Officer under Manipur surveillance' (Roy, 1958, p. 100).

What is less known, if not forgotten, is that the demarcation of the boundary between Manipur and the Chin Hills arbitrarily awarded several villages which were under the dominance of the Kamhau-Sukte to Manipur. As pointed out earlier, the power and control of the chief over a particular village/villages or places can only be judged through the maintenance of 'tribute-relation' (Pershits, 1979). With regard to the case in question, Carey admitted, 'By the delimitation of the Manipur boundary Howchinkup lost several villages which his forefathers had conquered and which up to that time had paid him a nominal tribute' ([1896] 1932, p. 112). Two years before the boundary delimitation, Captain G.B. Stevens, 4th Madras Pioneers and commander of the Kamhau Column, had visited all the villages of northern Chin Hills, including those of Thado, Zou and Guite villages. He went up to Tonglawn (Tornlongs) and Losau (Losow), where the Guite clan had moved from Mualpi, to extract slaves from their possession. Thus villages which had clearly paid tribute to the paramount ruler of northern Chin Hills were, after the boundary delimitation, found inside Manipur.[21] The villages which were arbitrarily awarded to Manipur by the Boundary Commission include 19 Zou villages, 15 out of 21 Thado villages and 13 Guite villages.[22] As a result of the boundary demarcation the 'Thado tribe', Carey later remarked, 'now drops out of my books as well as the 'Yo' and 'Nwite (including the Vaipe) which are now included in the Kuki or Kongjai hills of Manipur' ([1896] 1932, p. 112).

VIII Conclusion

It may be argued that the way to understand the power, influence and territorial extent of a particular king/chief before modern cartography came into application is through 'tribute-relation'. While memorial stones are undoubtedly markers of some historical/commemorative events, it cannot necessarily be a marker of border unless it was substantiated by tribute relation. The only supportive condition where a memorial stone could be a marker of border is when the king/chief who erected such stones, as a result of any event, exacted tribute/taxes from that particular area/region where the memorial stone has been erected. But in the absence of any tribute relation in the aftermath of its erection, a memorial stone simply remains a commemorative stone to mark a particular event and signifies nothing else. As discussed earlier, the memorial stones erected in the name of the Maharajah of Manipur in 1872/3, no matter its content, cannot be considered a marker of a border without proof of maintaining tribute relation between the so-called conqueror and conquered in the aftermath. It was only in 1894 that the British formally demarcated Manipur and Chin Hills boundary through the process of modern cartography thereby separating the same people into different administrative units.

As mentioned earlier, terms such as *migrant*, *foreigner* or *outsider* are labels which emerged as a result of a shallow understanding of the process of border making, if not political expediency. I would argue that the predicament which continues to haunt the hills–valley people in Manipur today is nothing but a colonial legacy and the problem of border making which did not take into account the interest of the communities on the ground. Therefore, it would be hard to understand the question of indigeneity or belonging, especially in the Indo-Burma borderland, without taking into consideration the inclusion or exclusion of populations as part of border making. As argued earlier, I would reiterate that the incorporation of tribes of the southern frontier hills in Manipur was, to borrow Sanjib Baruah's phrase, 'a matter of historical accident' (2008, p. 15) and, as Robert Reid also says, a 'natural administrative convenience' ([1942] 1974, p. 19). Therefore, while the indigeneity of the tribes who lived or settled in the India-Myanmar borderland even before the demarcation of the boundary is out of the question, the question of their 'belonging', it must be reiterated, was the making of the colonial rulers and cartographers who arbitrarily decided their fate through boundary demarcation in 1894. That neither the creation of British Burma as a separate administration from India in 1937 nor the Indian Independence Act, 1947 make any change in the 1894 Manipur–Chin Hills boundary demarcation is a fact which also means the tribes on that frontier area had been unilaterally divided by the colonial rulers for 'administrative convenience' (Pau, 2020). Therefore, it is important to properly understand the historical process of border making and the inclusion and exclusion of populations by the Boundary Commission and surveyors before one is tempted to include or exclude someone or to blindly tag them as 'outsider', 'foreigner' or 'migrant' in their own land. To conclude, it is apt to quote Mahmood Mamdani who says: 'Cultural communities rooted in a common past do not necessarily have a common future. Some may have a diasporic future. Similarly, political communities may include immigrants and thus be characterised by cultural diversities, even if there is a dominant culture signifying a history shared by the majority. The point is that political communities are defined, in the final analysis, not by a common past but by a resolve to forge a common future under a single political roof, regardless of how different or similar their pasts may be' (2001, p. 661).

Notes

1 The three bills are the Manipur Land Reforms and Land Revenue (7th Amendment) Bill, 2015, the Manipur Shops and Establishment (2nd Amendment) Bill, 2015 and the Manipur Protection of Peoples Bill, 2015. For a discussion on this, go to https://www.huffpost.com/entry/politics-of-3-bills-and-9_b_9147904
2 Indigenous and Tribal Population Convention, 1989 (No. 169) Part I, Article I. See https://www.ilo.org/dyn/normlex/en/f?p=NORMLEXPUB:12100:0::NO::P12100_INSTRUMENT_ID:312314
3 Assam State Archives (ASA), Governor Secretariat (GS), Lib/R007/S3/81: Diary and Report of the Manipur Boundary Commission 1894 by Lieutenant W. H. Dent, Printed by the Superintendent, Government Printing, Burma, August 1894.
4 Ibid.
5 ASA, GS, Lib/R007/S3/81.
6 Frontier posts of Manipur in 1871 were located at Kowpum, Limetak, Bishenpoor, Moirung Hills, Koomos Chumbupoong and Koongshangkool in the hills and Muttarook, Tseklapi (headquarters), Shoogonoo, Mangchangoway, Kengyang and Koongamaroo. See NAI, FDPA, August 1872, No 83; From Major-General W. F. Nuthall, Political Agent, Munnipoor to C. U. Aitchison, Esq., C.S.I., Secretary to the Government of India, Foreign Department, no. 59 dated 12 April 1872.
7 Carey and Tuck, p. 120.
8 NAI, FDPA, August 1872, No 83; From Major-General W. F. Nuthall, Political Agent, Munnipoor to C. U. Aitchison, Esq., C.S.I., Secretary to the Government of India, Foreign Department, no. 59 dated 12 April 1872.
9 Ibid.
10 FPAP August 1872, No.83.
11 ASA, GS, Lib/ R007/S3/81: Diary and Report of the Manipur Boundary Commission 1894 by Lieutenant W. H. Dent, Printed by the Superintendent, Government Printing, Burma, August, 1894.
12 ASA, GS, Lib/R007/S3/81: Diary and Report of the Manipur Boundary Commission 1894 by Lieutenant W. H. Dent.
13 *Annual Administration Report of the Munnipoor Agency, for the Year ending 30th June 1873*, Published by Authority, Foreign Department Press, 1874, p. 7.
14 FEAP, September 1893, No. 8; From Major H. Maxwell, Political Agent and Superintendent of State, Manipur (on leave) to the Secretary to the Chief Commissioner of Assam, 1 February 1893.
15 FEAP, October 1893, No. 34; From B.S. Carey, Political Officer, Chin Hills, to the Chief Secretary to the Chief Commissioner of Burma, 28 September, 1892.
16 FEAP, October 1893, No. 129 & 130.
17 FEAP, October 1893, No. 131.
18 ASA, GS, Lib/R007/S3/81.
19 ASA, GS, Lib/R007/S3/81.
20 FEAP, October 1894, No. 247: From B.S. Carey, Political Officer, Chin Hills to the Chief Secretary to Chief Commissioner of Burma, 16 March 1894.

21 FEBP, January 1893, Nos. 1–17. See, Appendix D: From Captain G. B. Stevens, 4th Madras Pioneers, (late) Commanding Kanhaw Column, to the Assistant Adjutant-General, Myingyan District, Fort White, 17 April 1892.
22 FEAP September 1893, No. 80. Also see (Carey & Tuck [1896] 1932: 112).

References

Agnew, John. (2008). Borders on the mind: reframing border thinking. *Ethics & Global Politics*, 1(4), 175–91.

Baruah, Sanjib. (2008). Territoriality Indigeneity and Rights in the North-east India. *Economic and Political Weekly*, 43(12/13), 15–19, March 22–April 4.

Beteille, Andre. (1998). The Idea of Indigenous Peoples. *Current Anthropology*, 39(2), 187–92, April.

Carey, B. S. and H. N. Tuck. ([1896] 1932). *The Chin Hills*, vol. I. Aizawl: Tribal Research Institute.

Khai, Sing Khaw. (1995). *Zo People and their Culture*. Churachandpur: Published by KhampuHatzaw.

Mackenzie, Alexander. ([1884] 2001). *History of the North East Frontier*. New Delhi: Mittal Publications.

Mamdani, Mahmood. (2001). Beyond Settler and Native as Political Identities: Overcoming the Political Legacies of Colonialism, *Society for Comparative Study of Society and History*. 651–64.

McCulloch, William. ([1859] 1980). *Valley of Manipur*. New Delhi: Gian Publications.

Pau, Pum Khan. (2020). *Indo-Burma Frontier and the making of the Chin Hills: Empire and Resistance*. London: Routledge.

Pemberton, Robert Boileau. ([1835] 2000). *Eastern Frontier of India*. New Delhi: Mittal Publication.

Pershits, Abraham I. (1979). Tribute Relations, in S. Lee Seaton and H.J.M. Claessen (eds.) *Political Anthropology*. The Hague: Mouton Publishers. 140–56.

Reid, Robert. ([1942] 1974). *History of the Frontier Areas Bordering on Assam*. Guwahati: Spectrum Publications.

Roy, J. (1958). *History of Manipur*. Imphal.

Sukte, Laibu Bawl. (1996). *Sukte beh leh Tedim Gam Tangthu*. Tedim: Published by the author.

Xaxa, Virginias. (1999). Tribes as Indigenous People of India. *Economic and Political Weekly* 34(51), 3589–95, December.

Chapter 15

Between Legality and Illegality

Citizenship and the Chakmas in North-East India

Anindita Ghoshal

> *We are very worried about our future as we and our forefathers have suffered long enough because of Partition. We oppose any move to disturb, dismember or dislodge the Chakma community from the State any further.*
>
> – statement of the Arunachal Pradesh Chakma *Gaonburah* (village headman) Association.[1]

1 Backlog

The construction of Kaptai Lake, the largest artificial lake in Bangladesh and a popular tourist destination, was constructed for hydroelectric power generation in the Rangamati district of Chittagong Hill Tracts (CHT). The dam was necessary for the Karnafuli Hydropower Station project that was completed around the year 1962. But at the ground level, it left the worst impact on the *paharis* or *jummas* (indigenous tribals) of the CHT. The Chakmas and Hajongs were the major tribes inhabiting the CHT. They made desperate appeals to the Central Government of Pakistan based in Karachi and the local authorities in East Bengal to save them from that man-made disaster. But such pleas fell onto deaf ears of the West Pakistani authorities. The industrial development project ended up submerging at least 54,000 acres of agricultural lands of the *pahari* or *jumma* people. Over 100,000 *paharis* were displaced from their place of origin; their respective homes, hills and habitats, and it led to the forced migration of thousands of Chakma and Hajong families to the other side of the Bengal borderland in search of new settlements, homes and identities. Therefore, for those *pahari/jhumma* families, Kaptai Lake has remained as a site of a heartbreaking event called *Bor Porong* or 'the great exodus'.[2] The Chittagong Hill Tracts remained as the blind spot during both the Pakistan and Bangladesh phases, though because of different reasons. Even the War of Liberation couldn't provide them with adequate space, for floating ideas of their notion of freedom (Naeem, 2010, p. 3). It is rather replicated by the same kinds of hegemony about language, security and regional autonomy for the *jumma* people of the CHT.

DOI: 10.4324/9781003345152-21

Samari Chakma (2018), a Chakma *jhumma*, a former lawyer by profession, as well as an activist of the Chittagong Hill Tracts herself, has collected oral narratives of six eyewitnesses of this particular heartbreaking event. She collected stories o f those people, whose lives have been changed forever by the construction of the Kaptai Dam, who left CHT and had to take shelter as refugees in Arunachal Pradesh. She could publish those first-hand accounts in her book *Kaptai Bandh: Bor Porong – Duburider Atmokothon* (Kaptai Dam: The Great Exodus – Autobiography of the Drowner).[3] The story of one of her respondents might be useful here to set the tone of this particular chapter, primarily for defining the key problems of Chakmas and Hajong refugee families who reside in Arunachal Pradesh as stateless persons till date:

My name is Priya Bala Chakma, and I am 65 years old. When I got married in 1958 at the age of 17, I said goodbye to my father's village and moved to my in-laws' house in Burighat village near Rangamati district. The construction of the Kaptai Dam started a few years ago. I was surprised to hear that all the cultivable lands in our village would be submerged. Maybe we would also have to leave this village and go far away. I couldn't fully comprehend what would drown and who was behind this. When I asked about it, my father replied,

> *[F]ar away from the town of Rangamati, the government was building a 'goda' (meaning dam) at the mouth of the big river (Karnafuli). All that was left was to install a gate on this dam. When the gate was closed, the massive stream of the Karnafuli would not be able to flow. As a result, the water level in all the rivers surrounded by the hills would rise. The low agricultural lands we depend on for our livelihoods would be submerged due to the rising water level.*
>
> *Our lives were threatened. My father said if these places went underwater, we have to leave this house, this village and this hill. Maybe we would need to migrate to the neighbouring country.*

Many of the villagers could not believe that the water of the dam would travel miles away and engulf our village. Although some landowners were given forms to start the process of applying for replacement land elsewhere, many could not decide what was the right thing to do. It seemed that everyone had nothing thing to do except talk about this. When are they closing the gate? And we waited . . . and waited. Still, so much work left! Arranging new places to take refuge, fixing boats to survive in the event of a sudden flood, securing our cattle, and whatnot! In the meantime, we shifted to a new home (in-laws' house) built up the hill, leaving the big house near the plains so that we would not sink into the water.

At last, that critical moment came. It started raining just like a wet gloomy day in the rainy reason. It rained all day and night. The water started to rise slowly. When a severe storm hit us, the water level rose swiftly, submerging everything under the water. I woke up in the morning and saw water everywhere. It was still raining. Everyone knew that the day had come. In time the water engulfed everything. Everyone was trying to save their lives, taking refuge in unknown places. There was no time to think clearly and decide accordingly. Nobody had time to say goodbye to neighbours. Luckily, the boats had been arranged before. When the water rose, our relatives from downhill came to our house by boat. Following them, we reached Larna Para in Khagrachari District.

I lost contact with my father and siblings. Many years later, I came to know via a relative that my father, three brothers and one sister had all set off to Arunachal Pradesh in India after the event. There they were struggling hard just to survive. I didn't even know then that my father had died on the way to Arunachal. Because of Kaptai Dam, all our siblings were separated during the early 1960s. Some of us were able to reunite after two or three decades. This didn't happen to all of us. Maybe it will never happen, as I am growing old.[4]

II Journeys: A Beginning towards the End

The Chakma and Hajong refugees of Arunachal Pradesh have become a comparatively known but unofficial category of stateless people in South Asia. In spite of the fact that India is the largest refugee absorbent country in the whole of South Asia, still the root of the problem is, being the host of substantive asylum seekers and refugees, India has never and is not a signatory to the 1951 Refugee Convention or the 1967 Protocol. These two international mandates were chiefly

> relating to the Status of Refugees and to seek, from Executive Committee members parties to either or both of these instruments, general information about the methods of implementation adopted in their countries, and the successes achieved, or particular obstacles encountered.[5]

Although India has offered or in some cases provided shelter in form of asylum to many marginal communities in their mother countries like, Partition displaced refugees from West and East Pakistan, Tibetans, Tamil refugees from Sri Lanka, Bhutanese refugees from Nepal, Afghans, Rohingya or other refugees from Myanmar and refugees from Somalia, the Democratic Republic of Congo and Sudan, in one way or the other (Sen, 2015, p. 1). But India neither tried to frame any comprehensive rehabilitation policies for the protection of the refugees nor designed any definite legal policies for the asylum seekers. While the Indian state does not offer any de facto protection to refugees, the absence of any international mandate or at least any declared legal framework for refugee protection makes the status of the refugees, stateless persons and asylum seekers a precarious one. There is no domestic procedure or definite law to protect the security issues or interests of the refugees in India. Therefore, the final fate of the refugees is determined by the protections ensured by the Indian Constitution. But, the approach of the centre and respective state governments towards both the refugees and stateless persons were always kind of ad hoc, and their marginal status is based on the goodwill of the government in power. Therefore, the lack of legal responsibility of the state to the protection of refugee rights led to a mounting refugee crisis while the legally settled refugees claimed citizenship status.

For this particular case study, continuous demand to get citizenship rights couldn't resolve the crisis of the Chakma and Hajong refugees in Arunachal Pradesh. Rather, their suffering caused by the organized political marginalization efforts by the tribal domiciles of the Arunachal Pradesh and their constant deprivation from the political right and left these refugees to the edge. The tribals of Chittagong Hill Tracts were the worst sufferers of the policies of the Pakistan government before 1971; they were more disillusioned under the notion of Bengali nationalism after the creation of Bangladesh. They were compelled to leave their place of origin. Their migration from then East Pakistan to North-Eastern states like Arunachal Pradesh, Tripura and Mizoram was consented to by the then Government of India. But the Chakmas and Hajongs had to remain as 'stateless persons' in Arunachal Pradesh, as the Citizenship Act of 1955 was never 'applicable' in their case. With this background, this article aims to portray how they fell amidst the state–centre binaries, faced local undercurrents, resentments from the domicile tribals and socio-economic threats. This chapter aims to explore the reasons behind the floating condition of the Chakma and Hajong refugees of Arunachal Pradesh. It attempts to understand their current status between legal and illegal parameters, concerning their citizenship. Hence, the pertinent point to start writing this chapter should start with some questions. For example, what is their current legal status? What is the actual number of these refugees? What is their argument to define their deserving rights? Are they at all eligible to call them citizens of Arunachal Pradesh? How to define their issues of challenges? It tries to argue that the present generations of the Chakma and Hajong refugees became the victim of the state suppressions. They were neither refugees nor migrants. The Indian state even never declared them officially as 'stateless persons' by following any international mandate or deciding any concrete legal policies for them. Because of the policies and contemporary politics around the whole of North East India and the state–centre relations, they are suffering. For the Chakma and Hajong refugees, the current situation in Arunachal Pradesh was like the pre- and post-1971 situation in the CHT. It's like another history of continuous expansion of aggressive identity politics, a strange kind of nationalism, a different story of encroachment, marginalization of the Chakmas and Hajongs and further fear of displacement in future from Arunachal to the other states of the North East or somewhere else in India.

III CHT: The *Paharis* and *Jhummas*

The CHT (*Parbotto Chottogram* in Bengali) was previously known as *Jum Bungoo* and *Jum Mahal*, yet the most popular term to denote this particular area even before the colonial period was *Kapas Mahal*. Comprising mainly of three districts, Rangamati, Khagracherri and Banderban, the CHT is geographically an isolated region in the then East Bengal (now Bangladesh). Four rivers, Feni, Karnafuli, Sangu and Matamuri, have created a fertile valley in this region. Although the CHT region occupies almost 10 per cent of the total area of Bangladesh, the population of these three areas together makes only 1 per cent of the total population (Bhattacharchaya, 2001, p. 321). With a population of 350,000, the Buddhist Chakmas were the most dominant or majoritarian community among a dozen ethnic minorities living in the CHT. The other majority groups are Marma and Tippera, while the minorities, such as the Mro, Lusai, Khumai, Chak, Khyang Bawn, Pankhua, Hajong and Reang, were constituted other indigenous tribal communities. From perspectives like cultural affiliation and kinship relation, the entire tribal population, can be divided into two major categories. The South Asian model influenced some while others were inclined to the South-East Asian model (Schendel, 1992, p. 106). For example, Chakmas are more Indianized and their practice of Buddhism has been adopted from different Hindu *pujas* within their fold (Sattar, 1983, pp. 384–395).

Different rulers have redrawn the political map of CHT several times as a result of the frequent annexation of the region. The Mughals first initiated to encroach upon the CHT region, because of its strategic peripheral location. Mughal rulers had shown interest in this tiny peripheral region, which was famous for its elephants (Bhattacharyya, 1991, p. 73). They annexed the CHT in 1666 after a prolonged war with the hill people and convinced them to pay a regular tax, levied on trade between Chittagong hills and plains. Although in return, they agreed to provide them with the right to local autonomy. The first authentic source about this region is the account of Hamilton Buchanon, which stated that the predominant Buddhist origin of the tribes of CHT became an 'ideological bridge' between the hill people and Buddhist India on one hand and Myanmar (Burma) on the other (Schendel, 1994, pp. 64–67) The British, too, had difficulties extending their control into the CHT, and in 1860, the CHT was brought fully within the ambit of the British Empire. The British introduced several administrative changes in this region and simplified the judicial procedure. The most important reform was the CHT Regulation of 1900, which is known as the *CHT Manual*. This regulation divided the Chittagong district into three circles: the Chakmas, the Bohmong and the Mong. The significant aspect of this *Manual* was that rule 52 of the regulations had strictly prohibited the settlement of outsiders in the CHT. The prohibition in the transfer of land to non-indigenous people was another significant recommendation and they mentioned the use of 'permit system' in this region. In 1920, a new administration was formed under the CHT (amendment) Regulation. It declared the district as an 'Excluded Area'. In legal language, which meant the independence of general administration. Rule 52 was later repealed in 1930, and a permit was no longer required for entering the CHT. However, in 1935, the Government of India Act declared it a 'totally excluded area' (Chakma, 1986, pp. 140–162)

IV Partition of 1947 and Gradual Transition in the CHT

The Partition of 1947 separated Bengal and Punjab. The creation of borderland by dissecting this region has given the first political blow to the *pahari* and *jumma* people of CHT. By creating the Radcliffe Line, the non-Muslim majority of CHT first gained independence as a district of India. But later, it declared to be transferred to the Pakistani administration (Ali, 1993, p. 176). The reason for the sudden change of this particular decision was to provide a hinterland to the port at Chittagong including the Karnafuli river, which was vital for the commercial and strategic interest to this port. The inhabitants of CHT even hoisted the flag of India, but the Pakistani army marched in on August 18, 1947. The Indian flag was immediately taken down (Schendel, 2005, pp. 48–49) By this decision, CHT was handed over to East Pakistan, with 98 per cent of its population comprising dominantly Buddhists and other ethnic communities. It marked the beginning of a constant repressive policy to the people of CHT under the West Pakistani regime. The authorities and the central government supported the influx of a Bengali-speaking Muslim population from the plain areas to CHT, as it was not densely populated in comparison to the other regions of East Pakistan. The first Constitution of Pakistan adopted in 1956 recognized the CHT as an 'Excluded Area'. CHT lost its special status under the Pakistan Constitutional Amendment Act of 1963 (Mukherji, 2000, pp. 32–33). This enables non-indigenous people not only to enter but also to acquire lands in the CHT. By such unfair activities, from a relatively economically self-sufficient and politically semi-autonomous region, the CHT was turned into a peripheral area even within East Pakistan.

The story of marginalization of the Chakmas and Hajongs uprooted refugees can trace back to the post-Partition days. With the inclusion of CHT into Pakistan, the Chakmas and Hajongs were suddenly exposed to unanticipated political and religious persecution. Economic policies were made for implementation in this region, and consequent exploitation started in the early 1950s, when the Pakistani regime undertook industrial developmental projects in the CHT with the help of foreign capitals (Kanitkar, 2000, pp. 102–103). Those projects were not benevolent for the hill people. It was aimed at weakening the claim of the *pahari* and *jumma* people to special status on grounds of their own unique history and issues of ethnicity (Sopher, 1963, pp. 342–343). The first effort to modernize this region was through the construction of the Karnaphuli Paper Mill at Chandragona in

1953 with support of a huge loan from the World Bank. The next one was Pakistan's most ambitious project, the Kaptai Hydroelectric project between 1959 and 1963. When the first one led to the 'millions of tons of bamboos and soft wood cut' in the CHT for the purpose of producing paper, the second one encroaches on 52,000 acres of settled cultivable land, which was about 40 per cent of the total arable land in CHT (Singh, 2010, p. 41).

These two incidents largely led to one of the biggest displacements of ethnic tribals from CHT during the Pakistan period. It was one of the highest percentages of up-rootedness in the history of modern South Asia. Almost 100,000 people were compelled to leave that area and they were never properly rehabilitated in their homeland. The 'Census of Un-rehabilitated Displaced Persons' conducted surveys in 1959. The report stated about the settlement of Bengali Muslim refugee families in Chittagong, Chandraghona and Kaptai (Department of Works, 1959, p. v). These displaced hill people were fending for themselves when the erstwhile Government of East Pakistan failed to pay them any sort of compensation. Many of the Chakmas had left with any choice other than a support of survival by *jhum* cultivation or remained as 'internally displaced people' in and around the CHT. But, about 40,000 Chakmas could not meet up the minimum requirement for survival and crossed over to India for immediate security and permanent shelter. Their intention was to settle down in the neighbouring areas or any states of India like Tripura and Mizoram, where other tribal communities of similar origin had been residing for a long time (Basu Ray Chaudhury, 2003, p. 254). In fact, the *jhumma* population had been isolated over large areas in the native CHT in the adjoining areas of Tripura and Mizoram for the administrative purposes designed by the British. The Government of Tripura did not encourage the displaced Chakmas to settle down within the state but accommodated them initially in a refugee camp in Manughat (Basu Ray Chaudhury, 2003, p. 255). Finally, the Government of India contemplated a scheme to put up the refugees in the deserted land of the North-East Frontier Agency (popularly known as NEFA), now Arunachal Pradesh. The centre tried to arrange transport facilities for them to some rarely populated districts of Arunachal Pradesh. Although the vital motive given by the governor in Assam was to erect a human wall in view of the potential Chinese threat following the Sino-Indian War of 1962. A 'white paper' published by the Arunachal government quotes Vishnu Sahay, then Governor of Assam, telling then Assam chief minister Bimala Prasad Chaliha in a letter dated April 10, 1964: 'It occurred to me that we may get trouble between the Mizos and Chakmas in the Mizo district. These Chakmas would be quite suitable people to go into the Tirap division of NEFA where there is easily found vacant land.'[6] P N Luthra, then Adviser to the Governor, informed NEFA officials on April 21, 1965: 'Settlement of (these) people in NEFA will also help in developing the pockets that are lying unused and unoccupied. Besides, the presence of stretches of vacant land along the border is strategically not desirable'[7]

Apart from the *jumma* origin issue, the Government of India started considering some other factors too. The Centre assumed, as the local populace of Arunachal Pradesh were of the same religious belief and in case of necessity, a section of these people could be utilized in future by the Indian army and intelligence agencies (Basu Ray Chaudhury and Biswas, 1997, pp. 140–141). There were lots of similarities between these two hilly areas. As Arunachal Pradesh has enjoyed a 'Special Protected Area' status like CHT since the pre-independence period, the ethnic lifestyle of both the communities and their religious beliefs and practices were considered definite reasons behind the decision. Thus, the *pahari* and *jumma* people of CHT were kind of assured to continue with their religious and cultural prolongation as '[t]he Chakma refugees are Buddhists and some of the locals are also Buddhists' (Basu Ray Chaudhury and Das, 2011, p. 2). Thus, initially, these refugees were settled in the agency areas where there were rehabilitation schemes designed for them. The first batch accommodated in the Tirap division of Changlang district of the NEFA in the vacant lands. Between 1964 and 1969, a huge population from Chakma and Hajong communities got settled themselves with support from the then Central Government along with the erstwhile NEFA administration in Lohit and Subansiri districts (Government of Arunachal Pradesh, 1996, p. 4). They acquired 10,799 acres of land in these three districts, with due financial assistance from the central government for their rehabilitation. But, by only three decades, the refugee population rose more than 400 per cent, while their number has gone up to 65,000 in different districts of Arunachal Pradesh and 33,000 refugees spread over several camps in India's North East (Ghosh, 2004, p. 33).

V Politics of Ethnic Cleansing: Repressive Policies

It is the irony of the fact that on both sides of the Bengal borderlands, the marginal *pahari* and *jumma* people faced trouble along with constant discrimination by the respective state governments. For example, the discriminatory attitude of the Pakistan state towards them did not end up with the independence in 1971 and the emergence of a third country in a row. The new nation state, Bangladesh, didn't fetch any change in the fate of indigenous ethnic communities from CHT. They again became the victim of Bengali nationalism. They faced similar treatment from the Awami League chief, Prime Minister Sheikh Mujibur Rahman. While they demanded Constitutional recognition of their identities, he instructed them 'to forget their ethnic identities' (Chakma, 2010, pp. 10–12). Constant denial about the recognition of Chakmas, Hajongs and other ethnic communities as their citizen, on the new constituted Government's part, had two-fold reasons. The then Awami League leaders were upset with the role of the indigenous habitants of CHT played in the War of Liberation, as their chief, Chakma Raja Tridev Roy, chose to support West Pakistani administration/troops. The new policymakers of Bangladesh were under the impression that some of the tribal *jummas* were even recruited as *razakars* by the West Pakistani authorities against the native *Mukti Bahini*. The Awami League government was not sympathetic towards them. The 1972 Constitution of Bangladesh did not include a provision of recognizing the distinct identity of the indigenous ethnic populace living in the CHT (Chakma, 2014, p. 114). Another point of reluctance was on the government's part. It derived from the fact that their 'ideology of Bengali nationalism' in a way facilitated the rapid growth of outsiders, the Bengali settlement in CHT, chiefly in the reign of General Zia-ur-Rehman and General Ershad (Mutsuddhi. 1992, pp. 114–115). It led to the sheer tradition of extreme cases of violation of human rights in CHT for the tribals. This is the key reason why the *Pahari* people of CHT treat Manabendra Narayan Larna as the 'father of the *Jhumma* nation', as he initiated to launch the Parbattya Chattogram Jana Shonghati Samiti (PCJSS) in 1972. They still can remember his popular saying, 'Under no definition or logic can a Chakma be a Bengali or a Bengali be a Chakma. As citizens of Bangladesh, we are Bangladeshis, but we also have a separate ethnic identity, which unfortunately the Awami League leaders do not want to understand' (Gulrukh, 2010, p. 9). This quote became a myth in the tribal/ethnic communities of Bangladesh. Samari Chakma however wrote that after 1979 'the nature of persecution started changing. Instead of Army doing things directly, the Government brought Settler Bengalis from the plain lands. The reasons were completely political. Our lands started becoming grabbed by Bengalis. We could do nothing against this hostile attack by the Government' (Chakma, 1996, p. 20).

On the other side of the Bengal borderlands, the situation was different for them too. Under the Indira-Muzib agreement of 1972, it was decided that India and Bangladesh would not be liable and legally responsible for all those migrants who would enter India after March 25, 1971. Therefore, the Chakma and Hajong refugees who came to India before that time frame would be considered for the grant of Indian citizenship. But on January 21, 1972, the NEFA was made a Union Territory with a chief commissioner as per the provisions of the North-Eastern Areas (Re-Organization) Act, 1971 (vide annexure XX; Kumar, 1996, p. 52). Indira Gandhi at Ziro, which was the headquarters of the erstwhile Subansiri district, formally inaugurated it. As K. A. A. Raja visualized it, it led to further growth of political institutions in Arunachal Pradesh (Lego, 2008, p. 61). But these developments exaggerated the problems of Chakmas and Hajongs related to their prior refugee-hood and the question of citizenship immensely. The Citizenship Act of 1955 was never implemented for their cause. In fact, ever since the All NEFA Students Union, the forerunner of all Arunachal Pradesh Students Union (AAPSU) was formed; the Chakma issue was top on their agenda.[8] The genesis of the anti-foreigners movement in Arunachal Pradesh can be traced back to 1975, when the People's Party of Arunachal (PPA) raised its voice against the Chakmas for the first time during the first election of the Agency Council. As Arunachal was Union territory, the PPA raised the issue that if the Chakmas and Hajongs were accorded citizenship status and voting rights, they might be the deciding factor in the elections in those districts, where they were numerically dominant (Singh, 2010, pp. 84–85) According to the People' Rights Organization, the Chakmas have been suffering forcible eviction and arson since the early 1970s. But, the Chakmas and Hajongs remained 'stateless' even after the amendment of the Indian Citizenship Act of 1985. They have been constantly denied citizenship, which was illegal and systematically deprived of other fundamental rights since the time of their resettlement (Basu Ray Chaudhury, 2003, p. 259)

Apparently, this problem started with a letter from the minister of state for home, P. M. Sayeed to Nyodak Yonggam, a Rajya Sabha member on July 7, 1994. He mentioned the centre's decision to consider the grant of citizenship status to Chakmas and Hajongs refugees in the light of the pact of 1972. According to the Centre, the Chakma, Hajong and Tibetan refugees had been settled in the Arunachal Pradesh in consultation with the then NEFA administration (Saikia, 1994, p. 3311). As expected, the home minister's letter ignited a spark to the prevailing AAPSU sentiments. After one month, the situation underwent a drastic change. AAPSU served notice to all migrant communities, the Chakmas, Hajongs, Tibetans, other Bangladeshi migrants and Nepalis to quit Arunachal Pradesh by September 30, failing which a 'direct action' was threaded. With the active support of the state government, they argued that Arunachal became a 'dumping ground' for all 'developmental' and 'environmental' refugees and 'unwanted people of the Northeast'. AAPSU launched a direct movement named 'Refugee Go Back' that consistently held the view that the refugees were 'foreigners' in their land. They organized a rally with leaders and supporters from all political parties of the state. The then chief minister of Arunachal, GegongApang, set December 31 as a deadline for the centre to evict those refugees from the State, though 94% of the Chakmas and Hajongs settled in Arunachal Pradesh by the Government of India. In 1980, the State Government imposed a ban on their employment. They stopped issuing any type of certificate to them. All trade licenses issued to them from the late 1960s were seized. In fact, their employment options were sealed off completely.

In 1991, the state government started discontinuing the issuance of ration cards to them, when most of them always lived in extreme poverty. In 1994, the state government began closing and burning down schools in these areas, affecting denying the Chakmas and Hajongs their right to education (Hazarika, 1994, p. 1). Health facilities in the Chakmas and Hajong areas became a kind of non-existent. The state government made their point clear to the central government that these refugees had to be moved elsewhere in the country, arguing that they did not come from a neighbouring district or province of India. Indeed, they came with a settlement to NEFA and the central government. After such incidents, the People's Union for Civil Liberties (PUCL) started requesting both the state and central government to look after the issues of persistent conflicts. They treated the matter as a formal complaint and the Ministry of Home Affairs sent a note to National Human Rights Commission (NHRC) in favor of granting them citizenship. The Government of Arunachal Pradesh contended before the Supreme Court showing that all these allegations regarding the well-being of the refugee families were wrong. Finally, in 1996, the state government ought to protect the life and liberty of the refugees living in the region. Against this background, in 1998, 27 Chakmas submitted citizenship applications to the deputy commissioner of Changlang district, although the staff refused them immediately, as the higher authorities instructed the respective officials not to entertain any such cases. They tried to resubmit the same applications directly to the Union Home Ministry. But even more than two years after those incidents, the Chakmas and Hajongs refugees were not successful in acquiring citizenship. In 1999, the Committee for Citizenship Rights of the Chakmas of Arunachal Pradesh (CCRCAP), a representative organization of them urged the home minister, L. K. Advani, to intervene on the whole issue urgently and direct the Election Commission of India to include the Chakmas and Hajongs in the electoral rolls of Arunachal Pradesh, who were citizens by birth (Government of Arunachal Pradesh, 1996, p. 11). But both governments had made no move to include them in the electoral rolls.

VI Question of Citizenship in Arunachal Pradesh

The current citizenship question of the Chakma and Hajong refugees in Arunachal Pradesh is rooted in the conflicts, which emerged between the politics of India and Pakistan, and later, in Bangladesh, which engendered the expulsion of the Chakma and Hajong people from their traditional homelands. The AAPSU's key argument was, it was the Indian government that violated the legal provisions that prohibit people from outside Arunachal Pradesh from entering the state (Prasad, 2007, p. 1376). As per the verdict in 1996, a total of almost 4,637 Chakma and Hajong refugees applied for citizenship right between the years 1999 and 2002, but they were not allowed by the local authorities to join the verification process.[9] The conflict between the idea of domicile people versus outsiders was the key reason behind not providing them with their due right of citizenship, as they were not socially acceptable there. In response to a 'Right to Information' application in 2014, by Rahant Chakma, the Ministry of Home Affairs, North-East Division, the Government of India, provided the fact that apart from a large number of land encroachment cases, there were 220 registered criminal cases against them and report further confirmed that the Chakma concentrated in Changlang and Lohit districts were severely affected with 'organized crime' (Debnath and Debnath, 2020, p. 146). Over the decades, the political alienation of these refugees extended their sense of deprivation and marginalization.

In 2015, the Supreme Court of India directed the Government of India to confer citizenship rights to the refugees settled in Arunachal Pradesh. An all-party meeting in Itanagar discussed the court's order, and said they were not against Indian citizenship for Chakmas and Hajongs, but objected to their permanent settlement in Arunachal, and their exclusion from Inner Line Permit provisions. All parties are unanimous that permanent settlement would contravene the Bengal Eastern Frontier Regulation, 1873, Scheduled District Act, 1874, Assam Frontier Tract Regulation, 1880, Assam Frontier Forest Regulation, 1891, Chin Hills Regulations, 1896, and Assam Frontier (Administration & Justice) Regulation, 1945 (1 of 1945). AAPSU's argument was, the court's order would dilute the constitutional safeguards for the indigenous communities of the state, and pose a threat to their identity and culture. Therefore, the state government decided to file a review petition in the Supreme Court.[10] The Citizenship (Amendment) Bill of 2016 created further upstir in the region as this bill seemed to grant citizenship to refugees from minority communities, namely Hindus, Sikhs, Jains, Parsis, Christians and Buddhists, after their six years of stay in India. By all probable situations, the Citizenship (Amendment) Bill would be made the Chakma and Hajong refugees eligible to get all constitutional rights, including ownership of land. But Arunachal is among the states exempted from the CAA since it has an inner line permit to regulate the entry of outsiders.

Not only that, but all political parties of Arunachal Pradesh also unanimously oppose the demand for citizenship by the refugee population on the grounds that, besides stretching resources, it would change the demographic composition of the state, and threaten the identity and culture of the indigenous people, chiefly the smaller tribes of the region. Many believed that the Chakma and Hajong communities would eventually demand Scheduled Tribe (ST) status, which would lead to reductions in the number of seats reserved for the indigenous tribes in education and government jobs.[11] Many suggestions and other options came out in form of feasible suggestions. The key opinion was, the Central government might choose to establish a middle ground by making certain provisions such as 'Limited Citizenship' available to the Chakma-Hajong people, primarily so that the rights of the local indigenous population would be not get diluted. Under this, the Chakma-Hajong refugees would be granted citizenship rights, including Inner Line Permits required by non-locals in Arunachal Pradesh to travel and work. However, they would neither be given ownership of lands, nor ST status.[12] But even as the original immigrants await citizenship, many of their descendants born in India who are eligible for citizenship by birth are struggling to enrol as voters. However, the refugees were given voting rights in 2004. The latest records for Bordumsa-Diyun and Miao, which account for 90 per cent of the Chakma and Hajong population in Arunachal, say there are only 4,293 Chakma and Hajong voters. According to a state survey conducted in 2016 states that the total populations of the Chakma and Hajong refugees are 65,851.[13]

During the COVID-19 pandemic, the situation got worsened and the Division Bench of Justice N. Kotiswar Singh and Justice Manish Choudhury heard a Public Interest Litigation (PIL) filed by Indrajit Chakma who raised a concern that refugees belonging to Chakma, Hajong and other communities living in the three districts are not getting food supplies. However, it has been submitted by D. Ghosh, the counsel for the petitioner, that in spite of such statement made by the advocate general, Arunachal Pradesh, as well the observation made by this court, nothing has been done for providing food grains to the people of Chakma, Hajong and other communities living in Changlang, Papumpare and Namsai.[14] Taking note of allegations of 'massive hunger and starvation' faced by the two communities during the national lockdown; DoNER's joint secretary Rambir Singh on April 29 drew the attention of Arunachal Pradesh's chief secretary Naresh Kumar towards the allegation. Yet, according to Suhas Chakma, director of the New Delhi–based Rights and Risks Analysis Group (RRAG), 'for the last 56 years, Chakmas and Hajongs have faced discrimination as a matter of state policy'.[15] According to the National People's Party, the door for Chakmas should be closed, as Chakma-Hajong issue may turn Arunachal Pradesh tense again.[16] In August 2021, the central and state governments declared their plan to planned to relocate Chakma and Hajong refugees from Arunachal. While the AAPSU continues to oppose citizenship to the Chakma and the Hajong, they always stated the way Tobom Dai, the union's general secretary, put his point 'if citizenship has to be given, move them elsewhere. There is already pressure on indigenous groups because of their population explosion'.[17] After the declaration of both the Central and state governments, the All Nyishi Students' Union (ANSU) supported this move and they termed the step as 'a bold move to resolve permanent solution on vexed issue'.[18] Chakma and Hajong groups rejected the proposed relocation move vehemently. The Chakma Development Foundation of India (CDFI) wrote to Prime Minister Narendra Modi, Union home minister Amit Shah, Rashtriya Swayamsevak Sangh (RSS) chief Mohan Bhagwat and chief ministers of Arunachal Pradesh and Assam, Pema Khandu and Himanta Biswa Sarma, respectively, opposing the move. The letter mentioned that in his Independence Day speech, Khandu had mentioned that Chakmas and Hajongs would be settled outside Arunachal. It added that Union law minister Kiren Rijijuhas stated in public meetings that members of both communities will have to leave the state. Chakma Rights and Development Organisation (CRDO) opposed the relocation move and instead asked the centre to create a separate Union territory for Chakmas and Hajongs in the areas of Arunachal where they are settled at present. In a press release, they mentioned, "It hurts us badly when after 57 years of rehabilitation we are branded as 'refugees' by none other than the CM himself. We were 'refugees' at one point, long ago before the resettlement in NEFA but are like any other citizens of the country now."[19]

VII Conclusion

The weak demographic and economic structures of the states where the refugees were settled began to feel pressure more from the beginning of the twenty-first century. And, the xenophobic tiny indigenous tribal population of Arunachal Pradesh began to consider the refugees as 'encroachers'. The limited means were to be shared by both groups, which created acute tensions. The politicization of demographic issues, so typical of northeast India, soon generated a fear that the Chakma refugees might at a certain point outnumber the indigenous tribals, thereby usurping the political hegemony of the latter. The hostility towards the refugees intensified with the declaration of the centre's intention of granting these refugees Indian citizenship (Nag, 2005).[20] The question is if the Tibetans who fled to Arunachal Pradesh on their own can be given Indian citizenship, why cannot the Chakmas and Hajongs, who had migrated from undivided India? The central government had settled the Chakmas and Hajongs in the state, and they have the same right to all the facilities, without any type of discrimination based on social, economical, political and legal factors. It is a clear case of discrimination for political gains of a few AAPSU and core committee leaders in Arunachal Pradesh (Prasad, 2007, p. 1379). The Supreme Court has recognized the citizenship rights to the Chakmas and Hajongs, the popular argument of the indigenous communities of the state remained as, the continued presence of the Chakmas and the Hajongs has 'started threatening the fragile eco-system of the State of Arunachal Pradesh' (Basu Ray Chaudhury and Samir Kumar Das, 2011, p. 2)

The decadal growth rate of the Chakmas, according to Census figures, has been 25 per cent, compared to the state average of 36.83 per cent. In Arunachal Pradesh, although their number was sharply increased, their recognition even as citizens is a distant dream, while in the neighbouring other North-Eastern states, namely Assam, Meghalaya, Mizoram, and Tripura, the Chakmas are recognized as Scheduled Tribe (Debnath and Debnath, 2020, p. 139). Because of the cultural integration of the Arunachali identity was different with its diverse ethnic characters, the Chakmas and Hajongs remained as aliens there. Unlike the other North-Eastern states, the nature of the regional politics became different. The sharp rise of the numbers of the migrant Chakma and Hajongs left a visible impact on the politics of ethnicity between the local native people and outsiders. The crux of the problem lies in the fact that the rights claims of the Chakma refugees come into conflict with the rights claims of the indigenous tribes with a distinct way of life. The present generations of the Chakma and Hajong communities became the victim of the State suppressions. The Chakmas of Arunachal Pradesh are the perfect instance of the category of *de facto* stateless persons, per the definition decided by the United Nations High Commission for Refugees, who remain outside the country of their nationality and hence is unable or for valid reasons unwilling to avail themselves of the protection of the motherland. They were neither refugees nor migrants by birth, but because of their identities, policies and politics of the state–centre relations and policies, they are suffering till today.

Notes

1 https://www.thehindu.com/news/national/other-states/bid-to-deport-60000-chakmas-from-arunachal-slammed/article36055227.ece. Accessed on 23rd October, 2021.
2 https://www.thedailystar.net/views/in-focus/news/memories-lives-villages-under-water-2147836. Accessed on 11th November, 2021.
3 Samari, Chakma. (2018). *Bor Porong*, Comrade Rupak Chakma Memorial Trust, Narankhya, February, 2018.
4 https://globalvoices.org/2021/10/16/indigenous-artist-depicts-the-hidden-history-behind-the-creation-of-bangladeshs-kaptai-lake/. Accessed on 11th November, 2021.
5 https://www.unhcr.org/excom/scip/3ae68cbe4/implementation-1951-convention-1967-protocol-relating-status-refugees.html. Accessed on 28th November, 2021.
6 https://indianexpress.com/article/explained/why-chakmas-and-hajongs-are-indias-nowhere-people/. Accessed on 23rd October.
7 https://indianexpress.com/article/explained/why-chakmas-and-hajongs-are-indias-nowhere-people/. Accessed on 23rd October.
8 The students' union in the North East Frontier Agency (NEFA) first established in 1947 at Pasighat, east Siang district of Arunachal Pradesh by a few Adi and Mishing (tribes of Arunachal Pradesh) students was called the 'Adi-Mishing' Student Union (AMSU) with its headquarters at Pasighat. After the creation of the union territory in 1972, and its naming as Arunachal Pradesh, the NEFA students' union was also renamed the Arunachal Pradesh Students Union (AAPSU). For details see (Prasad, 2007,1373) Students' Movements in Arunachal Pradesh and the Chakma-Hajong Refugee Problem, *Economic and Political Weekly*, April 14, 2007, p. 1373.
9 Seetharaman, G. (2017). Government's flip-flop leaves Chakma and Hajong refugees on wings of hope. The Economic Times, September 24. Retrieved from https://economictimes.indiatimes.com/news/politics-and-nation/governments-flip-flopleaves-chakma-and-hajong-refugees-on-wings-of-hope/articleshow/60810196.cms. Accessed on April 11, 2018.
10 https://indianexpress.com/article/explained/why-chakmas-and-hajongs-are-indias-nowhere-people/. Accessed on 23rd October, 2021.
11 https://sprf.in/a-question-of-citizenship-the-case-of-the-chakma-hajong-refugees/. Accessed on 23rd October, 2021.
12 https://sprf.in/a-question-of-citizenship-the-case-of-the-chakma-hajong-refugees/. Accessed on 23rd October, 2021.
13 https://economictimes.indiatimes.com/news/politics-and-nation/for-chakma-hajong-refugees-citizenship-struggle-continues/articleshow/74033643.cms?from=mdr. Accessed on 23rd October, 2021.
14 https://www.indialegallive.com/top-news-of-the-day/news/chakma-refugees-arunanchal-pradesh-ration-card-food-grains/. Accessed on 23rd October, 2021
15 https://thefederal.com/covid-19/before-covid-19-chakma-hajong-tribes-of-arunachal-battled-a-stormy-migration/?doing_wp_cron=1635017378.3146469593048095703125. Accessed on 23rd October, 2021.

16 https://www.deccanherald.com/national/east-and-northeast/chakma-hajong-issue-may-turn-arunachal-pradesh-tense-again-1023782.html. Accessed on 23rd October, 2021.
17 https://economictimes.indiatimes.com/news/politics-and-nation/for-chakma-hajong-refugees-citizenship-struggle-continues/articleshow/74033643.cms?from=mdr. Accessed on 23rd October, 2021.
18 https://arunachaltimes.in/index.php/2021/08/31/ansu-welcomes-move-to-relocate-chakma-hajong-refugees/. Accessed on 23rd October, 2021.
19 https://www.hindustantimes.com/cities/others/chakma-groups-reject-proposed-relocation-move-from-arunachal-pradesh-write-to-pm-modi-101629740848589.html. Accessed on 23rd October, 2021.
20 Sajal Nag. (2005). The Killing Fields: Mapping Conflicts and Violence in North East India, Unpublished Report submitted to Oxfam (India), It was Commissioned By Oxfam under its Violence Mitigation and Amelioration Project, Oxfam (India).

References

Ali, S. Mahmud. (1993). *The Fearful State: Power, People and Internal War in South Asia*. London & New Jersey: Zed Books.

Basu, Ray Chaudhury Anasua and Das, Samir Kumar. (2011). A *Report on the State of Being Stateless: A Case Study of the Chakmas of Arunachal Pradesh*. Kolkata: Calcutta Research Group. February.

Basu, Ray Chaudhury Sabyasachi. (2003). "Uprooted Twice: Refugees from the Chittagong Hill Tracts", in Samaddar, Ranabir. (ed.) *Refugees and the State: Practices of Asylum and Care in India-1947-2000*. New Delhi: Sage Publications, 249–80.

Basu, Ray Chaudhury Sabyasachi and Biswas, Ashis K. (1997). "A Diaspora is Made: The Jummas in the North-East India", in Bhaumik, Subir, Guhathakurta, Meghna and Basu Ray Chaudhury, Sabyasachi. (ed.) *Living on the Edge: Essays on the Chittagong Hill Tracts*. Katmandu: South Asia Forum for Human Rights, 139–66.

Bhattacharchaya, Swapna. (2001). "The refugee-generating Chittagong Hill Tracts: past, present and future", in Sanjay, K. Roy. (ed.) *Refugees and Human Rights: Social and Political Dynamics of Refugee Problem in Eastern and North-Eastern India*. New Delhi: Rawat Publications, 317–44.

Bhattacharyya, Suchintya. (1991). *Genesis of Tribal Extremism in Tripura*. New Delhi: Gian Publishing House.

Census of Un-rehabilitated Displaced Persons in Chittagong, Chandraghona and Kaptai, (1959). Department of Works, Housing and Settlement (Housing and Settlement). Dacca: Government of East Pakistan.

Chakma, Ananda Bikash. (2014). "Peacebuilding in the Chittagong Hill Tracts (CHT): An Institutionalist Approach". *Journal of the Asiatic Society of Bangladesh (Hum.)* 59(1), 111–38.

Chakma, Bhumitra. (2010). "Structural Roots of Violence in the Chittagong Hill Tracts". *Economic and Political Weekly*, XLV(12).

Chakma, S. (1986). *Prasanga Parbatya Chattagram* (in Bengali). Calcutta: Nath Brothers.

Chakma, Samari. (1996). "Untitled (Translated by Hana Shams Ahmed, from "PaharerRuddhokontho", Hill Women's Federation)", in Naeem Mohaiemen. (ed). *Between Ashes and Hope: Chittagong Hill Tracts in the Blind Spot of Bangladesh Nationalism*. Dhaka: Drishtipat Writers' Collective.

Chakma, Samari. (2018). *Kaptai Baadh: Bor Porong – Duburider Attokothon.* (Kaptai Dam: The Great Exodus – Autobiography of the Drowned) Narankhya: Comrade Rupak Chakma Memorial Trust, February.

Debnath, Kollol and Debnath, Kunal. (2020). "Chakma Refugees in Arunachal Pradesh: Their Inclusion and Setback", in Sourav Kumar Das and Nidhi Chowdhary. (ed.) *Refugee Crises and Third-world Economies: Policies and Perspective.* Emerald Publishing Limited, in collaboration with Belur Research Association of Social Science, Bingley.

Ghosh, Partha S. (2004). *Unwanted and uprooted: A Political Study of Migrants, Refugees, Stateless and Displaced of South Asia.* New Delhi: Samskriti.

Gulrukh, Saydia. (2010). "The Other Shahid Minar", in Naeem Mohaiemen (ed.) *Between Ashes and Hope: Chittagong Hill Tracts in the Blind Spot of Bangladesh Nationalism.* Dhaka: Drishtipat Writers' Collective, 9–10.

Hazarika, Sanjoy. (1994). "The Chakmas Flight to Nowhere". *Indian Express.* October 17.

Kanitkar, Satish. (2000). *Refugee Problem in South Asia.* New Delhi: Rajat Publications.

Kumar, B. B. (1996). *Re-Organization of North-East India (Facts and Documents).* New Delhi: Omsons Publications.

Lego, N. (2008). *Local Self Government in Arunachal Pradesh (Early Times to 2008).* Itanagar: Published by the Author.

Mohaiemen, Naeem. ed. (2010). *Between Ashes and Hope: Chittagong Hill Tracts in the Blind Spot of Bangladesh Nationalism.* Dhaka: Drishtipat Writers' Collective.

Mukherji, Saradindu. (2000). *Subjects, Citizens and Refugees: Tragedy in the Chittagong Hill Tracts (1947-1998).* New Delhi: Indian Centre for the Study of Forced Migration.

Mutsuddhi, Chinmoy. (1992). *AshantaParbotyaChattagram O AnanyaPrasanga* (in Bengali). Dhaka: AgamiPrakashani.

Nag, Sajal. (2005). The Killing Fields: Mapping Conflicts and Violence in North East India, Unpublished Report submitted to Oxfam (India), Commissioned By Oxfam under its Violence Mitigation and Amelioration Project, Oxfam (India).

Prasad, Chunnu. "Students' Movements in Arunachal Pradesh and the Chakma-Hajong Refugee Problem". *Economic and Political Weekly.* April 14, 2007.

Saikia, Anup. (1994). "Arunachal Pradesh: Tensions OverChakma Issue". *Economic and Political Weekly*, 29(53), 3311, December 31st.

Sattar, Abdus. (1983). *In the Sylvan Shadows.* Dhaka: Bangla Academy.

Sen, Sreya. (2015). "Understanding India's Refusal to Accede to the 1951 Refugee Convention: Context and Critique". *Refugee Review: Re-conceptualizing and Forced Migration in the 21st Century*, 2(1, https://refugeereview2.wordpress.com/opinion-pieces/understanding-indias-refusal-to-accede-to-the-1951-refugee-convention-context-and-critique-by-sreya-sen/

Singh, Deepak K. (2010). *Statelessness in South Asia: The Chakmas between India and Pakistan.* New Delhi: Sage Publications.

Sopher, David F. (1963). Popular Dislocation in the Chittagong Hills". *Geographical Review*, LIII(3), 337–62, July.

Schendel, Willem Van. (1992). "The Invention of the 'Jummas': State Formation and Ethnicity in Southern Bangladesh". *Modern Asian Studies*, 26(1), 95–128.

Schendel, Willem Van. (1994). *Francis Buchanan in Southeastern Bengal.* (translated in Bengali by AyubSalahuddin as *DakhinpurbaBanglay Francis Buchanan*). Dhaka: International Centre for Bengal Studies.
Schendel, Willem Van. (2005). *The Bengal Borderland: Beyond State and Nation in South Asia.* London: Anthem Press, pp. 48–49.
White Paper on Chakma and Hajong Refugee Issue. (1996). Itanagar: Government of Arunachal Pradesh, March 12.

Index

Pages followed by n refer notes.

Aam Aadmi Party (AAP) 189, 192
Agamben, G. 48, 59, 63, 66, 68n12
Agarwala, Jyoti Prasad 74, 147–148
Agnew, John 248
Ahmed, Fakhruddin Ali 103
Ahmed, Hafiz 75–77, 80
Ahmed, Khabir 75
Ahmed, Sara 43–44, 49
Ahom state 132, 142n6
Akhlaq, Mohammad 194
Ali, Aman 80–81
Aligarh Muslim University (AMU) 185, 192, 194
All Arunachal Pradesh Students Union (AAPSU) 268–273, 274n8
All Assam Gana Sangram Parishad (AAGSP) 137
All Assam Minorities Students Union (AAMSU) 75
All Assam Students Union (AASU) 74–75, 105, 108, 121–122, 137, 139
All India Trinamool Congress (AITMC) 163, 167, 174, 177–179
All India United Democratic Front (AIUDF) 123
All Nyishi Students Union (ANSU) 272
Ambedkar, Babasaheb 168, 208
Ameen, Furquan xiii–xiv, 12, 183–195
Amnesty International 56, 107
Anti-CAA protests 184, 186–188, 190, 192–195, 203, 207, 210–211
Anti-outsiders movement 91
Arendt, H. 59, 66, 68n11
Arunachal Pradesh: Chakma and Hajong refugees of 262–263; citizenship 270–272
Asian Legal Resource Centre 107
Asom Gana Parishad (AGP) 128, 138–139, 152
Asomiya identity 128, 141
Asomiya intelligentsia 132, 135
Asomiya middle-class leadership 130–131, 141
Asomiya nationalism 130–131, 141; historicity 132–136; as ideological construct 129–132
Asom Jatiya Mahasabha 102, 135
Asom Jatiyatabadi Dal (AJD) 136–137
Asom Jatiyo Maha sabha 102
Assam: amended Citizenship Act 129; anti-immigrant movement in colonial 108; autonomous council for communities 92; citizenship discourse in 128–129; colonialism in 30, 132, 140; communities under sixth schedule 92; East/Eastern Bengal 73, 134, 157; Hindu and Muslim Bengalis in 101–102; Hindu nationalism 141; illegal migrants to 97; immigration 100, 134; labour from Bengal 99–100; Miya Muslims in 145, 147–150, 153, 155–157, 158n2; Mode of nation making 108–109; Muslim identity and citizenship question in *see* Muslim Assamese; NRC in 5, 28, 97, 123–124, 184, 240; Politics of citizenship 136–140; Population 100; Refugees in 100–102; *Sammillita Mahasabha* case 5, 28, 105, 123, 158n8; Tribal/tribal areas 92, 108, 125
Assam Accord 10, 27, 97–98, 121–122, 125, 129, 131, 137–138

The Assam Anti-Foreigners Agitations 121
Assam Assembly 98, 104
Assamese: and Bengalis 134–135, 141; citizenship rights 5; exceptionalism 102–104; Hindus 102; identity 101; language 72, 74–75, 77–80, 85, 93, 99; national identity 129; race 134; society 5, 30, 74, 138, 148–149
Assamese civil society in rebellion 130
Assam Movement (1979–85) 74, 148, 151
Assam Official Language Act 1960 74
Assam Pradesh (Provincial) Congress Committee (APCC) 135
Assam Provincial Muslim League 136
Assam Sanmilita Mahasangha 5, 28, 105, 123, 158n8
The Assam Tribune 98, 142n11
Assam Valley 98, 114, 120, 135
Association for the Refugees in India (AFRI) 163, 177–179
Azad, Abdul Kalam xiii–xiv, 9, 71–85

Banerjee, Debjani 40
Bangladesh government 175–176
Bangladesh Rifles (BDR) 175–176
Barak Valley 92, 147, 156–157
Barooah, Dev Kanta 117
Barooah, Nirode K. 127n26–127n30, 127n35
Baruah, Sanjib Kumar 130
Basumatari, Dharanidhar 115
Bengal borderlands 66
Bengal Eastern Frontier Regulation, 1873 125
Bengali: anti-Bengali riots 102; functionaries 99; Hindus 97; language 133; migrants 57–59; population in Assam 101
Bengal Provincial Congress 135
Bengal renaissance 132, 140
Bharatiya Janata Party (BJP) 6, 109, 123, 129, 137, 139–141, 163; power in 2014 124–125
Bhasaner char and repatriation 56–57
Bhattacharya, Nandini xiii–xiv, 9, 55–68
Bhutan Citizenship Act, 1985 239–240
Bhutanese government 223
Bhutanese Nepalese 237–238
Bhutan State Congress (BSC) 238
Bodoland Autonomous Council (BAC) 138
Bodoland Territorial Council (BTC) 138
Bongal Kheda movement 108
Border Police Organization 137, 152
Borders/borderlands 25–27
Border Security Force (BSF) 175–176
Bordoloi, Gopinath 119, 127n26–127n30, 127n35
Brahmaputra Valley 100, 133–135, 139–141
Brihattar Banga Samrajya 135
British Gorkha Army 233, 241

Cachar Column 253–254
Calcutta 132–135
Caste Hindu Asomiya 135–136, 141
Caste Hindu Assamese 10, 85, 104, 109
Census Act of 1948 105
Central Tibetan Administration (CTA) 13
Césaire, Aimé 79, 81
Chakma and Hajong refugees 260–263
The Chakma Development Foundation of India (CDFI) 272
Chakma Rights and Development Organisation (CRDO) 272
Chakma, Samari 261, 268
Chakraborty, Gorky xi, xiii–xiv, 3–14, 16–32, 67n3, 71–85
Chakravorty, Gayatri, Spivak 82
Chaliha, Kuladhar 117
Chaliha, B. P. 103, 117, 120, 266
char: alterities of refuge space 63–66; Bengali migrants 57–59; Eurocentricity 59–63; geopolitical realities of 55; ideational *ghar* 56; repatriation to *Bhasaner* 56–57; territorial ontology 56
char-ghar 55–56
Chatterjee, Anasua xiii, xv, 12, 201–212, 212n9
Chatterjee. Himadri xiii, xv, 11–12, 163–180
Chatterji, Joya 30
Chaudhuri, Rohini Kumar 114–115, 117, 126n11–126n12
Chaudhury, Moin-ul-Haque 103
Chinese Communist Party (CCP) 218
Chinese Indians 49–50
Chittagong Hill Tracts (CHT) 260–261, 263; Paharis and Jhummas

264–265; partition of 1947 and gradual transition 265–267; politics of ethnic cleansing 267–269
Chowdhury, Rita 41, 48–51
Chowdhury, Samik Roy xiii, xvii, 3–14, 16–32
citizenship: around the world 71; Chinese Indians 49–50; citizens of India 131; cultural 157; functional and relational dimension of 17–21; humanitarian aspects 40; Japanese American experience 44–48; literature 16; malleability 16; regime 23; and statelessness *see* citizenship and statelessness; and territoriality 16–17
Citizenship Act of 1955 103, 263
Citizenship Amendment Act (CAA) 6, 14n2, 29, 39, 50–52, 109, 163, 190, 201, 207; 2003 163, 170–171, 178; 2016 231; 2019 12, 140, 167, 171, 177–178, 183, 211n3
Citizenship Amendment Bill (CAB) 6, 39, 50–52, 124, 129, 139–140, 247
Citizenship and statelessness: emotion and affect 41–44; Monica Sone's *Nisei Daughter* 44–48; Rita Chowdhury's *Chinatown Days* 48–51
Citizenship discourse in India 3–4, 8; Assam and Bangladeshi 27–30; non-citizen 30–32; outsider in borderlands 25–27; outsider within 22–25; postcolonial 20–21; spatial dimension of 22
citizenship discourse in South Asia: crisis of statelessness 57; nation 19–22; outsider 22–25
The Citizenship (Registration of citizen & Issue of National Identity Cards) Rules 2003 103
The Citizenship Rules 2009 103
City of refuge 60–61
Colonialism 10, 132, 140
Colonial project of peasantization 134, 141
Committee for Citizenship Rights of the Chakmas of Arunachal Pradesh (CCRCAP) 270
Communist Party of India (Marxist) (CPIM) 80, 137, 142n8, 163, 167, 179
Constitution of Bangladesh, 1972 268
COVID-19 pandemic 53n5, 187, 210, 272
Dalai Lama 13, 218–219, 222, 226–227
Dam, Kaptai 261
Dandakaranya 172–174
decolonisation 12, 20, 24, 59
Delhi: BJP 192–193; court 194; Muslims from Old Delhi 193; north-east 192; police 185, 193–194; Seelampur-Mustafabad area 192; Shaheen Bagh *see* Shaheen Bagh, Delhi
Delhi Minorities Commission (2020) 193
Delhi's Jamia Millia Islamia: Delhi police 185; Jamia Nagar's Shaheen Bagh locality 186; Uttar Pradesh police 185
Derrida, J. 22, 59–60, 68n12
Deshi Muslims 153
Detention by Tribunals Act, 1983 (IMDT) 27–28, 85, 103–104, 151
Dewan, Maniram 133
Dharmaraja 231
Dorje, Orgyen Trinley 227
Dorji, Kazi Lhendup 235–236
Doubtful Voter (D voter) 104, 124, 152–155, 157
Drig Lam Namzha 237, 239
Drukpa: identity 242; Lamas 231; Nepalis(ese) in Drukpa Sikkim 234–237; Nepalis(ese) migration into Drukpa Bhutan 237–240
Dutta, Binayak xiii, xv, 10–11, 110n4, 112–127

East/Eastern Bengal 10–11, 73, 157, 102, 106, 112–113; Muslims of 119, 124
Eastern Himalayas: colonial migration 232–234; history of 231–232; postcolonial migration and Drukpa identity *see* Drukpa; states, Sikkim and Bhutan 230
East Pakistan 101, 112; Hindu refugees 115–116; migration 113–118
Ekbalpur protest 184, 188–189
Election Commission of India (ECI) 152
electoral rolls (ERs) 137–138
ethnicity 39, 44–45, 47, 56, 60, 84, 109, 157, 265, 273
Eurocentricism of refugium 59–63

foreigner 50–51
The Foreigners Act (1946) 27–29, 120, 151

The Foreigners (Tribunal) Amendment order 2012 103
The Foreigners Order 1948 103
The Foreigners (Tribunals) Order, 1964 103, 120, 152
Foreigners Tribunals (FTs) 74, 120, 129, 139, 152, 183
foreign nationals 104, 109, 121, 136–137, 139, 142n9
Foucault, Michel 47
Free Tibet 223–224

Gandhi, Mohandas 61
Gazette of India 124, 127n46
Ghising, Subash 240
Ghoshal, Anindita xiii, xv, 13–14, 260–275
Globalisation 9, 17–18, 32n1, 71
Goalpara 135, 141n1
Gogoi, Ranjan 77
Gogoi, Tarun 105
Gohain, Hiren 130
Goria-Moria-Deshi-JatiyaParishad 155
Goria Muslim community 148, 153, 155
Gorkhaland 240–242
Gorkhas 13, 233, 241
Goswami, Manu 21, 32n5, 122
Government of Assam 92, 100, 103, 118–119, 121, 124
Government of India 103, 112, 115–116, 118, 120–121, 123, 236, 255, 271
Guha, Amalendu 130–131, 149
Gujarat 7, 95, 185
Guwahati High Court 106–107, 123

Hasina, Sk. 67n6
Hau, Kam 251–252, 254
Hindu Bengalis 141, 142n10; as refugees 135–136
Hinduized Nepalis(ese) 232–233
Hindutva politics 128, 185, 202
Home Affairs Standing Committee 179
Home Fire 71
Hughes, Langston 79–80
Hussain, Ashraful 78, 83
Hussain, Kazi Sharowar 80, 83
Hussain, Shalim M 73, 77, 80
Hydari, Akbar 98

Identity Cards 103, 121
illegal migrants 27–28, 31, 157
India: citizenship anxiety of Nepalis 240–242; Hindutva 11; legal membership 4; partition of 126; and patriotism 118; process of state formation 20
India Against Corruption (IAC) movement 6–7
Indian citizenship law 4, 25, 27
Indian Civil Liberties Union (ICLU) 191
Indian Evidence Act, 1872 107
Indian Independence Act, 1947 257
Indian National Congress (INC) 131, 134, 136–141, 163, 167, 174, 177, 179
Indian nationalism 21–22, 27, 94, 147
Indian state 6, 19, 21, 28–31, 57–58, 62, 92, 108, 136, 147, 179, 204, 237, 240–243, 262–263
Indo-Bangladesh border 175–176
Indo-Burma borderland 257
Indo-Pakistan war, 1965 149
Inner Line Permit (ILP) 140, 141n1, 247
International Labour Organization (ILO) 248–249

Jaffrelot, C. 211n2
Jamia Coordination Committee 190
Jamiat-ul-Ulama-e-Hind 120
Janata Congress 235
Janata Party 136–137, 142n6–142n7, 142n9
Jan Lokpal Bill 6
Jantar Mantar, Delhi 7, 165
Japanese American experience 44–48
Joint Action Committee for Bengali Refugees (JACBR) 163, 165, 170, 177–179
Joint Committee on Inner Line Permit System (JCILPS) 247
Jorhat Sarvajanik Sabha 142n2

Kabaw Valley 249–250
Khan, Siraj 76–77, 80
Khup, Hau Cin 255
Koch Rajbongshi 152, 183
Kolkata's Muslims: anti-CAA protests 207; margins of city 203; neighbourhood of Park Circus 205–207; ordinary Muslims 204–207, 210; protesters at Park Circus 209–210
Kyi, Aung San Suu 58, 68n10

Lahiri-Dutt, Kuntala 67n2
Lahiri, Himadri xiii, xv–xvi, 9, 39–53
Lahore Resolution (1940) 101
Lama, Jigme Yeshi xiii, xvi, 13, 217–228
Laskar, Kaifia Ancer xiii, xvi, 12, 115, 183–195
Left Front government 165, 167, 171–174, 176
Lhasa government 218, 226
Lhatshampas 238, 240
Lok Sabha 124, 177, 247; elections 129, 136, 139–140
Lucknow 192
Lushai Expedition in 1871–72 252–254

Mackenzie, Alexander 251
Maharajah of Munnipoor 254
Mahatma Gandhi 94–95
Mamdani, M. 155
Manipur 13, 91; boundary demarcation 254–255; frontier posts and memorial stone 252–254; ill-defined border 249–250; ILP 247; indigenous/tribal people 248–249; Kam Hau and dominance 251–252; Maharajah of Manipur in 1872/3 257; reconfigured frontier 255–256
Manipur–Lushai Treaty 253
Marshall, T. H. 230
Massumi, B. M. 41
Matua Mahasangha (MM) 164, 169–170, 177–178, 180
Matua Namasudra activism 11–12
Matua Namasudra community 163–168, 171, 178; *see also* Namasudra community
McConnell, F. 217
McCulloch, William 250, 255
minority communities 29, 41, 113–114, 116, 118, 124, 185, 235, 271
Mirzapur of Uttar Pradesh 62
Misra, Tilottama 130
Miya identity 73, 77–78, 80–82
Miya Muslim community 72–74, 77–78, 81, 83–85; *char-chaporis* 153; Kamala Khatun 153
Miya Muslims 145, 147–150, 153, 155–157, 158n2
Miya poetry 52; emergence of 72; *Everyday On The Calendar Is Nellie* 79; ghost nation 82; Harlem Renaissance 79–80; *I am a Negro* 79; *Miya* dialect 78, 81; movement 76, 78, 80; *My Son Has Learnt to Cuss like the City* 76–77; poetics, politics and polemics 83–85; right to have rights 83; state and power 83
Mouffe, C. 22
Mullan, C. S. 11, 134, 142n4
Munnipore Government 249–250
Muslim(s): citizenship 201; between citizenship and media 183–195; community 5, 11; Datia, Dhulu, Tulu and Muchis 156; Dhakaiya and Chatgaiya families 150; *Dhakkya* 150; from East Pakistan 116; enactment of the CAA 185; Goria and Moria 150, 155–156; immigrants 136; neighbourhood 186, 205, 212n5, 212n7; population 10; population in Assam 147; in post-partition India 184; right-based *vs.* lived citizenship 202–203; Syed, Deshi and Julha 155–156
Muslim Assamese: and Assamese Identity 146–149; citizenship and history of violence 149–151; complexities of citizenship 151–154; context of Assam 156–157; good Muslim and bad Muslim 154–156
Myanmar 57–58

Na-Axomiya (neo-Assamese) 74, 85
Nag, Sajal xii–xvi, 10, 91–110, 275n20
Namasudra community: Dalapatis 168, 171, 178; identity 168; Left Front government 171–174; Matua 164–168, 171, 178; Namas 169; refugee activism 163, 169; refugees 165, 172; scepticism 168, 171
Namgyal Dolkar, Lhagyari 225
National Human Rights Commission (NHRC) 107, 270
national identity 25, 32n4, 66, 96, 131, 225
nationalism: humanism 96; human race 95; identity 96–97; Indian 95; spirit of 95; Western-type nationalism 94
National League for Democracy (NLD) 57
National Population Register (NPR) 183
National Register of Citizens (NRC) 6, 14, 25, 29–31, 39, 50–52, 58, 63, 68n13, 72, 129, 137, 139, 142n10, 148–149, 153–156, 207; NRC 1951 75, 105–106, 153–154; in Assam 5, 28, 97, 123–124, 184, 240; enumeration of 107–108; by Gogoi government 105; revised 98; upgradation 109

nationhood 94, 96
Nehru, Jawaharlal 50, 93, 102, 113, 119, 125, 127n25
Nehru–Liaquat Ali Pact 101–102, 106
Nellie massacre in 1983 74, 151
Nepal 13, 104, 219–221
Nepali festival of *Dasain* 238
Nepalis(ese) migration 230; into Drukpa Bhutan 237–240
Nepalis of Darjeeling hills 232, 240–243
Nepalis of India 240–242
New media 190–191
Nikhil Bharat Bangali Udbastu Samiti (NIBBUS) 178
Noakhali Riots, in October, 1946 115
non-citizen 30–32
Non-Muslim migrants 116
North-East Frontier Agency (NEFA) 266–269, 272, 274n8
North-East India 13–14, 91–92, 126
Northern Chin Hills 251, 255–256
Nowgaong Ryot Sabha 142n2
NRC Seva Kendra 75

Omvedt, Gail 130

Pakistan Constituent Assembly 114–115
Pandey, Gyanendra 22, 74
Park Circus, Kolkata 12, 184, 187–189, 191, 194–195; Muslims 205–211
Patel, Sardar 113, 126n3, 126n8
Pathan, Shofiul. Alom xiii, xvi, 11, 145–158
Pau, Pum Khan xiii, xvii, 13, 247–259
People's Liberation Army (PLA) 218
People's Party of Arunachal (PPA) 268
People's Republic of China (PRC) 217–218
People's Union for Civil Liberties (PUCL) 269
Plain Tribal Council of Assam (PTCA) 142n6–142n7
post-colonial Assam 149; BJP to power in 2014 124–125; burden of partition 113–118; ethno-linguistic politics 118–123
postcolonial India 23, 29, 112
Prevention of Infiltration from Pakistan (PIP) 103, 110n4, 120, 150
Public Law Contract 10, 129, 140
Purbanchaliya Lok Parishad (PLP) 136–137

Radhakrishnan, R. 40
Rahim, Abdur 80
Rahman, Gazi 80, 82
Rajah Chunder Kirtee Sing Maharajah 253
Rajya Sabha 124, 140
Rakhine state 56–58; *see also* Rohingya
reflexive ethnography 146
Reid, Robert 257
Republican Party of India (RPI) 172–173, 179
Reyaz, Mohammad xiii, xvii, 12, 183–195
Rohingya: migrants 57; populace 58; refugees 56, 68n9; repatriation 67n1
Roychoudhury, Ambika Giri 102, 119
Rudra, Kalyan 66, 68n15

Saadulla government 100
Sachar Committee Report (2006) 201–202, 211n1
Saha, Biswanath xiii, xvii, 13, 230–243
Sarabari Begum judgement 28, 32n7
Sarangi, Saurav 65
Sarmah, Bhupen xiii, xvii, 10, 128–142
Self-identity 83
Self interest 94
Shaheen Bagh, Delhi 5, 12; dadis and mothers of 186–187; Jamia Millia Islamia 185–186, 192; Park Circus, Kolkata 187–188; protesters 188–189
Shamsie, Kamila 71
Sheikh, Abdul Mazid 80
Shillong 91, 233
Sikkim Citizenship Order 1975 236
Sikkim Congress 235
Sikkimese Nepalis(ese) 234–237
Sikkim National Congress (SNC) 235
Sikkim Sangram Parishad (SSP) 236
Sikkim State Congress (SSC) 234
Sinha, S. K. 104
16th Tibetan Parliament in Exile (2016–2021) 220
slur *Miya* 72, 83–85
social media 12, 76–78, 190–191, 194, 212n15
Sone, Monica 41, 44–48
statelessness 9, 39–41, 45, 50, 57, 71
Sultana, Rehna 80
Supreme Court of India 5, 27–28, 77, 97, 107, 123–124, 149, 271
Surma Valley 135, 141n1

Sylhet: in province of Assam 114; transfer to Pakistan 98–99, 101
Sylhet Referendum 98, 125

Tagore, Rabindranath 61, 64–65, 68n14, 94
Tezpur Ryot Sabha 142n2
Thado tribe 254, 256
Thakur, Harichand 167
Thakur, Mamatabala 167, 177–178
Thakur, Manjul Krishna 167
Thakur, Pramatha Ranjan 167
Thakur, Shantanu 167
Thakur, Subrata 167
Tham, Lailin 49
36th Constitutional Amendment Act in 1974 236
Thokchom, Sunanda 247
Tibetan(s): Buddhism 227–228, 241, 243n3; and citizenship in India and the West 224–226; CTA and Tibetan citizens in exile 219–223; Dalai Lama's government 218; in Dharamsala 223, 225; national identity 225; nationalism 222; PRC 217–218; Shakespeare's Hamlet 217
Tibetan Government in exile (TGiE) 217
Tibetan People's Deputies (ATPD) 220, 227
Treaty of Titaliya, 1817 233
Treaty of Tumloong 1861 233
Treaty of Westphalia, 1648 230
Tribal League 135, 142n5

Ujoni Asom Rajya Parishad (UARP) 142n6
United Liberation Front of Assam (ULFA) 108, 138
United Nations High Commissioner for Refugees (UNHCR) 56, 58, 68n8, 273
United Nations Human Rights Commission (UNHRC) 31, 107
United Progressive Alliance (UPA) 6, 211
Unlawful Activities (Prevention) Act 189
Upper Assam Association 142n2
Upper caste Hindus 132–133, 138, 141
Uttar Pradesh 62, 147, 183, 185, 189, 192

Vaghaiwala, R. P. 107, 149
Van Gennep, Arnold 32n3
van Schendel, W. 63, 66

Wadud, Aman 77
Wangchuck, Jigme Dorji 238
Wangyal, Lobsang 225
West Bengal 11, 65–66, 113; anti-immigrant consensus 171–179; and Bangladesh 175–176; BJP issue 166–167, 171; Dalit communities 164; Dalit organizations 169; Government of 167; legislative assembly 167; Matua Mahasangha 164, 169–170; Matua Namasudra community *see* Namasudra community; Namasudra population in 164
Western Assam 152, 157

Yamamoto, Hisaye 46

Zedong, Mao 217
Zia-ur-Rehman 268

www.ingramcontent.com/pod-product-compliance
Ingram Content Group UK Ltd.
Pitfield, Milton Keynes, MK11 3LW, UK
UKHW021308260926
475702UK00048B/910
9781032347127